MASTERS OF WAR

By the same author

Israel's Political–Military Doctrine (1973)
Weak States in the International System (1981)
The Diplomacy of Surprise (1981)
Clausewitz and Modern Strategy (ed.) (1986)
*Strategic and Operational Deception in
The Second World War* (ed.) (1987)
Leaders and Intelligence (ed.) (1988)
War, Strategy and Intelligence (1989)
Intelligence and Military Operations (ed.) (1990)

MASTERS OF WAR

Classical Strategic Thought

MICHAEL I. HANDEL

Professor of Strategy, US Naval War College

THIRD REVISED AND EXPANDED EDITION

FRANK CASS
LONDON · PORTLAND OR.

First published in 1992
Second edition published in 1996
Third revised and expanded edition published in 2001 in Great Britain by
FRANK CASS PUBLISHERS
Newbury House, 900 Eastern Avenue,
London IG2 7HH

and in the United States of America by
FRANK CASS PUBLISHERS
c/o ISBS, 5824 N E Hassalo St
Portland, Oregon 97213–3644

British Library Cataloguing in Publication data
Handel, Michael
Masters of War: classical strategic thought. 3rd edn.
1. Sun Zi   2. Clausewitz, Carl von, 1780–1831
3. Military art and science – History
I. Title
355'.02'09
ISBN 0-7146-5091-9 (cloth)
ISBN 0-7146-8132-6 (paper)

Library of Congress Cataloging-in-Publication data
Handel, Michael I.
Masters of War: classical strategic thought / Michael I. Handel.—
3rd rev. and expanded edn.
p.   cm.
Includes bibliographical references and index.
ISBN 0-7146-5091-9 (cloth). — ISBN 0-7146-8132-6 (paper)
1. Military art and science—History.   2. Sun-tzu, 6th cent. B.C.
Sun-tzu ping fa.   3. Clausewitz, Carl von, 1780–1831. Vom Kriege.
4. Jomini, Antoine Henri, baron de, 1779–1869. Précis de l'art de
la guerre.   I. Title.
U27.H36   2000
355.02—dc21   00-035874

Third Revised and Expanded Edition

Typeset by Regent Typesetting, London
Printed in Slovenia on behalf of
Midas (UK) Printing Ltd.

To Jill,
Yael, Benjamin, Ethan and Sarah

Contents

List of Maps, Figures, and Tables

PULLOUT MAPS AND CHARTS

FIGURES

TABLES

Acknowledgements

There cannot be a more exciting and creative place for thinking about, writing on, and teaching strategy than the Department of Strategy and Policy at the U.S. Naval War College. For their stimulating discussions and 'strategic excitement' I thank all of my civilian and military colleagues past and present. I am particularly indebted to the Chairman of the Department, Professor George W. Baer, without whose support I could not have brought this new edition into print.

The development and growth of the third edition of *Masters of War* owes much to Professor Bradford A. Lee, for a number of comments and suggestions and for elaboration of his concept of the theory of victory; to Professor David E. Kaiser, for many arguments on various issues in *On War*, especially our discussions on Clausewitz's trinitarian analysis; to Professor William C. Fuller, for his comments on the Weinberger Doctrine, and the culminating point of victory in Napoleon's invasion of Russia; to Professor John H. Maurer, particularly for a number of comments on Chapter 18; Professor Alberto R. Coll, for his valuable advice and for sharing unusual travel adventures; and Professors Steven T. Ross, Thomas M. Nichols, Thomas G. Mahnken, Andrew R. Wilson, and John A. English. Among my military friends and colleagues I would like to thank in particular Captain Bryan Lucas, Captain Robert E. McCabe, Commander (Ret.) Lisa B. Squire, Colonel Neil Hartenstein, Captain James P. Butler, Captain Dorothy K. Grant, and my friend Captain (Ret.) James O'Rourke.

I have also benefited greatly over the years from the challenging arguments and tough questions posed by American and foreign students, particularly in my Clausewitz elective. I cannot fail to mention my student Captain James Dell for giving me the hardest time of them all. He represents so many other students who have made teaching such a rewarding experience.

As always, I would like to thank Professor Richard K. Betts, Director of the Institute of War and Peace at Columbia University, and John Ferris, Chairman of the History Department at Calgary University, for their encouragement and support. In the United Kingdom, I would like to express my gratitude to RAF Official Historian Sebastian Cox, for his good advice, gracious hospitality, friendship, and humor; Professor Andrew Lambert of King's College, London, for his comments on Chapter 18, especially Corbett's work; my publisher, Stewart Cass, for his encouragement and support; and my editor, Andrew Humphrys, for his dedication.

In addition, I would like to thank all of the librarians at the U.S. Naval War College for their cheerful and efficient help with my research and numerous queries.

Finally, I want to thank my wife, Jill, for her inspired insights, criticism, and editorial help. This book is dedicated to her and to our children, Yael, Benjamin, Ethan, and Sarah, with all of my love and gratitude.

MICHAEL I. HANDEL
Department of Strategy and Policy
U.S. Naval War College
Newport, RI
June 2000

And as water has no constant form there are in war no constant conditions.
Sun Tzu, *The Art of War*

War is more than a true chameleon that slightly adapts its characteristics to the given case.
Clausewitz, *On War*

Introduction

When first comparing the works of Sun Tzu and Carl von Clausewitz, I assumed that these two great theorists of war represented what scholars have traditionally held to be the radically different Eastern and Western approaches to the art of war. Yet after a careful study of these two 'opposing paradigms', I concluded that the basic logic of strategy, like that of political behavior, is universal. To say otherwise would be akin to asserting that Russia, China, Japan, and the United States each follow distinct theories of physics or chemistry. Nevertheless the logic of war also differs from that of the natural sciences because it is based, as Jomini aptly put it, on '. . . *nothing but usages, the principles of which are unknown to us*'. That is to say, the conduct of war is based less on a formally developed theory and more on intuition, experience, and an understanding of the rules or 'laws' of action.

The development of the study and theory of war is (and probably will always remain) in a pre-Newtonian, pre-scientific, or non-formal stage. However, even as the laws of gravity operated irrespective of their discovery by Newton, the universal logic of war still exists whether or not it is codified. In the absence of a formal strategic theory, political groups or states have had to construct one based on their own historical experiences and particular strategic and geographic environments. As this book shows, however, despite the fact that each political group or state developed its own strategic concepts, none could defy the as yet unarticulated universal logic of strategy with impunity; this in turn meant that they independently and ineluctably arrived at similar conclusions.

On a normative level, for example, every war must be decided upon and directed by the political leadership. Political leaders are charged with developing a coherent policy and clear objectives to be executed by a subordinate military group or organization (the primacy of politics in waging war). Likewise, any war conducted in a rational, instrumental manner requires the meticulous correlation of ends and means; the identification of a strategic and/or operational center of gravity and the

xvii

recognition that, while success on the battlefield should be exploited to the fullest, every offensive reaches a culminating point of victory after which further action could become counter-productive. To these we can add the advisability of avoiding a war with more than one major enemy at a time and the observation that, all other things being equal, a shorter decisive war is always preferable to a war of attrition. Finally, the support of the people should be mobilized and maintained throughout the war. Such insights into the fundamental logic of war were equally apparent to Sun Tzu, Thucydides, Machiavelli, Clausewitz, and Jomini – as much as they ought to be to the leader of any tribe or state at war.

All of these classical theorists can be said to have contributed significantly to the traditional strategic paradigm for the understanding and direction of war. This paradigm is based on the following assumptions and observations:

(1) Since it serves the *political interests* of the state (or group or tribe), war almost always has a rational purpose, at least initially. This also explains why the political and not the military leaders should always be in control and direct the war on its highest level.

(2) Although war should not be the first resort, it is not always the last resort either. Under certain circumstances, war provides the most effective or even the only way to protect or enhance the interests of the state or group.

(3) The rational aspects of war involve, *inter alia*, the establishment of clear goals: cost/benefit calculations concerning the utility or merit of a particular war are made continuously. Ideally, wars should be won as quickly as possible at the lowest possible cost.

(4) Despite its normative emphasis on waging war as rationally as possible, the classical strategic paradigm recognizes that many factors can limit the rationality of the calculations made. Among others, these include friction, chance and uncertainty, uncontrollable passions, incompetence, and the irrational behavior of leaders or groups. In addition, it acknowledges that wars can begin on the basis of rational cost/benefit calculations and expectations of promoting the state's interests – and then lose any semblance of a rational direction as they spin out of control. Furthermore, this paradigm recognizes the fact that war can at times be waged rationally to achieve non-rational objectives.

(5) Political, diplomatic, economic, or other activities used to

pressure the enemy do not cease with the onset of hostilities and may be as important as military means. Furthermore, the traditional paradigm recognizes that *military victory alone* is not enough. Military achievements must be consolidated by political and diplomatic means, since the victory achieved must be made acceptable to the enemy in order to achieve a better peace.

(6) Finally, the traditional paradigm as based on the observation of human nature and historical evidence, is pessimistic. It assumes that war cannot be abolished, that conflict and violence are part and parcel of the relationships among nations and groups. Thus, although *some* wars can be prevented, war in general cannot be relegated to history alone.

In recent years, this classical paradigm has become the target of increasing criticism, although none of its detractors has proposed a convincing alternative. This makes it all the more important for students of strategy to better acquaint themselves with the classical works on war.

The universality of strategic logic does not, however, mean that strategy is something apart from specific geographic, economic, or other factors, or that all political groups or nations will be able to learn and implement the inherent 'laws' of war with equal effectiveness or determination. States or political groups will often deviate from the imperatives dictated by the logic of strategy and will, so to speak, defy the laws of gravity. But while defying the laws of gravity leads to immediate or unpleasant repercussions, the contravention of strategic imperatives may not be so readily apparent. Thus the occasional deviation from the universal logic of strategy may be corrected in time or may bring success in the short run through unexpected actions, but, in the long run, consistent defiance of the logic of strategy brings defeat and decline.

Wars are not clashes between abstract entities, each rigidly adhering to a universal logic of strategic action. Political groups or nations can be fast or slow to learn the correct strategic lessons from their experiences and, even if they learn the correct lessons, they may be led by inept leaders pursuing personal and not necessarily rational or carefully calculated objectives; furthermore, the military or population may not be ready to make the necessary sacrifices or follow the decisions of the political leadership. Therefore, in addition to discerning the universal logic of strategy and war in general, the statesman and strategist must always understand the unique nature of the particular war he is fighting;

he must know his enemy and himself in order to be able to foresee how his opponent might deviate from the rational conduct of war. A realistic strategist can never assume that his opponent will behave only according to the logical or rational imperatives of strategy. This was recognized by Clausewitz when he said '. . . **war is not waged against an abstract enemy, but against a real one who must always be kept in mind**' (Clausewitz, *On War*, p. 161).

* * *

In recent years, most of the new ideas on warfare, as discussed in the professional military literature, have focused on the growing role of advanced military technology. In fact, the study of military technology seems to have largely *replaced* the study of the political, social, and strategic dimensions of war. For many, the advantages offered by advanced military technology represent the realization of a long-awaited panacea for the complex political and strategic problems of waging war.

The current military literature abounds with discussions of 'the Revolution in Military Affairs' (RMA), 'information warfare', 'information superiority', 'information dominance', 'cyber-war', 'true battlespace transparency', 'post-heroic war', 'dominant battle awareness', and so on. Given the actual and perceived success of the high-tech wars against Iraq and, more recently, against the Serbs over Kosovo, this is not surprising. Precision bombing and the extensive use of cruise missiles in these instances produced spectacular victories at an incredibly cheap cost in terms of human casualties. As a result, all seem to point to new forms of war dominated by the successful exploitation of high-tech military technologies.

Indeed, modern military technology boasts astounding new possibilities that were not even dreamed of a few decades ago and appears to confer a *great* and *unilateral* material advantage upon those who dominate research and production in this area (i.e., the United States, NATO, and perhaps Russia in some dimensions). While such technological advances should of course be fully exploited whenever possible, past and more recent experience also points to the limits of what can be achieved by technological superiority alone. There are, however, at least four points that must be considered before the role played by the latest military technologies in the Gulf War and in Kosovo is accepted as a model for future wars. After all, the particular political, social, and military/technological environment that provided optimum conditions for the success of state-of-the-art technology will not necessarily be present in future conflicts.

First, we must remember that the great military success enjoyed by the United States and its allies in the Gulf War as well as in Kosovo was not equally matched by political success. Ultimately, war is about 'compelling the enemy to do our will', that is, achieving our political objectives in order to translate a military victory into a political environment better than that which existed before the resort to force. From this point of view, both the Gulf War and the war in Kosovo produced only mixed success in the long run and in some ways even proved counterproductive. The fact that peace and stability on the victor's terms were never achieved clearly illustrates the meaning of Clausewitz's subtle observation that '**in war the result is never final**'. In other words, success and finality in war depend more on political wisdom than on military success. This point, like those that follow, is not intended to suggest that technology is unimportant. It is simply there to remind us that technology, while of the greatest importance, is still only the *means*; as such, it is always secondary to the political and strategic non-material dimensions of war. Thus, technological and material victories are inseparable from the political and 'strategic' dimensions, but in the final analysis they are at best only a necessary but rarely sufficient condition for a final and complete victory. For the victors in most recent wars, the preponderance of attention paid to technological and material success, with its concomitant neglect of strategic and policy failures, has indeed prevented the achievement of their ultimate long-range objectives.

Second, the resounding military victories over Iraq and Serbia were achieved against nations that, for political and social (as well as technological) reasons, were not able to fight back on equal terms. In both instances, the defeat of these states was hastened by the exceptionally poor performance of their leaders in developing their strategies, mobilizing their own people, and motivating their own military organizations. Military technologies undoubtedly made a decisive contribution to the victories achieved and actually performed better than expected. It is of course easier to fight against an opponent whose 'trinity' is in disarray and out of equilibrium. How much of these victories can be attributed to the fact that the United States and its allies were fighting against isolated regimes run by incompetent leaders whose populations lacked the will to fight or support their own governments? Could such quick and cheap victories have been achieved against dedicated, resolute opponents such as the North Vietnamese, the Afghanis, or the Chechens? Being exceptional, ideal conditions for the uncompromised application of military power will not always be present in the future. Even the most advanced military technologies need considerable time, which is seldom allowed by the political environment, to achieve their full impact. Political counter-pressure typically limits the time available to launch a unilateral attack before other powers begin to interfere.

A third point is that the defeated states and neutral observers will surely learn their lessons too. Having concluded that they cannot expect to win in a conventional 'high-intensity', 'high-tech' war against the United States and its allies, these states will determine that their 'comparative strategic advantage' lies elsewhere, in 'low-intensity', 'low-tech' political subversion, terrorism, and related methods of war. If these states successfully identify such effective counter-measures, then they will, depending on the circumstances, be able to neutralize or reduce the relevance and effectiveness of many of the most modern high-tech weapons along with those strategies based on their performance. High-tech war is most effective in major, conventional wars against an enemy who takes a similar approach. But the wars of the future may not all be high-tech wars in which similarly equipped enemies face each other. In addition, other less technologically advanced states may try to neutralize or deter advanced 'high-tech' states from waging war by demonstrating the will to use 'low-tech', chemical, biological, and even nuclear weapons of mass destruction. (Iraq is the first clear example of this trend; Iran, Syria, Libya, North Korea, and other states are likely to follow such a strategy in the future.) The readiness of such states to employ crude weapons of mass destruction may quickly reduce the appetite of high-tech military powers to wage war. Under such conditions, the high-tech military power involved may raise its own threshold for going to war when the dangers of escalation and the estimated costs appear unacceptably high. This is certainly one type of circumstance in which low-tech can defeat high-tech.

A fourth point is that other states (for example, Russia and China) which closely follow the success of U.S. 'high-tech' weapons in action will gradually develop equally effective state-of-the-art weapons and counter-measures. At that point, and in all cases where both sides have comparable advanced military technologies, no state will have an advantage over its opponents (as is now often assumed in the literature);[1] consequently, new high-intensity conventional wars between them may become prolonged and costly. Once a conventional high-tech war is fought between technologically equal opponents, the pace and accuracy of the destructive power wielded will increase, but their advanced technological capabilities will not give either side any particular advantage.

Many of the latest military theories and doctrines assume tacitly or explicitly that the wars of the future will be waged with perfect or nearly perfect information and intelligence ('information dominance'). These theories envision a scenario in which the technologically advanced side, with flawless command, control, and communications, will always identify and hit targets with precision. Yet this vision is a chimera, because it implies that friction in war will be greatly reduced if not eliminated. By definition, friction cannot be eliminated when two (or more) forces clash, for movement alone creates friction. Those who labor under the illusion that information can be monopolized by one side need to re-examine the complexities of war as described so long ago by Sun Tzu, Thucydides, Clausewitz, and many other classical theorists. There is no better remedy for the plethora of these recent theoretical works on war than a careful reading of the classics. While the outward shape and material dimensions of war may shift continuously, the essence of war remains unchanged. War will thus remain a dynamic and reciprocal activity in which various advantages are gained and lost as both sides adapt to successive challenges. War simply cannot be reduced to algebra or to an exact science.

Hence, the classical theory of war as discussed in this volume constantly reminds us of the complex and reciprocal nature of war; of its moral and non-rational dimensions; of friction, uncertainty, chance, and luck; and, of course, of its political character. As permanent elements that cannot and will not disappear, these dimensions of war play a critical role in defining its very nature. As Clausewitz says, '. . . **action [in war] is no mathematical construction, but has to operate in the dark, or at best in the twilight**' (Clausewitz, *On War*, p. 545). Perhaps *some* of the darkness has been lifted, which means that war is now fought more in the twilight than in darkness, but war is still not fought in 'broad daylight'. As soon as one side endeavors to lift the darkness, his opponent works just as hard to increase it through secrecy, deception, or any other available counter-measures. As a result, darkness and twilight, with an occasional ray of sunshine, will perpetually constitute the environment of war.

Clearly, each state should still try to exploit the latest technology even while remaining mindful of its inherent limits. Technology is only a means in war, which cannot produce complete victory and success by itself. In an age of staggering material and technological progress and change, when we instinctively search for technological and scientific 'rational' solutions, it has become more important than ever to identify those dimensions that have remained constant. *Paradoxically, therefore, it is now more, not less, critical to study the classical works on war.*

* * *

In this third edition of *Masters of War* I have added many new references to Clausewitz's *On War* as well as some new ones to Sun Tzu's *The Art of War*. I have also for the first time expanded the discussion of the military works of Mao Tse-tung, which I find to be in many ways as important and original as any of the classical works on strategy. Mao's work is actually much closer in spirit and content to that of Clausewitz, particularly his discussion of questions such as the nature of war, the problem of theory and practice, protracted war, and the role of the people in war. In many instances, as will be shown, Mao's theory of war strengthens the original thesis of this book, namely, that the logic of strategy and waging war is universal rather than parochial, cultural, or regional.[2]

I have also further expanded my discussion of, and references to, Machiavelli's work. Machiavelli has much to say about power, conflict, and war that is as original and worthy of attention as any of the classical works on war. His book on *The Art of War* includes an important discussion on the proper recruitment and mobilization of soldiers and officers for defense of their homeland. Machiavelli's insistence that one's military possess patriotic motivation (i.e., the mobilization of the people) rather than a mercenary incentive represents the beginning of a trend that would ultimately lead to the French Revolution and Clausewitz. But, since he does not go as far as to consider a *levée en masse*, or the total mobilization of the population, Machiavelli's advice on this matter represents a transition from the earlier feudal period of war to the modern age. True to his reputation, Machiavelli actually has more to say than Sun Tzu on the importance of deception in war. In his other works, particularly *The Prince* and *The Discourses*, he makes many interesting observations on issues ranging from understanding the nature of war through identification of its 'principles', and military leadership, to chance, luck, and friction in war.

The first of the new chapters in this expanded edition concerns the importance of identifying the correct nature of war. This chapter examines Clausewitz's approach to understanding the nature of war through application of his conceptual framework, or trinitarian analysis, then compares his approach with that of other classical theorists. It is in this context that I discuss Sun Tzu's concept of strategy as identification of a comparative strategic advantage over the enemy and fighting on one's own terms. Undoubtedly, the idea behind Clausewitz's emphasis on identifying the true nature of war and using his trinitarian analysis (i.e., what we would now call a 'net assessment process') is to determine one's own and the enemy's relative strengths and vulnerabilities (i.e., identifying one's comparative advantage as a basis for strategic planning). While Clausewitz provides us with elegant questions and an analytical method for identifying one's comparative strategic advantage, he never explicitly addresses the need to do so. Sun Tzu, on the other hand, addresses the issue explicitly and provides us with his conclusions regarding what is most important. But, unlike Clausewitz, Sun Tzu does not provide us with the reasoning sequence that led him to his insights on this issue. Consequently, Clausewitz and Sun Tzu are best read together as complementary texts.

Another new chapter explores the surprisingly complex problem of war termination. This topic has attracted increased interest from political and military decision-makers because the military successes in the Gulf War and Kosovo somehow failed to achieve the desired political goals in the war termination process. To be sure, although the problem of when and how to terminate a war was as difficult and important in the past as in recent history, it unfortunately did not receive enough attention in the classical literature on war. (Clausewitz's *On War* does not include a special chapter on the problem of war termination, but it *does* have more to say about this subject than previously supposed in numerous references scattered throughout the book.)

A third new chapter, on Corbett, Clausewitz, and Sun Tzu, includes a discussion of some of the issues that concerned Corbett as a naval strategist. Here I also briefly address Clausewitz's discussion of *limited war* and limited war by contingency. To my surprise, despite Corbett's extensive references to, and reliance on, Clausewitz's *On War* for the development of his arguments, I have concluded that Corbett's work is actually much closer to Sun Tzu's *The Art of War*, despite his lack of familiarity with it.

The fourth new chapter addresses what Clausewitz refers to as the 'moral factors' in war. For Clausewitz, these 'moral factors' consist of the non-material, metaphysical, non-linear, non-quantifiable dimensions that permeate every facet of war. This subject has traditionally received much more attention in the German literature on Clausewitz than it has elsewhere. In addition, a new short chapter on theory and practice in war according to Clausewitz and Mao has been included.

I have also added an appendix that explores Clausewitz's study of war as a *Gestalt* and as a complex system of interrelated concepts. By summarizing his systematic study of war in two 'flow charts', I was better able to sort out some of the issues involved as well as provide a heuristic stimulus for further discussion. *This most definitely does not, however, constitute an attempt to reduce Clausewitz's ideas to a mechanical formula. It merely points out possible links between his various concepts.*

Among sections added to existing chapters, I have included one on Mao's *terminal point of retreat* (i.e., the identification of the transition from retreat to defense, and eventually to a counter-attack). This subject clearly relates to Clausewitz's discussion of the culminating point of victory and his own interest in the transition from the defense to the offense. The section on the role of deception in war has been expanded as well.

The bibliography has been updated, while the index has grown considerably. Given the fact that none of the classical works on strategy and war has a detailed conceptual index such as this, I hope that the reader will find the index useful as a general reference to the works of Clausewitz, Sun Tzu, Jomini, and now also Mao.

As mentioned earlier, Clausewitz observed that **'in war the result is never final'**. The same can be said of the study of classical works on strategy. Like all other classical works of art and philosophy, they are open to different interpretations according to the background, interests, and perspective of a particular reader. Thus, there can be no final, definitive interpretation or understanding of the works of Sun Tzu, Clausewitz, or Jomini. Accordingly, in the following chapters I do not claim to present any 'final' or dogmatic interpretation – simply the interpretation that makes the most sense to me *at this time*.

1

Strategy: Past Theories, Modern Practice

In some professions, a single classical work has long served as the cornerstone upon which later generations of scholars and practitioners could build their own theories. For novices, such classical treatises provide an insightful point of departure and help to define an area of study; for experts, they represent a standard for the evaluation of all other studies in the field. Examples of such treatises are Machiavelli's *The Prince* in the study of politics; Thucydides' *The History of the Peloponnesian War* in history; Newton's *Principia* in science; and Adam Smith's *The Wealth of Nations* in economics.

Some works – particularly those on the natural sciences or in fields that lend themselves to a more rigorous quantitative analysis (such as economics) – are eventually either subsumed into, or discredited by, later studies, while many others in the humanities will always be as valuable as the day they were written. The study of warfare represents neither extreme, for it examines the immutable qualities of human nature as well as the constantly changing material and technological dimensions of military conflict. Strategists are therefore fortunate to have at least two enduring classical texts: Sun Tzu's *The Art of War* and Clausewitz's *On War*.[1]

Imagine what it would be like if scientists, physicians, or even economists were to rely on a text written over 150, let alone 2,000, years ago as the most valuable source of instruction in their profession. Yet this is precisely the case in the study of war, a fact that is especially ironic because no other area of human activity – the better understanding of which could determine the future of the human race – has been so transformed by rapid technological advances.

The longevity and pre-eminence of *The Art of War* and *On War* may be attributed to two main factors. The first, already mentioned, is that the underlying logic of human nature, and by extension of political action, has not changed throughout history. Although undoubtedly valid, this explanation does not account for the revolutionary changes that have occurred in the material environment of war, in which the world can now be destroyed in a matter of minutes; victory is often impossible and meaningless; the range of weapons is the entire globe; the relationship between the offense and defense continuously shifts; no two wars are ever alike, at least materially; and the involvement of whole populations has become unavoidable. All of these material – and consequently social and political – changes cannot be ignored and should therefore be incorporated into a new comprehensive theory of war. The second factor is the greatly increased complexity of modern warfare. Sun Tzu and Clausewitz already viewed war as infinitely complex in their own times, but modern technological developments have added an entirely new dimension of uncertainty; and this has so obfuscated the fundamental principles of strategy that constructing the type of relatively simple framework which sufficed in the pre-industrial age is now impossible.

The technological revolution in war that began to accelerate at a geometric pace after the mid-nineteenth century created a situation not unlike that facing scholars in the natural sciences: that is, the proliferation of specialized fields of research and the exponential growth in knowledge made it extremely unlikely that a single expert could cultivate an in-depth understanding of all the developments taking place. Just as it would hardly be possible to write one book encompassing the whole of modern science, it would be exceedingly difficult to compress all that is known and relevant about war into a single tome. And although no one has yet succeeded in writing a new, comprehensive study of war – despite a number of heroic attempts – such an undertaking nevertheless poses a worthy challenge.

*   *   *

Renewed interest in Sun Tzu and Clausewitz in recent years has yet to result in the publication of a detailed comparison of their writings. It is, however, easy to understand why strategists might be reluctant to embark on such a task. After all, few scholars are equally accomplished in the fields of Chinese history, culture, and language as well as European history at the turn of the nineteenth century. Since I am neither a sinologist nor an expert in eighteenth- and nineteenth-century European history, this book specifically examines the *ideas* developed by Sun Tzu and Clausewitz; it is based on a *content analysis* of *The Art of War* and *On War* that does not include a more general historical, philosophical, cultural, or linguistic study. As a result, these two texts are quoted extensively in the interest of allowing their authors to speak for themselves.

In modern works on strategy, the prevailing perception of Sun Tzu and Clausewitz is that they epitomize opposing, culture-bound approaches to the study and conduct of war. While *The Art of War* and *On War* certainly reflect their cultural and historical contexts, this study concludes that the extent of the differences hitherto assumed to exist between the two has been exaggerated. Ultimately, the logic and rational direction of war are universal and *there is no such thing as an exclusively 'Western' or 'Eastern' approach to politics and strategy*; there is only an effective or ineffective, rational, or non-rational manifestation of politics or strategy.

This edition also includes a number of references to Jomini's *The Art of War*. Jomini has traditionally been assumed to represent the positivistic if not mechanical approach to the study of warfare, but a careful comparison of Jomini's work with those of Sun Tzu and Clausewitz indicates that these three strategists are mostly in agreement on the fundamental issues. When Jomini asserts that military success can be achieved through the proper understanding and accurate application of three or four general principles, he is referring to the lower operational level alone; he makes it clear that on the highest levels, the conduct of war *'far from being an exact science, is a terrible and impassioned drama . . .'* (Jomini, *The Art of War*, p. 344).[2] Indeed, closer scrutiny of Jomini's treatise reveals the tension in his work between the non-scientific nature of the conduct of war on the higher level, and his attempt to demonstrate that war can be directed scientifically on the lower levels. But even Jomini, to reconcile this tension, insists that it is crucial to find an inspired commander whose intuition or *coup d'oeil* (as he, like Clausewitz, calls it) will ensure the correct application of his principles of war. And since the proper application of these principles ultimately depends on the intuition of a gifted individual, this indicates that even for Jomini, war is and will forever remain an art.

This edition also incorporates extensive references to Machiavelli's thoughts on war.[3] The concepts and observations that he developed

3

early in modern European history serve as a 'bridge' between earlier works on war such as those by Sun Tzu, Thucydides, or Polybius on the one hand, and Clausewitz and Jomini on the other. Machiavelli's work is also important because it illustrates the similarities, conceptual unity, and universality of strategic thought. Thus Machiavelli's emphasis on the central role of deception in war is very close to that of Sun Tzu, while his insistence on the primacy of politics as the driving force of war is identical to that of Sun Tzu and Clausewitz. In addition, the inclusion of Mao Tse-tung's military writings in this edition further emphasizes the universal logic of strategic theory. As will be demonstrated, the strategic theory of Mao is actually much closer to that of Clausewitz than to that of Sun Tzu.

The value of a comparative analysis is that it demonstrates the basic unity of the study of strategy and war, and also allows us to better understand these works on their own terms: each can be viewed from a broader perspective, and issues that would otherwise be obscured can be clarified. As explained in the text below, for example, Sun Tzu greatly values deception and surprise while Clausewitz regards them as largely impracticable; but a comparison of Clausewitz and Jomini on the same issue shows that both believe surprise is difficult to achieve and that deception is almost always a waste of time and resources. This indicates that Clausewitz's opinion on these matters is not so much idiosyncratic as a reflection of the general experience at the turn of the nineteenth century, when tremendous growth in the size of military formations had not yet been supported by corresponding improvements in mobility or communications. As a result, the effectiveness of deception and surprise was reduced for a time; but subsequent technological advances soon fundamentally altered the specific circumstances that had caused Clausewitz and Jomini to form negative opinions of surprise and deception. Moreover, the stalemate, immobility, and senseless carnage of the First World War eventually prompted a search for new solutions and 'force multipliers'. By the Second World War, Sun Tzu's (and Machiavelli's) assertion that *'all warfare is based on deception'* indicated that his positive conclusions on this subject were more relevant to our own time as well as to a general theory of war.

Significantly, Jomini *does* differ from Clausewitz in his acute awareness of the actual and potential importance of modern weapons technology; in a sibylline passage, he predicts that the weaponry of the future is likely to have a more decisive impact on the outcome of war.

> *The superiority of armament may increase the chances of success in war: it does not, of itself, gain battles but it is a great element of success . . . The armament of armies is still susceptible of great improvements; the state which shall take the lead in making them will secure great advantages . . . The new inventions of the last twenty years seem to threaten a great revolution in army organization, armament, and tactics. Strategy alone will remain unaltered, with its principles the same as under the Scipios and Caesars, Frederick and Napoleon, since they are independent of the nature of the arms and the organization of the troops . . . The means of destruction are approaching perfection with frightful rapidity. The Congreve rockets . . . the Perkins steam-guns, which vomit forth as many balls as a battalion, – will multiply the changes of destruction, as though the hecatombs of Eylau, Borodino, Leipsic, and Waterloo were not sufficient to decimate the European races.*
>
> *If governments do not combine in a congress to proscribe these inventions of destruction, there will be no course left but to make the half of an army consist of cavalry with cuirasses, in order to capture with great rapidity these machines; and the infantry, even, will be obliged to resume its armor of the Middle Ages, without which a battalion will be destroyed before engaging the enemy.*
>
> *We may then see again the famous men-at-arms all covered with armor, and horses also will require the same protection.*
>
> (Jomini, *The Art of War*, pp. 47–49)

What Jomini perceived as the quickening pace of technological evolution was in fact the nascent Industrial Revolution. By discerning the dynamic nature of military inventions and its influence on the shape of battle, Jomini in some respects grasps the essence of technological changes that were only fully discussed after the First World War by experts such J. F. C. Fuller and Tom Wintringham; in other respects, however, his vision of future technology is grafted to, hence bound by, the military capabilities of his own time. Nevertheless, Jomini provides us with a link between earlier classical strategic theory as represented by Sun Tzu and Clausewitz on the one hand – and that of the modern world on the other.

As partial and fragmented as Jomini's vision of the future of military technology may have been, it was prophetic in comparison with Clausewitz's seemingly static view of the material world. Clausewitz believed, perhaps correctly for his own time, that the most profound changes in war were political and social, not material:

> **Very few of the new manifestations in war can be ascribed to new inventions or new departures in ideas. They result mainly from the transformation of society and the new social conditions.**
>
> (Clausewitz, *On War*, p. 515)

> **Clearly the tremendous effects of the French Revolution abroad were caused not so much by new military methods and concepts as by radical changes in policies and administration, by the new character of government, altered conditions of the French people, and the like.**
>
> (Clausewitz, *On War*, p. 609)[4]

Writing well into the industrial age, Mao Tse-tung had to warn the military about the dangers of overreliance on material and technological factors in war:

> . . . this is the so-called theory that 'weapons' decide everything', which constitutes a mechanical approach to the question of war and a subjective and one-sided view. Our view is opposed to this; we see not only weapons but also people. Weapons are an important factor in war, but not the decisive factor; it is people, not things that are decisive. The contest of strength is not only a contest of military and economic power, but also a contest of human power and morale. Military and economic power is necessarily wielded by people.
>
> (Mao Tse-tung, *Selected Military Writings*, pp. 217–218)

In a time when many military men and strategists tend to regard material and technological factors as a panacea, Clausewitz's and Mao's observations serve as increasingly important caveats.

The staggering complexity of military conflicts has also made it impossible to avoid numerous internal contradictions – whether real or apparent – in formulating a general theory of war. The works of Sun Tzu, Clausewitz, and Jomini are certainly not devoid of such internal contradictions, tensions, and inconsistencies, the identification of which shows that the paradoxical nature of war defies complete understanding or 'final' codification. In many ways, the contradictions within each of these works are more interesting than the contradictions between them. The strategist's objective is not necessarily to resolve or eliminate every anomaly, but rather to understand why wrestling with these questions can bring better insight into the nature of war. (See Appendix A.)

Sun Tzu, for example, relies heavily on deception as a 'cheap' solution, if not a panacea, for many of the problems encountered in warfare. But deception is not as decisive as he assumes, for he seems to ignore the fact that there is no monopoly on the art of deception which, like the proverbial two-edged sword, can cut both ways. Sun Tzu then extols victory without bloodshed as an ideal, yet disregards the fact (which is central to Clausewitz's theory) that a reluctance to shed blood may cause one side to play into his opponent's hands; that is, knowledge of the other nation's reticence to 'come to blows' might impel such an opponent to bluff by either pretending that he is prepared to make a greater sacrifice or apply even more force to effect a decisive victory.

Both Sun Tzu and Clausewitz insist that, for war to be conducted on a rational basis, politics must be in command; at the same time, they emphasize that the field commander must be afforded sufficient freedom of action to exploit local opportunities to the greatest advantage. Neither strategist, though, develops criteria to indicate the type of circumstances under which the field commander could justify disregarding orders. Admittedly, it would be impossible to establish unequivocal criteria applicable to every situation, but this does not obviate the necessity of attempting to do so.

Clausewitz discusses at length the tendency of war – in theory and in practice – to escalate to the extreme, yet he also identifies contradictory trends that limit war and attenuate its violence. Still, the relative strengths and relationships of these trends are not explained in an entirely convincing manner. Clausewitz on the whole emphasizes the superior strength of the defense although he admits that in the opening phases of a war, the attacker may enjoy a considerable advantage. He

7

does not, however, provide a definitive answer as to whether war can be won by the defense alone or if a counter-attack is always required. Such ambiguity is not a flaw as some might assume, for a realistic theory of war can never be streamlined and perfectly consistent. As Clausewitz recognizes, the art of command is to make choices in the midst of ambiguity. Those seeking to extract simple, unalterable, and universally applicable scientific principles from the complexity of war are bound to be disappointed when they encounter its inevitable paradoxes, contra-dictions, and tensions. To take an example from the Freudian theory of psychoanalysis, Freud's identification of the two coexisting but opposing instincts of Eros (the pleasure-driven life instinct) and Thanatos (the death instinct) in no way detracts from or invalidates his theory.

Jomini, as we have seen, believes that war on the operational level can be waged as a 'scientific activity' guided by a few basic principles; yet he also points out (without being aware of or simply ignoring the contra-diction) that their consistently successful application hinges on the role of the military genius.

Some of the contradictions that can be identified in these works are only apparent and can be explained, for example, by differences in the level of analysis. Intelligence may be reliable on the strategic level but not on the operational; surprise may be readily achieved on the tactical level but not on the strategic; and defense may be stronger on the tactical and operational levels but not necessarily on the strategic.

The probabilistic nature of war is such that what is true most of the time is not guaranteed to be true all of the time. This is illustrated by the paradoxical qualities of risk in war. When all parties to a conflict are con-vinced that a particular course of action would be extremely risky, they often dismiss it as a viable option. But as Clausewitz observes: '. . . **Boldness in war has its own prerogative . . . it is a genuinely creative force'** (Clausewitz, *On War*, p. 190). Boldness, daring, and risk-taking defy rational analysis and transcend all rules, which is what makes them so unpredictable and difficult to counter; therefore, a course of action known by both sides to be risky but dismissed by only one may, paradoxically, have a better chance of succeeding. This does not mean that risk-taking is always rewarded or, conversely, that caution is invariably the better choice. It simply means that in the unstructured, competitive, and probabilistic environment of war, some rules make sense some of the time but all rules cannot be followed all of the time. The secret of success for the creative military genius lies in knowing when to break the rules and when to heed them.

*   *   *

The Gulf War of 1990–91 demonstrated the enormous advantages that can result from unilateral technological superiority. Yet despite the impressive technological achievements of the American-led coalition, that war was not won solely by state-of-the-art military technology: more significantly, no modern war has been won by superior technology alone. Short, decisive wars have been won by a superior military doctrine, better planning, stronger motivation or the achievement of surprise, while prolonged wars have been won by more effective leadership, better cooperation among allies, greater actual and potential economic strength, and favourable topographical and geographical conditions. Of course, this does not mean that modern weapons technology is unimportant – just that technological factors alone have never determined the outcome of modern wars.[5] At best, superior military technology is a necessary, but never sufficient, condition to win wars. For example, the victories secured by Germany early in the First and Second World Wars were not simply the result of superior technology but rather of superior planning, leadership, motivation, and the high standards of the troops in the field. In the longer run, Germany was neither saved nor defeated by modern technology; instead, it was overwhelmed by the greater economic strength, resolve, and political cohesion of the allies arrayed against it. In much the same way, the superior technology and economic might of the United States was not decisive in the outcome of the Vietnam War.

The inability of the United States to win the war in Vietnam seriously undermined the self-confidence of the U.S. military establishment, prompting a soul-searching examination of why its far greater strength and advanced technology, as well as sufficient motivation, had not been enough to prevent the first such failure in modern American history. Even more interesting was the fact that the U.S. military had not lost any major military engagements on the battlefield. It was therefore evident from the start that this failure could not be explained in exclusively military terms; nor was improved technology the answer,

9

because military technology as such had rarely failed. Clearly, the solution had to lie elsewhere.

The American military then began to look for answers in the classical works on strategy and war. Above all, U.S. war colleges turned to Sun Tzu's *The Art of War* and even more importantly, to Clausewitz's *magnum opus, On War*. (In this undertaking they were aided by the publication of a new, more readable translation of *On War* by Sir Michael Howard and Peter Paret in 1976.) This new direction of inquiry eventually inspired a significant change at the highest levels of the American military and political leadership.

The faculties of the U.S. war colleges, and students who graduated in the late 1970s and early 1980s, gradually (and for some, reluctantly)[6] understood that war and politics could never be separated; that military victory does not automatically guarantee ultimate political victory; that all wars, in particular those that are prolonged, require the political support and consensus of the people in whose name they are waged; that the military is only one of the three elements essential for success in war (the others being the government and the people); and that without a harmonious balance among these three elements, wars cannot be won no matter how just the cause or how great the effort invested. They also discovered the danger of fighting a war with irresolute political backing (which is almost inevitable in any prolonged war given the nature of the American political system). Furthermore, they realized that gradual escalation and other difficulties imposed by various political constraints prevented the concentration of maximum force that was necessary from the start.

As they became more attuned to the need to identify and define political and strategic objectives as well as an operational center of gravity, they realized that if no such objectives could be identified, war ought, if possible, to be avoided. Other previously neglected but important non-material dimensions, such as the role of intelligence and deception in war, also received increased attention. Above all, bitter experience had indeed proved that it was '**imperative . . . not to take the first step without considering the last**' (Clausewitz, *On War*, p. 584).

The study of the classical works on strategy provided an excellent point of departure and a broader perspective from which to examine the lessons of the Vietnam War. Eventually, these collectively learned lessons – whether learned directly in the U.S. war colleges or through an 'osmotic process' – were 'codified' in the Weinberger Doctrine, which subsequently proved its value as a guide in the highest-level political and strategic decision-making processes preceding the war against Iraq. According to the Weinberger Doctrine, the following conditions should be met before the United States becomes involved in a military conflict:

(1) The vital interests of the United States or its allies must be at stake.
(2) Sufficient force should be applied to reflect unequivocally the intention of winning (i.e., no half-hearted measures).
(3) Political and military objectives must be clearly defined.
(4) Political and military objectives must be continuously re-assessed to keep cause and response in synchronization.
(5) Before troops are committed, there must be a reasonable assurance of support from American public opinion.
(6) A combat role should be undertaken only as a last resort.[7]

The first and sixth principles are directly related to the rational behavior of states (or the theory of *raison d'état*) on which the works of Clausewitz and Sun Tzu are ultimately based. The second principle, calling for the maximum concentration of force; the third, requiring a clear definition of political and military objectives; the fourth, calling for a continuous reassessment of political and military objectives; and the fifth, on the need to obtain the support of American public opinion, are all discussed at length in *On War*. While the concept of the Clause-witzian trinity (the need to achieve the proper equilibrium among the government, the military, and the people) lies at the core of the Wein-berger Doctrine, these uniquely American tenets ascribe even greater importance to domestic political support as a precondition for success in war. Nevertheless, it is not important whether the framers of this doctrine were conscious of the Clausewitzian nature of the doctrine or whether they unknowingly spoke prose. After all, one does not necessarily have to read *On War* to be a Clausewitzian, since most of his ideas can be arrived at independently through the application of logic and common sense. In any event, the Weinberger Doctrine reflects the adoption of Clausewitzian ideas and their adaptation to the post-

11

Vietnam War era. (For a more detailed and critical discussion of the Weinberger Doctrine, see Appendix B.)

Until the Gulf War, many strategic experts believed it would be impossible and impractical to meet most of the conditions set forth in the Weinberger Doctrine. It was assumed that if these principles were regarded as a *sine qua non* for entering a war, they would either serve as an excuse for avoiding war even when necessary or else would make it impossible to go to war even when desired. These reservations proved groundless, however, in the test of the Gulf War, when the Weinberger Doctrine was shown to be an outstanding framework for developing an effective strategy tailored to the American domestic political environment. President Bush, Defense Secretary Cheney, and the Chairman of the Joint Chiefs of Staff, General Powell, demonstrated that it was possible to fulfill all of the necessary political and military conditions; and by doing so, they made the military victory against Iraq possible.

To the public and even to many military experts, the Gulf War appears as a triumph of modern technology, or state-of-the-art weaponry. Yet while the important role of modern technology in this conflict should not be underestimated, the victory was first and foremost achieved by prudent political planning and preparations. As Jomini puts it: *'The superiority of armament may increase the chances of success in war: it does not, of itself, gain battles, but it is a great element of success'* (Jomini, *The Art of War*, p. 47).

Above all, it was the brilliant political leadership of President Bush that made this victory possible. He created the ideal political conditions for the U.S. military to wage war, first by mobilizing the support of the American public for his policies, then by maintaining that support throughout the war. He simultaneously proceeded to isolate Iraq through diplomatic action in the United Nations and elsewhere by building a broad and previously unthinkable coalition: however tenuously, this coalition brought together enemies such as the Arabs and Israelis, and the Soviet Union and China, as well as the traditional U.S. allies. The President set clear military objectives for the coalition and allowed diplomacy enough time to work before launching the war. While unequivocally establishing the primacy of the political level over that of the military, he was able to delegate the proper freedom of action to the military to prepare and implement military plans according to their best professional judgement. He resisted the temptation (that which Sun Tzu, Clausewitz, and Jomini all warn against) to allow excessive political interference in the lower-level details of fighting a war. The achievement of this delicate balance between political control on the one hand, and sufficient freedom of action for the military on the other is, as noted earlier, a rare feat for any statesman or political system. Finally, the timing of President Bush's decision in launching the war was ideal: the political and military strength of the U.S. and Allied troops was at its peak (enough time had been allowed for preparations and training). The cohesion of the alliance was as strong as it would ever be. This made possible the achievement of a perfect strategic, operational (and technological) surprise; and the ensuing war, was, as a result fought on the terms of the United States and its allies who also emerged with unprecedentedly low casualties. While the President laid the political groundwork for action, the U.S. military high command adhered to the principles of the Weinberger Doctrine, which provided the systematic justification and criteria for the U.S. military's traditionally cautious approach to involvement in new wars.[8]

Not surprisingly, particularly in view of its traumatic experience in the Vietnam War and the 1983–84 intervention in Lebanon, the U.S. military advised caution, preferring political and economic sanctions to the immediate resort to war. This initial reluctance, which was partially a reaction to the considerable exaggeration of Iraq's military strength in intelligence estimates, may have unwittingly encouraged a cautious approach.[9] In accordance with the Weinberger Doctrine, the U.S. military insisted on the need for patience and the importance of not beginning a war until military strength sufficient to achieve decisive results had been concentrated in the region. Once the U.S. military had prepared adequately, concentrated the necessary forces in the field, mobilized public opinion in America and the allied states, and established clear objectives, its early caution was replaced by a readiness for action and an eagerness to fight.

In this way, the study of the classical works on strategy had a substantial, even if indirect, influence on the success of the United States-led coalition in the Gulf War. Particularly for those at the highest levels of command, the study of *On War* and *The Art of War* was not, after all, an idle academic exercise.[10]

* * *

13

At times, the very simplicity of the concepts expounded by Clausewitz and Sun Tzu causes them to be ignored or misunderstood. One such deceptively simple idea is Clausewitz's emphasis on the need to understand the nature of each war (for a detailed discussion of this key concept, see Chapter 9 below):

> **The first, the supreme, the most far-reaching act of judgment that the statesman and commander have to make is to establish by that test [viewing war as an act of policy] the kind of war on which they are embarking: neither mistaking it for, nor trying to turn it into, something that is alien to its nature. This is the first of all strategic questions and the most comprehensive.**
>
> (Clausewitz, *On War*, pp. 88–89)

Jomini makes the same point even more succinctly:

> *We will suppose an army taking the field: the first care of its commander should be to agree with the head of state upon the character of the war.*
>
> (Jomini, *The Art of War*, p. 66)

Unlike Saddam Hussein, President Bush and the military leaders with whom he worked understood the political and technological nature of the impending war. Consequently, they fought it on their own terms at the greatest possible advantage to themselves, and won at the lowest possible cost while avoiding the protracted, indecisive conflict that Saddam Hussein had probably envisioned. Saddam Hussein, on the other hand, completely failed to comprehend the type of war he had provoked: without grasping the full significance of his political isolation, he expected the same doctrine and technology that had succeeded against Iran to perform as well against the United States. He seemed oblivious to the immense disparity between a technologically and militarily underdeveloped Iran that had been weakened by internal strife and the most sophisticated military machine in the world. Moreover, the vastly superior force led by the United States held the political, strategic, and operational initiative. Thus, Saddam Hussein was grossly mistaken in his belief that Iraq's victory over Iran was indicative of what he could achieve against the United States, which had learned well the lessons of Vietnam; he was also mistaken if he thought that the Iraqi people and military would embrace this cause with the tenacity of the Vietcong and the North Vietnamese Army. Assessing the determination or readiness of the Iraqi military to fight was also difficult for U.S. intelligence, which overestimated their morale and commitment to Saddam Hussein. The Iraqi leader could enforce his rule but, unlike Hitler, Stalin, or Napoleon, could not persuade his people to fight and die for him. Yet the readiness to fight is the key to success even in the age of advanced technology. Field Marshal Wavell recognized this when he listed it as one of the four most important lessons of war:

> The final deciding factor of all engagements, battles and wars is the morale of the opposing forces. Better weapons, better food, and superiority in numbers will influence morale, but it is a sheer determination to win, by whomever or whatever inspired, that counts in the end. Fine feathers may make fine birds, but fine battleships do not necessarily make fine sailors or we could never have dominated the Mediterranean against the greatly superior Italian fleet. Study men and their morale always.[11]

This point had been emphasized long before by Clausewitz:

> **If you want to overcome your enemy you must match your effort against his power of resistance, which can be explained as the product of *two inseparable* factors, viz. *the total means at his disposal and the strength of his will*. The extent of the means at his disposal is a matter – though not exclusively – of figures, and should be measurable. But the strength of his will is much less easy to determine and can only be gauged approximately by the strength of the motive animating it . . .**
>
> (Clausewitz, *On War*, p. 77)

The assessment of the enemy's will is as fraught with problems today as it was in Clausewitz's time. The danger is that modern intelligence analysts and commanders may focus on that which can be measured rather than on the critical but more elusive factor of will. Certainly one important lesson of the Gulf War is that a close examination of the enemy's will (requiring familiarity with his language, culture, and politics) is requisite. On this point, it can be said that both sides were equally remiss in their preparations.

Many lessons learned since the Vietnam War were profitably applied

15

in the Gulf War, but there are still some lessons to be learned on war termination. Often, a decisive victory on the battlefield is not final even in military terms. Despite the unprecedented military victory achieved over Iraq, the victory was incomplete in a political sense. Clausewitz observes that on the operational level

> **. . . the importance of victory is chiefly determined by the vigor with which the immediate pursuit is carried out. In other words, pursuit makes up the second act of the victory and in many cases is more important than the first. Strategy at this point draws near to tactics in order to receive the completed assignment from it; and its first exercise of authority is to demand that the victory should really be complete.**
>
> (Clausewitz, *On War*, p. 267)

The Gulf War was terminated prematurely because its center of gravity was incorrectly identified (according to traditional military terms) as the Iraqi armed forces, whereas the defeat of these forces was in fact only a preliminary condition for attacking the true political center of gravity: Saddam Hussein himself. The problem here was, in part, that in the Western tradition of war it is assumed that a political leader suffering such an ignominious defeat will either resign or be removed by others. But even if Saddam Hussein had been identified as the true objective of the war, American laws and political circumstances made it impossible to target a leader in this way.

On the higher political and strategic levels, Clausewitz reminds us that . . .

IN WAR, THE RESULT IS NEVER FINAL

> **even the ultimate [military] outcome of a war is not to be regarded as final. The defeated state often considers the outcome merely as a transitory evil, for which a remedy may still be found in political conditions at some later date.**
>
> (Clausewitz, *On War*, p. 80)

Simply put, achievements on the battlefield can only be consolidated through a concerted political and diplomatic effort that makes the outcome acceptable to the defeated side. (For a detailed discussion of Clausewitz on war termination, see Chapter 14 below.)

While strategists must understand the actual and potential contribution of technology to modern warfare, it is no less vital for them to study the environment in which this technology operates. In the age of advanced technology, there is a natural proclivity to overestimate the role of weapons and, as a result, to undervalue the non-tangible dimensions of strategy and war. Nevertheless, technology is not a panacea that exists in a political vacuum, and when treated as such (e.g., as in the cases of the United States in Vietnam or the Soviet Union in Afghanistan) it cannot succeed.

Nothing is a more helpful corrective for such tendencies than the works of Sun Tzu, Clausewitz, and other renowned strategists; these classics enable students to identify the central elements of warfare that have been obscured by the emergence of modern technology. Neither of these two great strategists states anything that cannot be understood intuitively by an intelligent, rational political or military leader who has never read their writings; but in a technologically-dominated world, little is left to intuition. It is therefore imperative for modern military commanders and strategists, who have spent most of their careers working with military technology, to peruse the works of Sun Tzu and Clausewitz. Having done so, they will be that much better equipped to understand the pivotal political and human dimensions of warfare.

2

Comparing Sun Tzu
and Clausewitz

Theory puts things known into a system. But this function is more than a matter of what the older positivism used to call 'economy of thought' or 'mental shorthand', and what today is expressed in terms of the storage and retrieval of information. It is true that the systematization effected by a theory does have the consequence of simplifying laws and introducing order into congeries of fact. But this is a by-product of a more basic function: to make sense of what would otherwise be inscrutable or unmeaning empirical findings. A theory is more than a synopsis of the moves that have been played in the game of nature; it also sets forth some idea of the rules of the game, by which the moves become intelligible.

. . . theory serves as matchmaker, midwife, and godfather all in one. This service is what is delicately known as the 'heuristic' function of theory.

Abraham Kaplan,
The Conduct of Inquiry,
pp. 302–303

. . . **a working theory is an essential basis for criticism.**
Clausewitz, *On War*, p. 157

Our aim is not to provide new principles and methods of conducting war; rather, we are concerned with examining the essential content of what has long existed, and to trace it back to its basic elements.
Clausewitz, *On War*, p. 389

In political history or international politics, certain fundamental principles and insights into human behavior are generally held to be universally applicable. In the theory of international relations, for example, the assumption that *all* nations share a need to protect and promote their vital interests – and therefore strive to maximize their power *vis-à-vis* potential adversaries – is the type of broadly applicable insight that enables international politics to exist as an autonomous discipline.[1] All foreign policy decision-makers face common problems in assessing their own relative power as well as the intentions and policies of other nations; to implement their policies, all must learn how to manipulate public opinion and how to function within complex bureaucratic and organizational milieux. In short, the discipline assumes that despite the multiplicity of approaches to the formulation of foreign policy throughout the world, many aspects of national behavior can be reduced to a common denominator. A similar assumption can be made in the study of strategy.

The gap between Sun Tzu's *The Art of War* (third or fourth century BC) and Carl von Clausewitz's *On War* (1832) could hardly be wider in terms of time, geographic conditions, and culture. Nevertheless, the differences in emphasis and, at times, substance between these two great strategists should not be exaggerated. Liddell Hart once observed that Clausewitz's *On War* '. . . did not differ so much from Sun Tzu's conclusions as it appeared to do on the surface'. But even Liddell Hart is off the mark when he asserts that 'Sun Tzu has clearer vision, more profound insight, and eternal freshness . . .' or suggests that 'Sun Tzu's realism and moderation form a contrast to Clausewitz's tendency to emphasize the logical ideal and "the absolute" . . .'. Liddell Hart then adds that if one were 'to pursue the logical extreme [of Clausewitz's line of thought] . . . the means would lose all relations to the end';[2] yet this is precisely the opposite of what Clausewitz argues! Liddell Hart is mistaken, not so much because he prefers Sun Tzu, but because his perception of Clausewitz as excessively abstract reflects a superficial acquaintance with *On War*.

This study endeavors to show that these two seemingly divergent works on strategy actually have as much in common as that which presumably separates them; indeed, their fundamental strategic logic is often the same, as is the 'logic' or 'rational calculus' of the Eastern and Western approaches to warfare in general. As Professor John K.

Fairbank has observed, 'much of China's military experience is directly comparable with experience elsewhere . . . Comparative studies will no doubt show up the sinological fallacy as to China's alleged uniqueness.'[3] Whether illusory or merely exaggerated, such differences between these two military thinkers have been thought to exist for some of the following reasons:

* Many strategists are more comfortable reading Sun Tzu rather than Clausewitz, whose methodology and style are not as easy to follow. *On War* therefore lends itself to facile, hence erroneous, comparisons because it is seldom read in its entirety.

* Sun Tzu's *The Art of War* may seem easier on first reading, but it is actually more difficult to understand in depth – while Clausewitz's *On War* is initially more difficult to read, but is actually easier to comprehend if perused carefully.

* Sun Tzu and Clausewitz do not employ the same definitions or frameworks in their studies of war. The wider scope of Sun Tzu's definition has led many a strategist unwittingly to compare apples and oranges.

* *On War* and *The Art of War* frequently approach the same subject or related subjects from different perspectives: that is, they discuss opposite sides of the same coin. As in the case of the proverbial blind men examining various parts of the same elephant, this magnifies the apparent divergence of opinion without changing the fact that there is actually much in common.

Among the aspects of *On War* and *The Art of War* to be compared are their frameworks; methodologies and styles; positions on the primacy of politics in the formulation of strategic policies and the decision to go to war; and analyses of a field commander's responsibilities compared with those of a political leader. Also examined are their evaluations of intelligence and deception; quantitative superiority; the relationship between the offense and defense; friction, chance, luck and uncertainty in war; and the rational calculus of war. (See Table 2.1 for the traditional perceptions of these two classical works.)

Table 2.1
Sun Tzu and Clausewitz as Opposing Paradigms of Waging War

	Sun Tzu	Clausewitz
THEIR PERSPECTIVES ON WAGING WAR	A *broad* perspective that includes a large variety of non-military means (e.g., diplomatic, economic, and psychological).	A *narrow* emphasis on the use of military means. Although the importance of other means is recognized, they are not the concern of the military leader.
THE ROLE OF FORCE	Force should be used sparingly and as the last resort.	The use of force is often both necessary and the most effective (i.e., preferred) method of achieving the political goals of the state. The maximum available force should be used from the outset to achieve decisive results in the shortest possible time.
THE IDEAL VICTORY	The greatest achievement is to win without fighting, to convince the enemy's forces to yield and if possible switch sides rather than be annihilated.	The shortest way to achieve one's political objectives is by the destruction of the enemy's forces in a major battle. (The principle of destruction.) Other, non-military methods of winning are recognized but are rarely effective.
PREFERRED METHOD OF WINNING	Extensive use of deception. Psychological war, non-violent methods. The center of gravity is the enemy's will and alliance system.	The maximum concentration of force at the decisive point of engagement. The center of gravity is the enemy's army.
ADVANTAGES AND DIS-ADVANTAGES OF THE THEORY	An idealized paradigm encouraging the strategist to achieve the least costly victories. This approach may lack realism and ignores the inevitable presence of violence in war. War can become an 'intellectual' or 'metaphysical' exercise. Deception or intelligence can become a panacea.	Realistic; relevant for most types of war. Greater awareness of the violent nature of war. Excessive reliance on the use of force can be more costly; may underestimate some non-material aspects of war (e.g., deception, intelligence).

SUN TZU, CLAUSEWITZ AND THE STUDY OF WAR

The Art of War is a succinct (fewer than 40 pages in English translation, or some 6,600 characters in the original Chinese text) statement on strategy written in the pithy style typical of Chinese classical writings. In contrast, the generally turgid and obscure *On War* is close to 600 pages long. Comprehension of Clausewitz's analytical framework requires repeated reading of *On War* from cover to cover. For example, Chapter 1 of Book I, 'What is War?', cannot be digested easily even after several readings; yet this chapter is the key to mastery of Clausewitz's framework and methodology. (See Appendix C.) No such concerted effort is required for any of Sun Tzu's chapters, each of which can be read independently. Unlike *On War*, *The Art of War* does not offer the reader a systematic explanation or step-by-step reconstruction of the logical process through which concepts are developed. From this point of view, *The Art of War* reads more like a manual intended as a compact guide for the 'prince' or higher-ranking military commander.[4] Thus, while Clausewitz leads the reader through a torturous and tortuous – though rewarding – reasoning process, Sun Tzu, for the most part presents the reader with his conclusions. Clausewitz puts it most clearly when he states:

> **It is precisely that inquiry which is the most essential part of any *theory*, and which may quite appropriately claim that title. It is any analytical investigation leading to a close *acquaintance* with the subject; applied to experience – in our case, to military history – it leads to thorough *familiarity* with it.** [emphasis in the original]
>
> (Clausewitz, *On War*, p. 141)[5]

> **Theory cannot equip the mind with formulas for solving problems, nor can it mark the narrow path on which the sole solution is supposed to lie by planting a hedge of principles on either side. But it can give the mind insight into the great mass of phenomena and of their relationships, then leave it free to rise into the higher realms of action.**
>
> (Clausewitz, *On War*, p. 578)

Whereas Sun Tzu tells the reader that an apple always falls from the tree to the ground (a fact), Clausewitz explains *why* the apple always falls to the ground (a theoretical explanation; gravity). For the reader of *On War*, then, it is the *learning process* that matters most; but for the reader of *The Art of War*, acceptance of conclusions is the principal requirement. However, Clausewitz's sophisticated methodology invites misunderstanding because it is not always easy to decipher. Chief among such methodological concepts is his ideal-type method, which is closely related to the dialectical method of comparing opposites in general and his ideal types in particular (see Appendix C and Chapter 13 for a detailed explanation). For example, Clausewitz develops a concept of the abstract, ideal type of 'total' or 'absolute' war. War in theory, as he calls it, is waged with all available forces and resources – and without interruption – until one side is able to dictate the terms of victory. For Clausewitz, the French Revolution and the Napoleonic Wars were recent reminders that reality could approach his ideal type of total war, but he was also well aware that wars are never fought with *all* available forces and resources, are frequently interrupted, and more often than not end indecisively. In short, war in reality is always limited to some degree.[6]

In the process of explaining how war in reality differs from war in the abstract, Clausewitz systematically develops his most creative and original insights into the nature of war (such as the primacy of rational, political cost/benefit calculations; the value of setting objectives and estimating the national resources to be invested; the concepts of friction and chance; and the dominant role of uncertainty [that is, lack of information and intelligence]). Clausewitz's 'Newtonian' methodology has often been misconstrued, not only because it is abstract and difficult to follow, but also because the author moves from one level to the other (for example, from the ideal to the real and back) without warning.[7] Labouring under this common misconception, Liddell Hart comments that '. . . his [Clausewitz's] theory in a way [is] . . . too abstract and involved for concrete-minded soldiers to follow the course of his argument, which *often turned back from the direction it seemed to be taking*'.[8] This somewhat naive reference to Clausewitz's dialectical analysis shows that Clausewitz's methodology is the weakness *and* the strength of his work. It also explains why the majority of professional military readers and scholars have seldom taken the time to cultivate a deeper understanding of *On War* as the philosophical/educational text that it is; instead, they have preferred to use it as a manual from which to select quotations that conveniently confirm their preconceived ideas. With this in mind, the German General Gunther Blumentritt once observed that to give *On War* to the military was like 'allowing a child to play with a razor blade' ('Clausewitz ist der Rasiermesser in der Hand eines Kindes').[9] This does not mean that Sun Tzu failed to develop many of the same sophisticated concepts; but some of Sun Tzu's concepts are more implicit (or are arrived at intuitively) while those of Clausewitz are constructed through an elegant logical process and discussed in more detail in the context of his general theoretical framework.

Thus, Sun Tzu also employs the ideal-type method, only in a less explicit, more limited fashion. Sun Tzu's recommendation that '. . . *in war the best policy is to take a state intact'* (Sun Tzu, *The Art of War*, pp. 77) and that *'to subdue the enemy without fighting is the acme of skill'* (Sun Tzu, *The Art of War*, pp. 77 and 79) is certainly an ideal to which any political or military leader should aspire, but no more than that. This is evident from Chinese history itself and from the fact that most of *The Art of War* is dedicated to a discussion of how to win by fighting. Clausewitz would surely agree in principle that victory without fighting or bloodshed is desirable; but he also recognizes that this is rarely possible and proceeds forthwith to examine the more likely alternatives. To many, Sun Tzu's statements on the desirability of victory without bloodshed appear to contradict Clausewitz's ideas; in fact, these two strategists are simply approaching the same issue from different perspectives. In the same way, many of the points on which Clausewitz and Sun Tzu seem to disagree can often be attributed to differences in emphasis, not substance. (See Chapter 11 and Appendix C for further development of some of these ideas.)

THEORY, CHANCE AND UNCERTAINTY

> **In short, absolute, so-called mathematical, factors never find a firm basis in military calculations. From the very start, there is an interplay of possibilities, probabilities, good luck and bad that weaves its way throughout the length and breadth of the tapestry. In the whole range of human activities, war most closely resembles a game of cards.**
>
> (Clausewitz, *On War*, p. 86)

Sun Tzu and Clausewitz would probably agree on the fundamental methodological assumption that war is an art, not a science – that each military problem has many potentially correct solutions (not just a single, optimal solution) which are arrived at through the military leader's imagination, creativity, and intuition. They would also agree that the tremendous complexity inherent in the study of war makes it impossible to formulate a positive theory of war even if a set of 'laws' or maxims can be said to exist. Any 'laws' or 'principles of war' have only a *relative validity* – never an absolute one.[10] (In any event, the application of such 'laws' ultimately depends on each leader's subjective interpretation.) Clausewitz, however, treats this critical issue much more explicitly since he devotes all of Book 2 to an analysis of the theory of war.

He observes, for example, that:

> **Efforts were therefore made to equip the conduct of war with principles, rules, or even systems. This did present a positive goal, but people failed to take adequate account of the endless complexities involved. As we have seen, the conduct of war branches out in almost all directions and has no definite limits; while any system, any model, has the finite nature of a synthesis. An irreconcilable conflict exists between this type of theory and actual practice.**
>
> (Clausewitz, *On War*, p. 134)

It is only analytically that these attempts at theory can be called advances in the realm of truth; synthetically, in the rules and regulations they offer, they are absolutely useless . . . They aim at fixed values; but in war everything is uncertain, and calculations have to be made with variable quantities. They direct the inquiry exclusively toward physical quantities, whereas all military action is intertwined with psychological forces and effects. They consider only unilateral action, whereas war consists of a continuous interaction of opposites.

(Clausewitz, On War, p. 136)

Anything that could not be reached by the meager wisdom of such one-sided points of view was held to be beyond scientific control: it lay in the realm of genius, *which rises above all rules.*

(Clausewitz, On War, p. 136)

The very nature of interaction is bound to make it unpredictable.

(Clausewitz, On War, p. 139)

Nor can the theory of war apply the concept of law to action, since no prescriptive formulation universal enough to deserve the name of law can be applied to the constant change and diversity of the phenomena of war.

(Clausewitz, On War, p. 152)

Given the nature of the subject, we must remind ourselves that it is simply not possible to construct a model for the art of war that can serve as a scaffolding on which the commander can rely for support at any time. Whenever he has to fall back on his innate talent, he will find himself outside the model and in conflict with it; no matter how versatile the code, the situation will always lead to the consequences we have already alluded to: *talent and genius operate outside the rules, and theory conflicts with practice.*

(Clausewitz, On War, p. 140)

> **For in the art of war, experience counts more than any amount of abstract truth.**
>
> (Clausewitz, *On War*, p. 164)[11]

As Clausewitz emphasizes, war is in all aspects a reflection of human nature, rife with non-rational motives; on its higher levels, it is a creative and practical activity based on innate talent and inspiration, in which the opponents act and react to real and imagined moves in unpredictable ways. Furthermore, even if the conduct of war itself is rational (e.g., the correlation of ends and means, and defining clear objectives), the ultimate political objectives of war can still be be irrational.

As distinct from other contemporary military theorists, Clausewitz sees war as an 'organic' – not 'inorganic' or 'mechanical' – activity. With this as his premise, it was inevitable for him to conclude that war could never be studied profitably as an exact science. He makes this plain in a profound discussion in Chapter 3 of Book 2 entitled 'Art of War or Science of War'. The object of science, he states, is *knowledge* (*Wissen* in German) while the object of art is *creative ability* (or 'knowing') (*Können* in German). He argues:

> **It is . . . consistent to keep this basis of distinction** [between knowledge and ability] **and call everything art whose object is *creative ability* for instance, architecture** [or war]. **The term science should be kept for disciplines such as mathematics or astronomy, whose object is *pure knowledge*.** [my emphasis]
>
> (Clausewitz, *On War*, p. 148)

> **Creation and production lie in the realm of art: science will dominate where the object is inquiry and knowledge. It follows that the term 'art of war' is more suitable than 'science of war'.**
>
> (Clausewitz, *On War*, pp. 148–149)

Just as an exact science cannot progress without the benefit of some artistic, creative elements, the 'practical' pursuit of an art (e.g., that of warfare) may contain or be based on 'discrete' scientific theories. Each discipline therefore combines, in varying degrees, the interwoven and inseparable elements of art and science. Therefore, although the practice of war is more an art than a science, this does not mean that it cannot be studied systematically or that some scientific methods cannot be applied to non-scientific disciplines (e.g., psychology, economics, political science, war).*

Thus, while Clausewitz reaches the conclusion that war is essentially an art that contains some scientific aspects, Jomini oscillates between his desire to construct a scientific theory of war and his admission that war is a creative activity ultimately based on experience and intuition. Although, in the end, Jomini leans toward the recognition that war is an art, he never fully acknowledges this fact. In the final analysis, Jomini, like Clausewitz, admits that '*every maxim has its exceptions*' (Jomini, *The Art of War*, p. 84).

Inevitably, this tension exists in all theoretical works on war: each author tries to develop a theory based on empirical, historical evidence although no theory of conventional war can ever constitute an accurate basis for either action or prediction. But in recognizing that war is an art, Clausewitz by definition acknowledges *the limits of our understanding of war*. And this very realization is of the utmost practical value, as it impels political and military leaders to approach the specific conditions of each war with an open mind, a mind ready to adapt old lessons to new or unprecedented circumstances. The correct application of insights culled from the study and theory of war therefore first requires a keen understanding of its *limitations*.

Although he does not include a direct, in-depth discussion of this subject, Sun Tzu recognizes – as the title of his book indicates – that it is impossible to predict the shape and course of a war through the mechanical application of immutable formulae. '*[Ho Yen-hsi]*[12] *Now in war there may be one hundred changes in each step*' (*The Art of War*, p. 83). '*And as water has no constant form, there are in war no*

---

* To be even more precise, Clausewitz reaches the conclusion that '. . . **strictly speaking, war is neither an art nor a science . . . rather it is part of man's social existence.**' This puts war somewhere between art and an exact science, but much closer to art. He goes on to compare war with commerce '**which is also a conflict of human interests and activities and is still closer to politics which in turn may be considered a kind of commerce on a larger scale**' (Clausewitz, *On War*, p. 149).

According to Clausewitz, three main characteristics distinguish war from both science and art: (1) war deals with *living* not *inanimate* forces; (2) war involves conflict – action and reaction – between opponents; (3) war involves a clash between asymmetrical interests (i.e., the inherently weaker and positive offense trying to acquire and expand, and the inherently stronger, negative defense trying to maintain what it has).

constant conditions' (Sun Tzu, *The Art of War*, p. 101). He then employs poetic metaphors to illustrate the infinite complexity of warfare:

> *The musical notes are only five in number but their melodies are so numerous that one cannot hear them all.*
>
> *The primary colours are only five in number but their combinations are so infinite that one cannot visualize them all.*
>
> *The flavours are only five in number but their blends are so various that one cannot taste them all.*
>
> *In battle there are only the normal and extraordinary forces, but their combinations are limitless; none can comprehend them all.*
>
> *For these two forces are mutually reproductive; their interaction as endless as that of interlocked rings. Who can determine where one ends and the other begins?*
>
> (Sun Tzu, *The Art of War*, pp. 91–92)

Sun Tzu, like Clausewitz, observes that the complexity and unpredictability of war are generated by the process of interaction.

> *[Mei Yao-ch'en] That which depends on me, I can do; that which depends on the enemy cannot be certain.*
>
> *Therefore it is said that one may know how to win, but cannot necessarily do so.*
>
> (Sun Tzu, *The Art of War*, p. 85)

> *Of the five elements, none is always predominant; of the four seasons, none lasts forever; of the days, some are long and some are short, and the moon waxes and wanes.*
>
> (Sun Tzu, *The Art of War*, p. 101)

In other words, the principles of war are understandable in theory, but there is no blueprint to guide in their application.

> *These are the strategist's keys to victory. It is not possible to discuss them beforehand.*
>
> (Sun Tzu, *The Art of War*, p. 70)

In the end, Sun Tzu reaches the same conclusion as Clausewitz: '*[Li Chu'uan] In the art of war there are no fixed rules*' (Sun Tzu, *The Art of War*, p. 93). Both agree that success depends on what Clausewitz terms the *coup d'oeil* (or intuition) of the military genius. Such talent can be refined through experience, but only in those who already possess the innate ability. Sun Tzu views war as an original art that requires imagination, intuition, and innovation: '*Therefore, when I have won a victory I do not repeat my tactics but respond to circumstances in an infinite variety of ways*' (Sun Tzu, *The Art of War*, p. 100). Both strategists would also agree that the conclusions reached in their respective works have only limited value; for, despite their sagacity, they cannot give the military professional concrete advice on how to apply their insights. Success in war hinges not on the mastery of theory by rote but rather on its judicious application – and this is ultimately determined by the military commander's intuition.

It is also interesting to compare Clausewitz's view on the educational value of theory with that of Jomini – one of his contemporaries:

> *Correct theories, founded upon the right principles, sustained by actual events of wars, and added to accurate military history, will form a true school of instruction for generals. If these means do not produce great men, they will at least produce generals of sufficient skill to take rank next after the natural masters of the art of war . . .*

> *I cannot too often repeat that the theory of the great combinations of war is in itself very simple, and requires nothing more than ordinary intelligence and careful consideration . . .*

> *These truths need not lead to the conclusion that there can be no sound rules in war, the observance of which, the chances being equal, will lead to success. It is true that theories cannot teach men with mathematical precision what they should do in every possible case; but it is also certain that they will always point out the errors which should be avoided; and this is a highly important consideration, for these rules thus become, in the hands of skillful generals commanding brave troops, means of almost certain success.*[13]

Since Jomini cannot seem to make up his mind whether war is an art or a 'science',[14] the tension between the two approaches remains unresolved. According to Jomini, war on the highest political and strategic levels cannot be studied or mastered as though it were a science; on the lower operational level, however, he believes it is possible to identify a set of fundamental rules or principles. And these principles, which have a general scientific validity, can be taught to every general. Yet as Jomini acknowledges, it is the artistic intuition of the military genius that determines whether these scientific principles are correctly applied.

> *Nothing is better calculated to kill natural genius and to cause error to triumph, than those pedantic theories, based upon the false idea that war is a positive science, all the operations of which can be reduced to infallible conclusions.* [15]

In his conclusions, he therefore observes that '*war in its ensemble is not a science, but an art*' (Jomini, *The Art of War*, p. 321).

3

The Definition of War:
A Question of the Level of Analysis

Perhaps the greatest source of confusion in comparisons of *On War* and *The Art of War* has been the failure to recognize that their authors use different analytical frameworks and definitions. Sun Tzu devotes considerable attention to concerns that precede war, discussing in detail the advantages of various diplomatic strategies. For him, diplomacy is the best means of attaining his ideal of victory without bloodshed. When advising that the enemy's plans should be attacked at their inception (pp. 77–78), Sun Tzu is presumably referring to diplomatic and political bargaining, negotiations, and deception, although he offers no further explanation. As the next best step, he recommends disruption of the enemy's alliances. When deprived of external support, the enemy can, he believes, be expected to abandon his plans for war or at least be more rapidly defeated in isolation (see Figure 3.1).

> *[Tu Yu] Do not allow your enemies to get together.*
>
> *[Wang Hsi] Look into the matter of his alliances and cause them to be severed and dissolved. If an enemy has alliances, the problem is grave and the enemy's position strong; if he has no alliances, the problem is minor and the enemy's position weak.*
>
> (Sun Tzu, *The Art of War*, p. 78)

Sun Tzu's framework is much broader than that of Clausewitz, whose treatise is specifically on the art of waging war, not on the workings of diplomacy before, during, and after war. For Sun Tzu, diplomacy and war are not just closely related – they comprise a continuous, seamless activity. For Clausewitz, however, they can also be independent of one another and may lack the unity envisioned in Sun Tzu's approach. Clausewitz's analysis begins at the point that diplomacy has failed and war has become unavoidable. Merely because Clausewitz largely omits diplomacy from the scope of his discussion does not mean that he

FIGURE 3.1
SUN TZU AND CLAUSEWITZ: A BROADER AND NARROWER CONCEPT OF WAR

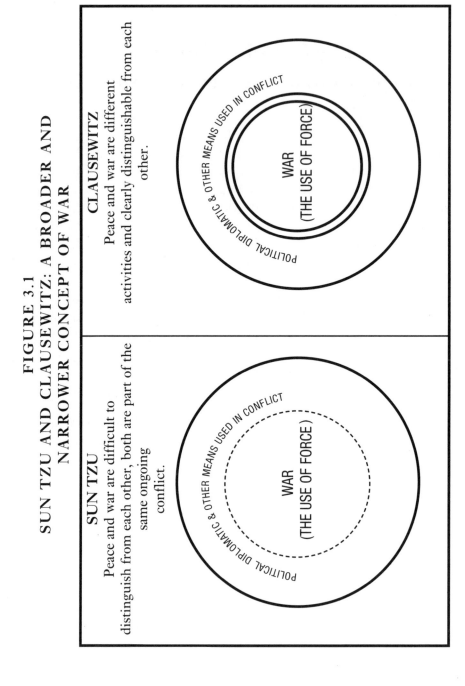

SUN TZU
Peace and war are difficult to distinguish from each other, both are part of the same ongoing conflict.

POLITICAL DIPLOMATIC & OTHER MEANS USED IN CONFLICT

WAR
(THE USE OF FORCE)

CLAUSEWITZ
Peace and war are different activities and clearly distinguishable from each other.

POLITICAL DIPLOMATIC & OTHER MEANS USED IN CONFLICT

WAR
(THE USE OF FORCE)

underestimates or ignores its significance. In fact, he plainly states that diplomacy (or politics) continues to play an important role throughout a war:

> **We also want to make it clear that war itself does not suspend political intercourse or change it into something entirely different. In essentials that intercourse continues irrespective of the means it employs . . . Do political relations between peoples and governments stop when diplomatic notes are no longer exchanged?**
>
> (Clausewitz, *On War*, p. 605)

Despite his reputation to the contrary, Clausewitz is aware, perhaps more than any other military thinker, that war is only one of the means (and not even an independent one) of achieving one's objectives when all else has failed. He defines war precisely in this context:

> **War is thus an act of force to compel our enemy to do our will.**
>
> (Clausewitz, *On War*, p. 75)[1]

> **War is a clash between major interests, which is resolved by bloodshed –** *that is the only way in which it differs from other conflicts.* [my emphasis]
>
> (Clausewitz, *On War*, p. 149)

> **Essentially war is fighting, for fighting is the only principle in the manifold activities generally designated as war.**
>
> (Clausewitz, *On War*, p. 127)

(For Clausewitz's other definitions of war, see Chapter 11, pp. 153–154, below.)

While Sun Tzu is primarily concerned with the conduct of war on the highest strategic level, Clausewitz focuses on the lower strategic/operational levels. What can be misleading is the fact that Clausewitz, who is best known for his ideas on the primacy of politics, actually devotes relatively little space (two out of eight books in *On War*) to the analysis of war on its highest level. The diplomatic or economic environment in which war takes place is just not within the scope of *On War*. For Clausewitz's military leader, the environment within which he

35

must strive for victory is a 'given'. In this sense, it is therefore inappropriate to compare these two treatises on identical terms.[2]

Clausewitz has also been accused of disregarding the economic and logistical dimensions of war. This criticism is not without merit, since logistics and economics are inextricably linked to strategy and war. Nevertheless, one must remember that Clausewitz, as mentioned earlier, confines his discussion to the conduct of war on the battlefield and takes the necessary economic and logistical support for granted (see Chapter 9, pp. 109–111). (But on his awareness of the logistical and economic preparations for war, see Book 5, Chapter 14, 'Maintenance and Supply', pp. 330–340.)

According to Clausewitz, it is possible, even advisable, to distinguish between the preparatory phases and the combat and operational phases of warfare.

> We clearly see that the activities characteristic of war may be split into two main categories: those *that are merely preparations for war*, and *war proper*. The same distinction must be made in theory as well . . . The knowledge and skills involved in the preparations will be concerned with the creation, training and maintenance of the fighting forces . . . The theory of war proper, on the other hand, is concerned with the use of these means, once they have been developed, for the purposes of war. All that it requires from the first group is the end product, an understanding of their main characteristics. That is what we call 'the art of war' in a narrower sense, or 'the theory of the conduct of war' or 'the theory of the use of the fighting forces'. For our purposes, they all mean the same thing. That narrower theory, then, deals with the engagement, with fighting itself, and treats such matters as marches, camps, and billets as conditions that may be more or less identical with it. It does not comprise questions of supply, but will take these into account on the same basis as other given factors.
>
> The art of war in the narrower sense must now in its turn be broken down into tactics and strategy. The first is con-

cerned with the form of the individual engagement, the second its use. [emphasis in the original]

(Clausewitz, *On War*, pp. 131–132)

In this context, it is instructive to compare Clausewitz's and Jomini's definitions of strategy. From a modern perspective, both would appear to describe more of what would today be considered the higher operational level of warfare rather than the strategic.[3] Clausewitz states:

> **Strategy is the use of the engagement for the purpose of the war. The strategist must therefore define an aim for the entire operational side of the war that will be in accordance with its purpose. In other words, he will draft the plan of the war, and the aim will determine the series of actions intended to achieve it: he will, in fact, shape the individual campaigns and, within these, decide on the individual engagements. Since most of these matters have to be based on assumptions that may not prove correct, while other, more detailed orders cannot be determined in advance at all, it follows that the strategist must go on the campaign itself. Detailed orders can then be given on the spot, allowing the general plan to be adjusted to the modifications that are continuously required. The strategist, in short, must maintain control throughout.**
>
> (Clausewitz, *On War*, p. 177)

Jomini defines strategy in these words:

> *Strategy is the art of making war upon the map, and comprehends the whole theater of operations. Grand Tactics is the art of posting troops upon the battlefield according to the accidents of the ground, or bringing them into action, and the art of fighting upon the ground in contradistinction to planning upon a map. Its operations may extend over a field of ten or twelve miles in extent . . . Strategy decides where to act . . . grand tactics decides the manner of execution and the employment of the troops.*
>
> (Jomini, *The Art of War*, pp. 69–71)

That Jomini's conception of strategy is what we would now classify as the operational level of warfare is made clear by another position later in the book:

> *Strategy, as has already been explained, is the art of bringing the greatest part of the forces of an army upon the important point of the theater of war or the zone of operations.*
>
> (Jomini, *The Art of War*, p. 322)[4]

Concepts of the different levels of warfare have changed over the years in response to advances in weapons technology and communications (that is, the appearance of longer-range weaponry, particularly air power, which can extend the war well beyond the front lines; and improved communications that permit direct real-time control over events on the front from far behind the combat zone). As war became more industrialized, factors such as the mobilization of all national resources, research and production, and diplomacy as well as the simultaneous direction of war on many fronts were increasingly seen as part of strategy.

Sun Tzu, on the other hand, views the political, diplomatic, and logistical preparations for war *and* the fighting itself as integral parts of the same activity. Consequently, he devotes as much attention to the environment in which war unfolds as to the battle proper. Clausewitz's more limited definition explains, in part, why it was so easy for his followers to forget that **'war is the continuation of politics by other means'**. By drawing an arguably artificial distinction, Clausewitz tends to overemphasize the centrality of combat at the expense of political preparations; his assumption that the logistical or economic dimensions of war would somehow take care of themselves, or the implication (as some of his adherents thought) that economic imperatives can be outflanked by victory on the battlefield, is indeed dangerous, as the Germans discovered in the First and Second World Wars. This narrow definition is even more misleading today, when technological innovation and scientific discoveries, as well as the production and distribution of fuel, food, weapons, and ammunition, are as crucial as one's performance on the battlefield. In this respect, Sun Tzu's (or even Jomini's)[5] comprehensive framework for the analysis of strategy and war is much more relevant to our own time than that of Clausewitz.

The consequences of the different levels of analysis used by Sun Tzu on the one hand, and Clausewitz and Jomini on the other, are best illustrated in their attempts to identify the key objectives for the most decisive defeat of the enemy. This is the subject of Chapter 5 below. (On the question of the level of analysis see also Appendix E.)

4

Clausewitz and Mao Tse-tung on Theory and Practice in War

> *These are the strategist's keys to victory. It is not possible to discuss them beforehand.*
>
> Sun Tzu, *The Art of War*, p. 70

> The influence of theoretical truths on practical life is always exerted more through critical analysis than through doctrine. Critical analysis being the application of theoretical truth to actual events . . . .
>
> Clausewitz, *On War*, p. 156

> . . . the step is always long from cognition to volition, from knowledge to ability.[1]
>
> Clausewitz, *On War*, p. 112

> [The] gap between principles and actual events . . . cannot always be bridged by a succession of logical deductions.
>
> Clausewitz, *On War*, p. 108

To make a fortune in business, one simply has to 'buy cheap and sell high'. This well-known advice seems clear enough, but if it were that easy to translate into reality, everyone in business would be wealthy. In much the same way, the theory of war is not that difficult to understand. The principles of war and the essence of good strategy are certainly no secret: they include familiar concepts such as avoiding a war on two fronts; defining clear objectives; identifying the principle of concentration, the culminating point of victory, or a center of gravity; achieving surprise; employing deception; and carefully planning military action on all levels with rational calculations. In war, as in business, it is not possible for all of the participants to succeed simultaneously, and certainly not in the long run.

Thus, although the principles and logic of waging war are widely known, their implementation is seldom straightforward or formulaic. Clausewitz never tires of reminding us that there is a **'great chasm between planning and execution'**, and that **'everything in war is very simple, but even the simplest thing is difficult'** (Clausewitz, *On War*, pp. 117–118; also pp. 146, 178). It is clear why any teacher of strategy or military affairs should be concerned with this question. After all, why should one write or teach about war (or business, or politics, for that matter), if there is no guarantee that anyone will be able to profit from this wisdom in practice? Mao Tse-tung also considers the question of theory versus practice at great length:

> To learn is no easy matter and to apply what one has learned is even harder. Many people appear impressive when discoursing on military science in classrooms or in books, but when it comes to actual fighting, some win battles and others lose them. Both the history of war and our own experience in war have proved this point.
>
> (Mao Tse-tung, *Selected Military Writings*, pp. 84–85)

> The concentration of troops seems easy, but is quite hard in practice. Everybody knows that the best way is to use a large force to defeat a small one, and yet many people fail to do so . . .
>
> (Mao Tse-tung, *Selected Military Writings*, p. 131)

The short answer to this problem is that some knowledge and a few good insights are still better than nothing. And although such knowledge cannot produce perfect answers in the real world, it does at least provide the practitioner with some general or specific guidance while preparing him to some degree for the uncertainties and difficulties he will encounter.

The wide gap between theory and practice arises from the unpredictable nature of war, and the fact that it can never be waged as an exact science. (The reasons why war is an art not a science are discussed throughout this book. See, for example, Chapter 2, pp. 25–32.) A military strategist contemplating the complexity of war must consider factors such as the staggering number of variables involved; the fact that key elements cannot be clearly measured, isolated, or controlled; the reciprocal nature of action and reaction; the role of friction, chance, and luck; the effects of secrecy and deception; the best way to deal with inadequate or unreliable intelligence; the paradoxical nature of risk; and the influence of moral factors. War therefore always consists of *unique* *situations* that can be resolved only through *subjective analysis*, which, by its very nature, cannot be readily incorporated into a theory of war because it depends on creativity, talent, intuition, and experience. Action in war, particularly on the operational level, can rarely be based on *objective analysis* alone. Thus, the inherently non-linear, unpredictable nature of war means that the gap between theory and practice can never be completely bridged, although it can sometimes be narrowed: *this, in a way, is the subject of the entire operational theory of war.* Proposed operational solutions range from the principle of concentration to the meticulous preparation of flexible plans and contingency plans; logistical preparations; the acquisition of better real-time intelligence; and the use of secrecy and deception (while preventing the enemy's use of the same). (These are discussed in depth elsewhere in the text. See Chapter 15.)

In this context, however, it is interesting to compare the theoretical 'solutions' proposed by Clausewitz and Mao. Clausewitz aspires to close the gap between theory and practice by relying on the *experience and intuition* of the military commander. Mao, in addition to relying on experience, hopes to find the solution in '*objective-scientific*' *estimates and analysis* of the military situation. At first glance, Clausewitz and Mao appear to be advocating diametrically opposed solutions – one largely subjective, and the other largely objective. In truth, however, these two approaches overlap and are essentially subjective; furthermore, both ultimately fail to find a satisfactory solution.

Clausewitz is a great believer in the value of experience because he knows that the theoretical understanding of war has its limitations, that even the best theory does not hold all of the answers. Referring to his own theory, Clausewitz says:

No logical [theoretical] conclusion has been avoided; but whenever the [theoretical] thread became too thin, I have preferred to break it off and go back to *the relevant phenomena of experience.* Just as some plants bear fruit only if they do not shoot up too high, so in the practical arts, the leaves and flowers of theory must be kept close to its proper soil – experience.

(Clausewitz, *On War*, p. 61, Note to an
Unpublished Manuscript on the Theory of War)

Theory is secondary in the sense that it is derived from the observation of reality.

. . . A satisfactory theory of war [is] one that will be of real service and never conflicts with reality. It only needs intelligent treatment to make it conform to action, and to end the absurd difference between theory and practice that unreasonable theories have so often evoked.

(Clausewitz, *On War*, p. 142)

Theory is content to refer to experience in general to indicate the origin of the [theoretical] method, but not to prove it.

(Clausewitz, *On War*, p. 171)

. . . The idea we wish to convey . . . will always have its origins in the impressions made by the sum total of the phenomena of war, rather than in speculative study.

(Clausewitz, *On War*, p. 138)

These [theoretical] truths must be rooted in experience. No theorist, and no commander, should bother himself with psychological and philosophical sophistries.

(Clausewitz, *On War*, p. 137)

. . . Theoretical truth must have been derived from military history or at least checked against it . . . A great advantage offered by this method is that theory will have to remain realistic: it cannot allow itself to get lost in futile speculation, hairsplitting, and flights of fancy.

(Clausewitz, *On War*, p. 144)

> In almost any other profession, a man can work with truths he has learned from musty books . . . It is never like that in war.
>
> (Clausewitz, *On War*, p. 147)

> . . . In the art of war, experience counts more than any amount of abstract truths.
>
> (Clausewitz, *On War*, p. 164)

The primacy of 'empirical evidence' and experience is central to Clausewitz's theory of war. In today's high-tech wars, theory almost inevitably *precedes* reality and experience because technological innovations are introduced at an accelerated pace and each war differs substantially from the last. This widens the gap between theory and practice, generating increasingly unrealistic theories or doctrines of war. At times, practice *is even considered an unnecessary part* of this process. In this sense, modern theories of war are being developed more as 'thought experiments' (*Gedankenexperiment*) or Nintendo-style war games than as reflections of actual experience. Thus, planning for modern conventional war will in the future be based less on experience and more on 'laboratory' experiments and computer exercises. This trend is inevitable but problematic. If Clausewitz's approach to the study of war is correct, and war is dominated by the reciprocal interaction of living actors, the new approach to developing theories of war is likely to fail in confrontations between equally capable opponents.

It is not surprising, therefore, that Clausewitz sought to narrow the gap between theory and practice by relying on the experience, talent, and intuition of the commander (see Chapter 16, pp. 265–271). In a world of friction, 'a force that theory can never quite define', instinct and experience provide the only solution.

> Only the experienced officer will make the right decision in major and minor battles at every pulsebeat of war. Practice and experience dictate the answer: this is possible, this is not.
>
> (Clausewitz, *On War*, p. 120)

> Is there any lubricant that will reduce this abrasion [i.e., friction]? Only one, and a commander and his army will not always have it readily available: combat experience.
>
> (Clausewitz, *On War*, p. 122)

45

Experience can be obtained directly, through combat, military exercises, and training, or indirectly through vicarious experience such as sending observers to learn from the wars of other nations. But experience alone is not enough. Since different commanders will not profit equally from the same experience, talent is needed as well.

> . . . It is natural that military activity, whose plans are based on general circumstances, are so frequently disrupted by unexpected particular events, should remain largely a matter of talent, and that theoretical *directives* tend to be less useful here than in any other sphere . . . For lack of objective knowledge one has to trust talent or luck . . . *Talent and genius operate outside the rules, and theory conflicts with practice.*
>
> (Clausewitz, *On War*, p. 140)

> All theories, however, must stick to categories of phenomena and can never take account of a truly unique case; this must be left to judgment and talent.
>
> (Clausewitz, *On War*, p. 139)

So, how does experience in war narrow the gap between theory and practice? Clausewitz's answer resembles the solution that Mao is seeking, namely, the ability to make objective, 'rational' decisions in war. Experience, Clausewitz argues, 'will . . . **provide a degree of objectivity** . . .' (Clausewitz, *On War*, p. 137). Yet, although experience can indeed provide a certain degree of objectivity for the decision-maker, it can also make his decision more subjective by predisposing him to a particular reaction to a certain stimulus. Hence, experience can be as much of a hindrance as an asset when it reduces the commander's incentive to take new and different circumstances into account.

Another problem arises when a commander applies experience on one level of warfare to practice on another. The experience of Napoleon and Hitler served them well on the operational level, but proved counterproductive when applied to the strategic level, where it led to the 'tacticization of strategy' (see Appendix E, pp. 353–360). Clausewitz recognizes that such experience is less useful at the higher levels of warfare:

> **Routine** [an important form of experience for Clausewitz] **will be more frequent and indispensable, the lower the level of action. As the level rises, its use will decrease to the point where, at the summit, it disappears completely. Consequently, it is more appropriate to tactics than to strategy.**
>
> (Clausewitz, *On War*, p. 153)

Indeed, for Clausewitz (though less so for Mao), the gap between theory and practice is more of a concern on the operational than on the strategic level.

Ultimately, though, Clausewitz's 'solution' is unsatisfactory and incomplete. Perhaps he places too much emphasis on the role of experience, which in turn depends on the problematic concept of the talented military genius. History teaches us that there are few such geniuses. A talented military genius might put his experience to its *best* use by learning to discern when it is and is not relevant.

Mao's theory places experience in an equally important position.

> Experience is essential . . . and failure is indeed the mother of success. But it is also necessary to learn with an open mind from the experience of others; and it is sheer 'narrow empiricism' to insist on one's own personal experience in all matters and, in its absence, to adhere stubbornly to one's own opinion and reject other people's experience.
>
> (Mao Tse-tung, *Selected Military Writings*, p. 121)

> All military laws and military theories which are in the nature of principles are the experience of past wars . . . We should seriously study these lessons . . . We should put these conclusions to the test of our own experience, assimilating what is useful, rejecting what is useless, and adding what is specifically our own.
>
> (Mao Tse-tung, *Selected Military Writings*, p. 87)

> Neither a beginner nor a person who fights only on paper can become a really able high-ranking commander; only one who has learned through actual fighting in war can do so.
>
> (Mao Tse-tung, *Selected Military Writings*, p. 87)

For Mao, however, closing the gap between theory and practice means conducting a 'scientific' analysis of the situation. He believes that the value of the principles of war and military manuals lies in their ability to warn the commander against 'subjectively committing mistakes through too rigid an application of principles' (Mao Tse-tung, *Selected Military Writings*, p. 85). 'The crux is to bring the subjective and the objective into proper correspondence with each other' (Mao Tse-tung, *Selected Military Writings*, p. 85). Why is it so difficult to perceive reality with a modicum of objectivity? In their haste to achieve victory, military commanders and strategists tend either to underestimate or to overestimate both their own power and that of the enemy. They often want to achieve impossible victories or else prefer to remain on the defensive long after they should have moved on to the offensive.

> All of the experience of the ten months of war proves the error both of the theory of China's inevitable subjugation and of the theory of China's quick victory. The former gives rise to compromise and the latter to the tendency to underestimate the enemy. Both approaches to the problem are subjective and one-sided, or in other words, unscientific.
>
> (Mao Tse-tung, *Selected Military Writings*, pp. 188–189)

> A careless military man bases his military plans on his own wishful thinking and hence his plans are fanciful and do not correspond with reality.
>
> (Mao Tse-tung, *Selected Military Writings*, p. 86)

Unlike Clausewitz, Mao does not believe in innate genius or a special talent, but in a careful, 'rational' study of the circumstances and environment, in 'the concrete analysis of concrete conditions' coupled with a readiness to learn and adapt quickly (Mao Tse-tung, *Selected Military Writings*, p. 94, quoting Lenin). For Mao, then, there is less genius and more hard work:

> In real life, we cannot ask for 'ever-victorious generals' who are few and far between in history.
>
> (Mao Tse-tung, *Selected Military Writings*, p. 85)

> The initiative is not an innate attribute of genius, but is something an intelligent leader attains through open-minded study and correct appraisal of the objective conditions and through correct military and political dispositions. It follows that the

initiative is not ready-made but is something that requires conscious effort.

(Mao Tse-tung, *Selected Military Writings*, p. 161)

This wisdom in sensing changes and choosing the right moment to act is not easily acquired; it can be gained only by those who study with a receptive mind and investigate and ponder diligently. Prudent consideration of the circumstances is essential to prevent flexibility from turning into impulsive action.

(Mao Tse-tung, *Selected Military Writings*, p. 163)

Mao believes that a thorough and careful *net assessment* can indeed produce an objective or accurate assessment of reality. He makes this clear in one of the longest sections, in which he also refers to Sun Tzu's theory of war:

The laws of war, like the laws governing all other things, are reflections in our minds of objective realities: everything outside of the mind is objective reality. Consequently, what has to be learned and known includes the state of affairs on the enemy side and that on our side, both of which should be regarded as the object of study, while the mind (the capacity to think) alone is the subject performing the study. Some people are good at knowing themselves and poor in knowing the enemy, and some are the other way round; neither can solve the problem of learning and applying the laws of war. There is a saying in the book of Sun Tzu, the great military scientist of ancient China: 'Know the enemy and know yourself, and you can fight a hundred battles with no danger of defeat' which refers both to the stage of learning and to the stage of application, both to knowing the laws of the development of objective reality and to deciding on our own actions in accordance with these laws in order to overcome the enemy facing us.

(Mao Tse-tung, *Selected Military Writings*, p. 88)

Mao's belief that it is possible to conduct an objective, rational analysis can be attributed not only to Sun Tzu but also to dialectical materialism and the Marxist belief that history and politics can be studied successfully on a scientific basis. Is Mao's belief in an objective, detached analysis of military action more reliable than Clausewitz's reliance on talent, genius, and experience? Not really. Particularly in military affairs, reality is surprisingly elusive. In fact, the higher the level of decision-making, the more reality is likely to be distorted by wishful thinking, political considerations, ideological biases, poor intelligence, past experience, partial information, and individual and organizational interests. The vast body of literature on this topic largely agrees that misperceptions of political and military reality are as common as accurate assessments.[2]

No one could be more aware of such problems than Mao, who was involved in directing a war that lasted almost two decades. Political leaders, and military commanders and strategists who are being pressured to change their current strategy in a protracted, indecisive war will be sorely tempted to take shortcuts to end the conflict. Periclean, Fabian, or Maoist strategies in their early phases always call for disengagement, avoidance of battle on the enemy's terms, and prolonged delays in action. Consequently, identifying the circumstances and trends in a prolonged conflict occupies a central position in Mao's theory of war. He spends more time discussing this subject, especially the pathologies of the process, than any other strategist does.

> Epistemologically speaking, the source of all erroneous views on war lies in *idealist* and *mechanistic* tendencies . . . People with such tendencies are subjective and one-sided in their approach to problems. They either indulge in groundless and purely subjective talk, basing themselves upon a single aspect or temporary manifestation [and] magnify it with similar subjectivity into the whole of the problem . . . Only by opposing idealistic and mechanistic tendencies and taking an objective all-sided view in making a study of war can we draw correct conclusions on the question of war.
>
> (Mao Tse-tung, *Selected Military Writings*, p. 195)

In the case of the Communist Party in the People's Republic of China and the Red Army, Mao considers two basic groups of pathologies that can often (though not exclusively) be identified with the right or left wing of the party. The first group consists of conservatives who, because of a lack of confidence caused by early defeats, tend to overestimate the enemy's strength. As a result, they leave the initiative to the enemy ('only retreat, never advance') (Mao Tse-tung, *Selected Military*

Writings, p. 245). Their tendency to remain on the defensive even when the situation calls for a gradual transition to the offensive unnecessarily prolongs the war. Suffering from what Mao derogatively terms *guerrilla-ism* or *retreatism*, such military conservatives so prefer irregular or guerrilla warfare that they cannot bring themselves to make the transition to regular warfare (or 'mobile war', as Mao calls it).

On the left side of the spectrum, Mao identifies those whose overweening ideological zeal causes them to underestimate the enemy's strength while overestimating their own. Their arrogance feeds their desire prematurely to accelerate the transition from one phase of war to another, particularly from irregular, guerrilla warfare to regular, conventional warfare. Mao describes this approach, which inevitably results in premature offensives and costly defeats, as 'striking with two "fists" in two directions at the same time' (Mao Tse-tung, *Selected Military Writings*, p. 95). Governed by the 'only advance, never retreat' mentality (Mao Tse-tung, *Selected Military Writings*, p. 245), these impulsive 'adventurists' are convinced that they can easily 'wipe out the enemy before breakfast' (Mao Tse-tung, *Selected Military Writings*, p. 143). Mao warns that such wishful thinking and strong motivation are simply not enough (Mao Tse-tung, *Selected Military Writings*, p. 144):

> The exponents of quick victory . . . are . . . likewise wrong. Either they completely forget the contradiction between strength and weakness, remembering only the other contradictions, or they exaggerate China's advantages beyond all semblance to reality and beyond recognition, or they presumptuously take the balance of forces at one time and one place for the whole situation, as in the old saying, 'A leaf before the eye shuts out Mount Tai.'
>
> (Mao Tse-tung, *Selected Military Writings*, p. 206)

> In the end, Mr. Reality will come and pour a bucket of cold water over these chatterers, showing them up as mere windbags who want to get things on the cheap, to have gains without pains . . . There is no magic short-cut.
>
> (Mao Tse-tung, *Selected Military Writings*, pp. 218–219)

According to Mao, these 'left opportunists' are those who were 'mechanically opposed to employment of defensive military measures [which] was nothing but infantile thinking' (Mao Tse-tung, *Selected Military Writings*, p. 102). Mao refers to both types of subjective errors as 'the theories and practices of hotheads and ignoramuses' (Mao Tse-tung, *Selected Military Writings*, p. 113). And yet, from the greater attention he devotes to mistakes on the left (i.e., the premature transition from guerrilla warfare to conventional war, and from the defense to the offense), it is clear that Mao considers the mistakes of this group to be far more damaging. This makes sense for a military theorist who developed a new theory of protracted war and saw no hope for a quick victory because of the prevailing conditions in China and the strength of his enemies.

As with all of Mao's theoretical writings on war, once we strip away his Marxist jargon, we are left with two universal, opposing approaches to the management of war (the other being that of Clausewitz). One proposes to close the gap between theory and practice by experience and innate talent – the other to try an 'objective', scientific analysis. The question of the relationship between the theory and practice must be of primary concern to anyone writing a major work on these aspects of warfare. There is perhaps no other profession in which the discrepancy between theory and reality is so great. While the theory of war is relatively simple, its implementation never is.

As Raymond Aron has put it, the study of war is, in the end, about praxeology (i.e., *the theory of practical activity and human conduct*). Ultimately, therefore, every student of war must deal with the problem of how any such theory translates into reality. The difference between Mao and Clausewitz on this question is that Mao not only developed but also implemented his own theories. But since Mao's 'objective' approach is as problematic as Clausewitz's 'subjective' solution, it is best to seek a balanced answer that integrates both. As dynamic conflict between living forces whose actions, reactions, and interactions tend towards chaos, war is dominated by a level of uncertainty that ensures a perpetual gap between theory and practice.[3]

5

'Attacking the Enemy's Plans' and the Concept of 'The Center of Gravity': Eastern Psychology and Western Mechanics

Finding and attacking the most critical point in the enemy's position is another problem that inevitably occupies every strategist. Among the many ideas Clausewitz develops in his attempt to grapple with this problem is the concept of the center of gravity (discussed at length in *On War*, Book 8, pp. 597–599 and p. 617; and Chapter 27 of Book 6, pp. 484–487). As we shall see, Sun Tzu develops a number of similar solutions though he ranks them in an entirely different order of priority. The juxtaposition of their ideas presents an outstanding opportunity to observe how these strategists *think along parallel lines* even as it demonstrates some of the unavoidable conflicts stemming from their different methodologies and levels of analysis.

In this instance, Clausewitz borrows a concept from the world of Newtonian physics (as he does with the concept of friction) and applies it to the world of strategy and military operations; and while Sun Tzu is as remote as he could be from the world of Newtonian physics,[1] he arrives – two millennia before Clausewitz – at similar solutions to the problem of designing the most effective strategy.

As in other cases, Clausewitz develops the concept of the *center of gravity* more systematically and in greater depth than Sun Tzu: that which is explicit in Clausewitz's work is only implicit in Sun Tzu's. Clausewitz invites the reader to follow every step in the development of his idea; Sun Tzu presents the reader with a text of interrelated aphorisms but omits an explanation of the logical process used to arrive at his conclusions. With logic and detailed empirical evidence as his starting point, Clausewitz defines the center of gravity:

What the theorist has to say here is this: one must keep the dominant characteristic of both belligerents in mind. Out of these characteristics a certain center of gravity develops, the hub of all power and movement, on which everything depends. That is the point against which all our energies should be directed . . . *If the enemy is thrown off balance, he must not be given time to recover.* Blow after blow must be aimed in the same direction: the victor, in other words, must strike with all his strength and not just against a fraction of the enemy's. [Only] . . . by constantly seeking out the center of his power, *by daring all to win all*, will one really defeat the enemy. [my emphasis]

(Clausewitz, *On War*, pp. 595–596; for another detailed discussion, see also pp. 485–486)

(Note Clausewitz's emphasis on the importance of taking high risks to succeed, as well as on his insistence on not allowing the enemy to recover, subjects that will be addressed below.) Jomini presents a similar definition of the same concept, which he refers to as *decisive strategic points* or *objective points* (Jomini, *The Art of War*, pp. 85–92, 328–330, 337). He elevates the concept to even greater importance than Clausewitz does, viewing it as one of the two '*immutable principles of strategy*'. (In today's terminology, he is actually discussing the *operational* level.[2])

This employment of the forces should be regulated by two fundamental principles: the first being, to obtain by free and rapid movements the advantage of bringing the mass of the troops against fractions of the enemy; the second, to strike in the most decisive direction, that is to say, in that direction where the consequences of his defeat may be most disastrous to the enemy, while at the same time his success would yield him no great advantages. The whole science of great military combinations is comprised in these two fundamental truths.

(Jomini, *The Art of War*, pp. 328–329)

Strategy, besides indicating the decisive points of a theater of war, requires two things: 1st, that the principal mass of the force be moved against fractions of the enemy's, to attack them in *succession; 2nd, that the best direction of movement be adopted, that is to say, one leading straight to the decisive points already known . . .*

(Jomini, *The Art of War*, p. 331)

Sun Tzu, on the other hand, does not describe any such concept in detail, but instead offers general, somewhat cryptic advice:

> ***Thus, what is of supreme importance in war is to attack the enemy's strategy.***
>
> ***[Li Ch'uan] . . . The supreme excellence in war is to attack the enemy's plans. All the generals said: This is beyond our comprehension.***

(Sun Tzu, *The Art of War*, pp. 77–78)

The ambiguity of Sun Tzu's solution compels his readers to make a concerted effort to identify the best possible strategy. In this instance, Sun Tzu provides the question marks while, for once, Clausewitz furnishes the answers.[3] What, then, are some of the objectives or targets Clausewitz and Sun Tzu identify as proper centers of gravity in a strategic or operational plan for war?

For Clausewitz, typically, the most important center of gravity is the enemy's army.[4] In some cases, as in those of great military leaders whose entire careers depended on their military success, victory on the battlefield was everything:

> **For Alexander, Gustavus Adolphus, Charles XII, and Frederick the Great, the center of gravity was their army. If the army had been destroyed, they would all have gone down in history as failures.**

(Clausewitz, *On War*, p. 596)

In Chapter 27 of Book 6, Clausewitz reiterates this point.

> **Our position, then, is that a theater of war, be it large or small, and the forces stationed there, no matter what their size, represent the sort of unity in which a single center of gravity can be identified. That is the place where the decision should be reached; a victory at that point is in its fullest sense identical with the defense of the theater of operations.**

(Clausewitz, *On War*, p. 487)

Similarly, in his list of measures most critical for defeat of the enemy, the destruction of the enemy's forces comes first: '**1. Destruction of his army, if it is at all significant**' (Clausewitz, *On War*, p. 596). The cross-references Clausewitz makes between Chapter 27 of Book 6 and Chapter 4 of Book 8 reveal that he views the concept of the center of gravity *primarily as an operational concept*. Elsewhere one can find many examples of explicit statements to this effect; for example, '. . . **The battle must always be considered as the true center of gravity of the war**' (Clausewitz, *On War*, p. 248); '**There is . . . no factor in war that rivals the battle in importance**' (Clausewitz, *On War*, p. 261); and '**The major battle is therefore to be regarded as concentrated war, as the center of gravity of the entire conflict**' (Clausewitz, *On War*, p. 258; see also p. 260). In Chapter 1 of Book 8, he repeats and emphasizes once again the same point: '**We concluded that the grand objective of all military action is to overthrow the enemy – which means destroying his armed forces. It was therefore possible to show . . . that battle is the one and only means that warfare can employ. With that, we hoped, a sound working hypothesis had been established**' (Clausewitz, *On War*, p. 577). Many readers use this concept indiscriminately on both the operational and strategic levels, but a concept that is useful on the operational level can easily become mechanical or simplistic on another (see also the discussion in Chapter 11 below, p. 144).

Identification of the enemy's army as the single most important center of gravity is even more heavily emphasized by Jomini, who bases his purely operational concept on Napoleon's experience. In language resembling that of Clausewitz, he argues:

> *As to the objective points of maneuvers – that is, those which relate particularly to the destruction or decomposition of the hostile forces . . . this was the most conspicuous merit of Napoleon . . . He was convinced that the best means of accomplishing great results was to dislodge and destroy the hostile army, since states and provinces fall of themselves when there is no organized force to protect them . . . Where a party has the means of achieving great success by incurring great dangers, he may attempt the destruction of the hostile army, as did Napoleon.*
>
> (Jomini, *The Art of War*, pp. 89–90)

It is interesting to note that, whereas both Clausewitz and Jomini emphasize the desirability of taking high risks once the proper center of gravity has been identified, Sun Tzu's preferred center of gravity implies the need to avoid the risks associated with the use of force if possible.

One thing, however, is clear – for Sun Tzu the destruction of the enemy's army is only of secondary or tertiary importance: '*The next best* [mentioned in third place!] *is to attack his army*' (Sun Tzu, *The Art of War*, p. 78). For Sun Tzu, attacking the enemy's plans and his alliances comes long before attacking his army: his center of gravity is therefore on a different, much higher plane. After a war has begun, however, it is reasonable to assume that attacking the enemy's army would become a higher priority for Sun Tzu as well.

Clausewitz ranks capturing the enemy's capital second in importance:

> **In countries subject to domestic strife . . . the center of gravity is generally the capital . . . [and] 2. [The] seizure of his capital if it is not only the center of administration but also that of social, professional, and political activity.**
>
> (Clausewitz, *On War*, p. 596)

Once again Jomini agrees with Clausewitz:

> *All capitals are strategic points, for the double reason that they are not only centers of communications, but also the seats of power and government.*
>
> (Jomini, *The Art of War*, p. 87)

> *In strategy, the object of the campaign determines the objective point. If this aim be offensive, the point will be the possession of the hostile capital, or that of a province whose loss would compel the enemy to make peace. In a war of invasion the capital is, ordinarily, the objective point.*
>
> (Jomini, *The Art of War*, p. 88)[5]

Sun Tzu and Clausewitz analyse this concept only as it relates to the offensive – either before initiating the war, in the early planning phases, or during the implementation of offensive operations. But Jomini alone discusses the center of gravity in the context of a *defensive* strategy, as a concept equally important for the defender.

In the defensive, the objective point, instead of being that which it is desirable to gain possession of, is that which is to be defended. The capital, being considered the seat of power becomes the principal objective point of the defense . . .

(Jomini, *The Art of War*, p. 89)

In Sun Tzu's estimation, the enemy's cities are the least desirable and most costly objective: '*The worst policy is to attack cities. Attack cities only when there is no alternative*' (Sun Tzu, *The Art of War*, p. 78).[6] Clausewitz's emphasis on taking a capital when it is crucial to the enemy's capacity to wage war must not be understood as a recommendation for either siege warfare or wars of attrition: rather it should be considered in the context of his time, when major cities had become national centers controlling large states. Clausewitz was not referring to limited wars between feudal kings and smaller warring states or cities. Moreover, it is safe to assume that Clausewitz would urge the *occupation* (not the prolonged siege) of a capital *after* the enemy's army had been weakened or even defeated, much like the capture of Vienna after the Battle of Ulm (1805) or Berlin after the decisive Battle of Jena (1806).

Clausewitz places attacking the enemy's alliances third in his list of suitable targets:

In small countries that rely on large ones, it [the center of gravity] **is usually the army of their protector. Among alliances, it lies in the community of interest . . . As a principle . . . if you can vanquish all your enemies by defeating one of them, that defeat must be the main objective in the war. In this one enemy we strike at the center of gravity of the entire conflict.**

(Clausewitz, *On War*, p. 596)

3. Delivery of an effective blow against his principal ally if that ally is more powerful than he.

(Clausewitz, *On War*, p. 596)

Clausewitz recognizes that the weakest link in a coalition can be the ability of allies to cooperate and that it is often possible to divide them either politically or militarily. As he puts it elsewhere:

One country may support another's cause, but will never take it so seriously as it takes its own. A moderately-sized

force will be sent to its help; but if things go wrong, the operation is pretty well written off, and one tries to withdraw at the smallest possible cost.

(Clausewitz, *On War*, p. 603)

There is a decided difference between the cohesion of a *single* army led into battle under the personal command of a *single* general, and that of an *allied* force extending over 250 or 500 miles, or even operating against different fronts. In the one, cohesion is at its strongest and unity at its closest. In the other, unity is remote, frequently found only in mutual political interests, and even then rather precarious and imperfect; cohesion between the parts will usually be very loose, and often completely fictitious.

(Clausewitz, *On War*, p. 486)

Clausewitz ranks attacking the enemy's alliances third primarily because *On War* is not about diplomacy. Therefore, the other means by which conflicts can be won are not within the scope of his discussion. Furthermore, Clausewitz is convinced that in most instances, allied support is viewed as secondary, since nations only initiate wars if they believe they can win with their own strength. And even if an alliance or common interest among allies *is* identified as a center of gravity, Clausewitz sees this as a chiefly *military*, not diplomatic, problem in which an alliance is weakened by the infliction of such heavy costs on one of the allies that he is obliged to quit the war.

In direct contrast to Clausewitz and Jomini, Sun Tzu places the highest priority on defeating the enemy (preferably by non-violent means) *before* the war breaks out. After recommending that one attack the enemy's strategy at its inception, he advises that '. . . *The next best thing is to disrupt his alliances*' (Sun Tzu, *The Art of War*, p. 78). The disruption of the enemy's alliances is thus recommended *before* the attack on his army. In sum, Sun Tzu's first priority of winning diplomatically by disrupting the enemy's alliances is Clausewitz's last; and even then, Clausewitz's method of disrupting the enemy's alliance is for the most part military not diplomatic. (See note 3 for a detailed discussion of this point.)

Clausewitz also refers to two other possible centers of gravity which he does not discuss in detail. These, he states, are most useful in

59

popular uprisings '[where the center of gravity] **is the personalities of the leaders and public opinion**' (Clausewitz, *On War*, p. 596). These two possible centers of gravity deserve more careful attention, for the enemy's leader can become the most obvious center of gravity in more than popular uprisings. The wars of Napoleon with which Clausewitz was so familiar should have drawn his attention to the fact that only the removal of Napoleon as the leader of France finally brought the wars of the French Revolution to an end. Until then, no defeat on the battlefield could accomplish this. In more recent history, long after Germany's defeat in the Second World War had become inevitable, the war could not be terminated as long as Hitler was still in power. And in the 1990s, the defeat of the Iraqi army has not terminated the conflict with Iraq. As long as Saddam Hussein remains in power, this conflict must inevitably continue.

Public opinion has become an even more important center of gravity in modern warfare, particularly in prolonged guerrilla wars of attrition. Neither France nor the United States was beaten decisively on the battlefield in Indochina, Algeria, or Vietnam – yet eventually these wars became so unpopular at home that they were ultimately decided by the loss of public support.

Although Sun Tzu does not mention the possibility of identifying the enemy's leader or public opinion as an important objective, it is reasonable to assume that both could be included in his attack on the enemy's strategy. The reverse order of priority assigned by Sun Tzu and Clausewitz to the different centers of gravity is summarized by Table 5.1.

In one way at least, Clausewitz's discussion of the concept of the center of gravity brings him closer to Sun Tzu's type of thinking. Clausewitz claims that if the center of gravity is correctly identified on the various levels of warfare, victory can be achieved more efficiently at a lower cost – that by the judicious application of less force, more can be achieved. This is why he states that

> it is therefore a major act of strategic judgment to distinguish these centers of gravity in the enemy's forces and to identify their spheres of effectiveness.
>
> (Clausewitz, *On War*, p. 486)

Table 5.1
Sun Tzu and Clausewitz's Reversed Priorities in Identifying 'Centers of Gravity' for Strategic and Operational Planning in War

	SUN TZU	CLAUSEWITZ
THE LEVEL OF ANALYSIS AND DISTINCTION BETWEEN PEACE AND WAR	*Centers of gravity are identified primarily on the highest political and strategic levels. The distinction between war and peace is blurred, the two coexist, conflict is permanent.*	*Centers of gravity* are identified primarily on the operational and to a lesser extent also on the strategic level. The distinction between war and peace is sharp and clear, conflict is interrupted.
THE DEVELOPMENT OF THE CONCEPT OF *THE CENTER OF GRAVITY*	*The concept of the center of gravity is only implied, not explicitly developed. The analysis is based on experience, intuition, and empirical evidence. The conclusions are partly ambiguous and are provided primarily as a metaphor. Guidance for action is general.*	The concept of *the center of gravity* is developed theoretically, explicitly, and systematically and is based on Newtonian physics. The concept is clearly defined and is intended to provide concrete guidance for action – not only as a metaphor.
PREFERRED MEANS FOR IMPLEMENTING STRATEGY	*The preferred means for implementing strategic plans are non-military (i.e., diplomatic, economic, political intrigues). Recommends the conservation and whenever possible the minimum use of force (Li).*	The means of defeating the enemy are primarily military. Force (coercive violence) is used extensively (*Gewalt*), other means are recognized but not considered in detail.
OBJECTIVES IDENTIFIED AS POSSIBLE *CENTERS OF GRAVITY* BY ORDER OF PRIORITY	Centers of gravity *by order of priority:* *1. To attack the enemy's strategy or plans before the outbreak of war or use of force.* *2. Disrupt his alliances before the outbreak of war.* *3. Attack the enemy's army.* *4. Attack the enemy's cities as last resort.*	*Centers of gravity* by order of priority: 1. The destruction of the enemy's army. 2. The seizure of his capital. 3. The delivery of an effective *military* blow against his principal ally. Other: 4. The enemy's leader. 5. The enemy's public opinion.

Jomini agrees:

> *The greatest talent of a general, and the surest hope of success, lie in some degree in the good choice of these points* [i.e. objective points and decisive strategic points].
>
> (Jomini, *The Art of War*, p. 89)

Clausewitz's systematic development of the center of gravity concept with reference to the principles of Newtonian physics is at once its strength and its weakness. His rigorous argument, with its distinctly defined structure, often attracts those with a tendency to lift ideas out of context; the unfortunate result is a crude, mechanistic interpretation. This is ironic because Clausewitz more than any other strategic thinker, *generally* rejected the simplistic application of the methods, laws, and procedures of the natural sciences to the conduct and study of war. Yet Clausewitz's center of gravity is more susceptible than his other concepts to a mechanistic interpretation because in this instance, he develops it not as a metaphor, but as concrete guidance for action.

In this case, Sun Tzu's brevity and less precise development of a similar idea is also the source of his argument's strength. The ambiguity of his statement that '*the supreme excellence in war is to attack the enemy's plans*' obliges the reader to reflect in greater depth and work harder on deciphering the meaning of his statement. Instead of providing his readers with manual-like advice, it is Sun Tzu, not Clausewitz, who here presents his readers with an inspiring metaphor rather than with a formula for strategic and operational planning.

Many of the points on which these three strategists disagree concerning the selection of priorities for action and planning in war must be attributed to their different levels of analysis. Clausewitz and Jomini, who developed the concept of the center of gravity primarily as an operational concept, naturally focus their attention on the use and application of forces once hostilities have broken out. Sun Tzu, who concentrates on the highest political and strategic levels and is interested in securing a bloodless victory *before* the outbreak of war, assigns a higher priority to the use of non-military means and the conservation of force. Thus, while Clausewitz identifies most of the objectives in planning for war as physical – the enemy's army, his capital, and the use of force – Sun Tzu is most concerned with the non-tangible aspects of war such as the enemy's will and morale, his alliance systems, or his political plans.

The analysis to this point has emphasized the differences in approach between these two strategists. However, as we shall see below, when Clausewitz and Sun Tzu discuss war itself on the same level of analysis, they arrive at many similar conclusions.

6

The Primacy of Politics and the Military Commander

The aim of policy is to unify and reconcile all aspects of internal administration as well as of spiritual values . . . Policy of course is nothing in itself; it is simply the trustee for all these interests against other states . . . In no sense can the art of war ever be regarded as the preceptor of policy . . . We can only treat policy as representative of all interests of the community.

Clausewitz, *On War*, pp. 606–607

No major proposal required for war can be worked out of ignorance of political factors; and when people talk, as they often do, about harmful political influence on the management of war, they are not really saying what they mean. Their quarrel should be with the policy itself not with its influence.

Clausewitz, *On War*, p. 608

Since ancient times there has never been a war that did not have a political character . . . war cannot for a single moment be separated from politics.

Mao Tse-tung, 'On Protracted War', pp. 226–227

War, as Sun Tzu comments in the opening sentence of *The Art of War*,

> *is a matter of vital importance to the State; the province of life and death; the road to survival or ruin. It is mandatory that it be thoroughly studied.*
>
> (Sun Tzu, *The Art of War*, p. 63)[1]

Hence, war should not be a ritual or an instrument to redress petty grievances, but rather an activity to serve the interests of the state – not those of a single individual.[2]

> *If not in the interests of the state, do not act. If you cannot succeed, do not use troops. If you are not in danger, do not fight.*
>
> (Sun Tzu, *The Art of War*, p. 142)

> *A sovereign cannot raise an army because he is enraged, nor can a general fight because he is resentful. For while an angered man may again be happy, and a resentful man again be pleased, a state that has perished cannot be restored, nor can the dead be brought back to life.*
>
> *Therefore, the enlightened ruler is prudent and the good general is warned against rash action. Thus the state is kept secure and the army preserved.*
>
> (Sun Tzu, *The Art of War*, pp. 142–143)

> *. . . The general who understands war is the Minister of the people's fate and arbiter of the nation's destiny.*
>
> (Sun Tzu, *The Art of War*, p. 76)

Sun Tzu clearly recognizes the supremacy of *raison d'état* over all other considerations. War is a rational activity of the last resort (the *ultima ratio*) that correlates ends and means to enhance the vital interests of the state: it is a political activity as we understand it today.[3] The decision to initiate war is therefore political and must be made by political – not military – leaders.

> *And therefore it is said that enlightened rulers deliberate upon the plans, and good generals execute them.*
>
> (Sun Tzu, *The Art of War*, p. 142)

Normally, when the army is employed, the general first receives his commands from the sovereign . . . He receives the sovereign's mandate and in compliance with the victorious deliberations of the temple councils reverently executes the punishments ordained by Heaven.

(Sun Tzu, *The Art of War*, p. 102)

If a general who heeds my strategy is employed he is certain to win. Retain him! When one who refuses to listen to my strategy is employed, he is certain to be defeated. Dismiss him!

(Sun Tzu, *The Art of War*, p. 66)

The ideal military leader holds his personal interests in abeyance while wholeheartedly serving his political leaders and a political purpose.

And therefore the general who in advancing does not seek personal fame, and in withdrawing is not concerned with avoiding punishment, but whose only purpose is to protect the people and promote the best interests of his sovereign, is the precious jewel of the state . . . [Tu Mu] . . . Few such are to be had.

(Sun Tzu, *The Art of War*, p. 128)

Clausewitz also views war as an activity not to be embarked on lightly or for the wrong reasons:

War is no pastime; it is no mere joy in daring and winning, no place for irresponsible enthusiasts. It is a serious means to a serious end . . .

(Clausewitz, *On War*, p. 86)

(Mao Tse-tung makes a similar remark: 'for it should be understood that fighting the enemy is no joke' (Mao Tse-tung, *Selected Military Writings*, p. 164).)

Clausewitz is well known for his emphasis on the primacy of politics in the conduct of war, which is a rational instrument of the state *only* if it serves a political purpose. The following are some of his less quoted aphorisms on this subject:

When whole communities go to war – whole peoples, and especially *civilized* peoples – the reason always lies in some

political situation, and the occasion is always due to some political object. War, therefore, is an act of policy ... Policy ... will permeate all military operations, and, in so far as their violent nature will admit, it will have a continuous influence on them ... War is not a mere act of policy but a true political instrument, a continuation of political activity by other means ... The political object is the goal, war is the means of reaching it, and means can never be considered in isolation from their purpose.

(Clausewitz, *On War*, pp. 86–87)

Politics ... is the womb in which war develops – where its outlines already exist in their hidden rudimentary form, like the characteristics of living creatures in their embryos.

(Clausewitz, *On War*, p. 149)

War is only a branch of political activity, that ... is in no sense autonomous ... The only source of war is politics – the intercourse of governments and peoples ...

War cannot be divorced from political life; and whenever this occurs in our thinking about war, the many links that connect the two elements are destroyed and we are left with something pointless and devoid of sense.

(Clausewitz, *On War*, p. 605)

At the highest level the art of war turns into policy – but a policy conducted by fighting battles rather than by sending diplomatic notes ...

No other possibility exists, then, than to subordinate the military point of view to the political.

We can now see that the assertion that a major military development, or a plan for one, should be a matter for *purely military* opinion is unacceptable and can be damaging. [emphasis in original]

(Clausewitz, *On War*, p. 607)

A comparison of these statements with the earlier excerpts from Sun Tzu illustrates that the concepts for which Clausewitz is most renowned are all set forth by Sun Tzu in *The Art of War*. Clausewitz, however, analyses them in more detail and may express them in more elegantly worded aphorisms. Although the theoretical frameworks of *On War* and *The Art of War* agree that, ideally, politics should always be in command, both also acknowledge that the unique nature of warfare often makes this impossible. In an age when real-time communications did not exist, the need to make quick decisions, exploit opportunities or avoid defeat often caused local military developments to overrule remote political control. (From the vantage point of communication, control, and hence also command, the wartime environment of Sun Tzu had far more in common with that of Napoleon and Clausewitz than that of Napoleon and Clausewitz has in common with our own era.) Like politics, command on the battlefield is the art of the possible which requires the exploitation of fleeting opportunities or the avoidance of imminent disaster. (With modern communications, this is true to a lesser extent.) The negative consequences of Hitler's interference in Rommel's decisions or in the battle of Stalingrad, for example, are well known. Another famous yet possibly apocryphal example was President Carter's direct intervention in the aborted raid on Iran.

Accordingly, both Sun Tzu and Clausewitz recognize that, in exceptional circumstances, the military commander in the field must overrule political orders. In this, Sun Tzu is perhaps the most emphatic:

> *[Chia Lin] No evil is greater than commands of the sovereign from the court.*
>
> (Sun Tzu, The Art of War, p. 81)

> *He whose generals are able and not interfered with by the sovereign will be victorious.*

> *[Tu Yu] To make appointments is the province of the Sovereign; to decide on battle, that of the general . . .*

> *[Ho Yen-hsi] To say that the general must await the commands of the sovereign in such circumstances is like informing a superior that you wish to put out a fire. Before the order to do so arrives, the ashes are cold . . .*

> *[Ho Yen-hsi] To put a rein on an able general while at the same time asking him to suppress a cunning enemy is like tying up the*

69

Black Hound of Han and then ordering him to catch elusive hares.

(Sun Tzu, *The Art of War*, pp. 83–84)

There are occasions when the commands of the sovereign need not be obeyed.

[Ts'ao Ts'ao] When it is expedient in operations the general need not be restricted by the commands of the sovereign.

When you see the correct course, act; do not wait for orders.

[Chia Lin] . . . a general prizes opportune changes in circumstances.

The orders of a sovereign, although they should be followed, are not to be followed if the general knows they contain the danger of harmful superintendence of affairs from the capital.

(Sun Tzu, *The Art of War*, pp. 112–113)

If the situation is one of victory but the sovereign has issued orders not to engage, the general may decide to fight. If the situation is such that he cannot win, but the sovereign has issued orders to engage, he need not do so.

(Sun Tzu, *The Art of War*, p. 128)[4]

Although Clausewitz devotes less attention to this problem, he also notes that at times, operational considerations must take precedence over the primacy of politics. To paraphrase Clausewitz's famous metaphor, the grammar (that is, lower-level military considerations) will dictate the logic (that is, political objectives).[5]

> That, however, does not imply that the political aim is a tyrant. It must adapt itself to its chosen means, a process which can radically change it . . .

> War in general, and the commander in any specific instance, is entitled to require that the trend and designs of policy shall not be inconsistent with these means. That, of course, is no small demand; but however much it may affect political aims in a given case, it will never do more than modify them.

(Clausewitz, *On War*, p. 87)

Policy, of course, will not extend its influence to operational details. Political considerations do not determine the posting of guards or the employment of patrols. But they are more influential in the planning of war, of the campaign, and often of the battle.

(Clausewitz, *On War*, p. 606)

Only if statesmen look to certain military moves and actions to produce effects that are foreign to their nature do political decisions influence operations for the worse. In the same way as a man who has not fully mastered a foreign language sometimes fails to express himself correctly, so statesmen often issue orders that defeat the purpose they are meant to serve. Time and again that has happened, which demonstrates that a certain grasp of military affairs is vital for those in charge of general policy.

(Clausewitz, *On War*, p. 608)

Machiavelli agrees with Clausewitz and Sun Tzu on the wisdom of delegating the maximum possible freedom of action to the field commander. According to Machiavelli, Roman history best illustrates the commendable results to be expected from this course of action. The authority of Rome's field commanders

. . . was of the most unlimited character, so that the Senate reserved to itself no other power than that of declaring of new wars and ratifying treaties of peace, all other matters being remitted to the arbitrament and power of the consul . . . All the details of the campaign were left to the discretion and authority of the consul, who could bring on a battle or not, and lay siege to this or that place, as seemed to him proper . . . It was eminently wise . . . for although there were many of the senators who had great experience in war, yet not being on the spot, and not knowing the endless particulars which it is necessary to know to counsel wisely, they would have been liable to commit the most serious errors in attempting to instruct the consul.

(Machiavelli, trans. Christian E. Detmold, *Discourses*, 2.33, Modern Library Edition, 1950, pp. 394–395. Alternatively, see Machiavelli, trans. Allan Gilbert, *Discourses*, vol. 1, pp. 417–418)

Machiavelli believes that Italian city-states' 'micro-management' of the field commanders of his own day was a principal cause of their many defeats at the hands of outside invaders. 'The republics of the present day . . . act very differently [from the Romans] so that if their generals . . . wish merely to place a battery of artillery, they [the republics] want to know and direct it.' He then sarcastically calls this, 'A system which is worthy of about the same praise as their conduct in all other respects, and which has brought them to the condition in which they now find themselves' (Machiavelli, *Discourses*, 2.33, Modern Library Edition, p. 395).

A corollary of the Italian republics' desire to control the minutiae of their field commander's decisions was their refusal to allow these commanders to take any initiative or risks.

> When these indolent princes or effeminate republics send a general with an army into the field, the wisest order they think they can give him is never to risk a battle and above all things to avoid a general action . . . Such orders as much as say to him, 'Give battle at your enemy's convenience but not at your own.'
> (Machiavelli, *Discourses*, Modern Library Edition, pp. 444–445)

In today's world as in Machiavelli's, the desire to minimize risks and avoid casualties through war by 'remote control' can produce similar restraints on the freedom of field commanders with equally disastrous results.

Deciding *when* to disobey a direct political order is the most critical decision a military commander must make at times, yet Sun Tzu and Clausewitz do not develop any criteria for taking such decisions. Factors the commander should consider are: local circumstances; the risks involved; the degree to which military control is centralized; the quality of communications; his intuition and experience; and, finally, what he can gain or lose in battle. The leader, on the other hand, should distinguish between political and professional military considerations, resisting the temptation to impose his views in 'purely professional' situations. This is what Professor Samuel Huntington has referred to as objective control (political non-interference) versus subjective control (political interference) in professional military questions.[6]

Sun Tzu and Clausewitz recognize that the ideal of political considerations remaining in command is not always attainable. The realities of war are such that the 'grammar of battle' will frequently dictate modifications in the political objectives of war; for as Clausewitz explains in the following passage, the success of political objectives usually rests on the achievement of objectives at the lower operational or even tactical levels.

> **Where the tactical results of the engagements are assumed to be the *basis* of all strategic plans, it is always possible, and a serious risk, that the attacker will proceed on that basis. He will endeavor above all to be tactically superior, in order to upset the enemy's strategic planning. The latter, therefore, can never be considered as *something independent*: it can only become valid when one has reason to be confident of tactical success. To illustrate briefly what we mean, let us recall that a general such as Bonaparte could ruthlessly cut through all his enemies' strategic plans in search of battle, because he seldom doubted the battle's outcome.** [Which is, of course, a good explanation for Napoleon's neglect of the higher strategic level of warfare.] **So whenever the strategists did not endeavor with all their might to crush him in battle with superior force, whenever they engaged in subtler (and weaker) machinations, their schemes were swept away like cobwebs ... Bonaparte was well aware that everything turned on tactical results ... *That is why* we think it is useful to emphasize that all strategic planning rests on tactical success alone and that – whether the solution is arrived at in battle or not – this is in all cases the actual fundamental basis for the decision.**
>
> (Clausewitz, *On War*, p. 386)

Consequently, military commanders will claim with some justification that the imperatives of battle demand greater freedom for them to make their own decisions in the field. At the same time, the abuse of such freedom may lead to the '*tacticization of strategy*' or to the *de facto* primacy of military over political considerations for the duration of the war (as, for example, occurred in Germany before and during the First World War). (See Appendix E.)

Jomini solves this problem by insisting on the primacy of operational and military considerations over political control once war has begun.

The best example of this principle in practice was the attitude of the German General Staff as represented by Schlieffen, Falkenhayn, Hindenburg, and Ludendorff. Jomini's position on this question is consistent with his belief that the study and practice of war on the operational level should be approached as a 'science', in accordance with the principles he set forth. For once war can be waged 'scientifically', it follows that the 'scientist' (that is, the professional military commander) and not the political leader, is the best qualified to interpret and apply the 'laws' of warfare. Thus, those who hold to this belief also establish, *de facto*, the primacy of military over political leadership.

> *A general whose genius and hands are tied by an Aulic Council five hundred miles distant cannot be a match for one who has liberty of action, other things being equal.*
>
> (Jomini, *The Art of War*, p. 42; see also p. 60)

In language closely resembling that of Sun Tzu, Jomini states that if the sovereign's general is

> *... interfered with and opposed in all his enterprises* [he] *will be unable to achieve success, even if he have the requisite ability. It may be said that a sovereign might accompany the army and not interfere with his general, but, on the contrary, aid him with all the weight of his influence.*
>
> (Jomini, *The Art of War*, pp. 52–53)

> *In my opinion, councils of war are a deplorable resource, and can be useful only when concurring in opinion with the commander, in which case they may give him more confidence in his own judgment, and, in addition, may assure him that his lieutenants, being of his opinion, will use every means to insure the success of the movement. This is the only advantage of a council of war, which, moreover should be simply consultative and have no further authority; but if, instead of this harmony, there should be difference of opinion, it can only produce unfortunate results.*
>
> (Jomini, *The Art of War*, p. 58)

Unlike Jomini, neither Sun Tzu nor Clausewitz dedicates enough attention to civil–military tensions in wartime. Sun Tzu in particular cannot come to a definitive conclusion on the matter of political control *versus* the delegation of independent decision-making authority to the commander in the field; on the whole, though, he favors the latter. In the end, both Sun Tzu and Clausewitz seem to assume that the enlightened political leader will be in overall command of the war, while refraining from direct interference in lower-level operational decisions. In other words, the ideal political leader will discern when and how to grant the commander just enough freedom of action to be able to make the best possible professional decisions on his own initiative. Unfortunately, the assumptions of Sun Tzu and Clausewitz on this subject have often proved to be wrong.

The complexity, interrelationships and non-hierarchical nature of the links among the three levels of war are illustrated in Figure 6.1 (see also Appendix E).[7]

FIGURE 6.1
THE THREE LEVELS OF WAR AS A COMPLEX MODEL OF INTERACTION

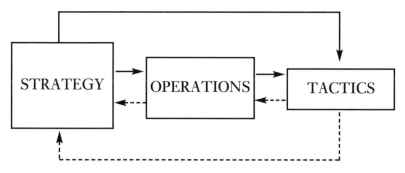

7

The Rational Calculus of War: Correlating Ends and Means

It is a common mistake in going to war to begin at the wrong end, to act first and to wait for disaster to discuss the matter.

Thucydides, *The History of the Peloponnesian War*, Book 1, Section 78, p. 52

Whoever makes war through choice or ambition has the intention of making gains and keeping them, and of acting in such a way as to enrich his city and his country and not to make them poor. He must, then, both in the gaining and in the keeping, take care not to spend, but rather to do everything to the profit of the public.

Machiavelli, *Discourses*, p. 341

If war is a means of achieving political objectives, the fulfillment of these objectives requires the careful, continuous correlation of means and ends. Sun Tzu approaches this issue through the development of what modern literature refers to as the 'pure rational decision-making model'.[1]

Weigh the situation, then move.

(Sun Tzu, *The Art of War*, p. 106)

Now the elements of the art of war are first, measurement of space; second, estimation of quantities; third, calculations; fourth, comparisons; and fifth, chances of victory.

Quantities derive from measurement, figures from quantities, comparisons from figures, and victory from comparisons.

(Sun Tzu, *The Art of War*, p. 88)

In this highly systematic decision-making process, factors such as objectives and comparisons of relative strength are evaluated carefully in considering various courses of action and in estimating the probability of victory. Clausewitz argues that:

> **No one starts a war – or rather, no one in his senses ought to do so – without first being clear in his mind what he intends to achieve by that war and how he intends to conduct it.**
>
> (Clausewitz, *On War*, p. 579)

> **He [the belligerent] would act on the principle of using no greater force, and setting himself no greater military aim, than would be sufficient for the achievement of his political purpose.**
>
> (Clausewitz, *On War*, p. 585)

Clausewitz explains why the 'rational calculus' of war is an ongoing process:

> **Of even greater influence on the decision to make peace is the consciousness of all the effort that has already been made and of the efforts yet to come. Since war is not an act of senseless passion but is controlled by its political object, the value of this object must determine the sacrifices to be made for it in magnitude and also in duration. Once the expenditure of effort exceeds the value of the political object, the object must be renounced and peace must follow.**
>
> (Clausewitz, *On War*, p. 92) (For an expanded discussion of the 'rational calculus of war' see Chapter 14 below.)

Perhaps because of his stronger belief in the value of intelligence or his faith in the benefits derived from observance of the proper religious rituals, Sun Tzu is convinced that rational calculations will usually bring about the intended results. In *The Art of War*, rational calculations are considered a virtual guarantee of success.

Clausewitz is much more pessimistic and realistic regarding the possibility of rationally calculating a war's outcome:

> **To discover how much of our resources must be mobilized for war, we must first examine our own political aim and**

that of the enemy. We must gauge the strength and situation of the opposing state. We must gauge the character and abilities of its government and people and do the same in regard to our own. Finally, we must evaluate the political sympathies of other states and the effect the war may have on them. To assess these things in all their ramifications and diversity is plainly a colossal task. Rapid and correct appraisal of them clearly calls for the intuition of a genius; to master this complex mass by sheer methodological examination is obviously impossible. Bonaparte was quite right when he said that Newton himself would quail before the algebraic problems it could pose.

The size and variety of factors to be weighed, and the uncertainty about the proper scale to use are bound to make it far more difficult to reach the right conclusion.

(Clausewitz, *On War*, pp. 585–586)

Both Sun Tzu and Clausewitz view war as an essentially rational activity involving the careful and continuous correlation of ends and means. At the same time, they are fully aware of the crucial effect of non-rational factors such as morale, motivation, and intuition. Clausewitz, however, appears to be more conscious of the difficulty of relying on rational calculations. As a result, he assigns a greater role to the unpredictable influence of elements such as friction, chance, unreliable intelligence, and sheer complexity. In his more limited expectations of the benefits flowing from rational calculations, Clausewitz is in many ways more realistic than Sun Tzu.[2]

On the other hand, Clausewitz assumes, in accordance with the tradition of *raison d'état*, that the political leadership will pursue a rational policy intended to benefit the state and maximize its power. This is of course one of the principal reasons for Clausewitz's insistence on the primacy of politics, and on war in general as an instrument of politics. But this idea, which Clausewitz never questions in *On War*, is much too simplistic. The fact that politics provides the purpose for waging war does not mean that the purpose itself is always rational. *Non-rational political objectives can be implemented by rational means.* As he should have known from the leadership of Napoleon, the objectives and strategic decisions of such leaders are not necessarily rational and may often

79

be intended to fulfill their personal or dynastic ambitions, not to promote the interests of the state.[3]

Indeed, Clausewitz, more than any other theorist of war, dedicates extensive attention to the non-rational, psychological, and intangible factors that always play such an important role in war. These are the subject of the following chapter.

8

Clausewitz on the Role of 'Moral Forces' in War

> It is even more ridiculous when we consider that these very critics usually exclude all moral qualities from strategic theory, and only examine material factors. They reduce everything to a few mathematical formulas of equilibrium and superiority, of time and space limited by a few angles and lines. If that were really all, it would hardly provide a scientific problem for a schoolboy.
>
> Clausewitz, *On War*, p. 178

> . . . Moral elements are among the most important in war . . . Unfortunately they will not yield to academic wisdom. They cannot be classified or counted. They have to be seen or felt.
>
> Clausewitz, *On War*, p. 184

It has often been argued that Clausewitz emphasizes the need to view war as a rational instrument, as a means for the leaders to promote and protect their state's vital interests.[1] From this accurate interpretation, however, some readers have then erroneously inferred that Clausewitz also considers it possible for *war itself* to be waged as a rational activity. In fact, Clausewitz, repeatedly reminds us that this is not so, for he knows that war in all of its dimensions is permeated by non-rational influences, or what he calls '**moral factors**' (*moralische Grossen*), '**spiritual forces**' (*geistigen Kräften*), or '**spiritual factors**' (*geistigen Grossen*), which '**cannot be classified or counted**' (Clausewitz, *On War*, p. 184).

For Clausewitz, these intangible, non-quantifiable 'moral factors' (not to be confused with morale, which is only one type of moral factor) are so intertwined with activity on all levels of war that we cannot even identify all of their complex interactions with each other and with the material elements. Some of these countless 'moral factors' include, for example, the personality, creativity, experience, and intuition of leaders; the passions and character of the people; the training and motivation of the military; the quality of the military doctrine; and the behavior of the troops under fire and their continued resistance following a defeat. (For a more detailed list of these factors, see Clausewitz, *On War*, p. 186.) In addition to the moral factors, 'neutral factors' such as friction, chance, uncertainty (the probabilistic nature of war), luck, poor intelligence, and, above all, the unpredictable nature of war combine to undermine the possibility of waging war as a purely rational activity. Indeed, many of these moral factors are already mentioned in discussions throughout this book, but a special chapter such as this is useful to further emphasize their importance in Clausewitz's theory of war.

Remembering the role of moral factors in war in today's wartime environment is critical for two reasons. First, most modern military organizations are so preoccupied with the material and technological aspects of war that they tend to overlook its 'moral' dimensions. The Vietnam War, the Gulf War, and more recently, the war against Serbia and the Russian war in Chechnya are recent examples of this mindset. Second, many military experts who have developed the current theories of 'information war', 'cyber-war', and the 'Revolution in Military Affairs' (RMA) often imply or suggest that war has been transformed into a rational activity that can be based on perfect or nearly perfect information; in this case, they claim, the precise execution of carefully laid pre-war plans combined with thorough preparations and use of state-of-the-art technology will make the outcome of war highly predictable. But to paraphrase Clausewitz, **'Recent events have scattered such nonsense to the winds'** (*On War*, p. 259).

There is, however, nothing new about the well-meaning but misguided desire to identify 'laws' or 'principles' of war that would eliminate the discomfiting uncertainties of warfare. **'Efforts'**, Clausewitz said, **'were . . . made to equip the conduct of war with principles, rules, or even systems. They did present a positive goal, but people failed to take adequate account of the endless complexi-**

ties involved . . . The conduct of war branches out in almost all directions and has no definite limits: while any [scientific] system, any model has the finite nature of a synthesis' (Clausewitz, *On War*, p. 134). But while this quest was, in the past, based on an attempt to distill scientific principles of war from past experience, today it springs from overconfidence in the panacea of a superior technology. One can see why access to better real-time communications; improved command and control; the collection of more intelligence on a greater number of targets; and the increased range and precision of weapons delivery might seem enough to dispel many of the uncertainties of the past.

Today, as much as in Clausewitz's time, there are still those who think that new and better theories of war can minimize the costs of waging war to the point where fighting and bloodshed will become unnecessary. This reflects a lack of realism bolstered by wishful thinking.[2] If anything, the role of moral factors has actually expanded in modern warfare (e.g., the influence of real-time mass media on public opinion). Moreover, war is and will remain a relentlessly reciprocal activity in which all participants can counter each other with different methods, weapons, and technologies. Thus, the arguments that Clausewitz makes against the 'scientific' military theories and 'predictable' wars of Bulow or Jomini remain relevant today. Objecting vehemently to such attempts to reduce war to a science, Clausewitz views such theories as **'intellectually repugnant'** (Clausewitz, *On War*, p. 134):

> They aim at fixed values [i.e., they do not understand the reciprocal and dynamic nature of war]; but in war everything is uncertain, and calculations have to be made with variable quantities. They direct the enquiry exclusively toward physical quantities [i.e., tanks, bridges, refineries, communications centers] whereas all military action is intertwined with psychological forces and effects [i.e., 'moral factors']. They consider unilateral action, whereas war consists of continuous interaction of opposites.
>
> (Clausewitz, *On War*, p. 136)

Instead of acknowledging the difficulties posed by the realities of war, such theorists artificially reduced its complexities to fit their theories or political/organizational agendas. This type of expediency is still widely practiced today.

> They [the theorists] soon found out how difficult the subject was, and felt justified in evading the problem by again directing their principles and systems only to physical matters and unilateral activity [i.e., the emphasis on technology in many of today's theories of war]. As in the science concerning the preparations for war, they wanted to reach a set of sure and positive conclusions and for that reason considered only factors that could be mathematically calculated.

> (Clausewitz, *On War*, p. 134)

A realistic theory of war cannot, however, be constructed on the basis of only a few selective quantifiable variables. It must take into account the moral as much as the material factors of war. 'Military activity is never directed against material force alone; it is always aimed simultaneously at the moral forces which give it life, and the two cannot be separated' (Clausewitz, *On War*, p. 137). Elsewhere, he states:

> The effects of physical and psychological factors form an organic whole which, unlike a metal alloy, is inseparable . . . In formulating any rule concerning physical factors, the theorist must bear in mind the part that moral factors may play in it . . . Most matters in this book are composed of equal parts of physical and of moral causes and effects. . . . One might say . . . that the physical factors seem little more than the wooden hilt, while the moral factors are the precious metal, the real weapon, the finely honed blade [or, more accurately, the 'sharpened blade'].

> (Clausewitz, *On War*, pp. 184–185)

Thus, Clausewitz argues that the moral intangible factors are in fact *more* important than the material factors. From the very first sentence of *On War*, Clausewitz makes it clear that one cannot separate the various material and intangible factors in war. War can only be studied as a whole, as a Gestalt (see Appendix D, pp. 345–352). 'In war', he says, 'more so than in any other subject, we must begin by looking at the whole; for here more than elsewhere, the part and the whole must always be thought of together.' (Clausewitz, *On War*, p. 75) He clarifies this point in Section 5, where he states that the military strength of any state is '. . . the product of two *inseparable* factors, viz. *The total* [i.e., material] *means at his disposal and the strength of his will* [i.e., the moral factors].' While the means can be quantified in most cases, 'the strength of the will is much less easy to determine and can only be gauged approximately . . .' (Clausewitz, *On War*, p. 77).

The inability to quantify the relative strength of 'moral factors' explains why most modern analysts prefer to focus on measuring capabilities related to technology and firepower, while some theorists primarily confine themselves to the theory of rational analysis. Conveniently ignoring the moral intangibles such as motivation or intentions, they search for success not where the problems exist but only where the data can be identified and quantified. 'Unfortunately, "moral factors" will not yield to academic wisdom. They cannot be classified or counted. They have to be seen or felt' (Clausewitz, *On War*, p. 184).

The estimation of moral factors must often be left to the intuition or experience of the military commander, or in today's world, the military analyst. This is why '. . . principles and opinions [in war] can seldom reduce the path of reason to a *simple line* [i.e., war . . . is not amenable to a linear type of analysis]. As in all practical matters, a certain latitude always remains . . . The man of action must at times trust in the sensitive instinct of judgment . . . which almost unconsciously hits on the right course' (Clausewitz, *On War*, p. 213 [my emphasis]). Thus, the complex interconnections in war can only be divined by *the intuition of the military genius*.

As with many of Clausewitz's most original concepts, his discussion of the role of moral factors in war is mainly concerned with the operational level of war: that is, the effect of intangible psychological factors on the outcome of a battle; and the difficulty of predicting their non-linear influence on the behavior of soldiers following an unexpected outcome. Moral factors also play an important part on the higher strategic level in determining, for example, the support of the people for a government under duress; and the readiness of the people to go on fighting a 'people's war' after a defeat. Furthermore, if we view moral factors as representing all intangible dimensions affecting the course of a war, we should include the ability of creative political and military leaders to devise an original strategy. Nevertheless, a careful reading of *On War* makes it clear that most of Clausewitz's discussion of the role of moral factors pertains to the lower operational and tactical levels.

> **Loss of moral equilibrium must not be underestimated merely because it has no absolute value and does not always show up in the final balance. It can attain such massive proportions that it overpowers everything by its irresistible force. For this reason, it may in itself become a main objective of the action . . .**
>
> (Clausewitz, On War, p. 232)

Moral factors therefore constitute one of the most important operational objectives in war. A successful attack on the enemy's moral equilibrium in battle is a powerful 'force multiplier' that cannot be understood in linear or quantitative terms.

> **The psychological effect of victory** [or achieving surprise or the enemy's loss of a key military leader] **does not merely grow in proportion to the amount of military forces involved, but does so at an accelerating rate.**
>
> (Clausewitz, On War, p. 232)

Nowhere does Clausewitz summarize this problem more cogently than at the end of the chapter on the culminating point of victory. How can the general identify the culminating point of victory? How can he assess the morale of his enemy?

> **He must guess, so to speak; guess whether the first shock of battle will steel the enemy's resolve and stiffen his resistance, or whether, like a Bologna flask, it will shatter as soon as its surface is scratched; guess the extent of debilitation and paralysis that the drying up of particular sources of supply and the severing of certain lines of communication will cause the enemy; guess whether the burning pain of the injury he has been dealt will make the enemy collapse or, like a wounded bull, arouse his rage; guess whether the other powers will be frightened or indignant, and whether and which political alliances will be dissolved or formed. When we realize that he must hit upon all this and much more by means of his discreet judgement, as a marksman hits a target, we must admit that such an accomplishment of the human mind is no small achievement. Thousands of wrong turns running in all directions**

tempt his perceptions; and if the range, confusion and complexity of the issues are not enough to overwhelm him the dangers and responsibilities may.

(Clausewitz, *On War*, pp. 572–573)

Although the number of possible permutations is much smaller on the strategic than the operational level, Clausewitz's observations apply to both. Furthermore, despite the availability of real-time information and communications, satellite photography and SIGINT (Signals Intelligence), the moral factors that need to be addressed and the judgments that must be made are not necessarily any easier now than in the nineteenth century. Did the President of the United States and his advisors correctly identify the culminating point of victory at the end of the Gulf War? Did he accurately assess the 'moral factors' involved? Whether he did or not remains open to debate, but all of the modern technology at his disposal certainly could not help him make a better decision.

Similarly, the expectations of top U.S. decision-makers in March 1999 that a few days of bombing would cause Slobodan Milosevic's government to 'shatter like a Bologna flask' proved to be embarrassingly wrong. Despite NATO's high-tech weaponry and near-perfect intelligence on Yugoslavian material capabilities, NATO grossly misjudged Yugoslav intentions and the strength of the 'moral factors' involved. The result was a prolonged and only partially effective air campaign that might have damaged the Kosovar Albanians and NATO as much as it did Serbia. An earlier example of a monumental strategic error that resulted from ignoring the role of moral, intangible factors in war was Hitler's expectation that a 'corrupt and decadent' Soviet Union would capitulate soon after the beginning of the Nazi invasion in June 1941. When Hitler hubristically compared his imminent attack on Russia to 'kicking a rotting door' he seriously underestimated Russia's power of resistance; Stalin's political and organizational capabilities; and the Soviet reaction to Nazi brutalities. Conversely, Hitler's overall strategy in the Second World War is an outstanding example of how the value of 'moral factors' can be mistakenly exaggerated at the expense of material/economic imperatives. Hitler's intoxication with his own early successes in the war convinced him that Germany's 'moral superiority', its superior military doctrine (the *Blitzkrieg*), German racial superiority, and his inspired leadership would crush any imaginable resistance. As a result, he did not hesitate to begin a war on two fronts – that is, to attack the Soviet Union before finishing the war in the West, and to declare war on the United States. Believing vainly in 'the triumph of the will', Hitler was defeated by superior material and economic strength, superior intelligence, and the determination of his 'inferior' opponents.

As much as Clausewitz emphasizes the role of moral factors in war, he can do no more than apprise us of their critical importance but cannot otherwise supply any concrete guidance on how to identify or measure them.

> **This type of knowledge cannot be forcibly produced by an apparatus of scientific formulas and mechanics; it can only be gained through a talent for judgment, and by the application of accurate judgement [i.e., experience] to the observation of man and matter.**
>
> (Clausewitz, *On War*, p. 146)

> **The appreciation and understanding of moral factors can only be perceived by the inner eye, which differs in each person, and is often different in the same person at different times.**
>
> (Clausewitz, *On War*, p. 137) (See also Chapter 16, pp. 265–272)

Therefore, although a good theory of war can never ignore 'moral factors', it cannot provide a fully satisfactory account of them either: that would be impractical and futile. Ultimately, Clausewitz argues, '**No theorist, and no commander should bother himself with psychological and philosophical sophistries**' (Clausewitz, *On War*, p. 137). Any attempt to classify or list the moral factors that influence war in detail can '**all too easily lead to platitudes, while the genuine spirit of inquiry soon evaporates and unwittingly we find ourselves proclaiming what everyone already knows**'. Therefore, Clausewitz makes it clear that he can treat the subject of 'moral factors' only '**in an incomplete and impressionistic manner, content to have pointed out . . . [their] general importance**' (Clausewitz, *On War*, p. 185). This fits perfectly with his observations on the value but also the limits of any theory of war. In closing his discussion on the role of moral factors, Clausewitz – to his credit — does not try artificially to impose a comprehensive and rigorous theory on the role of moral forces in war, much as he was probably tempted to do so.

FIGURE 8.1
LIMITS TO THE RATIONAL CONDUCT OF WAR

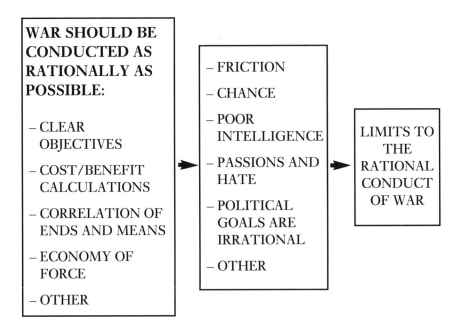

9

The Supreme Act of Judgment: Understanding the 'Nature of War' and the 'Trinitarian Analysis'

All planning, particularly strategic planning, must pay attention to the character of contemporary warfare.
Clausewitz, *On War*, p. 220

Unless you understand the actual circumstances of war, its nature and its relation to other things, you will not know the laws of war, or know how to direct war or to be able to win victory.
Mao Tse-tung, *Selected Military Writings*, p. 78

How . . . often have statesmen and officers, even in the most harmonious conference, been unable to decide on a coherent plan of war from inability to analyse scientifically the situation they had to face, and to recognize the general character of the struggle in which they were about to engage. That the nature of a war should be realized by contemporaries as clearly as it comes to be seen afterwards in the fuller light of history is seldom to be expected.
Julian S. Corbett, *Some Principles of Maritime Strategy*, pp. 5-6

THE NATURE OF WAR

In the conclusion of Chapter 1 of *On War*, Clausewitz briefly develops two of his best-known analytical concepts. The first explains the importance of knowing the 'kind of war' (i.e., *the nature of the war*) that one is about to fight, while the second proposes the *remarkable (or paradoxical) trinity* as the starting point for reaching such an understanding.[1] Although simple in principle, these two closely related concepts are frequently misunderstood.

The first analytical concept, introduced in Section 27, Book 1, explains that *every war is unique in some way*. '**Wars**', Clausewitz observes, '**vary with the nature of their political motives and the situations which give rise to them**' (*On War*, p. 88). It is therefore essential for key political and military leaders to understand *how* and *why* the impending war will differ from those in the past. If they fail to do so, they are unlikely to make the proper preparations, develop an optimal strategy, or wage the war effectively; and if they misconstrue the nature of the new war, these leaders are instead likely to fight the last war over again. Clausewitz puts it this way:

> **The first, the supreme, the most far-reaching act of judgment that the statesman and commander have to make is to establish by that test** [i.e., the political motives and special circumstances] **the kind of war on which they are embarking; neither mistaking it for, nor trying to turn it into, something that is alien to its nature. This is the first of all strategic questions and the most comprehensive** . . .
>
> (Clausewitz, *On War*, pp. 88-89)

Clausewitz returns to this subject toward the end of *On War*. In Book 8 on War Plans, he elaborates on his almost aphoristic comments in Section 27 of Chapter 1, Book 1. In Section 27, he emphasizes that the statesman and commander must work together to identify the kind of war on which they are embarking. Clausewitz's choice of words indicates that political and military analyses are equally important parts of this process. Nevertheless, his expanded discussion of the same subject in Book 8 stresses that war is first a political, not a military, matter. Consequently, the political leader, with the advice of the military commander, is responsible for identifying the *political nature* of the war. Will the political objectives on one or both sides be total or limited? Will the political leaders be able to mobilize the support of the people and for how long? Will they be able to attract the support of other states? Only by answering such questions and thereby arriving at a correct political understanding of a war can a leader develop successful strategic and operational plans. While crucial in and of themselves, military considerations are still subject to, and shaped by, the overriding political issues that define the nature of war. In Book 8, Clausewitz leaves no doubt about the relative importance of the civilian and military authorities:

> **Theory, therefore, demands that at the *outset of war, its character* [i.e., nature] *and scope should be determined on the basis of political probabilities.* The closer these political probabilities drive the war toward the absolute, the more the belligerent states are involved and drawn into its vortex, the clearer appear the connections between its separate actions, and the more imperative the need not to take the first step without considering the last.** [my emphasis]

(Clausewitz, *On War*, p. 584)[2]

In Chapter 6B of Book 8, Clausewitz explains why political considerations must ultimately take precedence over military considerations in determining the nature of a war:

> **Clearly the tremendous effects of the French Revolution abroad *were caused not so much by new military methods and concepts as by radical changes in policies* and administration, by the new character of government, altered condition of the French people, and the like. That other governments did not understand these changes, that they wished to oppose new and overwhelming forces with customary means: all these were *political errors. Would a purely military view of war have enabled anyone to detect these faults and cure them? It would not.* Even if there really had existed a thoughtful strategist capable of deducing the whole range of consequences simply from the nature of the hostile elements, and on the strength of these of prophesying their ultimate effects, it would have been quite impossible to act on his speculations.**

93

> Not until statesmen had at last perceived the nature of the forces that had emerged in France, *and had grasped that new political conditions* now obtained in Europe, could they foresee the broad effect all this would have on war; and *only in that way could they appreciate the scale of the means that would have to be employed, and how best to apply them.* [my emphasis][3]
>
> (Clausewitz, *On War*, p. 609)

Today, instead of the French Revolution and Napoleon, we could use the examples of the Vietnam War, the Gulf War, or the war against Serbia to reach the same conclusion; namely, that it was the *political circumstances* which first determined the unique character of each war, and which then either allowed or prevented the exploitation of the latest available military technologies.

Predicting the nature of a *future or ongoing* war sounds simple enough but is actually quite challenging. Many difficult questions (not only political ones) will have to be answered. Will the war be short or prolonged? Will it be a war of decision or maneuver, or a war of attrition? Will it be a conventional war, a guerrilla war, or a combination of both? Will it be a high-tech, low-tech, or 'no-tech' war? Will new weapons technologies favor the offense over the defense or vice-versa and at which phase of the war? How determined will the populations on both sides be? Will the war be fought for limited or unlimited goals, and by whom? What alliances will be formed and how will they endure under pressure?

The probability of answering these questions correctly increases in direct proportion to a leader's grasp of the political, psychological, sociological, material, and technological circumstances in which the war will take place. Furthermore, the decision-makers require excellent information not only on their own circumstances, but also on those of the opponent and his allies. This in turn requires reliable intelligence and the ability to conduct a comprehensive and objective net assessment. Even the most enlightened leadership in the best of circumstances will find that this is no mean feat, given the inescapable subjectivity of political biases, parochial interests, and wishful thinking.

Moreover, the *reciprocal nature* of all action in war means that attempts to grasp its complexities through a static, unilaterally based concept will never succeed. (In Sections 27 and 28 of Book 1, Clausewitz discusses how to understand the nature of war, but only from the perspective of one side. Yet a realistic approach must consider how one's adversary interprets the war as well.) Thus, perceiving the nature of a war is a reciprocal and dialectical process in which it is important to consider how one side's perspective and actions affect the other side's actions and reactions. These questions are difficult to answer, particularly when the adversary himself is not sure what he will do. Thus, the true nature of war can only be better understood *after* the war has begun, when it is then defined by a complicated series of interactions between the warring parties. Moreover, as events unfold, observers and strategic analysts will view the same situation in different ways. While it may or may not be easy to forecast the first few opening encounters, the initial assessments grow less accurate with each passing day. Just because perfection is unattainable, however, does not mean that attempts to assess the nature of a war are futile. After all, a level of 25 percent accuracy is still preferable to one of 10 percent or less.

Although Clausewitz does not make a direct statement to this effect, it is clear that the proper assessment of a war is a dynamic, ongoing process in which *initial predictions must be revised continuously*. Once political and military leaders develop the ability to recognize their own and the enemy's mistakes, they must then remain flexible enough to modify or even abandon their original strategy if necessary. This is, of course, much easier said than done.

In his essay on 'Strategy in China's Revolutionary War', Mao explains the need to regularly assess and reassess the nature of a war *based on what is actually happening*:

> The process of knowing a situation goes on not only before the formulation of a military plan, but also after. In carrying out the plan from the moment it is put into effect to the end of the operation, there is another process of knowing the situation, namely the process of practice. In the course of this process, it is necessary to examine anew whether the plan worked out in the preceding process corresponds with reality. If it does not correspond with reality, or if it does not fully do so, then in light of our new knowledge, it becomes necessary to form new judgments, make new decisions, and change the original plan so as to meet the new situation.[4]

The importance of adapting to the changing nature of war was recognized long ago by Machiavelli, who dedicates an extensive chapter to this subject in *The Discourses* (Book 3, Chapter 9). One aspect of this adaptability concerns a nation's ability to fit particular leaders to situations that most require their talents. 'He errs the least and will be most favored by fortune who suits his proceedings to the times.' For example, Machiavelli explains that Fabius Maximus was the ideal military leader for the early defensive phases of the Second Punic War against the tactically brilliant Hannibal because of his 'extreme caution and the slowness of his movements'; yet Fabius was no longer the right leader for the offensive phase of the war, when the balance of power tipped in Rome's favor. True to his disposition, Fabius opposed the Senate's approval of Scipio's more aggressive plan to switch the war against Carthage to Africa. But fortunately, Machiavelli tells us, '. . . Rome was a republic that produced citizens of various character and dispositions such as Fabius, who was excellent at the time when it was desirable to protract the war, and Scipio, when it became necessary to terminate it.' Thus, Machiavelli makes a sophisticated argument that republics or democratic regimes, which by their nature are able to change political and military leaders as the circumstances require, can better adapt to the continuously changing nature of war. By contrast, authoritarian regimes, which 'encourage' conformity and discourage innovation, are more likely to retain the same leaders, who by their nature and political culture are disinclined to meet change with flexibility. 'It is this', Machiavelli continues, 'which assures to republics greater vitality and more enduring success than monarchies have; for the diversity of the genius of her citizens enables the republic better to accommodate herself to the changes of the times than can be done by a prince.' But is there really a positive correlation between success in war and democratic government? This proposition appears plausible in the twentieth century, but would require more rigorous statistical analysis and further research to be proven correct.

Machiavelli then explains that the inability to adapt has two other explanations as well. The first 'is impossibility to change the natural bent of our characters'. The second 'is the difficulty of persuading ourselves, after having been accustomed to success by a certain mode of proceeding, that any other can succeed as well' (Machiavelli, *The Discourses* (Modern Library edn), pp. 442-443). The latter point is simply a question of hubris and habit. As Kenneth Boulding once put it, 'There is no failure like success and no success like failure.'

In Section 27 of Chapter 1, Book 1, Clausewitz simply ignores the substantial difficulties involved in identifying the nature of a future war. He does, however, indeed return to this issue in Chapter 3B, Book 8 on War Plans.

> To discover how much of our resources must be mobilized for war, we must first examine our own political aim and that of the enemy. We must gauge the strength and situation of the opposing state. We must gauge the character and abilities of its government and people and do the same in regard to our own. Finally, we must evaluate the political sympathies of other states and the effect the war may have on them. To assess these things in all their ramifications and diversity is plainly a colossal task. Rapid and correct appraisal of them clearly calls for the intuition of a genius; to master all this complex mass by sheer methodical examination is obviously impossible. Bonaparte was quite right when he said that Newton himself would quail before the algebraic problems it could pose.
>
> The size and variety of factors to be weighed, and the uncertainty about the proper scale to use, are bound to make it far more difficult to reach the right conclusion. We should also bear in mind that the vast, unique importance of war, while not increasing the complexity and difficulty of the problem, does increase the value of the correct solution . . .
>
> We must admit that an imminent war, its possible aims, and the resources it will require, are matters that can only be assessed when every circumstance has been examined *in the context of the whole* which of course includes the most ephemeral factors as well. We must also recognize that the conclusion reached can be no more wholly objective than any other in war, but will be shaped by the qualities of mind and character of the men making the decision – of the rulers, statesmen, and commanders, whether these roles are united in a single individual or not.
>
> (Clausewitz, *On War*, pp. 585–586)

The remainder of Chapter 3B, Book 8 discusses the nature of war in different periods of history, which can be explained not only by its inherent theoretical tendencies (as described in Chapter 1, Book 1) but also in the context of its particular time and place. (Nevertheless, the dynamics of war as described by the paradigm of the absolute war are valuable for explaining some aspects of war such as escalation, war termination, and civil-military tensions.)

The actual circumstances of a war are of course the most important for understanding its unique nature.

> **The theorist** [i.e., in this case, the political leader and commander] ... **must scrutinize all data with an inquiring, a discriminating, and a classifying eye. He must always bear in mind the wide variety of situations that can lead to war. If he does, he will draw the outline of its salient features in such a way that it can accommodate both the dictates of the age and those of the immediate situation.**
>
> **We can thus only say that the aims a belligerent adopts, and the resources he employs, must be governed by the particular characteristics of his own position; but they will also conform to the spirit of the age and to its general character. Finally** [and here Clausewitz returns to the importance of the abstract theory of war] **they must always be governed by the general conclusions to be drawn from the nature of war itself.**
>
> (Clausewitz, *On War*, pp. 593–594)

Comprehending the 'dictates of the age' and the 'spirit of the age and its general character' certainly depends on the intuition and insight of political and military leaders – not on a rigorous scientific analysis. Yet whatever the characteristics of wars throughout history, they always contain a common element, namely the basic logic of war or strategy. For example, the primacy of politics; the correlation of ends and means; the principle of concentration; and the role of friction will always be valid. *The theory of war itself does not change, only its application, which varies in emphasis according to specific circumstances.*

A few examples will help to clarify why it is so difficult to identify the nature of a war. Before the outbreak of the Peloponnesian War, Pericles estimated that the Spartans would soon give up after they had failed to lure the Athenians into a direct, decisive battle. As it turned out, the Spartans did not give up and the war lasted, off and on, for another 27 years. Pericles' confident predictions based on the superior economic strength of the Athenians also proved to be incorrect. Although he warned the Athenians not to embark on new expeditions before they had won the war in Greece proper, the Athenians launched their expedition to Sicily – an unwise move that soon ended their naval and military superiority. Nor did Pericles foresee that the Spartans would conclude a treaty with the Persians, ultimately giving them the naval strength to match that of Athens. Finally, Pericles failed to estimate the impact of his leadership and later, its absence, on the Athenian capacity to wage the war successfully. With his death came the end of his own strategy. In addition, it is not clear how he would have adapted his own strategy to the changing circumstances. What is certain, however, is that Pericles had no history of modifying his strategy to fit changing circumstances.

In more recent wars, from the American Revolution to the Vietnam War, such misapprehension of the nature of the war caused either serious setbacks or major defeats. In its war against the upstart American colonies, the British government failed to understand how its strategy would radicalize and mobilize the American people only as long as the fighting lasted. In the same way, the European powers, for as long as 15 years, did not fully recognize that new political circumstances and the mobilization of the people during the French Revolution now called for concomitant reforms of their own political systems (see Clausewitz, *On War*, p. 519). Even once they *had* perceived the changes wrought by the French Revolution, they were reluctant to introduce the necessary political reforms. This is because they feared that such reforms would jeopardize their own political stability. On the eve of the First World War, none of the warring states of Europe grasped how the Industrial Revolution and new technological developments had changed the face of modern war. As a result, they expected the war to be short, offensive, and decisive (despite evidence to the contrary from the American Civil War, the Boer War, and the Russo-Japanese War). They clung to the belief that modern technology favored the offense over the defense; and even when this proved to be incorrect, they could not bring themselves to adapt. In the Second World War, the British and French, for example, initially expected to fight a modified version of the First

99

World War because they never imagined developments such as the *Blitzkrieg*.

In Vietnam, the U.S. military waged a 'central front' high-tech, conventional war from beginning to end, which was evidence enough of its utter failure to understand the correct nature of the war. Unfortunately for the United States, the North Vietnamese saw that their comparative advantage lay in a lower-intensity guerrilla war combined with political subversion. U.S. strategists refused to acknowledge such factors as the limited effectiveness of their firepower and its counter-productive impact, despite mounting evidence that the American approach was wrong. Unable to perceive that the political dimension of the war mattered most, they failed to see how prolonging the war would adversely affect American public opinion. The U.S. military ended the war as it had begun, in a high-tech conventional mode. The North Vietnamese, on the other hand, learned from their mistakes and resorted to either conventional or guerrilla warfare as circumstances required. Current American military histories of the war in Vietnam show that, even in hindsight, experts disagree on the type of strategy that should have been developed to best suit the evolving nature of the war. Identifying the nature of a war before it has begun can be so complex that even the advantage of historical perspective is not enough to produce a consensus among experts.

Particularly in a prolonged war, forecasting the twists and turns of innumerable reciprocal interactions between opponents is daunting indeed. Moreover, friction, chance, and luck combine with the other distinct elements of a war to form its unique character. Why, then, does Clausewitz advise us to predict the kind of war that will emerge *as accurately as possible* even while he stresses its volatile nature? Clausewitz would answer that although no political or military leader can accurately predict the nature of war, it is nevertheless incumbent upon him to try. This maximizes his chance of establishing a sound basis for his strategic and operational planning as well as for his war preparations. Imperfect estimates are better than no estimates at all. Since war is a dynamic, ongoing process in which initial estimates are soon overtaken by unfolding events, the correct way to understand Clausewitz's advice is therefore in the context of his general argument on the uncertain nature of war. The following chart (Figure 9.1) illustrates how understanding the nature of war forms the basis for identifying one's

FIGURE 9.1

THE IMPORTANCE OF UNDERSTANDING THE NATURE OF WAR AS THE BASIS FOR ALL STRATEGIC PLANNING

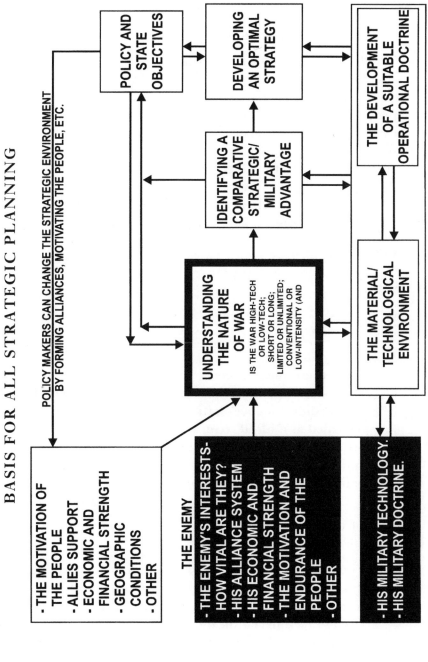

comparative strategic advantage, completing strategic planning, and analyzing almost all other important related issues.

THE TRINITARIAN ANALYSIS

Mindful of the complexity implicit in trying to understand a war in advance, Clausewitz sought to simplify this task through the introduction of his trinitarian analysis. Clausewitz begins Section 28 by reminding us that no two wars are identical because all undergo dynamic change and adaptation to a given environment. 'War', he states, 'is more than a true *chameleon* that slightly adapts its characteristics to the given case' (Clausewitz, *On War*, p. 89). Two millennia earlier, Sun Tzu had used a similar metaphor comparing the changeability and variety of war to that of water: '*And as water shapes its flow in accordance with the ground, so an army manages its victory in accordance with the situation of the enemy. And as water has no constant form, there are in war no constant conditions*' (Sun Tzu, *The Art of War*, p. 101).

In the trinitarian analysis, Clausewitz ingeniously reduces the infinite complexities of war to *three basic dominant tendencies*. Although each war is unique, all wars can nevertheless be better understood through a close examination of the role and interrelationship of these three tendencies.

> As a total phenomenon its [war's] dominant tendencies always make war a paradoxical trinity – composed of primordial violence, hatred, and enmity, which are to be regarded as a blind natural force; of the play of chance and probability within which the creative spirit is free to roam; and of its element of subordination, as instrument of policy, which makes it subject to reason alone.
>
> (Clausewitz, *On War*, p. 89)

Each of these three tendencies generally, but not exclusively, corresponds to one of three groups in society:

> The first of these three aspects mainly concerns *the people*; the second, *the commander and his army*; and the third, *the government*. The passions that are kindled in war must already be inherent in the people; the scope which the play of courage and talent will enjoy in the realm of probability

and chance depends on the particular character of the commander and the army; but the political aims are the business of the government alone.

(Clausewitz, *On War*, p. 89)

Each tendency is not, however, represented only by its corresponding group in every case. To assert, as Clausewitz does, that '**the political aims are the business of the government** *alone*' is unacceptable in modern democracies and was perhaps incorrect in Clausewitz's time as well (see also discussion in Chapter 10, pp. 128–129). In some instances, political aims might not be adequately addressed by the government, leaving the people or even the military to have the greatest impact on the formation of a guiding policy for the war. In the same way, although the element of passion, hate, and enmity must be present in the spirit and attitude of the people – it can also be expressed by the military and the government. On other occasions, the creative talent required for the management of chance and probability might be present in the political rather than the military leadership. Nevertheless, this does not change the fact that the intricate relationships among the three dominant tendencies define the nature of war. This raises the question of whether Sections 27 and 28 appear in the most logical order. Perhaps the development of the trinitarian analysis in Section 28 should precede the discussion of the nature of war in Section 27. Regardless, the two are so closely related that they cannot be fully understood separately.

If we assume that the three dominant tendencies are equally important, their relationship can be represented by an equilateral triangle. Yet the simplicity of this representation belies the complexity of war, since, as Clausewitz points out, the three dominant tendencies rarely carry equal weight; their relative intensity and relationships change according to the circumstances of each case.

> **These three tendencies are like three different codes of law, deep-rooted in their subject and yet variable in their relationship to one another. A theory that ignores any one of them or seeks to fix an arbitrary relationship between them would conflict with reality to such an extent that for this reason alone it would be totally useless . . . . Our task therefore is to develop a theory that maintains a balance**

103

between these three tendencies, like an object suspended between three magnets.

(Clausewitz, *On War*, p. 89)

FIGURE 9.2
THE THREE DOMINANT TENDENCIES OF WAR

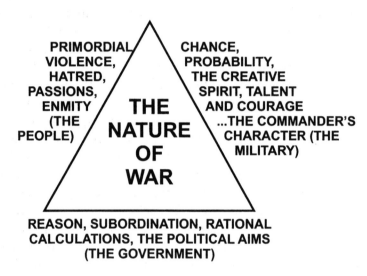

A more accurate depiction of the varying relationship among these three tendencies is a simple vector analysis, where the nature of a war is the outcome or 'vector' of the three dominant tendencies. Modern conventional war is best represented by a 'vector analysis' in which the importance of each tendency is roughly equal. In representing guerrilla warfare, however, the role of the people takes precedence over the role of the professional military (at least in the war's initial phases), while the role of the political leadership is as important as in a conventional war. The extreme case of an all-out nuclear war (high on Herman Kahn's[5] ladder of escalation) gives greatest weight to the government, since almost all of the decisions (given the short time available, the weapons used, and the need to strike first) would be made by political leaders. The military would play a small role (button-pushing), and the people would have little to do other than to suffer the consequences. Since no two wars are identical, the nature of each war has to be depicted by an individually designed 'vector analysis'.

FIGURE 9.3
THE TRINITY AS A 'VECTOR ANALYSIS' (CONVENTIONAL WAR)

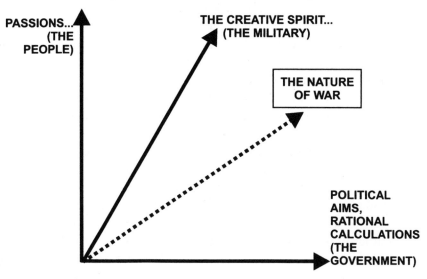

FIGURE 9.4
GUERRILLA WARFARE

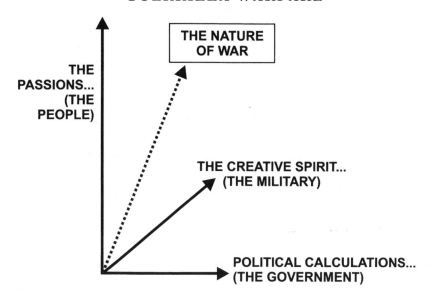

Clausewitz does, however, omit one important issue of which he was surely aware; namely, that *the nature of war can never be defined in isolation by one country alone* because it is shaped by the dynamic interaction among the belligerents' individual 'trinities'. Only by appreciating the importance of this interaction can the analyst hope to approach an accurate definition of a war's true nature. For example, during the Vietnam War, the passions, hatred, and motivation of the North Vietnamese and Vietcong outlasted those of the Americans, while the South Vietnamese government failed to mobilize the passions of its own people. Meanwhile, the Vietcong and North Vietnamese military creatively modified their strategies according to their level of success or failure on the battlefield. They fought guerrilla war or conventional war as dictated by the particular circumstances. By contrast, the U.S. military inflexibly waged a capital-intensive, high-tech, conventional war throughout: the emphasis was on firepower and a dogged determination not to adapt strategy and tactics to the circumstances at hand. On the political level, the U.S. government failed fully to mobilize the support of the American people and to articulate clear and consistent political aims to its own military (as claimed by Col. Harry Summers).[6] The South Vietnamese government certainly concentrated more on its own short-term survival without motivating its people or developing a political system for which the people would want to fight. At the same time, the North Vietnamese government promulgated clear aims with popular appeal; in addition, it effectively mobilized the support of world public opinion and created the political conditions that enabled its own military ultimately to win the war with a direct conventional onslaught on South Vietnam. In the long run, and for complex reasons that cannot be discussed in this context, the North Vietnamese 'trinity' proved more effective than that of the United States and South Vietnam.[7] Clearly, then, Clausewitz's otherwise continuous emphasis on the *reciprocal, interactive* nature of war suggests that understanding the nature of a war means understanding the interaction among *all* of the trinities of the warring states.

Another issue related to the trinitarian analysis bears mentioning. All three of the dominant tendencies that determine the nature of war are non-material, intangible, or metaphysical. Curiously, the trinitarian analysis makes no reference to the material, economic, or physical aspects of war. Perhaps in his desire to develop the most abstract or

FIGURE 9.5
THE NATURE OF EACH WAR IS DEFINED BY THE INTERACTION OF THE TRINITIES OF ALL PARTICIPANTS

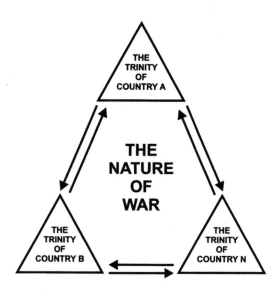

'pure theory of war', Clausewitz thought that the material (or today's technological) dimensions of war were secondary. **'It is clear'**, he states, **'that weapons and equipment are not essential to the concept** [i.e., pure theory] **of fighting, since even wrestling is fighting of a kind'** (*On War*, p. 127). Although 'moral factors' (see above, Chapter 8, pp. 81–89) are obviously very important, wars cannot be won by will alone. Since war is ultimately a clash of physical forces of all types, it cannot be understood without its physical, economic, and technological dimensions. Indeed, Clausewitz's most important definition of war emphasizes the physical and material nature of all war by its distinguishing characteristic of *violent force*. Throughout the text, he underscores the centrality of battle and the principle of destruction, all of which are obviously based on the extensive use of physical force. In the real world, war has always involved far more than just opposing wills.

Why did Clausewitz neglect the economic and material dimension of war? First, Clausewitz wrote a book on war itself, on how to fight and win. This book was written primarily for military leaders mainly concerned with the actual fighting of the war and not as much with the material/economic preparations that the government is assumed to have completed. Clausewitz explicitly refers to his approach as a **'narrower theory of war', 'the theory of the conduct of war', or 'the theory of the use of the fighting forces'** (Clausewitz, *On War*, p. 132).

> **The conduct of war has nothing to do with making guns and powder out of coal, sulphur, saltpeter, copper, and tin; its given quantities are weapons that are ready for use and their effectiveness. Strategy uses maps without worrying about trigonometric surveys; it does not inquire how a country should be organized and a people trained and ruled in order to produce the best military results. *It takes these matters as it finds them* in the European community of nations, and calls attention only to unusual circumstances that exert a marked influence on war.**
>
> (Clausewitz, *On War*, p. 144)

> **One would not consider the whole business of maintenance and administration as part of the actual conduct of war.**
>
> (Clausewitz, *On War*, p. 129; see also pp. 128–129 and p. 131)

But Clausewitz's narrower approach to the study of war is unsatisfactory as far as the higher political and strategic levels of waging war are concerned.

A second explanation is that, since Clausewitz lived before the age of the Industrial Revolution, he did not anticipate rapid technological changes in the fighting environment. As a result, he might have assumed that all sides would quickly adopt every new technological or material development or counter-measure, thereby negating the impact of technological innovation.

> **If the offensive were to invent some major new expedient – which is unlikely in view of the simplicity and inherent necessity that makes everything today – the defensive would also have to change its methods.**
>
> (Clausewitz, *On War*, p. 362)

Third, and perhaps most important, Clausewitz believed that the most important changes in war during and before his time were political and sociological. By contrast, the material and technological environment seemed relatively stable.

> **Very few of the new manifestations in war can be ascribed to new inventions or new departures in ideas. They result mainly from the transformation of society and new social conditions . . .**
>
> (Clausewitz, *On War*, p. 515)

A more accurate and comprehensive understanding of the nature of war should therefore incorporate a fourth dominant tendency, namely, a material, economic, and technological dimension. Factors such as the range of weapons from arrows to guns and rockets; the mobility provided by horses with stirrups, trains, tanks, helicopters, or aircraft; the precision of weapons used; the rate of firepower; and the quality and effectiveness of command, control, and information-processing systems have always played a central role in determining the nature of war. Technological developments and surprises have, particularly in modern warfare, added a very important qualitative dimension or force multiplier.

It can be argued that there is no need to add a fourth dominant tendency if we simply examine Clausewitz's trinity against a material background. But adding a fourth dimension seems more precise because it puts the material environment on an equal footing with the other three dominant tendencies, thus emphasizing its relative importance. Either way, the material dimension must be represented in any conceptual framework on the nature of war. (Jomini, for example, was far more aware of the potential impact of material and technological changes in war.)

Clausewitz's general omission of the material dimensions of war is thus a major weakness in his theory. After all, he defines war as a collision of material forces; and the wars of the French Revolution and Napoleon of his time clearly involved economic and material elements that decisively affected the course of events in the long run. These include the Continental system and the Continental blockade; the economic war between Britain and France (which drove Napoleon to

FIGURE 9.6
THE MATERIAL AND TECHNOLOGICAL
ENVIRONMENT: SQUARING THE TRIANGLE

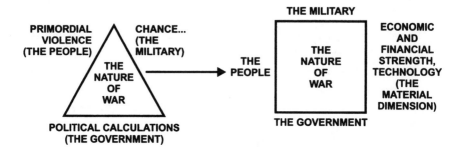

FIGURE 9.7
THE THREE DOMINANT DIMENSIONS OF
WAR IN THE CONTEXT OF A MATERIAL
ENVIRONMENT

Spain and Russia simultaneously and, ultimately, to his defeat); the British financial support of the various coalitions opposing Napoleon; British economic strength based on naval power and extensive trade outside Europe; and Napoleon's taxation of the occupied populations of Europe to finance his war effort.

Whether Clausewitz reflects a traditional German, 'romantic', emphasis on the moral dimensions of war (*moralische Grössen*) and the strength of will, or whether the Germans are Clausewitzians, does not matter as much as the fact that Germany's principal weakness in both world wars stemmed from its adherence to this 'narrower' concept of war. The Germans were in part defeated by their inefficiently managed war economy combined with the overestimation of their military performance and will to win – and the underestimation of Allied material and economic strength.

STRATEGY AS A SEARCH FOR A COMPARATIVE ADVANTAGE

> Pompaedius Silo: If you are a great general, come down and fight.
> Marius: If *you* are a great general, make me fight against my will.[8]

The process that we refer to today as 'net assessment' or 'correlation of forces' allows policymakers or strategists to identify their *comparative strategic advantages*, and devise a strategy that capitalizes on their own strengths and the enemy's weaknesses. In Chapter 6 ('Weaknesses and Strengths') of *The Art of War*, Sun Tzu makes the crucial yet subtle observation that the art of strategy should be based on exploiting a comparative advantage that enables one to dictate the terms or nature of the war. Fighting on one's own terms requires not only good intelligence (as emphasized by Sun Tzu on many occasions) but also cognizance of the enemy's preferred strategy and *his* reaction to one's own strategy. Needless to say, the enemy will go through the same estimative process. All other things being equal, the side that completes this 'net assessment' most carefully and objectively, and continues to reevaluate and adapt his strategy as the war progresses, will succeed by fighting more on his own terms.

True to his style throughout *The Art of War*, Sun Tzu provides us with concluding advice on exploiting our comparative advantage; there is no hint of the analytical process that led him to this point. Sun Tzu simply proceeds directly to the recommendation that we identify our comparative advantage and fight on our own best terms.

> *Therefore the clever combatant imposes his will on the enemy, but does not allow the enemy's will to be imposed on him.*
> (Sun Tzu, *The Art of War*, Giles trans., p. 42)

The Griffith, Ames, and Tai translations convey slight variations of the same passage:

> *And therefore those skilled in war bring the enemy to the field of battle and are not brought by him.*
> (Sun Tzu, *The Art of War*, Griffith trans., p. 96)

> *Thus the expert in battle moves the enemy, and is not moved by him.*
> (Sun Tzu, *The Art of War*, Ames trans., p. 123)

> *Therefore a skillful fighter keeps the initiative but on no occasion lets the enemy's will be imposed on him.*
> (Sun Tzu, *The Art of War*, Tai Mien-leng trans., p. 22)

In the Giles translation, the commentator Tu Mu clarifies this idea as follows:

> *One mark of a great soldier* [or strategist] *is that he fights on his own terms or fights not at all.*
> (Sun Tzu, *The Art of War*, Giles trans., p. 42)

A careful consideration of who can impose the terms of battle upon whom may result in one side's decision to avoid battle if possible. Knowing when to avoid battle is as important as knowing when to engage. '*He who knows when he can fight and when he cannot will be victorious*' (Sun Tzu, *The Art of War*, p. 82). This decision in turn depends upon the quality of intelligence available to the strategist or commander and upon the accuracy of his net assessment.

These statements on the importance of identifying a comparative advantage can be correlated with other more indirect statements to the same effect:

The skillful commander takes up a position in which he cannot be defeated and misses no opportunity to master his enemy.
(Sun Tzu, *The Art of War*, p. 87)

Anciently, the skillful warriors first made themselves invincible and awaited the enemy's moment of vulnerability. Invincibility depends on oneself; the enemy's vulnerability on him. It follows that those skilled in war can make themselves invincible but cannot cause an enemy to be certainly vulnerable.
(Sun Tzu, *The Art of War*, p. 85)

The latter statement is a reference to the reciprocal nature of action and reaction in war, for, regardless of how well it prepares for battle, one side can never be sure of the opponent's counter-moves or mistakes. The shrewd commander selects an advantageous position long before the battle begins. Once favorably situated, he can then compel the enemy to engage him on his preferred terms.

Anciently those skilled in war conquered an enemy easily conquered. . . . Thus a victorious army wins its victories before seeking battle. . . . He conquers an enemy already defeated.
(Sun Tzu, *The Art of War*, p. 87)

Ideally, fighting is the final and, in a way, the least important, phase of a successfully implemented strategy. The process of thinking, planning, and searching for a comparative advantage – not an impulsive rush to engage the enemy – lays the groundwork for victory.

For his part, Clausewitz never discusses the need to search for a comparative advantage as the basis for a sound strategy and success on the lower levels of war. He engages in a brilliant, systematic discussion on the importance of ascertaining the nature of war and of using the 'trinity' as an analytical tool, but leaves the need to identify one's comparative advantage and to fight on one's own terms as implicit concepts. After all, he who understands the nature of a war should also be able to identify his comparative advantages. In addition, Clausewitz's discussion of the relationship between the offense and defense, with the comparative advantage afforded by the defense, certainly relates to the same concept.

If . . . the use of every means available for pure resistance – gives an advantage in war, the advantage need only be

113

> enough to balance any superiority the opponent may
> possess . . . It is evident that this method, wearing down the
> enemy, applies to the great number of cases where the weak
> endeavor to resist the strong.

(Clausewitz, On War, p. 94)

One of the most important elements in the search for a comparative advantage is to make the war relatively more expensive for the enemy:

> [One] . . . question is how to influence the enemy's expendi-
> ture of effort; in other words, how to make the war more
> costly to him.

(Clausewitz, On War, p. 93)

Yet these ideas mentioned by Clausewitz are at best indirectly related to the search for a comparative advantage. By contrast, Sun Tzu makes an important and original contribution to the study of war when he explicitly develops this concept. Why engage the enemy on his own terms, where he is relatively stronger, when one can win by exploiting a comparative advantage? If an opponent holds the advantage in conventional warfare, one should wage a prolonged, low-intensity guerrilla-type of warfare. If an opponent is highly sensitive to changes in public opinion, one should try to prolong the war as much as possible. If, in modern times, for example, one's opponent has a significant advantage in fighting a high-tech war, one must search for a strategy that does not allow him to capitalize on it.

Although the history of war from antiquity to the present abounds with instructive examples, only a few will be mentioned here. Sparta's advantage over Athens in land warfare forced Pericles to search for a comparative advantage. His strategy was to avoid battle by refusing to emerge from behind the walls of Athens, in the hope that the Athenians would be able to hold out longer than the Spartans. Similarly, Hannibal's tactical and operational (but not strategic) brilliance inevitably led to the development of Fabius' strategy of avoidance and delay. This continued until the arrival of an equally brilliant Roman general Scipio, who favored a more aggressive strategy. Led by Scipio, the Romans moved over to the attack in Carthage where they finally defeated Hannibal. Each of these examples involved a contest between a strategy of annihilation and a strategy of attrition, to use Delbrück's terminology.

In the American Civil War, President Lincoln sought to exploit the Union's economic and numerical advantage over the Confederacy's superior fighting capabilities. He explains his thoughts on the search for a comparative advantage in a letter of 13 January 1862 to Generals Buell and Halleck. His words and ideas bear a remarkable resemblance to those used by Sun Tzu to describe the importance of dividing the enemy's forces (see Sun Tzu, *The Art of War*, p. 92).

> I state my general idea of this war to be that we have the greater numbers, and the enemy has the greater facility of concentrating forces upon the points of collision; that we must fail, unless we can find some way of making our advantage an over-match for his; and that this can only be done by menacing him with superior forces at different points, at the same time; so that we can safely attack, one, or both, if he makes no change; and if he weakens one to strengthen the other, forbear to attack the strengthened one, but seize, and hold the weakened one, gaining so much.[9]

This strategy, which caused the Union to expand its attacks in the west, so adroitly exploited the North's comparative advantages that the South could not find an answer to it. Despite operating on interior lines, the Confederacy was consistently hobbled by its economic weakness, inferior numbers, and inability to improve its railroads. Outstanding fighting machines or brilliant military opponents (e.g., the Spartans, Hannibal, Napoleon, the Confederacy, the German Wehrmacht) cannot be defeated in battles fought on their own terms.[10] But if the side that first appears to be weaker can find other methods, such as avoiding battle and stalling for a considerable time, building larger coalitions, or exploiting a materially superior position, then even a looming Goliath can be defeated eventually.

The search for a comparative advantage need not be confined to military strategy alone. The United States owed its initial successes in the Cold War to George Kennan's strategy of containment, which was

> calculated to apply American strength against Soviet weakness, thereby preserving the initiative while minimizing the costs. Fundamental [to Kennan's approach] was the notion of asymmetrical response – of applying one's own strengths against an

adversary's weakness, rather than attempting to match the adversary in all of his capabilities . . .[11]

Accordingly, the United States chose not to match the Soviet Union in direct military confrontation but primarily in the economic and technological arenas, where it could concentrate on rehabilitating Western Europe and Japan, on building 'an international order made up of independent centers of power, in which nations subjected to Soviet pressure would have both the means and the will to resist it themselves'.[12]

In the Gulf War, Saddam Hussein should have resorted to terrorism and subversion to accomplish his goals, since the United States clearly held the advantage in conventional high-tech war. If he had done so, Saddam Hussein would have been able to compete in an area where he possessed a comparative advantage. Similarly, in the Vietnam War, the North Vietnamese learned that they would do best in the conventional, high-tech war preferred by the United States if they waged a low-tech, prolonged guerrilla war. The North Vietnamese proceeded to exploit this comparative advantage until, in the end, their flexibility and readiness to make sacrifices enabled them to dictate the terms of battle and the nature of the war to the United States.

For the past 50 years, the Arab–Israeli conflict has also involved the constant search for a strategy that would allow each side to exploit its comparative advantage. The first four major, and partly also the fifth, Arab–Israeli wars (in 1948, 1956, 1967, 1973, and 1982–83) were conventional; each time, the Israeli advantage in this type of war increased. Gradually, the Arab states and Palestinians were forced to use, and later came to prefer, lower-intensity levels of war. First the Arabs initiated a guerrilla war, then an international terror campaign against Israel. The lower the level of violence, the more they could dictate the nature and terms of the war. But even on the lower levels of war, the Israelis prevailed. During the war in Lebanon (1982–85), the Israelis forgot the nature of their comparative advantage and became involved in a high-casualty, indecisive war through their own choice. They repeated this mistake in the 1990s during their war against the Hezbollah in southern Lebanon. Following the defeat of the PLO in Lebanon, the Palestinians were forced to discover an even lower level of war – the *Intifada* – which allowed them to capitalize on a comparative advantage against which Israel's conventional superiority proved irrelevant.

The interaction of the warring states, each searching for a comparative advantage, *defines the unique nature of each war*. Thus, Clausewitz's emphasis on the need to correctly identify the nature of war implies the need to identify one's own comparative advantage first. Given the dynamic nature of war, this is an ongoing process in which the more adaptable side that can identify the proper moment to switch from one strategy to another will eventually emerge triumphant.

10

The First Element of the Remarkable Trinity: The People in Arms

> In the eighteenth century . . . war was still an affair for governments alone, and the people's role was simply that of an instrument. At the onset of the nineteenth century, peoples themselves were in the scale on either side.
>
> Clausewitz, *On War*, p. 583

There is no doubt that Sun Tzu appreciates the importance of the three dimensions constituting Clausewitz's trinity and political framework. We have already seen that in *The Art of War*, Sun Tzu recognizes the primacy of politics in all major strategic decisions concerning the initiation, rational conduct, and termination of war. No less than Clausewitz, he pays close attention to the second dimension, which includes the role of the military in all technical details related to planning and leading troops in battle. What remains to be shown is that Sun Tzu also considers the mobilization of popular support as a prerequisite of success.

> *By moral influence I mean that which causes the people to be in harmony with their leaders, so that they will accompany them in life and unto death without fear of mortal peril.*
>
> *[Chang Yu] When one treats the people with benevolence, justice, and righteousness, and reposes confidence in them, the army will be united in mind and all will be happy to serve their leaders.*
>
> (Sun Tzu, *The Art of War*, p. 64)

Sun Tzu is particularly sensitive to the problem of losing popular support in prolonged wars:

When the army is engaged in protracted campaigns, the resources of the state will not suffice.

For there has never been a protracted war from which a country has benefited.

(Sun Tzu, *The Art of War*, p. 73)

Where the army is, prices are high; when prices rise the wealth of the people is exhausted. When wealth is exhausted the peasantry will be afflicted with urgent exactions.

With strength thus depleted and wealth consumed, the households in the central plains will be utterly impoverished and seven-tenths of their wealth dissipated.

[Li Ch'uan] If war drags on without cessation men and women will resent not being able to marry, and will be distressed by the burdens of transportation.

(Sun Tzu, *The Art of War*, p. 74)

Hence Sun Tzu's insistence that wars should be as short as possible, for clearly the longer a war drags on without decisive results, the more difficult it becomes to maintain the support of the people. Clausewitz agrees with Sun Tzu, remarking that it is absurd to spend any more time fighting a war than is absolutely necessary (Clausewitz, *On War*, p. 82).

Although both treatises underscore the necessity of striking the proper balance among the people, the army, and the government, Sun Tzu's discussion of these three elements is scattered while Clausewitz's analysis is once again more concentrated, systematic and explicit.

A comparison of Clausewitz and Jomini on the role of the people in war, however, is even more interesting. In a lengthy discussion, Jomini identifies three major causes for the mobilization and involvement of the people in war: religion, nationalism, or political ideologies. In *Wars of Opinion* (Section 7 of Chapter 1), he discusses nations that intervene in the affairs of other states (that is, wars of aggression and expansion) in the name of religious or political 'dogmas' (as he refers to ideologies). These wars, he declares *'are most deplorable . . . as they enlist the worst passions and become vindictive, cruel, and terrible'* (Jomini, *The Art of War*, p. 25). He then charges that so-called religious motives are usually no more than '*a pretext to obtain political power*' and that a bitter religious or secular dogma (ideology) '*excites the ardor of the people*' (Jomini, *The Art of War*, p. 25). Jomini also believes that military force and war are not suitable or effective in '*arresting an evil which lies wholly in the human passions*' and that only '*time is the true remedy for all bad passions and for all anarchical doctrines*'. Referring to the French Revolution, he remarks that '*to attempt to restrain such a mob by a foreign force is to attempt to restrain the explosion of a mine when the powder has already been ignited: it is far better to await the explosion and afterward fill up the crater rather than try to prevent it and to perish in the attempt*' (Jomini, *The Art of War*, p. 26). When intervening in the internal affairs of another country, one must, he cautions, be extremely careful to end the conflict as quickly as possible and avoid giving the impression that the independence and integrity of its territory are threatened.

Clausewitz, who also witnessed the wars of the French Revolution, observes that the unprecedented mobilization of the French people irreversibly changed the nature of warfare, which now more closely resembled his theoretical ideal type of absolute war:

> But these changes . . . were caused by the new political conditions which the French Revolution created both in France and in Europe as a whole, conditions that set in motion new means and new forces, and have thus made possible a degree of energy in war that otherwise would have been inconceivable.

> It follows that the transformation of the art of war resulted from the transformation of politics. So far from suggesting that the two could be disassociated from each other, these changes are a strong proof of their indissoluble connection.
>
> (Clausewitz, *On War*, p. 610)

> The French Revolution surprised us in the false security of our ancient skills, and drove us from Chalons to Moscow . . . Woe to the government, which, relying on half-hearted politics and a shackled military policy, meets a foe who,

> like the untamed element, knows no law other than his own power!
>
> (Clausewitz, *On War*, p. 219)
> (See also discussion in Chapter 14 below, pp. 200–202.)

The rise of this formidable 'untamed element' had signalled the rapid obsolescence of the old forms of doing battle:

> **The old way was a half-and-half affair; it was an anomaly, since in essence war and peace admit of no gradations.**
>
> (Clausewitz, *On War*, p. 603)

> **The elemental fire of war is now so fierce and war is waged with such enormous energy that even the regular periods of rest have disappeared, and all forces press unremittingly toward the great decision.**
>
> (Clausewitz, *On War*, p. 313)

> **It is true that war itself has undergone significant changes in character and methods, changes that have brought it closer to its absolute form.**
>
> (Clausewitz, *On War*, p. 610)

As Clausewitz explains, the appearance of the *levée en masse*, much like the release of the nuclear genie over 150 years later, could not be undone:

> **Will this [new, intensive, total type of warfare] always be the case in the future? From now on will every war in Europe be waged with the full resources of the state, and therefore have to be fought only over major issues that affect the people? Or shall we again see a gradual separation taking place between government and people? Such questions are difficult to answer . . . but . . . once barriers – which in a sense only consist of man's ignorance of what is possible – are torn down, they are not easily set up again. At least when major interests are at stake, mutual hostility will express itself in the same manner as it has in our own day.**
>
> (Clausewitz, *On War*, p. 593)

Elsewhere, Clausewitz seems convinced that the new changes in the nature of war are irreversible:

> **The bounds of military operations have been extended so far that a return to the old narrow limitations can only occur briefly, sporadically, and under special conditions. The true nature of war will break through again with overwhelming force, and must, therefore, be the basis of any permanent military arrangements.**
>
> (Clausewitz, *On War*, p. 313)

> **Now that governments have become conscious of these resources, we cannot expect them to remain unused in the future.**
>
> (Clausewitz, *On War*, p. 270)

As we shall see below, Jomini too was intrigued by the same question: that is, whether the forces unleashed by one war would inevitably become the rule in the future.

The most illuminating ideas on the role of the people in war are found in Clausewitz's and Jomini's analyses of guerrilla warfare (which Jomini discusses under the rubric of *National Wars*, while Clausewitz prefers the term *The People in Arms*).[1] Jomini considers national wars to be the most difficult because they are fought '*against a united people . . . filled with a noble ardor and determined to sustain their independence*' (Jomini, *The Art of War*, p. 29).

> *The difficulties in the path of an army in wars of opinions as well as national wars are very great and render the mission of the general conducting them very difficult.*
>
> (Jomini, *The Art of War*, p. 30)

As Clausewitz explains, '. . . **it is the natural law of the moral world that a nation on the brink of an abyss will try to save itself by any means**' (Clausewitz, *On War*, p. 483). When defeated, under occupation by a foreign power or in desperate straits, the entire population can be mobilized to resist the invading force. A guerrilla war will not necessarily be directed by the government at first, but will most often be the outgrowth of a spontaneous uprising.

In discussing the geographical, topographical, and other conditions necessary for the success of guerrilla warfare, Jomini is primarily influenced by the Spanish popular uprising against Napoleon.

> *The control of the sea is of much importance . . . If the people possess a long stretch of coast, and are masters of the sea or in alliance with a power which controls it, their power of resistance is quintupled . . . In mountainous countries the people are the most formidable; next to these are countries covered with extensive forests . . . Defiles and large forests, as well as rocky regions, favor this kind of defense.*
>
> (Jomini, *The Art of War*, p. 30)

Nevertheless, it is Clausewitz who manages to distill the essence of guerrilla warfare and the conditions for its success:

> **By its very nature, such scattered resistance will not lend itself to major actions, closely compressed in time and space. Its effect is like that of the process of evaporation: it depends on how much surface is exposed. The greater the surface and the area of contact between it and the enemy forces, the thinner the latter have to be spread, the greater the effect of a general uprising. Like smoldering embers, it consumes the basic foundations of the enemy forces . . .**
>
> **The following are the *only* conditions under which a general uprising can be effective:**
>
> 1. **The war must be fought in the interior of the country.**
> 2. **It must not be decided by a single stroke.**
> 3. **The theater of operations must be fairly large.**
> 4. **The national character must be suited to that type of war.**
> 5. **The country must be rough and inaccessible, because of mountains or forests, marshes, or the local methods of cultivation.**
>
> (Clausewitz, *On War*, p. 480)

It is interesting to note that although Mao Tse-tung was influenced by Sun Tzu, the main elements of his theory on guerrilla warfare can be found in the first two pages of Clausewitz's chapter, 'The People in Arms'. This subject is not discussed by Sun Tzu, who argues that no country has ever benefited from a protracted war; if anything, this is an argument against guerrilla war.[2]

Clausewitz and Jomini also believe that there is another condition that can contribute significantly to the effectiveness of a guerrilla war – namely, the direction and support of a core group within the regular army.

> **To be realistic, one must therefore think of a general insurrection within the framework of a war conducted by the regular army and coordinated in one all-encompassing plan.**
>
> (Clausewitz, *On War*, p. 480)

> **A commander can more easily shape and direct the popular insurrection by supporting the insurgents with small units of the regular army. Without these regular troops to provide encouragement, the local inhabitants will usually lack the confidence and initiative to take to arms.**
>
> (Clausewitz, *On War*, p. 482)

> *The difficulties* [of fighting against a popular uprising] *are particularly great when the people are supported by a considerable nucleus of disciplined troops. The invader has only an army; his adversaries have an army, and a people wholly or almost wholly in arms, and making means of resistance out of every thing, each individual of whom conspires against the common enemy* . . .
>
> (Jomini, *The Art of War*, p. 31)

The views of Clausewitz and Jomini on this subject are unmistakably colored by their military backgrounds. Although direction by a centralized command and control is advisable for any guerrilla movement, it is not clear that regular officers (as opposed to civilian leaders) are best suited for such a task. The traditional education of professional military officers as well as their career patterns and failure on the battlefield (without which there would be no need for a popular insurrection) do not necessarily enhance (and may even detract from) their ability to conduct a successful guerrilla war.

Both strategists may also have been influenced by a fear that the excessive radicalization of the people in arms – who discover their own

125

strength in the process of fighting an outside enemy – might eventually cause them to turn against their own government. This might at least partially explain their recommendation that the control of guerrilla operations be retained by a nucleus of the regular army.

Clausewitz and Jomini define the nature of guerrilla warfare in a strikingly similar way. Each recognizes that it is extremely difficult for a regular military force to win against a mobilized nation; each also identifies the same types of conditions that would support such a war and indicates the desirability of command and control by a core regular force.

Of the two, only Jomini sees the enormous potential of guerrilla war as a strategy of choice – as a preferred, autonomous course of action, rather than as the last-resort, auxiliary effort envisioned by Clausewitz. Jomini hated the 'barbarity' of guerilla warfare and, as a professional soldier, knew the difficulty of winning such wars; but he did not permit his personal distaste for people's wars to influence his conclusion that this form of warfare might become dominant in the future. In a prescient paragraph, he observes:

> The immense obstacles encountered by an invading force in these wars have led some speculative persons to hope that there should never be any other kind, since then wars would become more rare, and, conquest being also more difficult, would be less a temptation to ambitious leaders. This reasoning is rather plausible than solid; for, to admit all its consequences, it would be necessary always to be able to induce the people to take up arms . . . how [then] could it be known when and how to excite the people to a national war?
>
> (Jomini, *The Art of War*, p. 33)

This is exactly what happened in the Chinese revolution in the 1930s and after the Second World War in the former European colonies and the Third World. As Jomini hinted, *how* to mobilize the people to fight a brutal, costly, and prolonged war became one of the most important theoretical problems in the vast body of literature on guerrilla warfare. Nevertheless, the mobilization of the people was not as much of an obstacle as Jomini had hoped and has actually become easier since the Second World War. The problem of motivating the people has been solved through numerous approaches including nationalistic and communist propaganda; the threat of an enemy at one's borders; the actions of a revolutionary elite that begins the struggle; outside military support; and coercion and terrorism.[3]

Jomini adds one important dimension to his analysis of 'national wars' that is, not surprisingly, missing in Clausewitz's: the role of intelligence. Here Jomini departs from his preference for the offense and makes a convincing argument that guerrilla warfare favors the defense. (Clausewitz also considers guerrilla war to be defensive and therefore includes his chapter 'The People in Arms' in Book 6 on 'Defense'.) According to Jomini, those engaging in national wars enjoy a decisive natural advantage as far as intelligence is concerned. These are his perceptive comments:

> *Each armed inhabitant knows the smallest paths and their connections; he finds everywhere a relative or friend who aids him; the commanders also know the country, and, learning immediately the slightest movement on the part of the invader, can adopt the best measures to defeat his projects; while the latter, without information of their movements and not in a condition to send out detachments to gain it, having no resources but in his bayonets, and certain safety only in the concentration of his columns, is like a blind man; his combinations are failures; and when, after the most carefully concerted movements and the most rapid and fatiguing marches, he thinks he is about to accomplish his aim and deal a terrible blow, he finds no signs of the enemy but his campfires: so that while, like Don Quixote, he is attacking windmills, his adversary is on his line of communications, destroys the detachments left to guard it, surprises his convoys, his depots, and carries on a war so disastrous for the invader that he must inevitably yield after a time.*
>
> (Jomini, *The Art of War*, p. 31)

Jomini closes his analysis of national wars by expressing his nostalgia for the days when war was a 'simple', less brutal affair carried on among gentlemen, not entire nations:

> *As a soldier, preferring loyal and chivalrous warfare to organized assassination, if it be necessary to make a choice, I acknowledge that my prejudices are in favor of the good old times when the French and English Guards courteously invited each other to fire*

first, – as at Fontenoy, – preferring them to the frightful epoch when priests, women, and children throughout Spain plotted the murder of isolated soldiers.

(Jomini, *The Art of War*, pp. 34–35)

Clausewitz's important discussion of the political mobilization of the people since the French Revolution and the role of the people in guerrilla warfare is, unfortunately, scattered throughout the entire book. A special chapter on the role of the people in modern warfare would have allowed Clausewitz to develop his insights in greater depth, but as it stands, Clausewitz's diffuse treatment of this subject must be studied with two important caveats in mind.

First, citizens of modern democracies would not accept Clausewitz's assertion that **'the political aims are the business of the government alone'** (*On War*, p. 89). In a modern democracy, the political aims and direction of the war are clearly the concern of the people as well. Even though the people do not participate directly in the routine political conduct of a war, they do insist on participating in its long-term direction. Even in wartime, the people participate in elections and otherwise contribute to the ongoing national debate on the war's expected costs and benefits, and its bearing on national interests and desired political objectives. Furthermore, in a free and open society, the people will, unlike in Clausewitz's time, be able to express their views on these issues through the mass media or otherwise.

The second point concerns the influence of modern mass media and real-time communications technology on the role of the people in war. Today, when real-time communications bring the horrors of war into every home, political and military leaders (i.e., the two other dimensions of the 'trinity') are obliged to pay attention to continuously shifting public opinion. Public approval certainly cannot be taken for granted, since even one negative incident broadcast on television can severely erode a formerly solid base of support. Examples of this are the famous execution of a Vietcong guerrilla by a South Vietnamese police officer during the Tet offensive and CNN's report that the U.S. air attack on the Al Firdos bunker in Baghdad (13 February 1991) had killed many civilians. This report immediately caused the cancellation of such air attacks in Baghdad for the duration of the war.[4]

While Clausewitz recognizes the need to mobilize the people's support in war, he seems to take their continuous political support for granted once the war has begun. While he would agree that little or no popular support or passion hurts the war effort, he says nothing about the people's direct impact on governmental policies. Clausewitz seems to assume that the government will be able to persuade the people to support for its policies, but not that the people will significantly influence the government. While such a position is both theoretically and practically unacceptable today, it reflects the political realities of nineteenth-century Germany and Europe. (It is clear, though, that Clausewitz and the Prussian military reformers understood the need to give the Prussian people greater political freedom in order to mobilize their support. However, it does not appear that they went so far as to permit the people to influence the direction of the war itself.[5])

MACHIAVELLI AND CLAUSEWITZ ON THE ROLE OF THE PEOPLE IN WAR

The wars of the French Revolution and Napoleon are considered the first in modern European history to have exploited fully the energies of the entire population. The declaration of the *levée en masse* (the nation in arms)[6] therefore marks the beginning of modern total war. The *levée en masse*, which was declared by the Convention on 23 August 1793, called for the mobilization of all able-bodied citizens; it was later replaced by the *Loi Jourdan* of 5 September 1798, which required the registration and physical examination of all Frenchmen between the ages of 20 and 25.

Recognizing the significance of this development, Clausewitz assigned the people in war and the new political energies released by the French Revolution a central role in his theory. Indeed, as we have seen in this chapter, Clausewitz believed that this was the most important change in the nature of war that had occurred in his lifetime. Nevertheless, three hundred years earlier, Machiavelli pointed out the need for the Italian city-states to abandon their practice of relying on the services of foreign mercenaries and instead to mobilize the people in order to develop better and more reliable armies. Basically, Machiavelli argues that the city-state in which the people are unwilling to fight for their own interests is less likely to succeed in the long run. The *condottieri*, or soldiers of fortune, are, he warns, rapacious, violent, and fraudulent by virtue of their chosen profession. These qualities obviously make them poorly motivated soldiers with a vested interest in the continuation of violence in order to make a living. Furthermore, because they are not fighting for their own interests, they are also ill-disposed to risk their lives for their paymasters. If they are not paid on time or are offered better pay by the enemy, they might just as easily turn their weapons on their employer (see Machiavelli, *The Art of War*, pp. 573–576).

> A well-governed kingdom . . . must avoid such professionals because they alone are the ruin of the king and are altogether the servants of tyranny.
>
> (Machiavelli, *The Art of War*, p. 577)

> A city that makes use of foreign armies fears at once the foreigner she hires and the citizen . . . A city that uses its own forces fears only its own citizens.
>
> (Machiavelli, *The Art of War*, p. 585)

> The mercenary . . . [is] useless and dangerous; if a prince continues to base his government on mercenary armies, he will never be either stable or safe; they are disunited, ambitious without discipline, disloyal; valiant among friends, among enemies cowardly; they have no fear of God, no loyalty for men. Your ruin is postponed only as long as attack on you is postponed: in peace you are plundered by them, in war by your enemies. The reason for this is that they have no love for you nor any cause that can keep them in the field other than a little pay, which is not enough to make them risk death for you. They are eager indeed to be your soldiers as long as you are not carrying on a war, but when war comes, eager to run away or to leave.
>
> (Machiavelli, *The Prince*, p. 47)

(For Clausewitz's similar opinion on the *condottieri*, see *On War*, pp. 587–588.)

Conversely, citizen-soldiers are better motivated and more reliable since they are fighting for their own interests, and they can return to their peacetime occupations at the end of the war.

> A well-ordered city will then decree that this practice of warfare [i.e. by citizen-soldiers] shall be used at time of peace for exercise

and in times of war for necessity and for glory, and will allow the public alone to practice its profession as did Rome . . . Any city that conducts itself otherwise is not well-governed.

(Machiavelli, *The Art of War*, p. 576)

Indeed, in his exhortation to the Prince (Giuliano de Medici) to free Italy from the barbarians, he sees the essential condition as the building of a new citizen-army:

> She [Italy] must before all things as the true foundation of every undertaking, provide herself with her own armies, because there cannot be more faithful or truer or better soldiers . . . It is necessary, therefore, for her to prepare such armies in order with Italian might to defend herself against foreigners.
>
> (Machiavelli, *The Prince*, p. 95;
> also *The Discourses*, pp. 246–247.)

In calling for a citizen-army, Machiavelli was ahead of his time. This is recognized by Clausewitz, who sees the *condottieri* of Machiavelli's day as representing a period of transition from the feudal war to the modern era.

Over two hundred years after Machiavelli, and before Clausewitz's time, Jean-Jacques Rousseau, in his essay on *The Government of Poland*, also insists on the importance of a militia or citizen-army for every free nation.

> The state's true defenders are its individual citizens, no one of whom should be a professional soldier, but each of whom should serve as a soldier as duty requires. That is how they handled the military problem in Rome; that is how they handle it now in Switzerland; and that is how it should be handled in every free state . . .[7]

In Book 8, Chapter 3B of *On War*, Clausewitz surveys the relationship of the people and the government in war as it evolved until the outbreak of the French Revolution; in doing so he comments on the transformation of war brought about by the full mobilization of the people:

> **The end of the seventeenth century, the age of Louis XIV, may be regarded as the point in history when the standing army in the shape familiar to the eighteenth century**

131

reached maturity. This military organization was based on money and recruitment . . . A government behaved as though it owned and managed a great estate that it constantly endeavored to enlarge – an effort in which the inhabitants were not expected to show any particular interest . . . In the circumstances of the eighteenth century the people's part has been extinguished. The only influence the people continued to exert on war was an indirect one . . . War thus became solely the concern of the government to the extent that governments parted company with their peoples and behaved as if they were themselves the state . . . The means they had available were fairly well-defined and each could gauge the other side's potential in terms both of numbers and of time. War was thus deprived of its most dangerous feature – its tendency toward the extreme, and that of the whole chain of unknown possibilities which would follow. Not only in means . . . but also in its aims war increasingly became limited to the fighting force itself . . . There is no denying that it turned war even more into the exclusive concern of governments and estranged it further from the interests of the people . . . This was the state of affairs at the outbreak of the French Revolution . . . but in 1793 a force appeared that beggared all imagination. Suddenly war became the business of the people – a people of thirty millions, all of whom considered themselves to be citizens . . . The people became a participant in war; instead of governments and armies as heretofore, the full weight of the nation was thrown into the balance. The resources and efforts now available for use surpassed all conventional limits; nothing now impeded the vigor with which war could be waged . . . War, untrammeled by any conventional restraints, had broken loose in its elemental fury . . .

(Clausewitz, *On War*, pp. 587–593)

Clausewitz's discussion of the evolution of the armies of Europe[8] shows that it had taken three hundred years since Machiavelli's recommendations were made to build a true citizen-army. The prerequisite for this transformation was the political transition from a feudal system to enlightened despotism and the modern European state, and finally to the French Republic. Machiavelli's advice that free states should base their armed forces on their own citizens rather than on unreliable mercenaries is not a recommendation for a *levée en masse* (i.e., the extensive mobilization of the male population). Instead, it involves a smaller mobilization of a nationally based professional army whose patriotic soldiers are ready to fight for their own interests. The emphasis is on the recruitment of one's own citizens, not on expanding the mobilization itself. As such, therefore, the role of the people in support of the military in Machiavelli's political framework comes very close to that of the people in Clausewitz's 'trinitarian analysis'.

Machiavelli is well aware that not all of the people can fight or be trained to fight and that only those of the right age and physique are fit to serve, while those found eligible for service must be trained, disciplined, and led by others – presumably a core of professional soldiers (though not foreign mercenaries). The distinction therefore between the entire population as a base for recruitment and support of a smaller number of citizen-soldiers selected from it (i.e., the military) is clear.

The ability to recruit and maintain such a citizen-army is the responsibility of the government, whether led by a prince or an oligarchy such as that of Rome (which Machiavelli preferred). Machiavelli also observes the close link between the form of government and its ability to raise a good army ('. . . Wherever there are good soldiers there must be good government' (*Discourses* p. 202)). Good government is correlated with freedom, participation, and patriotism, which in turn inspire the citizen-soldiers' readiness to fight and die for their state. Thus, Machiavelli evinces an implicit awareness of the need to strike a proper balance among *the government*, *the people*, and *the citizen-army* (the military) as the necessary condition for waging a successful war. The creative genius of Clausewitz lay in his ability to take an old idea (which surely preceded Machiavelli) and present it in the succinct theoretical framework of the 'remarkable' or 'paradoxical' trinity.

11

The Ideal and the Real: Victory Without Bloodshed and the Search for the Decisive Battle

For to win one hundred victories in one hundred battles is not the acme of skill. To subdue the enemy without fighting is the acme of skill.
  Sun Tzu, *The Art of War*, p. 77

Kind-hearted people might of course think there was some ingenious way to disarm or defeat an enemy without too much bloodshed, and might imagine this is the true goal of the art of war. Pleasant as it sounds, it is a fallacy that must be exposed . . .
  Clausewitz, *On War*, p. 75

Those skilled in war subdue the enemy's army without battle. They capture his cities without assaulting them and overthrow his state without protracted operations.
  Sun Tzu, *The Art of War*, p. 79

Everything is governed by a supreme law, the decision by force of arms . . .
  Clausewitz, *On War*, p. 99

Your aim must be to take All-under-Heaven intact.
  Sun Tzu, *The Art of War*, p. 79

The *violent resolution of the crisis*, the wish to annihilate the enemy's forces, is the first-born son of war.
  Clausewitz, *On War*, p. 99

The preceding quotations are generally thought to embody the essence of their authors' philosophies of war. At first glance they may appear to conflict, but actually Sun Tzu and Clausewitz do not disagree as much as is assumed on the need to resort to the ultimate means of battle and bloodshed. Moreover, they agree that the most rational way of waging

135

war is usually to fight for the shortest possible duration and win decisively if possible. Any other types of prolonged and indecisive battles are to be avoided.

The Art of War and *On War* were both written during historical periods characterized by the widespread use of military force. Each appeared at a time when earlier forms of ritualistic or limited warfare had given way to the more virulent forms of intensive or total war. In China, the transition from the ritualistic warfare of the Spring and Autumn period (722 BC to 481 BC) to the unremitting military conflict and political confusion of the Warring States period (403 BC to 221 BC) was far more gradual than that which took place in Europe from the limited wars of the eighteenth century to the French Revolution and Napoleonic wars of the nineteenth.[1] Since both Sun Tzu and Clausewitz lived during times when the use of force was the norm, they knew that it is usually necessary to 'break eggs' (resort to war) in order to make an 'omelet' (achieve the political ends of a state in a system of independent states). Why, then, does Sun Tzu, in apparent contrast to Clausewitz, praise the virtues of winning without having to do battle, and to what degree does he realize that this is rarely possible in practice?

Sun Tzu's emphasis on the use of force only as a last resort reflects Confucian idealism and the political culture that it spawned. In Professor Fairbank's words, Sun Tzu 'shares the early Confucian assumption as to the primacy of mental attitudes in human affairs. Like other classics produced by idealists amid the disorder of the Warring States period, it bequeathed its doctrines to the far different imperial age.'[2] Far from glorifying physical coercion and warfare, Confucius taught that 'the superior man, extolled in the classics as the highest product of self-cultivation, should be able to attain his ends without violence'.[3] These values represented the ideal that was expected to find its most sublime expression in the person of the emperor:

> For the emperor to resort to violence was an admission that he had failed in his own conduct as a sage pursuing the art of government. The resort to warfare (*wu*) was an admission of bankruptcy in the pursuit of the arts of peace (*wen*). Consequently it should be a last resort, and it required justification both at the time and in the record.[4]

Within this system there was no place for the dichotomy between public and private morality so familiar in the Western concept of *raison d'état*, which sharply distinguishes between individual ethics and those of the state and its leaders. The inseparability of public and private morality and the view that resorting to war signified the emperor's personal failure may also explain why the emperor typically left the actual fighting to the military. 'Chinese youth were given no equivalents of Alexander, Caesar, or Napoleon to admire or emulate. There was no youthful worship of heroism like that in the West.'[5]

On the other hand, Clausewitz, for whom Frederick the Great and Napoleon were paragons of military genius, argues for the unity of political and military direction on the highest level of war:

> **To bring a war, or one of its campaigns, to a successful close requires a thorough grasp of national policy. On that level strategy and policy coalesce: the commander-in-chief is simultaneously a statesman.**
>
> (Clausewitz, *On War*, p. 111)

Sun Tzu's idealistic preference for all other means short of war, be they politico-diplomatic, economic, or ideological, also reflects traditional Chinese attitudes, as Professor Fairbank explains:

> Operations on so many levels . . . were beyond the capacity of a purely military man. They were the natural province of the trained Confucian bureaucrat, who knew how to employ military force within the repertoire of statecraft. This fact alone kept the military in their place.[6]

> In old China, war was too complex a matter to be left to the fighting man, however well trained he might be. Its objective was not victory but the re-establishment of order, and for this the arts of peace were equally necessary.[7]

This does not mean that there were fewer wars throughout Chinese history or that once war had broken out, the logic of war in China differed markedly from that in the West.[8] As so often occurs, an immense gap existed between the ideal and the real, between theory and practice.

How is this Confucian idealism expressed in *The Art of War*? As noted earlier, Sun Tzu repeatedly emphasizes that '. . . *those skilled in war subdue the enemy's army without battle*' and that '*the best policy*

137

in war is to take a state intact' (Sun Tzu, *The Art of War*, p. 79). This reluctance to resort to force is also evident in the desire to minimize the casualties and costs associated with war once it has begun. Confucian idealism inspires the search for non-material 'force multipliers' that will bring victory with the minimal use of force. '*[Chang Yu:] . . . the force applied is minute but the results enormous*' (Sun Tzu, *The Art of War*, p. 95). In contrast, Clausewitz warns of the dynamics of escalation inherent in war: '**Since in war too small an effort can result not just in failure but in positive harm, each side is driven to outdo the other, which sets up an interaction**' (Clausewitz, *On War*, p. 585).

Throughout *The Art of War*, Sun Tzu stresses the need to wage war as economically and cheaply as possible (i.e., in the most *efficient* way). This seems quite sensible, except for the fact that carrying this idea too far can in fact prove counter-productive. War itself has never been and can never be a purely economic activity: it is not simply about making profits or avoiding losses, nor is it primarily about preventing the waste of resources or minimizing pain. A war that involves a nation's vital interests (i.e., its survival and future well-being) must be won as quickly as possible, often *regardless of the costs involved*. War is therefore ultimately more about achieving *effective* results (i.e., victory) and less about how much such success will cost. Clausewitz repeatedly warns us to beware of a *false economy*. He believes that war (certainly a total or unlimited war) calls for a greater effort than what appears to be the minimum necessary, since investing too little usually brings indecisive results or defeat. Such a defeat may have irreversible consequences or result in a renewal of the fighting once new armies have been raised.

Clausewitz's approach stems from a worst-case analysis, which means that it requires a higher initial investment but may actually prove to be cheaper in the long run. Given the uncertainty permeating warfare, this makes sense. The line between economy and false economy in war is difficult to define but easy to avoid if Clausewitz's warnings are taken into account. Thus, while Sun Tzu emphasizes the search for the most *efficient* way to win a war – Clausewitz clearly emphasizes the search for the most *effective* way to win a war.[9] Therefore, the greater the force one concentrates from the start, the less force one has to employ later on. This usually brings the reward of a shorter, less costly war. For Clausewitz, then, '**there is no higher and simpler law of strategy**

than that of *keeping one's forces concentrated, . . .* **to be very strong;
first in general, and then at the decisive point'** (Clausewitz, *On
War*, p. 204).[10].(See below, Appendix F, pp. 361–367.)

To paraphrase Clausewitz's sarcastic definition of maneuver, one
might say that Sun Tzu's force multipliers **'carry the idea of an effect
created out of nothing'** (Clausewitz, *On War*, p. 591). Among the
force multipliers recommended by Sun Tzu are maneuver; reliance on
intelligence; the extensive use of deception and diversionary measures to
achieve surprise; the 'indirect approach'; and the use of psychological
means to undermine the enemy's will to fight. (All of these measures,
particularly reliance on intelligence and deception, are important
elements in *The Art of War*, but in *On War* they receive negligible attention from Clausewitz, who considers them unreliable and impracticable.) (See Chapter 15 below.)

Sun Tzu offers this advice on the 'indirect approach':

> *He who knows the art of the direct and the indirect approach
> will be victorious. Such is the art of manoeuvring.*
> (Sun Tzu, *The Art of War*, p. 106)

> *[Ts'ao Ts'ao:] Go into emptiness, strike voids, bypass what he
> defends, hit him where he does not expect you.*
> (Sun Tzu, *The Art of War*, p. 96)

> *Thus, march by an indirect route and divert the enemy by
> enticing him with a bait. So doing you may set out after he does
> and arrive before him. One able to do this understands the
> strategy of the direct and the indirect.*
> *[Tu Mu] He who wishes to snatch an advantage takes a devious
> and distant route and makes of it the short way.*
> (Sun Tzu, *The Art of War*, p. 102)

Unfortunately, Sun Tzu does not explain in concrete terms *how* to
identify the 'best' indirect approach. If anticipated by the enemy, an
indirect approach paradoxically becomes the direct, and everything that
succeeds then becomes the indirect approach. Like all truisms, such
advice is too vague to be of much practical value. But even truisms can
make *some* positive contribution by fostering an appreciation for certain
attitudes, 'formulas', or actions that are not as self-evident as they first
appear or that are not easy to put into practice.[11] But, as Clausewitz

139

emphasizes, identification of the optimal indirect approach ultimately depends on the creative genius, the *coup d'oeil*, of the military leader. This in turn raises the perplexing question, as we shall see, of how to identify the 'military genius' in peacetime.

Unlike *On War*, *The Art of War* stresses psychological warfare; that is, erosion of the opponent's will to fight in order to achieve victory at a far lower cost (or no cost at all).

> *And therefore those skilled in war avoid the enemy when his spirit is keen and attack him when it is sluggish and his soldiers homesick. This is control of the mental factor.*
>
> (Sun Tzu, *The Art of War*, pp. 108

> *Do not thwart an enemy returning homewards. To a surrounded enemy you must leave a way of escape.*

> *[Tu Mu] Show him there is a road to safety, and so create in his mind the idea that there is an alternative to death. Then strike.*

> *Do not press an enemy at bay.*
>
> (Sun Tzu, *The Art of War*, pp. 109–110; see also pp. 132–133)[12]

Although Clausewitz does not attach the same degree of importance to the indirect approach and psychological warfare, he still cautions the reader against ignoring them entirely:

> **When we speak of destroying the enemy's forces we must emphasize that nothing obliges us to limit this idea to physical forces: the moral element must also be considered.**
>
> (Clausewitz, *On War*, p. 97)[13]

> **Destruction of the enemy's force is only a means to an end, a secondary matter. If a mere demonstration is enough to cause the enemy to abandon his position, the objective has been achieved . . . .**
>
> (Clausewitz, *On War*, p. 96)[14]

> **Battle . . . should not be considered as mutual murder – its effect . . . is rather a killing of the enemy's spirit than of his men.**
>
> (Clausewitz, *On War*, p. 259)

Clausewitz also recognizes the possibility – particularly in a limited war – of winning with less bloodshed by undermining the enemy's alliances and his morale.

> **But there is another way. It is possible to increase the likelihood of success without defeating the enemy's forces. I refer to operations that have *direct political repercussions,* that are designed in the first place to disrupt the opposing alliance, or to paralyze it, that gain us new allies, favorably affect the political scene, etc. If such operations are possible it is obvious that they can greatly improve our prospects and that they can form a much shorter route to the goal than the destruction of the opposing armies.**
> [emphasis in original]
>
> (Clausewitz, *On War*, pp. 92–93;
> see also Chapter 12 below, pp. 156–157)

According to Sun Tzu, a military leader skilled in the art of command must be able to create a situation in which he leaves his own troops no choice but to stand and fight, or die:

> *Throw the troops into a position from which there is no escape and even when faced with death they will not flee. For if prepared to die, what can they not achieve? Then officers and men together put forth their utmost efforts. In a desperate situation, they fear nothing; when there is no way out they stand firm.*
> (Sun Tzu, *The Art of War*, p. 134; see also p. 135)[15]

Although Clausewitz attaches the greatest importance to moral factors, to 'the strength of will' and numerous other non-material factors, he does not discuss various means of undermining enemy morale as much as Sun Tzu does. This may be because he sees this as self-evident; indeed, he would probably have considered many of the statements excerpted from *The Art of War* in this section to be too simplistic. Clausewitz's emphasis on the intellectual learning process, the raising of pertinent questions, and guidance of the reader through complicated arguments, seems to avoid the sort of maxims typical of *The Art of War*. Still, *On War* is not devoid of truisms, even though Clausewitz makes a more serious effort to explain their logical underpinnings. For example, his advice to be strong at the decisive point or his sophisticated development of the concepts of the culminating point of the attack or the center of gravity do not, in the end, leave the reader with more practical advice on their implementation. The difference between the two books is, however, that Clausewitz's systematic framework includes an *explicit* analysis of the role of the military genius and intuition in war, thereby providing better insight into those problems not otherwise susceptible to concrete advice.

Perhaps this is also the context in which to mention one more difference between Sun Tzu and Clausewitz. *The Art of War* continually informs the reader how the successful general can deceive and surprise his opponent and how he should gather good intelligence and undermine the fighting spirit of his enemy. Yet Sun Tzu seldom alludes to the fact that the enemy can be expected to follow the same advice. In this case, his one-dimensional analysis seems to assume that the enemy is passive and will not pursue similar stratagems.

Clausewitz, on the other hand, *emphasizes the reciprocal nature of war, that is, the action and reaction of equally capable enemies.* If both opponents are skilled in the art of war it is not as easy to assume that one will handily outmaneuver the other and win without bloodshed or achieve a less costly victory through deception. Clausewitz is wary of elaborate stratagems that underestimate the enemy:

> If we abandon the weak impressions of abstract concepts for reality, we will find that an active, courageous, and resolute adversary will not leave us time for long-range intricate schemes; but that is the very enemy against whom we need these skills most. It seems to us that this is proof enough of the *superiority* of the simple and direct over the complex.
>
> (Clausewitz, *On War*, p. 229)[16]

In general, but especially when one is faced with an equally strong and implacable enemy, Clausewitz recommends straightforward methods:

> The probability of direct confrontation increases with the aggressiveness of the enemy. So, rather than try to outbid the enemy with complicated schemes, one should, on the contrary, try to outdo him in simplicity . . . Whenever possible . . . we must . . . choose the shorter path. We must further simplify it to whatever extent the character and

situation of the enemy and any other circumstances make necessary.

(Clausewitz, *On War*, p. 229)

Clausewitz assumes, more than Sun Tzu, that since there are no easy unilateral solutions, it is impossible to succeed by applying '*little strength to achieve much*'. When reading *The Art of War* with its emphasis on victory without battle, on achieving less costly victories through deception, or on weakening the enemy's resistance, one should remember the comments of Frank Kierman in his essay, 'Phases and Modes of Combat in Early China'.

> This exaltation of the extraordinary stratagem may be a reflection of the Chinese scholar's (and historian's) repugnance of brute force. However sanguinary, warfare may have been more acceptable to the Chinese literati if it could somehow be represented as a kind of intellectual hand-wrestling, with the harsh facts of discipline, organization, armament, endurance, and bloodshed somehow minimized by that stress upon trickiness. It is only a short step from this to the idea that unusually successful generals are wizards possessed of a magical power to control nature and circumstance. This removes warfare still more from the everyday, accepted realm of experience, leaving that sphere to the rationalistic Confucian literati . . . And relegating the military enterprise to the sphere of fantasy encourages the sort of dreamlike armchair strategy which has marked Chinese military thinking so deeply down the centuries, into our own day.[17]

Clausewitz is not guilty of any of the above, for *On War* relates many lengthy, realistic descriptions of the horrors of war. Nor does he provide the reader with neat solutions to render combat unnecessary:

The decision by arms is for all major and minor operations in war what cash payment is in commerce. Regardless how complex the relationship between the two parties, regardless how rarely settlements actually occur, they can never be entirely absent.

(Clausewitz, *On War*, p. 97)

It is inherent in the very concept of war that everything that

143

occurs *must originally derive from combat.* [emphasis in the original]

(Clausewitz, *On War*, p. 95; see also p. 96)

Everything is governed by a supreme law, the decision by force of arms . . . To sum up: of all the possible aims in the war, the destruction of the enemy's armed forces always appears as the highest.

(Clausewitz, *On War*, p. 99)

The destruction of the enemy's forces must always be the dominant consideration in war.

(Clausewitz, *On War*, p. 230)

The destruction of the enemy forces is admittedly the purpose of all engagements.

(Clausewitz, *On War*, p. 236)

The objective of all military action is to overthrow the enemy – which means destroying his armed forces . . . [we] tried to make it absolutely clear that the destruction of the enemy is what always matters the most.

(Clausewitz, *On War*, p. 575)

The very concept of war will permit us to make the following unequivocal statements:

1. Destruction of the enemy forces is the overriding principle of war, and, so far as positive action is concerned, the principal way to achieve our object.
2. Such destruction can *usually* be accomplished only by fighting. [emphasis in the original]

(Clausewitz, *On War*, p. 258; see also Chapter 5 above, p. 56)

Clausewitz thus concedes that in rare instances one might be able to win without combat, but he considers this possibility to be so remote that it can be relegated to the realm of theory. In a telling critique of eighteenth-century wars, he argues that the possibility of victory without fighting was an aberration in the history of warfare. Even if such limited wars in which all participants played by the same rules were once possible in the Age of Reason, the French Revolution and subsequent total wars rapidly made ritualistic warfare appear absurd.[18]

Consequently, it would be an obvious fallacy to imagine war between civilized peoples as resulting merely from a rational act on the part of their governments and to conceive of war as gradually ridding itself of passion, so that in the end one would never really need to use the physical impact of the fighting forces – comparative figures of their strength would be enough. *That would be a kind of war by algebra.* [my emphasis]

(Clausewitz, On War, p. 76)

Combat is the only effective force in war; its aim is to destroy the enemy's forces as a means to a further end. That holds good even if no actual fighting occurs, because the outcome rests on the assumption that if it came to fighting, the enemy would be destroyed. It follows that the destruction of the enemy's force underlies all military actions; all plans are ultimately based upon it, resting on it like an arch on its abutment. Consequently all action is undertaken in the belief that if the ultimate test of arms should actually occur, the outcome would be *favorable.*

(Clausewitz, On War, p. 97)

ALL POSSIBLE ENGAGEMENTS ARE TO BE REGARDED AS REAL ONES BECAUSE OF THEIR CONSEQUENCES.

(Clausewitz, On War, p. 181; see also p. 489)

If a mere demonstration is enough to cause the enemy to abandon his position, the objective has been achieved. [my emphasis]

(Clausewitz, On War, p. 96)

One may admit that even where the decision has been bloodless, it was determined in the last analysis by engagements that did not take place but *had merely been offered.* In that case, it will be argued, *the strategic planning* of these engagements, rather than the tactical decision, should be considered the operative principle.

(Clausewitz, On War, p. 386; see also pp. 181, 311)

At one point, Clausewitz comes very close to admitting that a new

145

principle of war – of winning without fighting – may be possible, but he leaves us without final conclusions:

> **But armed resistance, by its diversity of possible combinations, can so change the appearance and vary the character of armed defense, especially in cases where** *there is no actual fighting* **but the outcome is affected by the fact that there could be, that** *one is almost tempted to think some new effective principle here,* **awaits discovery. The vast difference between savage repulse in a straightforward battle and the effect of a** *strategic web* **that prevents things from getting that far, will lead one to assume that a different force must be at work – a conjecture somewhat like that of the astronomers who deduced from the enormous void between Mars and Jupiter that other planets must exist. [my emphasis][19]**
>
> (Clausewitz, *On War*, pp. 385–386)

Yet despite the analogy to Newtonian physics and astronomy (see Chapter 5, note 1, pp. 382–386), no such new principle of bloodless victory can actually be 'discovered'. Clausewitz resists Sun Tzu's argument that a 'strategic web' is all that is needed to secure bloodless victories. In this instance, the comparison to Newtonian physics does not lead to the discovery of a new hidden law or principle after all; on the contrary, it leads to another 'Newtonian' conclusion (see Clausewitz, *On War*, p. 386); namely, that most victories are achieved as the result of a physical collision between two opposing forces rather than through the operation of ever so subtle 'strategic webs'.

Clausewitz also acknowledges the desire to win without fighting in his examination of the interaction between the attack and the defense (Book 6, Chapter 7). Here we find him arguing, paradoxically enough, that war always begins with the defender not the attacker.[20] Inasmuch as the attacker always wants to obtain his objectives without fighting, it is the defender's decision to resist the attack that leads to war:

> **Consider in the abstract how war originates. Essentially, the concept of war does not originate with the attack,** *because the ultimate object of attack is not fighting: rather, it is possession.* **The idea of war originates with the defense, which does have fighting as its immediate object, since fighting and parrying obviously amount to the same thing.**

> Repulse is directed only toward an attack, which is there-fore a prerequisite to it; the attack, however, is not directed toward defense but toward a different goal – possession, which is not necessarily a prerequisite for war. It is thus in the nature of the case that the side that first introduces the element of war, whose point of view brings two parties into existence, is also the side that establishes the initial laws of war. This side is the defense . . .
>
> (Clausewitz, *On War*, p. 377)

This is not meant to be an ethical or moral determination of fault or of which side causes the war. It is simply a good technical definition or description of how wars begin. In any case, Clausewitz considers the chance of winning without fighting to be so low that it is not of great concern.

The divergence between Clausewitz and Sun Tzu on the issue of victory without fighting is substantial. While Sun Tzu elevates it to an ideal, Clausewitz considers it to be a rare exception. Clausewitz's skepticism regarding the possibility of winning cheap and bloodless victories, using 'minute force' to achieve major results, or relying on non-material force multipliers as panaceas comes across unmistakably in his cynical comments on miraculous formulas for victory:

> Maneuvering the enemy out of an area he has occupied is not very different from this, and should be considered in the same light, rather than as true success of arms. These means are generally overrated; they seldom achieve so much as a battle, and involve the risk of drawbacks that may have been overlooked. They are tempting because they cost so little.
>
> They should always be looked upon as minor investments that can only yield minor dividends, appropriate to limited circumstances and weaker motives. But they are obviously preferable to pointless battles – victories that cannot be fully exploited.
>
> (Clausewitz, *On War*, p. 529)

None of this is meant to say that there should be any less activity in warfare. Tools are there to be used, and use will naturally wear them out. Our only aim is clarity and order; we are opposed to bombastic theories that hold that the most overwhelming surprise, the fastest movement or the most restless activity cost nothing; that they are rich mines which lie unused because of the generals' indolence. The final product may indeed be compared to that of gold and silver mines: one looks only at the end result and forgets to ask about the cost of the labor that went into it.

(Clausewitz, *On War*, p. 322)[21]

That is why governments and commanders have always tried to find ways of avoiding a decisive battle and of reaching their goal by other means or of quietly abandoning it. Historians and theorists have taken great pains, when describing such campaigns and conflicts, to point out that *other means* not only served the purpose as well as a battle that was never fought, but were indeed evidence of higher skill. This line of thought had brought us almost to the point of regarding, in the economy of war, battle as a kind of evil brought about by mistake – a morbid manifestation to which an orthodox, correctly managed war should never have to resort. Laurels were to be reserved for those generals who knew how to conduct a war without bloodshed; and it was to be the specific purpose of the theory of war to teach this kind of warfare . . . Recent history has scattered such nonsense to the winds.

(Clausewitz, *On War*, p. 259)

How are we to prove that usually, and in all the most important cases, the destruction of the enemy's forces must be the main objective? How are we to counter the highly sophisticated theory that supposes it possible for a particularly ingenious method of inflicting minor direct damage on the enemy's forces to lead to major indirect destruction; or that claims to produce, by means of limited but skillfully applied blows, such paralysis of the enemy's forces and control of his will-power as to constitute a significant shortcut to victory? Admittedly, an engagement at one point may be worth more than at another.

Admittedly, there is a skillful order of priority of engagements in strategy; indeed, that is what strategy is all about,
and we do not wish to deny it. We do claim, however, that
direct annihilation of the enemy's forces must always be
the *dominant consideration. We simply want to establish this
dominance of the destructive principle.*
(Clausewitz, *On War*, p. 228 [my emphasis]; see also pp. 130, 259)

We are not interested in generals who win victories without
bloodshed. The fact that slaughter is a horrifying spectacle
must make us take war more seriously, but not provide an
excuse for gradually blunting our swords in the name of
humanity. Sooner or later someone will come along with a
sharp sword and hack off our arms.
(Clausewitz, *On War*, p. 260)[22]

Nevertheless, this does not mean that Clausewitz prefers bloodshed
to other, cheaper methods *if* they are possible. The following statements
clarify his position:

The advantage that the destruction of the enemy forces
possesses over all *other means* is balanced by its cost and
danger; and it is only in order to avoid these risks that other
policies are employed. That the method of destruction
cannot fail to be expensive is understandable; other things
being equal, the more intent we are on destroying the
enemy's forces, the greater our own efforts must be. The
danger of this method is that the greater the success we
seek, the greater will be the damage if we fail. *Other
methods, therefore, are less costly if they succeed and less
damaging if they fail, though this holds true only if both sides
act identically . . .*
(Clausewitz, *On War*, pp. 97–98)

If the opponent does seek battle, this recourse can never be
denied him. A commander who prefers another strategy
must first be sure that his opponent either will not appeal
to that supreme tribunal – force – or that he will lose the
verdict if he does.
(Clausewitz, *On War*, p. 99)[23]

149

For Clausewitz, the *principle of destruction* is, all other things being equal, the shortest and surest way to defeat the enemy and impose one's will on him. Once the enemy's armed forces have been destroyed, it is clear that his resistance will come to an end. By *destruction*, Clausewitz does not necessarily mean physical eradication or devastation of the enemy; he is also referring to destruction of the enemy's will to go on fighting. In this sense, Clausewitz's idea of destruction does not differ radically from Sun Tzu's approach to war. The point Clausewitz makes is that unless armies are capable of destroying the enemy's force in theory and in reality, potentially and actually, they *cannot* achieve the state's political objectives .

Victory without fighting is, therefore, primarily relevant for the type of military conflict with which Sun Tzu would have been most familiar: dynastic wars waged for limited objectives rather than the total-ideological wars of the nineteenth and twentieth centuries. Thus, Clausewitz's assumption is that wars can be fought by other, non-violent means (which he does not specify) *only* when *both sides* have moderate objectives. He makes this point more emphatically in his instructions to the Crown Prince of Prussia:

> **In our plan of battle we must set this great aim: the attack on a large enemy column and its complete destruction. If our aim is low, while that of the enemy is high, we will naturally get the worst of it. We are pennywise and pound-foolish.**

> (Clausewitz, *Principles of War*, pp. 17–18)

But, as Clausewitz knows, no warring state wants to allow its enemy to win cheaply and without risk by these much-vaunted other methods (for example, diplomacy, economic blockades, bluffs and threats, and military demonstrations). A state in this position must normally convince the enemy that he cannot hope to triumph without a prolonged and bloody fight; such a state must also be prepared to escalate and dictate its own terms of battle. If it is weaker, its only chance is to convince the enemy that the war will not be worth his while (that is, deter him). To put it another way, the reciprocal relationship between states and the dynamics of war are such that if the first state realizes that the second will limit its effort to less costly methods – the first then has even more of an incentive to make the cost of war appear prohibitive. Hence,

Sun Tzu's normative recommendation that one should win cheaply and, if possible, without fighting, can logically and practically be only the exception, not the rule.

In sum, Clausewitz understood the logical fallacy of the idea that military commanders should strive to win wars by cheaper, non-military methods. In Book 1, Chapter 2 of *On War*, the only chapter to include a direct analysis of this problem, Clausewitz suggests that non-violent methods can succeed *only* if the enemy also intends to rely on a similar strategy: if this is not the case, he states, the advantage will always accrue to the side that is (or at least appears to be) ready to do battle despite the high cost in lives and resources.[24] The most persuasive argument against the ideal of the bloodless victory is that, in most instances, only a powerful demonstration of the readiness to resort to force will, paradoxically enough, achieve this end. Undoubtedly, the known desire to win without bloodshed only emboldens one's enemy. Clausewitz continues:

> **If he** [the enemy] **were to seek the decision through a major battle,** *his choice would force us against our will to do likewise* **[Clausewitz's emphasis]. Then the outcome of the battle would be decisive; but it is clear – other things again being equal – that we would be at an overall disadvantage, since our plans and resources had been in part intended to achieve other goals, whereas the enemy's were not. Two objectives, neither of which is part of the other, are mutually exclusive: one force cannot simultaneously be used for both. If, therefore, one of the two commanders is resolved to seek a decision through major battle, he will have an excellent chance of success if he is certain that his enemy is pursuing a different policy. Conversely, the commander who wishes to adopt** *different means* **can reasonably do so** *only* **if he assumes his opponent to be equally unwilling to resort to major battles. [my emphasis]**
>
> (Clausewitz, *On War*, p. 98)

> **If one side uses force without compunction, undeterred by the bloodshed it involves, while the other side refrains, the first will gain the upper hand.**
>
> (Clausewitz, *On War*, pp. 75–76)

This view [i.e., that wars can be won without actually fighting] is as petty as its subject. *In the absence of great forces and passions* it is indeed simpler for ingenuity to function; *but is not guiding great forces* [i.e. material and even more so ideological and spiritual motivation], navigation through storms and surging waves, a higher exercise of the intellect? That other, formalized type of swordsmanship is surely included and implicit in the more energetic mode of conducting war. It has the same relation to it as the movements on a ship have to the motion of the ship. It can *only be carried on so long as it is tacitly understood that the opponent follows suit.* But is it possible to tell how long this condition will be observed? The French Revolution surprised us in the false security of our ancient skills and drove us from Chalons to Moscow . . . Woe to the government, which, relying on half-hearted politics and a shackled military policy, meets a foe who, like the untamed elements, knows no law other than his own power! Any defect of action and effort will turn to the advantage to the enemy, and it will not be easy to change from a fencer's position to that of a wrestler. A slight blow may then often be enough to cause a total collapse. [my emphasis]

(Clausewitz, *On War*, pp. 218–219)[25]

Obviously, wars waged by both sides *to the full extent of their national strength* must be conducted on different principles from wars in which policy was based on the comparative size of regular armies. [my emphasis]

(Clausewitz, *On War*, p. 220)

This is how, without having read Sun Tzu, Clausewitz demolishes the idea that '*To subdue the enemy without fighting is the acme of skill.*' Therefore, if a Clausewitzian commander were to confront a commander who interpreted Sun Tzu's recommendations literally, the Clausewitzian would – all other things being equal – be in a better position to win. For this reason Clausewitz warns that

in war too small an effort can result not just in failure but

in positive harm [where] **each side is driven to outdo the
other, which sets up an interaction.**

(Clausewitz, *On War*, p. 585)

It should be noted that even if the enemy were to be subdued without fighting, Clausewitz would not consider such a victory to be war but rather deterrence, coercive diplomacy, blackmail, or deception. As the reader may remember from Chapter 3, Clausewitz considers war as '. . . **a clash between major interests which is resolved by bloodshed – that is the only way in which it differs from other conflicts'** (Clausewitz, *On War*, p. 149). **'Total non-resistance would not be war at all'** (Clausewitz, *On War*, p. 77). **'. . . the concept of fighting remains unchanged, that is what we mean by war'** (Clausewitz, *On War*, p. 127). **'. . . war is nothing but mutual destruction . . .'** (Clausewitz, *On War*, p. 236). **'The essence of war is fighting'** (Clausewitz, *On War*, p. 248). **'War is the impact of opposing forces'** (Clausewitz, *On War*, p. 205). (Another definition of war which emphasizes the element of uncertainty can be found on p. 103, where Clausewitz describes war as **'the domain of the unexpected'**.[26])

The weakness of Sun Tzu's approach lies in its implication that war can somehow be turned into a non-lethal intellectual exercise in which cunning and intelligence are central. On the other hand, an erroneous interpretation of Clausewitz's emphasis on force and the principle of destruction can cause force to be wielded too readily, without the careful consideration of non-military means; this would only make war more costly than necessary. But the choice need not be between either approach when an intelligent combination of both produces the proper balance.

Finally, although Clausewitz believes that his 'decisive battle' is generally the most effective way to achieve a state's political objectives in war, he also points out that it cannot be considered final in the long run unless the military victory is made *politically* acceptable to the defeated enemy.

A government must never assume that its country's fate, its whole existence, hangs on the outcome of a single battle, no matter how decisive. Even after a defeat, there is always the possibility that a turn of fortune can be brought about by developing new sources of internal strength or through the

> natural decimation all offensives suffer in the long run or
> by means of help from abroad.
>
> (Clausewitz, *On War*, p. 483)

Unfortunately, Clausewitz gave this important idea scant attention in *On War*. In the first chapter, Clausewitz does include a significant but often ignored section entitled 'In War the Result is Never Final'. **'Lastly'**, he states, **'even the ultimate outcome of war is not always to be regarded as final. The defeated state often considers the outcome merely as a transitory evil, for which a remedy may still be found in political conditions at some later date'** (Clausewitz, *On War*, p. 80).

His brief discussion of the limitations involved in the use of military force alone is overshadowed by lengthy, detailed analyses on *how* to achieve such 'decisive' military victories – victories that are, at best, only a necessary but never sufficient condition for securing long-range results in war. Here Clausewitz is his own worst enemy, for his military background and concentration on the military dimensions of war detract from his message on the higher political and strategic level. As a result, Clausewitz inadvertently misled many of his militarily oriented readers who relied on his authority and Napoleon's example in their chimerical search for the perfect decisive battle. Yet Clausewitz obviously knew that Napoleon never achieved a *final* victory, despite an unsurpassed record of military triumphs. It is ironic that no nation ignored this insight more than Germany in the First and Second World Wars (Bismarck's war of German unification being an exception).

In Clausewitz's defense, one could add that in the nineteenth century, on rare occasions, a decisive military victory might have been enough to terminate a war quickly. But, since the American Civil War, the use of this approach has revealed a gross misunderstanding of *the nature of modern war*. This has ultimately cost millions of lives and led to wars of attrition that were expected to be wars of decision.

12

Speed, Numerical Superiority, and Victory

> **The decision can never be reached too soon to suit the winner or delayed long enough to suit the loser.**
>
> Clausewitz, *On War*, p. 238

> Only numbers can annihilate.
>
> Nelson

> The aspiration 'to wipe out the enemy before breakfast' is admirable, but it is a bad way to make concrete plans to do so.
>
> Mao Tse-tung, *Selected Military Writings*, p. 143

Since the ideal of winning without battle is seldom realized, the strategist must try to determine the most effective way to achieve victory when bloodshed has become inevitable. Once Sun Tzu turns his attention to strategy in practice, his views on the art of war do not differ from those of Clausewitz as much as previously thought. Sun Tzu is also searching for the quickest, most decisive victory, which can be realized most directly through absolute numerical superiority in general or relative superiority at the decisive point of contact. It is, of course, the latter situation in which the qualities of superior generalship are brought to the fore. In order to win despite numerical inferiority, the 'military genius' (to use Clausewitz's terminology) must, for example, comprehend the potential contribution and limits of intelligence, the most effective way to use deception, and the fundamental distinctions between the offense and defense; further, he must be aware of the advantages conferred by terrain and weapons technology as well as those that cannot be gained solely through numerical superiority.

155

Victory is the main object in war. If this is long delayed, weapons are blunted and morale depressed. When troops attack cities, their strength will be exhausted . . . Thus while we have heard of blundering swiftness in war, we have not yet seen a clever operation that was prolonged.

(Sun Tzu, *The Art of War*, p. 73)

Determination and speed are essential elements of a decisive victory.

[Chang Yu] When you see the correct course, act; do not wait for orders.

(Sun Tzu, *The Art of War*, p. 112)

Therefore at first be shy as a maiden. When the enemy gives you an opening be swift as a hare and he will be unable to withstand you.

(Sun Tzu, *The Art of War*, p. 140)

Clausewitz too emphasized the importance of speed in war:

The second principle is the rapid use of our forces.[1] **Any unnecessary expenditure of time, every unnecessary detour, is a waste of strength and thus abhorrent to strategic thought. It is still more important to remember that almost the only advantage of the attack rests on its initial surprise. Speed and impetus are its strongest elements and are usually indispensable if we are to defeat the enemy. Thus theory demands the shortest roads to the goal.**

(Clausewitz, *On War*, p. 624)

Clearly, the purpose of the search for swift results in a decisive battle is to avoid becoming mired in prolonged wars of attrition.[2] The desire to bring a war to the quickest and most decisive victory is universal. As Mao Tse-tung reminds us:

Quick decision is sought in campaigns and battles, and this is true at all times and in all countries. In a war as a whole, too, quick decision is sought at all times and in all countries, and a long drawn-out war is considered harmful.

(Mao Tse-tung, *Selected Military Writings*, p. 143)

Unlike Sun Tzu, who scarcely discusses the bloody realities of war let alone the importance of annihilating the enemy forces, Clausewitz goes directly to the point:

> **The immediate object of an attack is victory.**
> (Clausewitz, *On War*, p. 545)

> **The destruction of the army is the key to his defeat.**
> (Clausewitz, *On War*, pp. 595–596)

> **Victory alone is not everything – but is it not, after all what really counts?**
> (Clausewitz, *On War*, p. 291)

> **We doubt whether Bonaparte in any of his campaigns ever took the field without the idea of crushing the enemy in the very first encounter.**
> (Clausewitz, *On War*, p. 261)

> **We do claim, however, that the direct annihilation of the enemy's forces must always be the *dominant consideration*.**
> (Clausewitz, *On War*, p. 228; see also p. 230)
> (See also Chapter 11 above, pp. 143–144.)

And how is a quick, decisive victory to be achieved? As illustrated in the foregoing quotations, Clausewitz believes that overwhelming numerical superiority is one of the few ways in which it is remotely possible to win without battle. As Clausewitz explains, numerical superiority, all other things being equal, is certainly the simplest way to win decisively:

> **In tactics as in strategy, superiority of numbers is the most common element in victory.**
> (Clausewitz, *On War*, p. 194)

> **Superiority of numbers admittedly is the most important factor in the outcome of an engagement . . . It thus follows that as many troops as possible should be brought into the engagement at the decisive point . . . This is the first principle of strategy.**
> (Clausewitz, *On War*, pp. 194–195)

The first rule, therefore, should be: put the largest possible army into the field. This may sound a platitude but in reality it is not.

(Clausewitz, *On War*, p. 195)

The best strategy is always *to be very strong*: first in general, and then at the decisive point . . . There is no higher and simpler law of strategy than that of *keeping one's forces concentrated*.

(Clausewitz, *On War*, p. 204)

Since in strategy casualties do not increase with the size of the forces used, and may even be reduced, and since obviously greater force is more likely to lead to success, it naturally follows that we can never use too great a force, and further, that all available force must be used *simultaneously*.

(Clausewitz, *On War*, pp. 206–207)

An impartial student of modern war must admit that superior numbers are becoming more decisive with each passing day. The principle of bringing the maximum possible strength to the decisive engagement must therefore rank rather higher than it did in the past.

(Clausewitz, *On War*, p. 282)[3] (See Appendix F below, 'Clausewitz's Principle of Concentration'.)

While victory is most easily effected through absolute numerical superiority, both Sun Tzu and Clausewitz show that what matters most is not an absolute numerical advantage but rather superiority at the decisive point, the point of engagement. An absolute quantitative advantage may not always translate into victory, particularly on the strategic level where no direct contact is made. Numerically inferior armies with capable leadership can therefore emerge victorious through the correct application of this concept.

In a minor engagement it is not too difficult to judge approximately how much force is needed to achieve substantial success, and what would be superfluous. In

strategy, this is practically impossible, because strategic success cannot be defined and delineated with the same precision.

(Clausewitz, *On War*, p. 208)

To achieve relative superiority at the point of contact is undoubtedly one of the greatest feats of the military genius:

Consequently, the forces available must be employed with such skill that even in the absence of absolute superiority, relative superiority is attained at the decisive point.

(Clausewitz, *On War*, p. 196; also p. 197)

The same idea is also expressed by Sun Tzu in *The Art of War*.

If I am able to determine the enemy's dispositions while at the same time I conceal my own, then I can concentrate and he must divide. And if I concentrate while he divides, I can use my entire strength to attack a fraction of his. There, I will be numerically superior. Then if I am able to use many to strike few at the selected point, those I deal with will be in dire straits.

(Sun Tzu, *The Art of War*, pp. 98–99)

Jomini includes identical advice in the second of his four fundamental principles of war: '*To maneuver to engage fractions of the hostile army with the bulk of one's forces*' (Jomini, *The Art of War*. p. 70).[4]

The fact that Clausewitz's discussion of force ratios and the superiority of numbers is concentrated in specific chapters of *On War* (Book 3, Chapter 8, 'Superiority of Numbers', pp. 194–197; and Book 5, Chapter 3, 'Relative Strength', pp. 282–285), while Sun Tzu's comments on these subjects appear throughout *The Art of War*, does not mean that Sun Tzu is any less conscious of their significance. Both maintain that the key to victory lies in relative superiority at the decisive point of engagement, but they differ on how this goal is best attained. Clausewitz stresses the '*positive*' approach of maximum concentration of one's own forces, but is less concerned with the enemy. Sun Tzu is chiefly concerned with the '*negative*' approach of preventing the enemy from concentrating his troops through reliance on stratagems that divide and disperse his forces. This leads Sun Tzu to a much greater appreciation of deception and diversion in war:

159

When he is united, divide him.

(Sun Tzu, *The Art of War*, p. 69)

The enemy must not know where I intend to give battle. For if he does not know where I intend to give battle he must prepare in a great many places. And when he prepares in a great many places, those I have to fight in any one place will be few.

And when he prepares everywhere, he will be weak everywhere.

[Chang Yu] He will be unable to fathom where my chariots will actually go out . . . or where my infantry will actually follow up, and therefore he will disperse and divide and will have to guard against one everywhere. Consequently, his force will be scattered and weakened and his strength divided and dissipated, and at the place I engage him I can use a large host against his isolated units.

(Sun Tzu, *The Art of War*, pp. 98–99)

Now when a Hegemonic King attacks a powerful state, he makes it impossible for the enemy to concentrate. He overawes the enemy and prevents his allies from joining him.

(Sun Tzu, *The Art of War*, p. 138)[5]

And in a rare reference to the positive approach more typical of Clausewitz, Sun Tzu states:

Concentrate your forces against the enemy and from a distance of a thousand li you can kill his general. This is described as the ability to attain one's aim in an artful and ingenious manner.

(Sun Tzu, *The Art of War*, p. 139)

By comparison, Clausewitz largely ignores the question of the enemy's perceptions. Placing little faith in intelligence, he instead prefers the one-sided but safer approach of concentrating his own troops. He asserts that as long as one achieves the greatest possible concentration, success will follow (assuming all other factors are equal). In a world of war dominated by uncertainty and poor intelligence, Clausewitz's planning is based on the maximum concentration of troops *regardless* of the enemy's own plans. Moreover, Clausewitz does not offer any further suggestion about *how* relative superiority at the decisive point is to be realized, and almost entirely disregards the potential of deception, which Sun Tzu believes is critical to success. The danger of Sun Tzu's approach, however, is that deception (as well as reliable intelligence) viewed as a panacea encourages an unrealistic quest for quick, cheap victories.

In fact, these two approaches should be combined. The possession of superior strength believed sufficient to ensure victory does not preclude recourse to deception, which can reduce the cost of victory in terms of lives, resources, and time. But human nature being what it is, powerful nations most often rely on direct, brute force to accomplish their objectives, leaving deception and stratagem to those whose perceived or actual weakness seems to give them no alternative.[6]

This observation also leads to the conclusion that the readiness to use deception is more a reflection of strength or weakness than of (in this case) Eastern or Western culture or historical experience. During the Second World War, for example, the Western military tradition and culture shared by the British and Germans clearly did not determine the extent of their enthusiasm for deception. At that time, the British, who were on the brink of defeat and could not mobilize as much military strength as the Germans, resorted extensively and effectively to the use of deception on all levels; meanwhile, the Germans, who were complacent in the knowledge of their superior strength and early victories, relied more on naked power than on their wits. Yet when the British were confident of their military might during their colonial wars in Afghanistan, the Boer War, or the First World War, they almost completely ignored deception. And although deception is far from an unknown quantity in Chinese military history, the Chinese did not hesitate to abandon its use and resort to large-scale frontal attacks in, for example, Korea and Vietnam. In much the same way, when the Israelis felt weak and vulnerable (in 1948, 1956, and 1967) they relied on deception as a matter of course; but once intoxicated by their resounding success in 1967, they later neglected its use (in 1973).

In addition, Sun Tzu enumerates the specific force ratios necessary to implement various types of operations, thus distinguishing indirectly between the relative strengths of the offense and defense:

> *He who understands how to use both large and small forces will be victorious.*
>
> (Sun Tzu, *The Art of War*, p. 82)

Consequently, the art of using troops is this: When ten to the enemy's one, surround him . . .

When five times his strength, attack him . . .

If double his strength, divide him . . .

If equally matched, you may engage him . . .

If weaker numerically, be capable of withdrawing . . .

[Chang Yu] If the enemy is strong and I am weak, I temporarily withdraw and do not engage.

(Sun Tzu, *The Art of War*, pp. 79–80)

Other conditions being equal, if a force attacks one ten times its size, the result is flight.

(Sun Tzu, *The Art of War*, p. 125)

As can be seen from these force ratios as well as from the following statements, Sun Tzu – like Clausewitz – sees the defense as the stronger form of war:

Invincibility lies in the defence: the possibility of victory in the attack.

One defends when his strength is inadequate; he attacks when it is abundant.

(Sun Tzu, *The Art of War*, p. 85)

Sun Tzu also implies that although the defense is the stronger form of warfare, it cannot in and of itself enable one to triumph over the enemy. Sooner or later, the defender who aspires to victory must move over to the attack (Sun Tzu, *The Art of War*, p. 85).

Clausewitz expresses the same ideas as follows:

We repeat then that the defense is the stronger form of war, the one that makes the enemy's defeat more certain.

(Clausewitz, *On War*, p. 380)

If defense is the stronger form of war, yet has a negative object, it follows that it should be used only so long as weakness compels, and be abandoned as soon as we are strong enough to pursue a positive object. When one has used defensive measures successfully, a more favorable balance

of strength is usually created; thus, the natural course in war is to begin defensively and end by attacking. It would therefore contradict the very idea of war to regard defense as its final purpose . . . .

(Clausewitz, *On War*, p. 358)

The transition to the attack is the culminating point of the defense.

A sudden powerful transition to the offensive – the flashing sword of vengeance – is the greatest moment for the defense.

(Clausewitz, *On War*, p. 370)

So long as the defender's strength increases every day while the attacker's diminishes, the absence of decision is in the former's best interest; but if only because the effects of the general losses to which the defender has continually exposed himself are finally catching up with him, the point of culmination will necessarily be reached when the defender must make up his mind and act, when the advantages of waiting have been completely exhausted.

(Clausewitz, *On War*, p. 383).[7] (For a detailed discussion, see Chapter 13 below.)

While Clausewitz develops a more sophisticated comparison of the offense and defense, he never tries to establish specific force ratios for undertaking certain defensive or offensive operations. Instead, his analysis remains on a higher methodological and conceptual plane. Nevertheless, both strategists agree that the defense is a stronger form of warfare that can be successfully waged with fewer troops; in addition, both caution against depending on numerical superiority alone.

In war, numbers alone confer no advantage. Do not advance relying on sheer military power.

(Sun Tzu, *The Art of War*, p. 122)

[Tu Yu] There are circumstances in war when many cannot attack few, and others when the weak can master the strong. One able to manipulate such circumstances will be victorious.

(Sun Tzu, *The Art of War*, pp. 82–83)

163

Clausewitz comments:

> **Superior numbers, far from contributing everything, or even a substantial part, to victory, may actually be contributing very little, depending on the circumstances.**
>
> (Clausewitz, *On War*, p. 194)

> **It would be seriously misunderstanding our argument to consider numerical superiority as indispensable to victory; we merely wished to stress the relative importance.**
>
> (Clausewitz, *On War*, p. 197)

> **To accept superiority of numbers as the one and only rule, and to reduce the whole secret of the art of war to the formula of numerical superiority at *a certain time in a certain place was an oversimplification that would not have stood up for a moment against the realities of life.***
>
> (Clausewitz, *On War*, p. 135)[8]

Both conclude that inspired generalship enables a numerically inferior army to win through the concentration of more troops at the decisive point (see Appendix F). This can be accomplished in many ways including better command and control, deception, stronger motivation and, in modern warfare, superior weapons technology and fire power.

In discussing the ideal-type of war (that is, absolute war), Clausewitz points out from the start that non-material factors are no less important than material means.

> **If you want to overcome your enemy you must match your effort against his power of resistance, which can be expressed as the product of two inseparable factors, viz., *the total means at his disposal and the strength of his will* [i.e., primarily his motivation to fight but also all other non-material elements of power]. The extent of the means at his disposal is a matter – though not exclusively – of figures, and should be measurable. But the strength of his will is much less easy to determine and can only be gauged approximately by the strength of the motive animating it.**
>
> (Clausewitz, *On War*, p. 77; see Chapter 8 above)

13

The Principle of Continuity and the Culminating Point of Victory: The Contradictory Nature of War†

> Strategy is the art of making use of time and space.
>
> Napoleon

> **If any time is lost without good reason, the initiator bears the loss.**
> Clausewitz, *On War*, p. 601

THE PRINCIPLE OF CONTINUITY

Based on common sense and experience, the *principle of continuity* is one of the oldest principles of war. (On the tactical level, it is sometimes referred to as the *principle of pursuit*, the exploitation of success or **'the utilization of victory'** (Clausewitz, *On War*, p. 570).[1]) This principle states that commanders must exploit an advantage by keeping the enemy under unrelenting pressure, thereby denying him respite or time to regain his equilibrium. The underlying logic is universal: it makes no sense for the side that has gained an advantage to give an opponent the chance to renew his resistance later on. Conversely, a principle of discontinuity is implied; that is, the defeated or weakened side has every interest in *disengaging* – whether through withdrawal, seeking a cease-fire, or prolonging negotiations – to build up his strength for the future.

Although Clausewitz develops the principle of continuity in greater detail and depth than any other military thinker, this concept is also recognized and discussed in brief references throughout *The Art of War*.

---

† The reader is advised to read Appendix C on Clausewitz's use of the ideal-type method.

This is despite the fact that Sun Tzu, unlike Clausewitz, did not write a special chapter on the suspension of action in war:

Keep him under a strain and wear him down.

[Li Ch'uan] When the enemy is at ease, tire him.

[Tu Mu] . . . Exhaust him by causing him continually to run about.

(Sun Tzu, *The Art of War*, pp. 68–69)

When torrential water tosses boulders, it is because of its momentum . . . Thus the momentum of one skilled in war is over-whelming, and his attack precisely regulated.

(Sun Tzu, *The Art of War*, p. 92)

When the enemy is at ease, be able to weary him . . . when at rest to make him move.

(Sun Tzu, *The Art of War*, p. 96)

[Tu Mu] . . . The military law states: Those who when they should advance do not do so . . . are beheaded.

(Sun Tzu, *The Art of War*, pp. 106–107)

Now to win battles and take your objectives, but to fail to exploit these achievements is ominous and may be described as 'wasteful delay'.

(Sun Tzu, *The Art of War*, p. 142)

As we have seen, the principle of continuity is also implied in Sun Tzu's emphasis on the need for speedy operations:

Speed is the essence of war. Take advantage of the enemy's unpreparedness . . .

(Sun Tzu, *The Art of War*, p. 134)

When the enemy presents an opportunity, speedily take advantage of it . . .

(Sun Tzu, *The Art of War*, p. 140; see also Chapter 12, pp. 155–164 above)

Clausewitz, like Sun Tzu, emphasizes the need for speed and the folly of wasting time in war: '**Any unnecessary expenditure of time, any detour, is a waste of strength and thus abhorrent to strategic thought**' (Clausewitz, *On War*, p. 624).

Advice that the ruler should delegate authority to the military commander in the field also has much to do with the need to continue action and exploit fleeting opportunities:

> *Chang Liao said: 'Our Lord is campaigning far away, and if we wait* [discontinuity, allowing the enemy to gain time] *for the arrival of reinforcements, the rebels will certainly destroy us. Therefore the instructions say that before the enemy is assembled we should immediately attack in order to blunt his keen edge and to stabilize the morale of our own troops.'*
>
> (Sun Tzu, *The Art of War*, p. 94)

Elsewhere, Sun Tzu and the commentator Tu Mu discuss the advantages and difficulties of a relentless hot pursuit:

> *It follows that when one rolls up the armour and sets out speedily, stopping neither day nor night and marching at double time for a hundred li, the three commanders will be captured.*
>
> (Sun Tzu, *The Art of War*, p. 103, and Tu Mu's comments, pp. 103–104)

The principle of continuity implies of course that when the enemy is weak, tired, or has been defeated, he will do his best to avoid battle and gain time. '*When the envoys speak in apologetic terms, he* [the enemy] *wishes a respite*' (Sun Tzu, *The Art of War*, p. 120). Sun Tzu observes that in such circumstances the enemy should not be allowed the time to prepare for a later engagement. Conversely, if one's own forces are not doing well, the commander must know when and how to elude the enemy. '*And if in all respects unequal, be capable of eluding him*' (Sun Tzu, *The Art of War*, p. 80).

The principle of continuity has been recognized implicitly and explicitly by many pre-modern theorists of war. Thucydides, for example, implicitly acknowledges its existence in the Corinthian speech, where he contrasts the dynamic, aggressive, and risk-taking Athenians, who created the conditions for success and then exploited them to the fullest, with the passive Spartans, who often missed the opportunity to exploit their victories.

> . . . there is promptitude on their side against procrastination on yours . . . They are swift to follow up a success, and slow to recoil from a reverse . . . they were born into the world to take no rest

167

themselves and to give none to others . . . you [Spartans] still delay, and fail to see that peace stays longest with those who are not more careful to use their power . . . let your procrastination end . . .

(Robert B. Strassler (ed.), *The Landmark Thucydides: A Comprehensive Guide to the Peloponnesian War*, Book 1, Sections 70–71, p. 40)

. . . The Lacedaemonians [Spartans] proved the most convenient people in the world for the Athenians to be at war with. The wide difference between the two characters, the slowness and want of energy of the Lacedaemonians, as contrasted with the dash and enterprise of their opponents, proved of the greatest service, especially to a maritime empire like Athens. Indeed, this was shown by the Syracusans, who were most like the Athenians in character, and also most successful in combating them.

(Thucydides, *The History of the Peloponnesian War*, Book 8, Section 96, p. 539)

Indeed, on the one occasion that the Athenians under Nicias behaved like Spartans, they probably caused the Sicilian expedition to fail. Having achieved strategic surprise when landing in Sicily, the Athenians should have attacked Syracuse immediately before it had time to prepare; instead, they let the opportunity slip by (Thucydides, *The History of the Peloponnesian War*, Book 6, Sections 42–50, pp.385–389). (This episode reminds one of two British failures to capitalize on initial successes during the landings in Gallipoli; the first on 25 April 1915 at Anzac Beach and the second on 6 August 1915 at Suvla Bay.[2])

The context of the Corinthian speech before the Spartan Assembly makes it clear that the principle of continuity can be applied to the strategic and policy levels as well as to the lower levels of military operations. In this case, a pre-emptive strategy is advocated, since allowing the enemy to prepare for war in peacetime is folly. Even on the lower operational levels of war, the principle of continuity has direct strategic implications because the continuous exploitation of success allows the quickest possible achievement of the war's objectives. A failure to exploit tactical and operational success will, on the other hand, lead to indecisive action and a prolonged war; ultimately, the original objectives of the war will not be achieved at all or will be achieved after much delay at a far higher cost.

Hannibal's failure to march on Rome – a move that would have exploited his victory at Cannae – is the most famous example of a lost opportunity that held the promise of longer-range strategic consequences.[3] In his *History of the Art of War*, Delbrück argues that Hannibal knew from the beginning of his campaign that he lacked the strength for a direct attack on Rome. If Delbrück is correct in dismissing Maharbal's accusation 'that Hannibal understood how to win but not how to exploit his victories . . .'[4] then Hannibal, as a strategist took unjustifiably high risks in which the possibility of exploiting any of his operational successes for strategic victory was always very slim.

Machiavelli is wiser on this score, suggesting that in the absence of further reinforcements from Carthage, Hannibal and the Carthaginians should have made peace with Rome on the basis of honorable conditions.[5] In another context, Polybius demonstrates that Hannibal understood the principle of continuity very well indeed.

Following a minor operational success soon after his arrival in northern Italy, the capture of Clastidium, and the defection of the Celts to his side, Hannibal realized that the momentum was on his side and that the Romans were not yet ready to face him in a major battle. Conversely, Publius Scipio, who reached the same conclusion, wanted to avoid battle. This is what Polybius remarks on Hannibal's desire to press his attack:

> Hannibal took much the same view of the case as Scipio and was therefore, unlike him, eager for battle because in the *first place*, he wished to avail himself of the enthusiasm of the Celts before it had at all gone off [i.e., before they redefected to the Roman camp]. In the *second place*, he wished to engage the Roman legions while the soldiers in them were raw recruits without practice in war. And in the *third place*, he wished to fight the battle while Scipio was still unfit for service [Publius Scipio was sick]. But most of all he wanted to be doing something and not let the time slip by fruitlessly. For when a general leads his troops into a foreign country and attempts what looks like a desperate undertaking, the one chance for him is to keep the hopes of his allies alive by continually striking some fresh blow.
>
> (Polybius, *On Roman Imperialism*, p. 140)

(Following this decision, Hannibal wins the battle of Trebia.)

Machiavelli is more concerned with the principle of continuity and the dangers of discontinuity on the lower tactical levels.

> When a general wins, he ought with all speed to follow up his victory, imitating in this manner Caesar, not Hannibal, who by standing still after he had defeated the Romans at Cannae, lost thereby the mastery of Rome. The other after victory never rested, but in pursuing his defeated enemies showed greater vigor and dash than in attacking them when they were unshaken. When he loses, a general should try to get some benefit from the loss, especially if some remnant of his army is left. Such opportunity can come from the negligence of an enemy, who after victory, often grows careless and gives you a chance to defeat him . . . [Conversely, when defeated in battle] you must take measures to keep your enemy from following you easily or must give him a good cause for hesitation . . . [Here Machiavelli has a number of suggestions for the defeated commander on how to gain time and prevent pursuit. First . . .] some generals when they knew they were losing, have ordered their officers to flee in different directions and by different roads, after giving orders where they were later to regather. They did this in order that the enemy, fearing to divide his army, would allow the safe escape of all or the greater part of the defeated army . . . [Second] . . . many have openly abandoned their most precious things, so that the enemy, delayed by the spoil, would give them more time for flight.
>
> (Machiavelli, *The Art of War*, pp. 655–656)

On the higher strategic level, Machiavelli observes that:

> when a wise prince hopes to obtain something from another, he does not, if the opportunity allows, give the other prince time for consideration, but manages to make him see the necessity for quick decisions . . .
>
> (Machiavelli, *Discourses* p. 523)

For Clausewitz, the principle of continuity is central to his ideas on the *ideal type of war* (or as he interchangeably refers to it, war in theory, war in the abstract, or absolute war) as well as to his discussion of war in practice on the operational level.

In Book 3, 'On Strategy in General' (which we would primarily consider today to be the operational level of war), Clausewitz dedicates an entire chapter, 'The Suspension of Action in War', to this subject (*On War*, 3, pp. 216–219), describing the principle of continuity in poetic prose.

> [In theory] . . . **suspension of action in war is a contradiction in terms. Like two incompatible elements, armies must continuously destroy one another. Like fire and water they never find themselves in a state of equilibrium, but must keep on interacting until one of them has completely disappeared . . . military action *ought* to run its course steadily like a wound-up clock . . .** [my emphasis]
> (Clausewitz, *On War*, p. 216; see also p. 579)

But it is actually in Chapter 1 of Book 1 where the principle of continuity is first introduced. Continuity or fighting without interruption is one of the most important differences between war in theory and in practice. As we shall see, the introduction and subsequent modification of the principle of continuity allows him to formulate some of his most important ideas or concepts on war (i.e., the difference between the attack and defense; the influence of human nature; the role of imperfect knowledge or poor intelligence; the probabilistic character of war; and ultimately, war's political nature).

Theoretically, the principle of continuity must be seen as the nexus of the three cases of interaction – (1) the maximum use of force, (2) the objective of disarming the enemy, and (3) the maximum exertion of strength – all of which lead to an extreme, to escalation, and in fact to *non-stop* war. Clausewitz begins by stating that each action in war must be completed as quickly as possible. (See Appendix C, p. 328.)

> **If every action in war is allowed its appropriate duration, we could agree that . . . any additional expenditure of time – any suspension of military action – seems absurd. In this connection, it must be remembered that what we are talking about is not progress made by one side or the other but the progress of military interaction as a whole.**
> (Clausewitz, *On War*, p. 82)

As long as neither side has achieved its goals and their opponents have not terminated the war, each has a reason to continue fighting for

171

its original objectives. Logically, there is only one reason to interrupt the fighting, and this is when one side is waiting for a more opportune situation. Clausewitz refers to this as the *principle of waiting* – the opposite of the principle of continuity.[6]

> [This] would never operate on more than one side since its opposite must automatically be working on the other. If action would bring an advantage to one side, the other's interest must be to wait.
>
> (Clausewitz, *On War*, p. 82)

As he puts it elsewhere:

> If we assume that both generals are completely cognizant of their own and the opponent's conditions, one of them will be motivated to act, which becomes in turn to the other a reason for waiting. Both cannot simultaneously want to advance, or on the other hand, to wait.
>
> (Clausewitz, *On War*, p. 216)

But what if both sides are equally strong or in balance? Not only is this very unusual, argues Clausewitz, but if it were true, the attacker – the side with the positive aim – would maintain the initiative. War would be interrupted only if the side with the positive aim were weaker than the defender; that is, despite the attacker's desire to continue his attack, his strength would not be sufficient. At this juncture, Clausewitz points out, the two sides should terminate the war. But as long as any change in the *relative strength* of the sides is anticipated in the near future, only one side can, by definition, gain from it when it occurs; therefore (assuming that both have equally good intelligence estimates) the side that will soon find itself at a disadvantage – should attack (i.e., the war would be fought without a break). Thus, whether or not a conflict will continue does not depend on the *balance* or *relative strength* at any given moment but rather on the positive or negative aims and projected power of the combatants. (See below, Chapter 14 on 'War Termination'.)

Clausewitz brings this example: if the side with the positive aim (the attacker) has seized part of the other's territory, the defeated party can either accept this as a *fait accompli* and agree to make peace, or he can stall until he is able to take action four weeks later. At this point, however, the winning side, assuming he possesses correct information on the other's intentions to resume fighting in a month, must continue fighting to prevent his opponent from stalling.[7]

> **If this continuity were really to exist in the campaign, its effect would again be to drive everything to extremes [in fact, a fourth case of interaction]. Not only would such ceaseless activity arouse men's feelings and inject them with more passion and elemental strength, but events would follow more closely on each other and be governed by a stricter causal chain. Each individual action would be more important, and consequently more dangerous.**
>
> (Clausewitz, *On War*, p. 83)

This comment touches upon a closely related question that concerns Clausewitz throughout *On War* – that is, whether war ought to be considered as a series of discrete events in which only the last event really matters or whether war is aggregative in nature (Clausewitz, *On War*, in particular Book 8, Chapter 3, p. 582, but also pp. 142, 182–183, 194, 211, 216–217, 386, 626).

In theory, therefore, war should be interrupted only rarely either when one side's victory has been accepted by the other, or when the attacker is weaker than the defender. Otherwise, war ought to continue without interruption. In reality, of course, war is frequently interrupted even when neither side has relinquished its original objectives. The most common explanation is 'that both are waiting for a better time to act' (Clausewitz, *On War*, p. 82), but Clausewitz has convincingly shown that this makes little theoretical sense.

> **War . . . seldom if ever shows such continuity. [Therefore, the interruption of action in war] . . . cannot always be an anomaly. Suspension of action in war must be possible; in other words, it is not a contradiction in terms.**
>
> (Clausewitz, *On War*, p. 83)

> **. . . action in war is not continuous but spasmodic. Violent clashes are interrupted by periods of observation . . .**
>
> (Clausewitz, *On War*, p. 219)

Clausewitz then offers the following modifications and explains why, in the real world, war involves as much inactivity, inaction, and interruptions as it does action and continuity.

The *first* modification distinguishes between the attack and defense, which do not simply represent opposite poles, yin and yang, but are inherently 'two different things'.[8] The only common ground the attack and defense have is when they interact:

> [The] . . . defense is the stronger form of war, the one that makes the enemy's defeat more certain.
>
> (Clausewitz, *On War*, p. 380)

> It is easier to hold ground than take it. It follows that the defense is easier than the attack, assuming both sides have equal means. Just what is it that makes preservation and protection so much easier? It is the fact that time which is allowed to pass unused accumulates to the credit of the defender. He reaps what he did not sow. Any omission of attack – whether from bad judgment, fear, or indolence – accrues to the defender's benefit.
>
> (Clausewitz, *On War*, p. 357)[9]

This difference in strength between the attack and defense now provides Clausewitz with one of the most important explanations for inaction in war, namely that even if both sides are numerically equal, the attacker, with the positive aim, cannot attack because the defender is in an otherwise stronger position. Furthermore, even if the attacker is numerically superior, he may not have enough of an advantage to compensate for the inherent superiority of the defense.[10] This can be described as follows: Let us assume that both sides have 100 divisions or units of strength and that the defense is twice as strong as the offense. Under these conditions the attacker is at a disadvantage and cannot expect to win even if he wants to take the initiative.

ATTACKER		DEFENDER
100	$\langle$	100×2

Therefore the result would be inaction. To match the superiority of the defense, the attacker needs a minimum of 200 divisions.

ATTACKER		DEFENDER
200	$=$	100×2

Yet even when the attacker's numerical superiority is enough to compensate for the inherent advantages of the defense, action or 'continuity' do not automatically follow. This leads to Clausewitz's *second* modification of the principle of continuity and to yet another crucial observation. This time the cause of inaction is *imperfect knowledge* (i.e., inadequate information or poor intelligence).[11] Here Clausewitz asserts that even if the attacker has the advantage, the dearth of accurate intelligence will cause him to be either unaware of it or unsure that it is enough to defeat his enemy.

> **There is still another factor that can bring military action to a standstill: imperfect knowledge of the situation. The only situation a commander can fully know is his own; his opponent's he can only know from unreliable intelligence. His evaluation, therefore, may be mistaken and can lead him to suppose that the initiative lies with the enemy when in fact it remains with him.**
>
> (Clausewitz, *On War*, p 84; also pp. 216–217)

In principle, as Clausewitz admits, poor intelligence should lead as much to action as to inaction, were it not for the *third* modifying factor of human nature. Under conditions of uncertainty, '**men are always more inclined to pitch their estimate of the enemy's strength too high than too low, such is human nature**' (Clausewitz, *On War*, p. 85). (The entire argument is briefly and perhaps more clearly repeated in Chapter 16 of Book 3, pp. 217–218.) When faced with uncertainty, most commanders almost instinctively tend to prefer a *worst-case analysis* – that is, they prefer inaction to action. Uncertainty (i.e., poor intelligence) and human nature thus combine to create further inaction. (See note 9 of Chapter 1, pp. 376–377.)

Typically, Clausewitz's analysis begins with an explanation of the reason that war is not fought continuously, even as it explores other closely interconnected insights and observations on the nature of war.

> [Inaction in turn has a moderating effect on] . . . **the progress of the war by diluting it, so to speak, in time by delaying danger . . . the slower the progress and the more frequent the interruptions of military action, the easier it is to retrieve a mistake, the bolder will be the general's assessments and the more likely he will be to avoid theoretical**

> **extremes** [i.e., the ideal type of war and the three cases of inter-action] **and base his plans** [in the absence of reliable information] **on probability and inference.**
>
> (Clausewitz, *On War*, p. 85)

Once action is determined by 'assessing probabilities' it is further removed from the inherent imperatives (or *necessary causes*) and certainties of the absolute or ideal type of war with which Clausewitz began.[12] But this chain reaction of ideas does not stop here: once war is based on the 'assessment of probabilities', one moves further into the world of risk-taking or, in other words, into the realm of gambling. His discussion of chance, which introduces an element of the gamble into every war, once again leads Clausewitz to the subject of human nature – this time to the fact that in a world dominated so much by chance – courage, daring, boldness, and trust in one's luck are essential qualities for a great commander. The recognition of the role of chance and its interaction with human nature ends the modification process that aligns theory with reality.

> . . . **Absolute, so-called mathematical factors never find a firm basis in military calculations . . . In the whole range of human activities, war most closely resembles a game of cards . . . the art of war deals with living and with moral forces. Consequently, it cannot attain the absolute, or certainty** [i.e., the ideal type of war, the absolute war]; **it must always leave a margin for uncertainty, in the greatest things as much as in the smallest.**
>
> (Clausewitz, *On War*, p. 86)

Indeed, the extent to which the principle of continuity diverges from the ideal depends on the intensity of the motives involved.

> **The greater the tensions that have led to the war, and the greater the consequent war effort, the shorter these periods of inaction. Inversely, the weaker the motive for conflict, the longer the intervals between actions.**
>
> (Clausewitz, *On War*, p. 85)

> **But usually one side is . . . more strongly motivated, which tends to affect its behavior: the offensive element will dominate, and usually maintain its continuity of action.**
>
> (Clausewitz, *On War*, p. 219)

176

Clausewitz believed that the wars of the French Revolution and even more so of Napoleon brought war in theory and in practice close enough to overlap (see above, Chapter 10, pp. 121–122).

> ... Warfare attained the unlimited degree of energy that we consider to be its elementary law. We see it is possible to reach this degree of energy; and if it is possible, it is necessary.
>
> (Clausewitz, *On War*, p. 217)

> The elemental fire of war is now so fierce and war is waged with such enormous energy that even these regular periods of rest have disappeared, and all forces press unremittingly toward the great decision.
>
> (Clausewitz, *On War*, p. 313)

On the operational level, Clausewitz believes that in practice, even when the attacker has imperfect information or has grown weaker, it is still preferable to maintain the initiative and continue without interruption. Time could easily work in favor of the opponent and once operations are brought to a halt, they are very difficult to resume.

> We hope to have made it clear that in our view an offensive war requires above all a quick, irresistible decision. If so, we shall have cut the ground from under the *alternative* idea that a slow, allegedly systematic occupation is safer and wiser than conquest by continuous advance ... It is of course easier to reach a nearby object than a more distant one. But if the first does not suit our purpose, a pause, a suspension of activity will not necessarily make the second half of the journey any easier to complete. A short jump is certainly easier than a long one; but no one wanting to get across a wide ditch would begin by jumping half-way.
>
> (Clausewitz, *On War*, p. 598)

After summarizing the traditionally accepted reasons for slowing or interrupting the momentum of an offensive, Clausewitz voices his opposition:

> All these are admirable aims, and no doubt they can make the offensive war easier; but they cannot make its results more certain. They usually camouflage misgivings on the

177

part of the general or vacillation on the part of the government . . . [All the advantages of waiting for reinforcements, resting, and so on will also work for the enemy.] **Our belief then is that any kind of interruption, pause, or suspension of activity is inconsistent with the nature of offensive war. When they are unavoidable, they must be regarded as necessary evils, which make success not more but less certain. Indeed, if we are to keep strictly to the truth, when weakness does compel us to halt, a second run at the objective normally becomes impossible; and if it does turn out to be possible, it shows that there was no need for a halt at all. When an objective was beyond one's strength in the first place, it will always remain so.**

(Clausewitz, *On War*, pp. 598–600)

Once a major victory is achieved there must be no talk of rest, of a breathing space, or reviewing the position or consolidating and so forth, but only of the pursuit, going for the enemy again if necessary, seizing his capital, attacking his reserves and anything else that might give his country aid and comfort . . . we demand that the main force should go on advancing rapidly and keep up the pressure.

(Clausewitz, *On War*, p. 625)

Once a pause has become necessary, there can as a rule be no recurrence of the advance . . . Every pause between one success and the next gives the enemy new opportunities. One success has little influence on the next, and often none at all. The influence may well be adverse, for the enemy either recovers and rouses himself to greater resistance or obtains help from somewhere else. But when a single impetus obtains from start to finish, yesterday's victory makes certain of today's, and one fire starts another. For every case of a state reduced to ruin by successive blows – which means that time, the defender's patron, has defected to the other side – how many more are there in which time ruined the plans of the attacker!

(Clausewitz, *On War*, p. 626; see also p. 599)

[Once victory] **has been won, one must ensure that it touches off a series of calamities which, in accordance with the law of falling bodies, will keep gathering momentum.**

(Clausewitz, *On War*, p. 478)

Moreover, Clausewitz eloquently describes the psychological advantages of pursuing a defeated enemy (as compared with the pursuit of an undefeated enemy).

The situation is completely different when a defeated army is being pursued. Resistance becomes difficult, indeed sometimes impossible, as a consequence of battle casualties, loss of order and of courage, and anxiety about the retreat. The pursuer who, in the former case had to move with circumspection, almost groping like a blind man, can now advance with the arrogance of the fortunate and the confidence of the demigod. The faster his pace, the greater the speed with which events will run along their predetermined course: this is the primary area where psychological forces will increase and multiply without being rigidly bound to the weights and measures of the material world.

(Clausewitz, *On War*, pp. 469–470)

Jomini agrees:

A pursuit should generally be as boldly and actively executed as possible, especially when it is subsequent to a battle gained; because the demoralized army may be wholly dispersed if vigorously followed up.

(Jomini, *The Art of War*, p. 242; see also Mao Tse-tung, *Selected Military Writings*, p. 123)

It is clear how much attention Clausewitz paid both in theory and in practice to the principle of continuity. On the whole, he discusses this principle on the higher operational level and less so on the strategic. Nevertheless, the principle has a great deal to offer the strategist and policymaker as well (as Clausewitz indicates). Once secured, an operational advantage must be translated into a strategic and political advantage, with pressure on the operational level bringing better and quicker results at the bargaining table (see Figure 13.2, pp. 186–187). To their detriment, U.S. policymakers and strategists during the wars in

179

Korea, Vietnam, and the Gulf seem to have forgotten this principle. In the spring of 1951, the U.S. offensive in Korea, first under General Ridgeway and later under General Van Fleet, which led to the defeat of the Chinese People's Liberation Army, came to a halt on the ground by June 1951 as soon as the Chinese and North Koreans indicated their readiness to negotiate. And since the Chinese and North Koreans were using this break in the fighting to recuperate and build up their defenses in depth, American negotiators soon found that the enemy was in no hurry to conclude an armistice. At this stage, however, it would have been much more costly for the United States to renew the ground offensive. Some have suggested that the United States should have continued its offensive further up to the narrow waist of Korea and terminated the war unilaterally at the place of its choice, but this may not have been necessary. Had the U.S. applied steady pressure on the defeated Chinese army while negotiating, the war might have terminated with a quick armistice. But by interrupting its advance *before* any agreement had been reached, the United States eliminated the Chinese and North Korean incentive to negotiate. As a result, the war persisted at an unavoidably high cost in lives.[13] In hindsight, it is evident that the Chinese, North Koreans, and North Vietnamese dangled the bait of negotiations in front of the Americans primarily to avoid defeat and prepare for the next round. While the communists in each instance coordinated their diplomatic and military actions in support of each other, this was not true for the United States. In each case, a desire to terminate the war as quickly as possible and reduce casualties ironically prolonged the war and increased costs. In an equally accommodating move, each time the United States began its negotiations with Hanoi in the late 1960s and early 1970s, it politely halted its strategic bombing. Often, if an opponent makes the condition that operations must come to a halt before negotiations begin, his real motives are suspect. Unless an agreement can be reached quickly or operations successfully renewed, negotiations and operations should always continue simultaneously until a satisfactory agreement has been concluded. This was understood by the Allies in the late fall of 1918, when they refused to stop their advance while negotiating with the Germans for an armistice. Ludendorff's change of heart in late October and readiness to renew the fighting certainly proved the wisdom of this decision.[14] (See Chapter 14 on 'War Termination' and Note 6, pp. 415–418.)

The Gulf War provides yet another example of military operations that were prematurely terminated. While the United States and its allies need not have marched all the way to Baghdad, *the threat* to do so, combined with steady pressure on the ground and in the air might have brought the war to a more satisfactory conclusion. The United States and its allies should have insisted that Saddam Hussein either resign and leave the country or stand trial as a war criminal (as in the trial, eventual abdication, and escape to exile of the Kaiser in 1918). In addition, the U.S. and its allies could have done far more to include in an agreement arrangements to protect the Kurds in the north and the Marsh Arabs and Shi'ites in the south. But the United States was eager to minimize casualties. (Most of its Arab allies would not have minded continuing the war at least until Saddam Hussein had been removed, although they were unlikely to admit this in public.) Instead, the outcome has caused much more death and suffering for millions of Iraqis while the dangerous presence of Saddam Hussein has not been eliminated. Clearly, the principle of continuity has as much to offer on the *strategic* as on the operational level of war.

THE CULMINATING POINT OF THE ATTACK/VICTORY

Finally, attention must be drawn to the fact that no principle of war can be valid at all times and that one principle may contradict or be in tension with other principles. The principle of continuity is no exception since it is in tension with Clausewitz's other important concept of the culminating point of the attack.[15]

Clausewitz states that as any attack continues to advance and succeed it also diminishes in strength. Moving progressively further from his own bases of supply, the attacker has to protect longer communications lines, his flanks become more exposed, his forces are less familiar with the terrain, the troops suffer from attrition in battle, and so on. With all other things being equal, the passage of time favors the defense and enervates the attack.

> **There is no growth of intensity in an attack comparable to that of various types of defense.**
>
> (Clausewitz, *On War*, p. 525)

> **Every attack will anyhow end in a defense whose nature will be decided by circumstances. These may be very favorable**

FIGURE 13.1
CLAUSEWITZ ON THE ADVANTAGES AND DISADVANTAGES OF INVADING THE ENEMY'S TERRITORY AND THE CULMINATING POINT OF VICTORY/ATTACK (SEE *ON WAR*, PP. 566–567)

The Advance of the Attacker Produces the Following Advantages

1. Normally the losses of the defending forces are heavier.
2. The defender loses fixed assets not lost by the attacker. (Depots, magazines, etc.)
3. The defender loses ground and hence resources.
4. The attacker can live at the enemy's expense.
5. The defender loses his inner cohesion and the smooth functioning of his forces.
6. Some allies are lost to the defender; others turn to the invader.
7. The defender is discouraged and to some extent disarmed.

The Advance of the Attacker Produces the Following Disadvantages

1. The invader has to besiege and assault the defender's fortresses.
2. The theater of operations now becomes hostile; it must be garrisoned.
3. The invader moves away from his sources of supply while the defender moves closer to his own. (Longer flanks and communication lines in the enemy's territory invite attacks and will have to be protected.)
4. The danger threatening the defender will bring allies to his aid.
5. The defender, being in real danger, makes the greater effort, whereas the efforts of the victor slacken off.

when the enemy forces have been destroyed, but where this is not the case, things may be very difficult.

(Clausewitz, *On War*, p. 525)

The attacker is purchasing advantages that may become valuable at the peace table, but he must pay for them on the spot with his fighting forces. If the superior strength of the attack – which diminishes day by day – leads to peace, the object will have been attained. There are strategic attacks that lead up to the point where their remaining strength is just enough to maintain a defense and wait for peace. Beyond that point the scale turns and the reaction follows with a force that is much stronger than that of the original attack. This is what I mean by the culminating point of the attack.

(Clausewitz, *On War*, p. 528)

The natural goal of all campaign plans therefore is the turning point at which the attack becomes defense. If one were to go beyond that point, it would not only be a *useless* effort which could not add to success. It would in fact be a *damaging* one . . .

(Clausewitz, *On War*, p. 570)

What matters therefore is to detect the culminating point with discriminative judgment.

(Clausewitz, *On War*, p. 528)

Both the principle of continuity and the concept of the culminating point of victory (or attack) are very perceptive – but at the same time contradictory. On the one hand Clausewitz advocates the full exploitation of a successful attack, but he also advises caution since the culminating point of victory is 'often . . . entirely a matter of the imagination [i.e., it cannot be identified objectively]'. Conceptually, if not practically, Clausewitz outlines the criteria for making the proper decision in identifying the culminating point of victory:

The obvious answer [in deciding where to stop the attack] is that superior strength is not the end but only the means. The end is either to bring the enemy to his knees or at least to deprive him of some of his territory – the point in that

183

> case being *not to improve the current military position* but to improve one's general prospects in the war and in the peace negotiations. Even if one tries to destroy the enemy completely, one must accept the fact that every step gained may weaken one's superiority – though it does not necessarily follow that it must fall to zero before the enemy capitulates. He may do so at an earlier point, and if this can be accomplished with one's last ounce of superiority, it would be a mistake not to have used it.
>
> (Clausewitz, *On War*, p. 570)

The culminating point of victory is not a theoretically *fixed* point, but a dynamically *fluctuating* point, whose correct identification depends on specific conditions and circumstances which can continuously change on the battlefield or even strategically. While Clausewitz's concept is clear (as the case always is) in principle – its application is very challenging in practice, i.e. the gap between theory and practice remains difficult to bridge (see Chapter 4 above).

This discussion can at least conceptually guide the commander in deciding whether he should follow the principle of continuity or obey the caveat of the culminating point of victory. This analysis is described in Figure 13.2 and Maps 1 and 2 at the end of this chapter.

How is the attacking commander to know which concept or principle to follow at which time? Clausewitz does not, and cannot, develop any specific criteria which give the commander the right decision. He offers only an empirical-psychological explanation indicating what the decision of most commanders is likely to be.

> This is why the great majority of generals will prefer to stop well short of their objective rather than risk approaching it too closely and why those with high courage and an enterprising spirit will often overshoot it and fail to attain their purpose. Only the man who can achieve great results with limited means [i.e., the military genius] has really hit the mark.
>
> (Clausewitz, *On War*, p. 573)

Usually, Clausewitz prefers the bold, daring, and risk-taking general, whom he encourages to pursue the enemy mercilessly without interruption or pause. But in this concluding observation on the culminating point of victory, Clausewitz suddenly states that daring commanders who have 'high courage and an enterprising spirit' will continue action 'and cross the threshold of equilibrium, the line of culmination, without knowing it' (Clausewitz, *On War*, p. 572), which means that they will *fail* to attain their purpose (Clausewitz, *On War*, p. 573); worse still, such a commander may actually suffer defeat because the end of a long offensive is the weakest form of the defense.

> One defensive is not exactly like another, nor will the defense always enjoy the same degree of superiority over attack. In particular this will be the case in a defense that follows directly the exhaustion of an offensive – a defense whose theater of operations is located at the apex of an offensive wedge thrust forward deep into hostile territory . . . It is clear . . . that a defense that is undertaken in the framework of an offensive is weakened in all its key elements. It will thus no longer possess the superiority which basically belongs to it.
>
> (Clausewitz, *On War*, pp. 571–572; see also p. 470)

Thus, even if by his temperament and inclination Clausewitz prefers the audacious commander, he has just explained why the worst-case analysis of the cautious commander can be superior to the high risks taken by the audacious commander. The former may fail to exploit his success to the fullest, but if he achieves less than he intended, he will at least be in a position to defend his acquisitions. The daring, high-risk commander who gambles *va-banque* will most likely be left with nothing. The best advice of course is to strike the perfect balance, to be a military genius, but if this is not possible then it is safer to be cautious (see also Chapter 17 below on 'Boldness and Calculation').

The concept of the *culminating point of victory* (i.e., on the highest operational and strategic level) is closely related to the *problem of war termination*. At the culminating point of victory, the victor has gone as far as he can without risking a reversal of fortune and attained the strongest possible position relative to his opponent: now he must consider the issue of war termination – how to consolidate his gains on the battlefield into enduring political results (i.e., a favorable, lasting peace). The proper implementation of both these concepts requires meticulous calculation of the current relative strength of both sides as well as the careful projection of anticipated trends in their relative strength. Even

185

FIGURE 13.2
THE CULMINATING POINT OF THE ATTACK/VICTORY

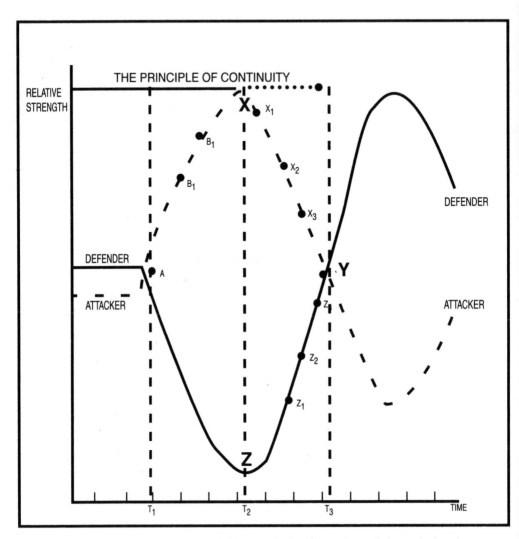

Figure 13.2 is a summary of Clausewitz's discussion of the culminating point of the attack/victory. The graphic presentation is designed to help the reader follow the development of his argument as well as the solution he offers to the problem of identifying this point in theory if not in practice.

The attacker (- - -) and defender (———) have roughly comparable strength when the war begins at point A (T_1). The attacker achieves strategic and operational surprise and rapidly advances. As the attacker continues to advance (from point A to X or from T_1 to T_2), he gathers strength while the defender weakens. As long as he can both advance and gain strength, his decision should be dictated by the principle of continuity. Gradually the defender regains his equilibrium while the attacker loses much of his momentum (beginning at point X (or T_2)) – his forces are getting further and further away from their bases of supply; his lines of communication are extended, and his flanks are exposed. At the same time the defender continues to fall back on his own supply bases; his communication lines become shorter, and the population friendly. Time works in his favor. At point X (or T_2) on the curve the attacker has reached the *peak of his power* relative to the defender, but as he begins to grow *relatively weaker* (from point X to X_1 to X_2 . . . X_3) (or from T_2 onward), the defender is becoming *stronger* (from points Z, to Z_2, Z_3 . . .) (or from T_2 onward). At point Y (or T_3) on the curve, the defender overtakes the attacker and the momentum of a counter-attack is on his side.

Where is the culminating point of attack/victory? Should the attacker move over to the defense at points B_1 or B_2 or X or X_1 . . . X_2 . . . X_3 *before* the defender grows stronger? Clausewitz argues that the culminating point of the attack/victory *cannot be determined in advance*. It depends on the circumstances . . . above all on whether the attacker has already or can still be expected to achieve his object. Clearly, for the attacker to stop at points B_1 or B_2 before his power has peaked is premature, but this does not matter if he has already attained his object. Clausewitz states (*On War*, p. 570) *that as long as the attacker is convinced he can attain his goal*, it makes no difference whether he stops at points X_1, X_2 or X_3 as long as he attains his objectives. *What matters is the achievement of the object, not the relative strength of the opponent.* Strength is only *a means not an end* (i.e., if the attacker can *win* or gain his object between point X and Y (or between T_2 and T_3) – the problem of the culminating point of victory is irrelevant). If, however, the attacker *cannot* (or is *not sure* whether he can) *achieve his object*, he should move over to the defense at point X, where his power is at its peak: this will give him the optimal defense in hostile territory. (In other words, if the attacker cannot win, the principle of continuity should guide him between points T_1 and T_2 as long as his power increases relative to that of his opponent. If, however, he can win, the principle of continuity should still guide him even if his relative strength is on the decline.)

In practice, of course, the commander can never pinpoint the exact strength of his own troops let alone that of his enemy. Therefore he does not know the shape of the curves, or the location of points X or Y. Only *the battle itself and hindsight* can tell him whether he judged the situation correctly – and sometimes not even then.

the most impressive military victories and resounding defeats are often only transitory. Yet this is seldom recognized by the now hubristic victor, who cannot imagine why he should deign to offer the defeated side fair and acceptable peace terms. That which is the culminating point of victory for one side may be the culminating point of defeat for the other. If it wishes to terminate the war quickly, the defeated side may be forced to negotiate from a position of weakness because it has no bargaining chips left. This and other difficulties inherent in the process of war termination are the focus of the next chapter.

CLAUSEWITZ ON THE TRANSITION FROM THE DEFENSE TO THE OFFENSE AND MAO ON THE 'TERMINAL POINT FOR THE RETREAT'

One need look no further than the Chinese Civil War and Japan's invasion of China to understand Mao's interest in the study of the defense. He knew that in such situations, a retreat into the interior of the country was the only way to restore the balance between the powerful attackers and the weaker Red Army. (Clausewitz, of course, witnessed the Russian army's withdrawal all the way to Moscow under Napoleon's pressure.) Mao's discussion of the drawbacks and advantages of such a retreat into the interior in 'Strategy in China's Revolutionary War' and 'On Protracted War' includes some of his most original arguments and theories of war. These essays are comparable to Clausewitz's Book 6 'On the Defense', particularly Chapters 25 and 26 on 'The Retreat to the Interior of the Country' and 'The People in War' (Clausewitz, On War, pp. 469–478, 479–483).

In his military writings, Mao examines, either directly or indirectly, many of the same issues raised by Clausewitz in his discussion of the 'principle of continuity' and the 'culminating point of victory'. Much like Clausewitz, he is interested in how to identify the *optimal timing* for the transition from one phase of war to another. Clausewitz is concerned with both the transition from the attack to the defense (i.e., the culminating point of victory and the attack) *and* the transition from the defense to the attack, while Mao, given the circumstances of the Chinese Civil War, is mainly interested in the latter. Mao first seeks to identify what he calls 'the terminal point for retreat' before turning his attention to what Clausewitz would have called 'the culminating point of the defense'.

Let us first briefly examine what Clausewitz has to say about the transition from the defense to the attack:

> **It is in the nature of things that a retreat should be continued until the balance of power is reestablished – whether by means of reinforcements or the cover of strong fortresses or major natural obstacles or the overextension of the enemy. The magnitude of the losses, the extent of the defeat, and, what is even more important, the nature of the enemy, will determine how soon the moment of equilibrium will return.**
>
> (Clausewitz, *On War*, p. 271)

> **Once the defender has gained an important advantage, defense as such has done its work. While he is enjoying this advantage, he *must* strike back, or he will court destruction. *Prudence bids him strike while the iron is hot* and use the advantage to prevent a second onslaught. How, when, and where that reaction is to begin depends, of course, on many other conditions which we shall detail subsequently. For the moment, we shall simply say that *this transition to the counterattack* must be accepted as a tendency inherent in defense – indeed, as one of its essential features. Wherever a victory achieved by the defensive form is not turned to military account, where, so to speak, it is allowed to wither away unused, a serious mistake is being made. *A sudden powerful transition to the offensive – the flashing sword of vengeance – is the greatest moment for the defense.* [my emphasis]**
>
> (Clausewitz, *On War*, p. 370)

> **While we [i.e., the defender deep in the interior of his country] may have more time and can wait until the enemy is at last at his weakest, the assumption will remain that *we shall have to take the initiative* at the end . . . so long as the defender's strength increases every day while the attacker's diminishes, the absence of decision is the former's best**

189

> interest; . . . the point of culmination will necessarily be
> reached when the defender must make up his mind and act,
> when the advantages of waiting have been completely
> exhausted. There is of course no infallible means of telling
> when that point has come; a great many conditions and
> circumstances may determine it.
>
> (Clausewitz, *On War*, p. 383)

Following a successful defensive campaign, the balance of power will
shift in favor of the defender, who must then, according to Clausewitz,
move rapidly over to the offensive to exploit the attacker's decline in
strength. Of course, the main problem is that it is not easy to identify
this point of transition or *culminating point of the defense*. The timing
must be weighed carefully. If the defender moves over to the attack
prematurely, he risks defeat or excessive losses; if he moves too slowly,
he wastes time and resources and allows his opponent either to consolidate his defensive position or to withdraw in good order, thus increasing the cost of the counter-attack or preventing it from achieving
decisive results. *Timing is everything.*

How can the culminating point of the defense be identified? Clausewitz would answer that this task must be left to the intuition of the military genius. While a correct decision is not guaranteed, the situation
itself is at least theoretically clear.

For Clausewitz, there are only two phases of war: defense and attack.
Once the attacker has exhausted his momentum, the counter-offensive
must begin immediately. The situation is akin to a zero–sum game, since
the defender's gain is the attacker's loss. Like 'fire and water' the conflict
must go on. This somewhat mechanical point of view of war to a large
extent reflects the realities of conventional/regular war in Clausewitz's
time. Clausewitz's conception of the attack and defense in a prolonged
campaign – the attacker pursuing the retreating defender – was obviously formed by his experience, observation, and generalizations drawn
from Napoleon's invasion of Russia. But Mao's very different experience is reflected in his more complex conception of a *process* of transition
from the defense to the offense.

Mao's first concern is to identify the point at which the retreat must
end and the regular defense may begin, with an eventual transition to
the counter-offensive. Mao refers to this point as '*the terminal point for
retreat*'.

The decision on the terminal point for retreat should depend on the situation as a whole. It is wrong to decide on a place which, considered in relation to only part of the situation, appears to be favourable for our passing to the counter-offensive, for at the start of our counter-offensive, we must take subsequent developments into consideration, and our counter-offensives always begin on a partial scale.

(Mao Tse-tung, *Selected Military Writings*, p. 116)

Like Clausewitz, Mao is interested in identifying the *optimal time* to complete the transition from one mode of war to another.

A well-timed retreat, which enables us to keep all the initiative, is of great assistance to us in switching to the counter-offensive, *when we have reached the terminal point of retreat*, we have regrouped our forces, and are waiting at our ease for the fatigued enemy. [my emphasis]

(Mao Tse-tung, *Selected Military Writings*, p. 120; see also p. 107)

Pinpointing the moment of transition from one phase of war to another, and particularly from the defense to the offense, is, however, a far more involved process for Mao. In the first place, Mao's theoretical model of warfare is not simply divided into a two–phase, defense/offense sequence, but rather into three phases. In Clausewitz's theory, there is by definition never a stable or prolonged state of equilibrium between the attacker and defender. In theory, as soon as the defender reaches the culminating point of the defense or the attacker reaches the culminating point of victory (one often implies the other), he *must* make the transition to the attack. As we have seen, this is the logic behind the principle of continuity and the view of war as a straightforward clash between 'fire and water' with no possible middle ground.

For Mao, the transition from one phase of war to another is a gradual, evolutionary process, not an abrupt change. The two sides may find themselves, for a shorter or longer period, in a position of equal strength or stable equilibrium. Mao outlines the three phases as follows:

The *first* covers the period of the enemy's strategic offensive and our strategic defensive. The *second* stage will be the period of the enemy's strategic consolidation and our preparations for the counter-offensive. The *third* stage will be the period of our

191

strategic counter-offensive and the enemy's retreat. *It is impossible to predict the concrete situation in the three stages . . .* [in which] the objective course of events will be exceedingly rich and varied with many twists and turns . . .

(Mao Tse-tung, *Selected Military Writings*, pp. 210–211)

Mao expresses a similar idea in his famous 16-character formula, in which he divides war into four phases:

> The enemy advances, we retreat;
> The enemy camps, we harass;
> The enemy tires, we attack;
> The enemy retreats, we pursue.
>
> (Mao, *Selected Military Writings*, p. 111) (lines 2 and 3
> can be seen as phase 2 of his three-phase model)

This makes it clear why identifying the 'optimal point' for the transition from one phase to another is so much more difficult and subtle in Mao's more complicated world.

(1) On the simplest level, while Clausewitz's strategist or commander must make one decision on the timing of the transition from the defense to the offense, Mao's commander must make at least two regarding the transition from the defense to a partial offensive, then from the partial offensive to a full offensive. This of course creates another opportunity to make mistakes.

(2) In Clausewitz's regular or conventional war, the transition is also easier to recognize than in Mao's world of protracted guerrilla warfare. In other words, it is easier to identify a decisive victory or defeat such as Austerlitz, Jena, or Waterloo in a conventional war than it is accurately to assess the aggregate results of a lengthy war of attrition with many clashes between smaller conventional and irregular forces. This is closely related to the next point.

(3) Mao's strategist makes a double transition between the second and third phases of war. He must gradually transform an irregular guerrilla force into a regular or conventional army. This daunting task requires the institution of different patterns of command and control, and the development of new tactics

and doctrine, as well as the acquisition and training in the use of new weapons. It also requires an entirely new psychological outlook on the part of the political and military leaders. *This is a true metamorphosis, not just a 'simple' transition.*[16]

Whereas Clausewitz's two-phase war seems somewhat oversimplified and 'mechanical', Mao's is a more 'organic' model that favors gradual growth and evolution over rapid transitions. Strategists should, however, remember that military success on one level by no means guarantees comparable results on another. The opponent who fails to fight a counter-guerrilla war effectively can still pack a powerful punch in conventional operations (e.g., as the North Vietnamese discovered in the 1968 Tet offensive). The immense difficulties and dangers inherent in fixing the optimal time for a transition from one phase of war to another explain why Mao pays so much attention to the question of theory and practice as well as to objective and subjective analysis (see Chapter 4, pp. 41–52).

FIGURE 13.3
CLAUSEWITZ'S TWO-PHASED WAR

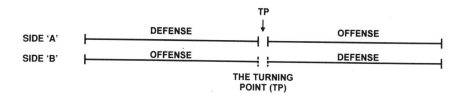

MAO TSE-TUNG'S THREE-PHASED WAR

Map 1 is the classic graphic presentation of Napoleon's invasion of Russia in 1812, as designed by the French engineer Charles Joseph Minard in 1861. This is a perfect example of what happens when a general goes beyond the culminating point of victory – an example that influenced Clausewitz's thinking as he developed the concept. For an outstanding analysis of Napoleon's invasion of Russia see William C. Fuller, Jr, *Strategy and Power in Russia 1600–1914* (New York: The Free Press, 1992), chapter 5, pp. 177–218.

Map 2 depicts a modern example of a situation in which both sides (i.e., the British and Germans in the Western Desert) press their attacks beyond the culminating point of the attack/victory. This results in a 'see-saw' campaign with each side losing the initiative to the opponent after an initial success. As the type of general who was ready to take great risks, Rommel certainly favored the principle of continuity over identification of the culminating point of attack/victory.

14

Clausewitz on War Termination

> Everyone may begin a war at his pleasure
> but cannot so finish it.
> > Machiavelli, *The Discourses* (Modern
> > Library Edition), p. 308

> **If we remember how many factors
> contribute to an equation of forces,
> we will understand how difficult it
> is in some cases to determine which
> side has the upper hand. Often it is
> entirely a matter of the imagination.**
> > Clausewitz, *On War*, p. 528

> *To win victory is easy; to preserve its
> fruits, difficult.*
> > Sun Tzu, *The Art of War*, Griffith trans.,
> > Appendix 1, p. 152.

With the exception of Machiavelli's *Discourses*, none of the classical works on strategy and theory of war discussed here devotes a special chapter to war termination. Pointing to the wisdom of a well-timed peace through compromise and negotiation, Machiavelli examines this subject in a chapter aptly titled 'Wise Princes and Republics Should Content Themselves with Victory; For When They Aim at More, They Generally Lose' (*The Discourses*, 2.27). In contrast, the other classical strategists focus on what they consider to be the conduct of war itself, assuming that war termination is a discrete post-war process which falls in the political leaders' bailiwick. Modern students of war and military professionals have, however, increasingly realized that understanding war termination, that is, the process of negotiating or dictating the terms of peace, should be their concern as well. This is because the demands made of one's adversary during the war and the conditions under which the war is ended directly affect the degree of resistance encountered. Key factors such as the enemy's incentive to end the war or his desire to resume fighting in the future; unlimited war aims (such as unconditional surrender) or limited war aims; and harsh or generous terms bear heavily on the belligerents' resolve either to conclude the war quickly or to continue fighting. (Many other factors also play an important role: for example, the initial goals set by the politicians; the absolute and relative costs of the war to each side; expectations about future success or failure on the battlefield; the prestige of the political and military leaders and how it relates to their continued survival in positions of power; public opinion; and the position of friendly allies or certain hostile states.)

The classical theorists of war of course agree that, all other things being equal, wars should be brought to the quickest possible termination, normally following a decisive victory. While this makes sense as far as it goes, it is not of much help to students of war termination. Of the classical works discussed here, Clausewitz's *On War* has the most to say on this subject. Clausewitz first draws a distinction between war termination in the ideal type of war, or war in theory, as compared to the same process in reality. In Clausewitz's ideal type of war (and often in a *total* or *unlimited war*), only one side can emerge victorious. **'The aim is to disarm the enemy . . .'.** Ideally, the enemy must be rendered **'. . . literally defenseless or at least put . . . in a position that makes this danger probable. . . . The ultimate aim of waging war . . . must be taken as applying to both sides'** (*On War*, p. 77). Clausewitz returns to the same theme in Book 8, Chapter 2:

> **. . . The natural aim of military operations is the enemy's overthrow, and that strict adherence to the** *logic of the concept can*, **in the last analysis, admit no other. Since both belligerents must hold that view, it would follow that military operations could not be suspended,** *that hostilities could not end until one or other side were finally defeated.* [my emphasis]
>
> (*On War*, p. 579)

In other words, the victor does not have to negotiate the conditions for peace, since he can dictate them. War termination in the ideal type of war, 'the absolute war', or unlimited total war, is a unilateral affair, not a reciprocal process of accommodation and recognition of each other's

196

vital common interests. The victor, in Clausewitz's words, can 'compel [the] . . . enemy to do [his] will' (*On War*, p. 75).

Although Clausewitz's ideal type of war is rarely manifested in its pure form, this zero-sum-game type of war termination represents the way in which Napoleon ended his wars. The well-known outcome was that Napoleon's brutal dictates were unacceptable to his opponents, who, as a result, were motivated to form one coalition after another until they eventually defeated him. Napoleon could not secure a lasting peace as long as he refused to recognize his opponents' legitimate interests. Clausewitz, who states that the ideal type of war seldom leads to an enduring peace settlement, recognized this fact.

There is another very important section of Chapter 1 Book 1 that addresses, albeit indirectly, the problem of war termination. Section 9 is a short but profound passage that represents the third modification of war in the abstract (see Appendix C below, pp. 327–328) This is how Clausewitz phrases it:

> *In war the result is never final.* **Lastly, even the ultimate outcome of a war is not always to be regarded as final. The defeated state often** *considers the outcome merely as a transitory evil,* **for which a remedy may still be found in political considerations at some later date.** [my emphasis]
>
> (Clausewitz, *On War*, p. 80)

Ironically, those who characterize Clausewitz as a bloodthirsty Prussian obsessed with the ultimate decisive battle are ignoring statements such as these that expressly preclude the possibility of final results from military success alone. Sun Tzu recognizes this concept when he states, *'Treat the captives well, and care for them.'* Understood in the broader context, this means that the successful strategist must, in victory, create a common interest with the defeated enemy in order to have a lasting peace (*The Art of War*, p. 76) *'This'*, Sun Tzu tells us, *'is called winning a battle and becoming stronger'* (*The Art of War*, p. 76). Sun Tzu then adds: *'Generally in war the best policy is to take a state intact; to ruin it is inferior to this'* (*Art of War*, p. 77). Taking the state 'intact' is interpreted to mean that the ultimate skill of the general lies in taking the enemy's state or forces intact, and incorporating them into one's own state or army.

For the results of victory to endure, they must be accepted as final by the defeated side, whose interests and concerns must be taken into account. The conditions of peace must be such that they appear generous or at least reasonable to the loser. An enduring peace is therefore as reciprocal as everything else in war is. The realization that war termination can never be accomplished by a unilaterally imposed, zero-sum-game *diktat* is one of the first and most powerful modifications of the ideal type of absolute war (see Appendix C, p. 327). Military victory alone is only a necessary but never a sufficient condition for a lasting termination of war, which, after all, can only be achieved through political means; that is, through a political process of accommodation in which the victor recognizes the interests of the defeated party and grants him peace terms he can accept for the long run. (In fact, military victory is often not even a necessary condition for winning or for securing better peace terms.) Finality in war depends on recognition of mutual interests, which is a political, not a military, process.[1]

History is replete with examples of decisive military victories that led nowhere because the victor was not ready to acknowledge the legitimate interests of the vanquished adversary. In fact, the more resounding the *initial victory*, the harder it is for the now hubristic victor, in the heady moment of triumph, to recognize the reciprocal nature of war termination. This also explains why the greatest victors paradoxically fail to obtain enduring results. Many military experts, strategists, and leaders *might* have read parts of Clausewitz's *On War*, but few have perceived the significance of Chapter 1, Section 9.

If the military victor does not offer the defeated adversary terms that are acceptable in the long run, the best that can be hoped for is something like a temporary cease-fire. The losing side will accept the results **'merely as a transitory evil'** to be tolerated until it can regroup and resume fighting for its vital interests. Clausewitz makes this clear elsewhere in *On War*:

> **Even after a defeat, there is always the possibility that a turn of fortune can be brought about by developing new sources of internal strength or through the natural decimation** *all offensives suffer in the long run* **or by means of help from abroad . . . It is the natural law of the moral world that a nation that finds itself on the brink of an abyss will try to save itself by any means.** [my emphasis]

> *(On War*, p. 483)

In the same vein, Machiavelli argues that agreements made under duress are not binding:

> There is no disgrace in disregarding promises that have been exacted by force. Promises touching public affairs, and which have been given under the pressure of force, will always be disregarded when that force no longer exists, and this involves no dishonor.
>
> (Machiavelli, *The Discourses*, p. 529)

The wisdom of showing 'magnanimity in victory and good will in peace'[2] has of course been recognized in other classical works on strategy and war. After the setback suffered by the Spartans at Sphacteria/Pylos and before the final battle commenced, envoys to the Athenians argued that goodwill and magnanimity would bring their conflict to an end and lead to an enduring peace:

> If great enmities are ever to be really settled, we think it will be, not by the system of revenge and military success, and by forcing an opponent to swear to a treaty to his disadvantage, but when the more fortunate combatant waives these his privileges, to be guided by gentler feelings, conquers his rival in generosity, and accords peace on more moderate conditions than he expected. From that moment, instead of the debt of revenge which violence must entail, his adversary owes a debt of generosity to be paid in kind, and is inclined by honour to stand to his agreement.
>
> (Thucydides, *History of the Peloponnesian War*, Strassler (ed.), Book 4, Section 19, p. 233)

In a discussion of Roman decision-making, Machiavelli explains that their solution to war termination meant choosing between two extremes: since a unilateral diktat imposed by the victorious side would not work in the long run, the Romans chose either to eradicate, disperse, and enslave their defeated enemies – or to grant them generous terms worthy of equals. To illustrate this point, Machiavelli, quoting Livy, describes the Roman treatment of the defeated inhabitants of Privernum, whose revolt had recently been put down.

> The people of that town sent many citizens to ask pardon from the Senate . . . [When] one of the Senators asked one of them what punishment he thought the Privernati deserved . . . the man answered: 'That which they deserve who think themselves worthy of liberty.' To this the Consul replied: 'And if we should remit the

199

penalty to you, what sort of peace could we hope to have with you?'
To which he replied: 'If you grant a good one, loyal and lasting; if
a bad one, not very long.' Therefore the wiser part of the Senate
. . . said 'they had heard the voice of one who was free and a man,
and they did not believe it possible for any people, or even an individual, to remain longer in a painful condition than they must.
Peace would be sure where willing men had made it, and where
they tried to get servitude, they could not hope to have loyalty.'

(Machiavelli, The Discourses, pp. 390–391)

The Senate then granted Roman citizenship to the Privernati because
they had shown themselves worthy of this status in their noble and
honest reply. The Roman Senate's prudent and magnanimous treatment of Privernum stands in marked contrast to the Athenian popular
democracy's reaction to the revolt in Mytilene. In this case, the
Athenians brutally crushed the rebels in order to deter other members
of the Delian League from making a similar mistake. While the Romans
gained a loyal ally, the Athenians only fuelled Mytilene's resentment,
which ultimately led to another, successful, revolt by a coalition of
Athens' enemies.[3]

Clausewitz makes yet another important point that explains why the
result in modern war is never final. Before the French Revolution, most
wars of the *ancien régime* were conducted between professional armies of
limited size for limited interests. Under such conditions, once an army
had been defeated on the battlefield, given the moderate demands of the
victor, it was relatively easy to agree on peace terms. Since the wars of
the *ancien régime* did not directly involve the people, it would have been
difficult to mobilize a new army in time to be of use.

> **War . . . became solely the concern of the government . . .
> The means they had available were fairly well defined, and
> each could gauge the other side's potential in terms both of
> numbers and of time. War was thus deprived of its most
> dangerous feature – its tendency toward the extreme . . . No
> great expansion [of the armed forces] was feasible at the out-
> break of the war. Knowing the limits of the enemy's
> strength, men knew they were reasonably safe from total
> ruin; and being aware of their own limitations, they were
> compelled to restrict their own aims in turn . . .**

The conduct of war thus became a true game, in which the cards were dealt by time and accident. In its effect, it was a somewhat stronger form of diplomacy, a more forceful method of negotiation in which battles and sieges were the principal notes exchanged. Even the most ambitious ruler had no greater aims than to gain a number of advantages that could be exploited at the peace conference . . . Not only in its means, therefore, but also in its aims, war increasingly became limited to the fighting force itself . . .

(Clausewitz, *On War*, pp. 589–591)

The comfortable formality of limited war 'by the rules' was soon shattered by the new, harsh reality of war governed by the passions of the people:

Suddenly war again became the business of the people . . . The people became a participant in war; instead of governments and armies as heretofore, the full weight of the nation was thrown into the balance. The resources and efforts now available for use surpassed all conventional limits; nothing now impeded the vigor with which war could be waged . . . War, untrammeled by any conventional restraints, had broken loose in all its elemental fury. This was due to the people's new share in these great affairs of state . . . .

(*On War*, pp. 592–593) (See also the discussion in Chapter 10 above, pp. 121–123.)

Once the energy and passions of the people had been mobilized, and major rather than secondary interests were at stake, the quick resolution of a war became much more difficult. Defeat could not be made acceptable to the losing side as long as the people refused to accept the results as final. After all, an impassioned citizenry could continue a war with or without their government's backing.

The stubborn resistance of the Spaniards . . . showed what could be accomplished by arming the people and by insurrection . . . The Russians showed us that one often attains one's greatest strength in the heart of one's own

> country . . . **All these cases have shown what an enormous
> contribution the heart and temper of a nation can make to
> the sum total of the politics, war potential, and fighting
> strength . . .**
>
> (*On War*, pp. 220)

Thus, although the wars of the French Revolution and in particular, Napoleon, seemed to make war more brutal and decisive, the mobilization of the people on both sides paradoxically impeded efforts to translate such victories into enduring results. Consequently, the politicians of the nineteenth and twentieth centuries found that, in order to wage war successfully, they had to mobilize the support of the masses, which could not always be reined in once unleashed. By contrast, the leaders of the *ancien régime*, who were not dependent upon the will of the people, could initiate as well as terminate wars according to their own decisions.

Only one chapter in *On War*, 'Purpose and Means in War', is at least partially dedicated to a direct examination of issues related to war termination. (Found in Chapter 2 of Book 1, this chapter also includes a discussion of *the principle of destruction* and the possibility or impossibility of *winning a war without fighting*.) The first three pages of this chapter begin with a succinct and thought-provoking, yet incomplete, discussion of at least four issues related to war termination. More so than elsewhere in *On War*, Clausewitz confines himself to an excessively rational, 'linear' approach while ignoring the 'non-linear' human dimensions that dominate the process. Indeed, human perceptions and misperceptions, fears, and wishful thinking as well as the psychology of tough bargaining undermine the entire rational basis of Clausewitz's concept of war termination.

In his treatment of this subject, Clausewitz concentrates on four interrelated issues:

(1) the three objectives that must be attained to end a war (pp. 90–91);
(2) the theoretical and actual grounds for making peace (pp. 90–91);
(3) the so-called rational calculus of war (p. 92);
(4) the optimal timing for the termination of war (the equilibrium analysis of war termination) (p. 92).

(1) In this chapter, as in the preceding one, Clausewitz still alternates

between the object of war in the abstract (p. 91), '**the strict law of inherent necessity**' (p. 91) or the '**pure concept of war**' – and war termination in reality. The issue first discussed by Clausewitz concerns the three objectives that must be fulfilled to disarm the enemy and compel him to make peace on one's own terms.

(a) *Destruction of the enemy's forces.* '**. . . They must be put in such a condition that they can no longer carry on the fight**' (p. 90).

(b) *Occupation of the enemy's country.* If this is not accomplished, then the enemy could renew the hostilities in the interior of the country '**perhaps with allied help**' (p. 90).

(c) *Breaking the enemy's will to continue fighting.* Of the three objectives, Clausewitz considers this to be the most important. For as the Napoleonic Wars amply demonstrated, the defeat of the enemy's army and even the occupation of his country will not result in a final peace agreement as long as the enemy's government and population have the will to go on fighting (p. 90).

Under most circumstances, though, the destruction of the enemy's army and the occupation of his country should bring the enemy to the negotiation table. The two objectives are often connected: that is, the defeat of the enemy's armed forces will naturally lead to the occupation of his country. But this is not always the case. Sometimes, the enemy withdraws to avoid battle, thereby allowing his territory to be occupied without the destruction of his armed forces.[4]

While the aim of each side, *in theory*, is to disarm the enemy in order to accomplish the war's political purpose, *in reality*, as Clausewitz suggests, many peace treaties have been concluded long before one of the belligerents has been rendered powerless. Oftentimes, particularly if one's enemy is much stronger, a resounding victory of this sort is not even possible. In theory, of course, a war between two sides unequal in strength seems futile, but in reality, it makes sense because the stronger side cannot always win at *a reasonable cost*.

(2) Theoretically, wars can be terminated following the defeat and disarming of one belligerent, but Clausewitz knows that this is rarely true in practice. '**War is often far removed from the pure concept postulated by theory. Inability to carry on the struggle, can in practice be replaced by two other grounds for making peace: the**

203

first is the *improbability of victory*; the second is its *unacceptable cost*' (*On War*, p. 91, my emphasis). Making peace because victory is improbable occurs when military 'gridlock' prevents either side from winning. Since the prevailing stalemate means that the war has no effective military solution, one or both sides should be amenable to negotiating a peaceful solution. The second reason for making peace is not that victory cannot be achieved but that the cost of achieving it is too high. This brings Clausewitz to his discussion of the 'rational calculus of war'.

(3) The improbability of achieving victory or the unacceptable costs of winning should lead to a peaceful resolution long before any of the belligerents can disarm his opponent. Consequently, the decision to terminate a war ought ideally or normatively to be determined by the costs and benefits of a war as indicated by Clausewitz's 'rational calculus of war'.

> Of even greater influence on the decision to make peace is the consciousness of all the effort that has already been made and of the efforts yet to come. Since war is not an act of senseless passion but is controlled by its political object, the value of the object [i.e., the expected benefit] must determine the sacrifices [i.e., costs] to be made for it in *magnitude* and also in *duration*. Once the expenditure of the effort exceeds the value of the political object, the object must be renounced and peace must follow.
>
> (*On War*, p. 92)

A schematic representation of the rational calculus of war is shown in Figure 14.1.

Figure 14.1 demonstrates that as long as the belligerent's position is located within the area of triangle ACD, at points 1, 2, or 3, for example, the continuation of the war makes sense because his benefits exceed his costs. If, on the other hand, at least one of the belligerents is within the area of triangle ABC, at points 4, 5, or 6, for example, the costs of continuing the war exceed any possible benefits, so he should end the war as soon as possible. A position on line AC indicates that the costs and benefits are equal: in this situation, the decision whether to quit the war or to continue fighting will depend on factors such as anticipated trends in the relative strengths of the belligerents or the importance of the interests at stake.

FIGURE 14.1
CLAUSEWITZ'S RATIONAL CALCULUS OF WAR

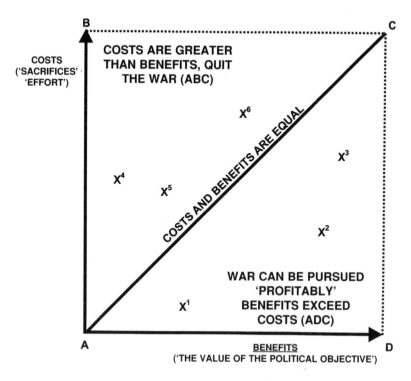

While the rational calculus of war makes sense in theory, it is far more difficult to follow in practice. (Only a few of the many reasons for this will be mentioned here. See also Chapters 7 and 8 above.) In the first place, it is no simple task to quantify the costs and benefits of a war. How many lives should be sacrificed in a fight for freedom or a fight to maintain the balance of power? What price should be paid for the conquest of territory or the preservation of national honor? What price will be paid by future generations? What are the short- and long-term economic costs? What are the peace terms, if any, offered by the enemy?

Furthermore, as the war unfolds, earlier estimates of the political, social, and economic costs and benefits change constantly. As the amount of effort invested grows with each day, it becomes progressively harder to calculate rationally, especially under the pressure of enemy demands. In this context, Clausewitz comments: **'The original political objects** can greatly alter during the course of the war and many finally change entirely since they are influenced by events and their probable consequences' (*On War*, p. 92). The dynamic, reciprocal, and dialectic nature of war wreaks havoc on static calculations. For example, all belligerents during the outbreak of the First World War expected that the war would be relatively short and entail reasonable costs relative to the anticipated benefits. But as the war progressed, the objective changed from the desire to alter the European balance of power, from border and territorial modification to a question of survival. After six months and hundreds of thousands of casualties, how could the German military and the Kaiser turn to the population and say, 'Sorry, the war did not turn out as we expected: the costs are too high and we must now quit the war as quickly as possible.'[5] When the very survival of the political leaders is at stake, it is that much more difficult, especially in a democracy, to admit to such colossal miscalculations. A more typical reaction is to raise the stakes, to invest more in the hope of obtaining ever more elusive benefits. The original political objectives of the war (e.g., territorial aggrandizement; defeat of an enemy; support of an ally) are thus often imperceptibly overshadowed by *personal political objectives.* Although Clausewitz recognizes that political leaders can make mistakes and go to war for their personal interests (*On War*, pp. 606–607), the 'rational calculus of war' is based on the false assumption that nations or leaders are always fighting for the national interest alone. (In fact, personal and national interests often become intertwined.)

Wishful thinking, wounded national and personal pride, inaccurate intelligence estimates, excessive faith in the performance of new weapons, and the expectation of outside help or of a decline in the enemy's morale may all suggest that even if present costs are exorbitant – the next offensive or the next phase of the war will nevertheless bring victory within reach. Despite staggering costs and the possibility of negligible benefits at best, the First World War dragged on from 1914 to 1918 until it was decided by the collapse of one side. This is how a war that begins as a 'calculated' or 'rational' limited enterprise often ends as an unmitigated disaster. (The Peloponnesian War, the American Civil War, and the Second World War are also outstanding examples, although the pitfalls of inaccurate initial calculations and the inability to control the course of events exist in almost all wars.) To this we can add that it might be relatively easier to make rational strategic decisions in limited war or military interventions involving only secondary or tertiary interests than in total war, which involves the state's vital interests and survival.

The passions involved, the desire to recoup investments made thus far, and the irresistible allure of wishful thinking all doom efforts to conduct war rationally. Even if the original calculations are rational, the war will become increasingly impervious to a rational approach as it progresses. When nations initiate wars, they often perceive their position to be somewhere within the borders of triangle ACD; but by the mid-course or final phases of the war, they are likely to find themselves in triangle ABC. Does this mean that Clausewitz's 'rational calculus of war' is an irrelevant exercise? Not entirely. Since Clausewitz knows that war cannot be waged according to purely rational calculations (see Chapters 7–8 above), his advice must be seen as a normative ideal advocating that responsible political leaders try to minimize the chance of continuing a politically senseless war. Finally, the decision to terminate a war – as in all other actions in war – also depends on the actions of the enemy. Even if one of the belligerents has, through rational calculations, decided that it is time to make peace, he may be prevented from doing so unless his opponent agrees or offers him reasonable terms. Unfortunately, that which one side deems rational is often not considered so by the other. Thus, Clausewitz raises the question of interaction between the two sides in reaching a decision on the 'optimal' point for termination of a war.

(4) When neither of the belligerents can bring the war to a decisive military conclusion (which is true of most wars), both sides must end the conflict through negotiations. If so, how do the respective positions of the belligerents affect the choice of the 'ideal' time to begin negotiations? The process of war termination reflects each participant's rational and irrational calculations and assessment of the other side's ability to continue fighting. In a mutual effort, they will have to end the war through interaction both on the battlefield and at the bargaining table. Clausewitz summarizes this process as follows:

We see then that if one side cannot completely disarm the other, the desire for peace on either side will rise and fall with the probability of further success and the amount of

effort these would require. If such incentives were of equal strength on both sides, the two would resolve their disputes by meeting halfway. If the incentive grows on one side, it should diminish on the other. Peace will result so long as their sum total is sufficient – though the side that feels the lesser urge for peace will naturally get the better bargain.

(*On War*, p. 92)

The give and take of this bargaining process is described in the following graphic presentation, Figure 14.2, which illustrates why the process of ending a war is so delicate and complicated.

FIGURE 14.2
THE OPTIMAL POINT FOR WAR TERMINATION

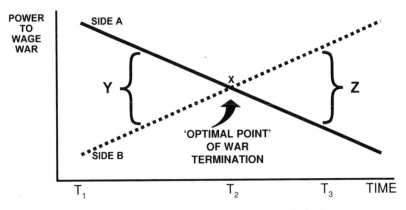

According to Clausewitz, when the belligerents' ability to wage war is about the same (at the 'optimal point' of war termination, point X at time T_2), they should have equal incentives to end the war. At all other points, as at T_1 or T_3, their unequal incentives give the stronger side the advantage at the bargaining table. (For example, at point T_1, Side A is stronger than Side B as indicated by power gap Y; at point T_3, Side B is stronger than side A as indicated by Gap Z.) In the preceding citation, Clausewitz assumes that the weaker or losing side always has a stronger incentive to make peace, which puts him in a weaker bargaining position. But this is not necessarily true. That which appears patently clear in a graph quickly loses its simplicity in the real world of human misperceptions and dynamic interaction.

In the first place, the perceptions of the warring parties rarely coincide: they usually differ in general outlook, available intelligence, hopes and expectations. The two sides may hold very different views of the same situation at the same time (see Figure 14.3). Therefore, even if both belligerents appear to be equally powerful to an objective outside observer (as in point X at T_2 on Figure 14.2), Sides A and B do not usually perceive each other in this way.

FIGURE 14.3
TWO DIFFERENT VIEWS OF THE SAME SITUATION

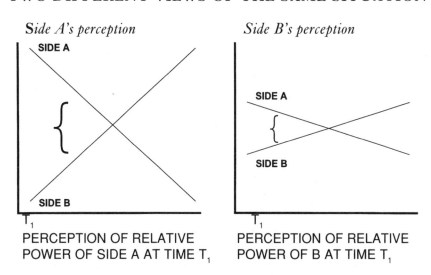

Side A's perception

SIDE A

SIDE B

T_1

PERCEPTION OF RELATIVE
POWER OF SIDE A AT TIME T_1

Side B's perception

SIDE A

SIDE B

T_1

PERCEPTION OF RELATIVE
POWER OF B AT TIME T_1

Only through negotiations can a mediator bring the perceptions of Sides A and B closer to one other so that an agreement can be reached. The exception is of course a decisive defeat, which removes all ambiguity from the situation. Tracing the power trends portrayed in Figure 14.2 allows us better to understand some of the paradoxes and obstacles inherent in the process of war termination. We can then readily see why the so-called 'optimal point' of war termination is not a true point of 'equilibrium', and why it is not the point where both sides have equal incentives to end the war.

As shown in Figure 14.2, point X is the 'optimal point' in time to terminate the war because each side's power is *momentarily* equal. Point X is, in reality, only *a point of intersection*, not of stable equilibrium. What matters most in a proper analysis of the adversaries' relative bargaining power is *not a point in time but rather dynamic trends*. If both sides have a reliable picture of trends in the war, then point X at T_2 shows a downward trend in Side A's power and an upward trend in Side B's power (see Figure 14.2). (A good example would be the position of the Allies versus that of the Axis powers from early to mid-1943.) Side B already knows that if current trends continue, the power projection by time T_3 should be squarely in its favor. Why, then, should Side B agree to terminate the war at time T_2 if it soon expects to be in a stronger position from which to dictate more favorable peace terms? And if the trends are as clear to both sides at time T_1 and power gap Y (which clearly favors Side A), then Side A should make a peace offer to Side B while Side A is still ahead. There are, however, many problems with this supposition. Although unmistakable when illustrated in Figure 14.2 at time T_1, these trends are rarely as clear in reality. Often, the winning side (Side A in this case) does indeed identify its advantage over Side B but erroneously considers it to be permanent or long term. This explains why Napoleon, the Confederacy in the American Civil War, Germany in the First and Second World Wars, and Japan in the Second World War had no interest in offering their opponents generous peace terms. Human behavior is not that rational. Suffering from what the Japanese called *the victory disease*, the victor is typically intoxicated by his recent success. Those who have enjoyed military success, particularly in a war's early phases, are seldom in a frame of mind to entertain the notion that they could suffer a serious setback. By the time they realize the actual long-range direction of the relative power trends, they will already be in a weaker bargaining position. In the meantime, at time T_1 and power gap Y, the weaker Side B will have a strong incentive to negotiate for peace because his impending good fortune may not be as obvious to him as it is on Figure 14.2. (Trends in the relative power positions as depicted in Figure 14.2 can normally be reconstructed with any degree of accuracy *only in hindsight*.[6])

In any event, Side B may not be very motivated to negotiate for two reasons. The first is that if he appears eager, he will weaken his bargaining position. As Clausewitz reminds us, **'If the incentive grows on one side it should diminish on the other'** (*On War*, p. 92). The second is that, as the weaker party, he wants time to improve his position on the battlefield in order to secure a better bargaining position. Paradoxically, therefore, the weaker, losing side, which *should* have the greater incentive to negotiate, feels compelled to continue fighting to appear stronger. (This may have been the Allied position in 1914–16 or in 1939–40.) This is even more likely to occur if the opponent suffers from a 'victory disease', which prevents him from offering reasonable terms to the weaker side. In this way, the desire to end a war by demonstrating one's resolve to continue fighting becomes a self-negating prophecy. Much of course depends on the conditions offered or demands made by the victor as well as on the importance of the interests and political aims involved. Clausewitz comments on this important set of 'variables' in Chapter 1 of Book 1:

> **The smaller the penalty you demand from your opponent, the less you can expect him to try to deny it to you; the smaller the effort he makes, the less you need to make yourself. Moreover, the more modest your political aim, the less importance you attach to it and the less reluctantly you will abandon it if you must.**
>
> (*On War*, p. 81)

He returns to this point in Chapter 2 of Book 1:

> **Not every war need be fought until one side collapses. When the motives and tensions are slight, we can imagine that the very faintest prospect of defeat might be enough to cause one side to yield. If, from the very start, the other side feels that this is probable, it will obviously concentrate on bringing about the probability rather than take the long way round and totally defeat the enemy.**
>
> (*On War*, p. 91)

There is also an implied correlation between the type of war and the possibility of ending it quickly or slowly. Clausewitz concludes that it is much easier to end a war in which both sides have limited interests and political objectives. On the other hand, a total or unlimited war in which the vital interests and survival of the belligerent states are at stake is obviously far more difficult to terminate. Of course, the political interests of both sides are not necessarily of comparable intensity or degree. Thus, although the Vietnam War was limited from the American point of view, it was not at all limited for the North Vietnamese. In this case, the militarily stronger side had a weaker incentive to continue fighting while its enemy was ready to pay a higher price. This explains why the war and the ensuing peace negotiations lasted so long. Furthermore, the Korean and the Vietnam Wars also represented the ideological clash of communism and the free world, an important ideological dimension that made their termination that much more difficult.

The prospects for a smoothly negotiated end to a war shrink if both sides reach a stalemate (see Figure 14.4). In this case, each fears that making concessions will imply weakness (e.g., the stalemated war on the Western Front from 1914 onward; the Korean War from April 1951 to June 1953; or the Iran–Iraq War).

FIGURE 14.4
A STALEMATED WAR

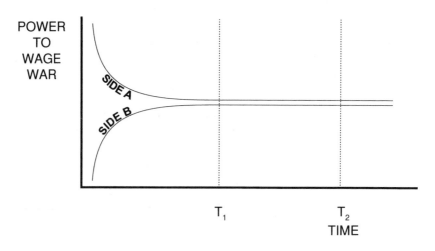

In hindsight, it appears that the 'optimal time' to make peace is at T_1, when the power trends do not favor either side (for example, after the Battle of the Marne or in the Korean War in June 1951). The problem is that (1) the warring parties do not usually know when they have reached a stable equilibrium point; and (2) both sides continue fighting in order not to appear too eager to negotiate. Each hopes that the stalemate will somehow be broken in the next offensive. As one might expect, the result is that the war continues apace even if neither side has much to gain. When both sides finally recognize (at T_2) that the war has deteriorated into a prolonged, indecisive stalemate, they are well beyond the original stable equilibrium point and more valuable resources have been squandered. The incentive to make peace under such conditions depends on the simultaneous recognition that each side is too weak to win. This rarely occurs during an early phase of the war, when both sides are generally well supplied and hoping for victory. Usually, it is only after much time and effort has been invested and both sides have exhausted their resources that they will begin negotiations.[7] (See Figure 14.7, p. 419.)

15

Deception, Surprise, and Intelligence

All warfare is based on deception.
Sun Tzu, *The Art of War*, p. 66

Plans and orders issued for appearances only, false reports designed to confuse the enemy . . . should not be considered as a significant independent field of action at the disposal of the commander.
Clausewitz, *On War*, pp. 202–203

Attack where he is unprepared: sally out when he does not expect you.
Sun Tzu, *The Art of War*, p. 69

It is very rare therefore that one state surprises another, either by an attack or by preparations for war.
Clausewitz, *On War*, p. 199

Know the enemy, know yourself; your victory will never be endangered.
Sun Tzu, *The Art of War*, p. 129

Many intelligence reports in war are contradictory; even more are false, and most are uncertain . . .
Clausewitz, *On War*, p. 117

This chapter examines three main topics – deception, surprise, and intelligence. The first two can be seen as subcategories of the last. Deception and surprise are closely related, as deception provides one of the most effective ways to achieve surprise. Surprise and deception in turn can presumably be avoided or prevented by timely, reliable intelligence.

Deception is one of the earliest and most basic defining characteristics of war. Sun Tzu deemed it a key factor long before the beginning of organized intelligence, and it was, in the earlier history of war, even more critical than in modern times. As perhaps the most ancient force-multiplier in history, deception before the premodern era was primarily left to the improvisation of the military commander – that is, to the creative genius and inspiration of a single individual. In the twentieth century, however, as war became inordinately complex and depended on the extensive use of real-time communications, deception for the most part had to be carefully prepared by specialized organizations.

For Sun Tzu and Machiavelli, war, and often politics as well, could be equated with deception. This cannot be said of Clausewitz and Jomini, who pointed out the occasional operational utility of deception but did not by any means consider it pivotal. In the early nineteenth century, success on the battlefield was decided by the concentration of superior forces at the decisive point. In the age of mass mobilization and large-scale battles, deception was perceived as a tool of no more than marginal importance. Neither Clausewitz nor Jomini foresaw the possibility of achieving surprise on the higher operational and strategic levels of land warfare. (Major surprises could, however, be achieved at sea as demonstrated by Nelson.)

Sun Tzu also shows the greatest appreciation for the role of intelligence, perhaps because he examines war from a wider perspective embracing the political and military aspects involved as well as the pre-war stages. Clausewitz shows scant appreciation for intelligence because he is concerned mainly with its value on the tactical and operational levels; indeed, the lack of real-time communications and the fluid nature of battle in his time did make intelligence unreliable in most cases.

It is the role of intelligence and the ability to obtain reliable information in real time that has changed the most since the classical works on strategy and war were written. This is a recent phenomenon, since the critical part played by intelligence in war and the establishment of immense intelligence bureaucracies began in earnest during the First World War. To this day, this subject has not been properly integrated into a modern theory of war although Handel and Ferris have made an attempt to show the influence of developments in modern intelligence on the theory of the art of war.[1] Thus, although modern intelligence has considerably altered the roles of uncertainty, friction, command, leadership, and 'luck' in war, the classical works that are the subject of this book still continue to determine much of the thought on these issues.

216

DECEPTION

> ... the most successful soldier will always
> be the man who ... carefully consulting
> his own means makes his attack not so
> much by open and regular approaches as
> by seizing the opportunity of the moment,
> and these stratagems, which do the greatest
> service to our friends by most completely
> deceiving our enemies, have the most
> brilliant name in war. [Brasidas before the
> attack on Amphipolis, summer 422]
>
> Thucydides, *The History of the
> Peloponnesian War*, Book 5, Section 9,
> pp. 306–307

> Nor do I believe that force alone will be
> enough, but fraud alone will be enough.
>
> Machiavelli, *Discourses*, p. 357

In *The Art of War*, the principal method of concentrating one's troops
while forcing the enemy to disperse his, is that of deception. (Deception
and diversion are not ends in themselves; they are the *means* of achieving surprise. And surprise is the ability to concentrate troops where the
opponent does not expect them.) By enabling the deceiver to conceal his
actual objectives, successful deception persuades the enemy to concentrate his forces in the wrong places, thereby weakening himself at the
decisive point of engagement.[2]

As any content analysis would quickly show, deception is the most
frequently discussed theme in *The Art of War*.[3] Sun Tzu's definition of
deception is very broad indeed: it includes both active and passive
measures, from elaborate deception plans, simple baits, and diversion,
to secrecy and concealment. According to Sun Tzu, deception must be
employed at all times (before and during war) and on all levels, whether
diplomatic (to drive a wedge between the enemy and his allies), political
(to sow the seeds of suspicion and discord in his army through political
subversion), or military.[4] (See Chart 5 between pp. 388 and 389.) The
starting point for such action must be a thorough understanding of
the enemy's innermost thoughts, expectations, and plans – and this is

derived from good intelligence and penetration of the enemy's camp by one's own spies.

. . . When capable, feign incapacity, when active, inactivity.

When near, make it appear that you are far away; when far away, that you are near.

Offer the enemy a bait to lure him; feign disorder and strike him.

(Sun Tzu, The Art of War, p. 66; also pp. 92–93)

Pretend inferiority and encourage his arrogance.

(Sun Tzu, The Art of War, p. 67)

[Ho Yen-hsi] I make the enemy see my strengths as weaknesses and my weaknesses as strengths . . .

(Sun Tzu, The Art Of War, p. 67)

Sun Tzu is acutely sensitive to the psychological factors that enable the enemy's perceptions to be manipulated; he knows that those convinced of their own superiority are usually oblivious to the need to be on guard against deception. Since most successful deception reinforces the existing beliefs and wishful thinking of the intended victim, the ruse most frequently mentioned by Sun Tzu is that of feigning weakness.[5] Such 'good news' is always welcomed by one's enemy, who is gradually lulled into a false sense of security. According to Sun Tzu, deception and diversionary operations on the battlefield should be carried out through controlled actions such as simulated disorder, withdrawals, and noise on or near the battlefield that can be directly observed by the enemy. On a higher level, false information can be 'fed' to the enemy through double agents or by what he terms expendable agents – those who are deliberately supplied with fabricated information and are then allowed to be captured by the enemy (Sun Tzu, *The Art of War*, p. 146).

Sun Tzu is definitely concerned about the need to avoid being deceived, but unfortunately cannot advise military leaders more specifically than this: '*When he pretends to flee, do not pursue*' or '*Do not gobble proffered baits*' (Sun Tzu, *The Art of War*, p. 109).[6] While this is good general advice, how is a military leader to know, in the heat of battle, whether the enemy is really retreating or only pretending to withdraw? And if he is unsure, should he assume that it is a ruse? Such an interpretation of Sun Tzu's statements can be risky because it re-inforces the predisposition of many field commanders to err on the side of caution and make worst-case assumptions regarding the enemy's intentions.

After all, Sun Tzu and (even more so) Clausewitz admire the commander who is not afraid to take high risks. As a result, such pre-cepts are of dubious practical value, for even skilled practitioners of the art of deception cannot avoid being ensnared by their enemy's carefully devised stratagems.

Similarly, while Sun Tzu warns of the danger posed by double agents and spies in general, he gives no reliable advice on how to distinguish between *bona fide* spies on the one hand and enemy-controlled agents on the other. Indeed, the persistent difficulty involved in attempting to expose deception is what makes it such an effective weapon.

In accordance with Sun Tzu's broader definition of war, a vital part of all deception operations takes place *before* the outbreak of hostilities. This type of political and diplomatic deception, which sabotages the enemy's alliances and internal cohesion, for example, is today referred to as disinformation and a fifth column.

> *[Chang Yu] Sometimes drive a wedge between a sovereign and his ministries; on other occasions separate his allies from him. Make them mutually suspicious so that they drift apart. Then you can plot against them.*
>
> (Sun Tzu, *The Art of War*, p. 69)

> *[Tu Yu] Do not allow your enemies to get together . . . Look into the matters of his alliances and cause them to be severed and dis-solved.*
>
> (Sun Tzu, *The Art of War*, p. 78)

> *[Chia Lin] Plans and projects for harming the enemy are not confined to any one method. Sometimes entice his wise virtuous men away so that he has no counsellors. Or send treacherous people to his country to wreck his administration. Sometimes use cunning deceptions to alienate his ministers from the sovereign. Or send skilled craftsmen to encourage his people to exhaust their wealth. Or present him with licentious musicians and dancers to change his customs. Or give him beautiful women to bewilder him.*
>
> (Sun Tzu, *The Art of War*, pp. 113–114)

The weight Sun Tzu assigns to pre-war deception operations and political subversion of all types also helps to explain his belief in the feasibility of attacking the enemy's plans at their inception, disrupting his alliances and resolving problems before they arise. (See *The Art of War*, particularly Chapter 3.)

A good deception plan, particularly on the operational and tactical levels, allows for quick adaptation to changing circumstances, even if it has been discovered. This capacity to continuously form new combinations is an important part of the psychology of deception that enables the deceiver to stay one step ahead of his opponent.

To keep the opponent perpetually off balance, Sun Tzu develops an elegant paradigm that combines operational or tactical maneuvers and deception. In its basic form, this type of action/deception paradigm calls for the simultaneous use of two independent but coordinated forces – one that pins down or diverts the enemy, and a second that delivers the decisive blow against a weak, now vulnerable point on the enemy's flanks. The first type of force, *cheng*, is various translated as *normal* or *direct* (trans. by Giles, Griffith); *straightforward* (Sawyer); regular (Huang); or *orthodox method* (Cleary). The second, known as *ching*, is translated as *extraordinary* or *indirect* (Giles, Griffith); *surprise* (Sawyer); *irregular* (Huang); and *unorthodox method* (Cleary).

Sun Tzu explains this manuever-cum-deception paradigm in Chapter 5 of *The Art of War*, Sections 3 to 12.[7] In the opening statement, Section 3 establishes that the proper use of direct and indirect forces is the key explanation for victory: *'That the army is certain to sustain the enemy's attack without suffering defeat is due to operations of the extraordinary and the normal forces'* (Sun Tzu, *The Art of War*, p. 91). As it stands, the opening statement is so subtle that it does not readily convey Sun Tzu's deeper meaning. This discussion of the *direct* and *indirect* (or the normal and extraordinary) must be understood as a reference to *two similarly structured forces that perform different functions*. However, these forces are also interchangeable, meaning that each can perform the function of the other when the deception as originally planned must be adapted to new circumstances. The commentators in *The Art of War* explain the advantages of this approach:

> *[Ho Yen-hsi]: I make the enemy conceive my normal force to be the extraordinary and the extraordinary to be the normal.*

Moreover, the normal may become the extraordinary and vice-versa.

(Sun Tzu, *The Art of War*, p. 91)

[T'ai Tsung]: A chi manoeuvre may be cheng, if we make the enemy look upon it as cheng; then our real attack will be ch'i and vice versa. The whole secret lies in confusing the enemy, so that he cannot fathom our real intent.

(Sun Tzu, *The Art of War*, trans. Giles, p. 35)

The next statement explains that this method allows the commander to *concentrate strength against weakness*: *'Troops thrown against the enemy as grindstone against eggs is an example of solid acting upon a void'* (Sun Tzu, *The Art of War*, p. 91). In Section 5, Sun Tzu then explains *how* the forces are used: *'Generally in battle, use the normal forces to engage; use the extraordinary to win'* (Sun Tzu, *The Art of War*, p. 91).

This flexibility allows the skillful commander access to an infinite number of combinations that can be revised continuously, thereby creating new and unpredictable situations to confuse the enemy (Sections 6 to 12).

(6) Now the resources of those skilled in the use of extraordinary forces are infinite as the heavens and earth, as inexhaustible as the flow of great rivers.

(7) For they end and recommence; cyclical, as are the movements of the sun and moon. They die away and are reborn; recurrent, as are the passing seasons.

(Sun Tzu, *The Art of War*, p. 91)

In Sections 8, 9, and 10, the infinite number of combinations that can be derived from musical tones, the primary colors, and various flavors (see also above, pp. 29–30) are used as similes for the innumerable combinations that are possible in war. In Sections 11 and 12, Sun Tzu returns to this idea:

(11) In battle, there are only the normal and extraordinary forces, but their combinations are limitless; none can comprehend them all.

(12) For these two forces are mutually reproductive; their

221

interaction as endless as that of interlocked rings. Who can determine where one ends and the other begins.

(Sun Tzu, *The Art of War*, p. 92)

The elegance of this scheme lies in the fact that even when the distraction or diversion has been exposed (which is rare in any case), it can still remain effective if quickly reversed. In other words, if the object of the deception discovers that the forces he is engaging in the first phase of battle have been intended as a distraction (the *cheng* force) and that the decisive attack (the *chi* force) is actually directed at his flank, he will switch his main force to protect his flank. Having observed this reaction, the deceiver can exploit the new situation to his advantage by changing the center of gravity – by changing his *cheng* forces into *chi*, and his *chi* into *cheng*. The 'discovery' of the deception plan thus causes the deceived party to change his plans, but in doing so, he still falls into a similar trap.[8]

This is a brilliant scheme if it can be implemented. As always in war, this is easier said than done. Much depends upon the deceiver's flexibility and capacity for improvisation, coordination, and good timing – and upon the deceived opponent's intelligence, caution, calculations, and improvised reactions. Should the adversary remain calm and level-headed despite being surprised, he could, through a balanced response, upset the deceiver's plans. Moreover, if all of the belligerents happen to be familiar with Sun Tzu's paradigm, such a deception may lose some of its potential.

It must be emphasized that this type of deception is most easily implemented on the tactical level, where the forces can be controlled by direct observation. It is more difficult on the operational level, and extremely difficult on the strategic level, where the control and timing of such an operation is cumbersome and switching forces from one area to another is much slower. The higher the level of warfare, therefore, the better the intelligence (in battle, real-time intelligence) the deceiver requires about his opponent's perceptions and reaction to the proffered bait. This means that, ideally, the deceiver must penetrate the top echelons of the enemy's command

Naturally, the target of the deceiver might be planning his own stratagems and manipulating the would-be deceiver through the use of double agents, disinformation, and counter-deception. By letting it be known that he has 'fallen' for a deception plot, the victim can thus cause the deceiver's own plan to backfire. This *MAD Magazine* 'Spy vs. Spy' scenario or infinite regression of deception, counter-deception, and counter-counter-deception is practically immune to exposure.[9] Eventually, the impossibility of distinguishing between signals and noise casts doubt on all of the intelligence received by both sides.

Today, air reconnaissance, satellites, and other longer-range methods of observation have made such deception schemes less practicable, particularly on the higher operational and strategic levels. They are now likely to succeed only when the object of the deception has lost his capacity to conduct longer-range reconnaissance. This is not unheard of. Nazi Germany's loss of air-control and air-reconnaissance capabilities after 1943 proved decisive in the success of Allied deception operations. More recently, Saddam Hussein's total loss of air reconnaissance in the Gulf War allowed the United States and its allies to implement deception plans without fear of discovery. During the Second World War, the Allies used the basic idea of *cheng* and *chi* on the highest operational and strategic levels: the invasions of Sicily and Normandy (the *chi* maneuver) were presented to the Germans as the 'diversion' (the *cheng*) when they were actually the main attack. Through Operation Mincemeat (one of the deception cover plans for the invasion of Sicily) as well as through their Double-Cross agents before the invasion of Normandy, the British allowed the Germans to 'discover' that these invasions were only diversions for the supposedly planned attack on Kalamata and Sardinia, and the attack on Pas de Calais. The difference between the Allied deception and Sun Tzu's paradigm is that, given the enormous scale of the operations, there was no possibility of turning the *cheng* into the *chi* (and vice-versa) should the Germans learn the truth. Moreover, the Allies (i.e., the British) carried Sun Tzu's paradigm even further. They presented the Germans with two forces, a *cheng* (in Sicily and Normandy) and a *chi* (in Sardinia, Kalamata, and Pas de Calais) but in this case, the *chi* forces were purely fictional. The Germans therefore reacted to a *chi* force that did not even exist. In a system that Sun Tzu would see as perfectly fitting his own theories, the Allies were able to achieve this because of their superior intelligence, particularly the Double-Cross System and ULTRA, which gave them excellent access to the innermost decisions of the German High Command.[10]

Clausewitz, however, puts little faith in the value of diversion and deception, which he sees as the last resort of the weak and desperate, not as the weapon of choice for all:

> To prepare a sham action with sufficient thoroughness to impress an enemy requires a considerable expenditure of time and effort, and the costs increase with the scale of the deception. Normally they call for more than can be spared, and consequently so-called strategic feints rarely have the desired effect. It is dangerous, in fact, to use substantial forces over any length of time merely to create an illusion; there is always the risk that nothing will be gained and that the troops deployed will not be available when they are needed.
>
> (Clausewitz, *On War*, p. 203)

> Plans and orders issued for appearances only, fake reports designed to confuse the enemy, etc. – have as a rule so little strategic value that they are used only if a ready-made opportunity presents itself. They should not be considered as a significant independent field of action at the disposal of the commander.
>
> (Clausewitz, *On War*, pp. 202–203)

> The weaker the forces that are at the disposal of the supreme commander, the more appealing the use of cunning becomes. In a state of weakness and insignificance, when prudence, judgment and ability no longer suffice, cunning may well appear the only hope. The bleaker the situation, with everything concentrating on a single desperate attempt, the more readily cunning is joined to daring. Released from all future considerations, and liberated from thoughts of later retribution, boldness and cunning will be free to augment each other to the point of concentrating a faint glimmer of hope into a single beam of light which may yet kindle a flame.
>
> (Clausewitz, *On War*, p. 203; see also p. 284)

It appears that the opinions of Clausewitz and Sun Tzu on the value of deception could not be further apart. How can Clausewitz's lack of interest in deception be explained? Once again, much of the answer lies in the level of analysis. Sun Tzu advocates using deception on all levels, including the highest political-strategic and operational levels, where it can be very effective; Clausewitz, however, analyses the utility of deception (or cunning as he calls it) primarily from the lower operational and tactical vantage points, where it is not only less certain but also less effective.

It must be remembered that Clausewitz's principal method of winning battles was through the concentration of superior force at the decisive point. This was the most important lesson of the Napoleonic wars. The use of diversions – the simplest and most common form of deception – inevitably reduced the number of troops available for the main effort; and given the difficulties in communication and control at the time, diversion operations served only to disperse one's troops without the certainty that they would succeed in deceiving the enemy. It was quite possible that the enemy might not even notice the diversion or that he might expose it as such. Thus, Clausewitz believed that it was preferable to secure victory by concentrating one's own troops.[11]

Interestingly enough, this is one of the few issues on which Clausewitz and Jomini are in full agreement. In almost identical language, Jomini states:

> However great may be the temptation to undertake such operations [i.e., diversions] as those enumerated, it must be constantly borne in mind, that they are always secondary in importance and that the essential thing is to be successful at the decisive points. A multiplication of detachments must, therefore, be avoided.
>
> (Jomini, *The Art of War*, p. 221)

> I understand by diversions to mean those secondary operations carried out at a distance from the principal zone of operations, at the extremities of a theater of war, upon the success of which it is sometimes foolishly supposed the whole campaign depends.
>
> (Jomini, *The Art of War*, p. 218)[12]

SURPRISE

> If we always knew the enemy's intentions beforehand, we should always, even with inferior forces, be superior to him.
>
> Frederick the Great[13]

In addition to discounting the importance of deception (which is the best means of surprising the enemy), Clausewitz is convinced that surprise on the strategic and higher operational levels is practically impossible.

> While the wish to achieve surprise is common and, indeed, indispensable, and while it is true that it will never be completely ineffective, it is equally true that by its very nature surprise can rarely be *outstandingly* successful. It would be a mistake, therefore, to regard surprise as a key element of success in war. The principle is highly attractive in theory, but in practice it is often held up by the friction of the whole machine.

> Basically, surprise is a tactical device, simply because in tactics, time and space are limited in scale. Therefore in strategy surprise becomes more feasible the closer it occurs to the tactical realm, and more difficult, the more it approaches the higher levels of policy.

> Preparations for war usually take months. Concentrating troops at their main assembly points generally requires the installation of supply dumps and depots, as well as considerable troop movements, whose purpose can be guessed soon enough.

> It is very rare therefore that one state surprises another, either by an attack or by preparations for war . . . Cases in which such surprises lead to major results are very rare. From this we may conclude how considerable are the inherent difficulties.
>
> (Clausewitz, *On War*, pp. 198–199; see also p. 246)

> The enemy force can never assemble and advance so secretly that the defender's first news of it would come from

his outposts. If that were to happen, one could only feel very
sorry for him.

(Clausewitz, *On War*, p. 454)

We say this in order to exclude certain vague notions about
sudden assaults and surprise attacks which are commonly
thought of as bountiful sources of victory. They will only be
that under exceptional circumstances.

(Clausewitz, *On War*, p. 545)

If surprise cannot be achieved, then deception serves no purpose. Once
we move from the higher to lower levels of warfare, surprise may be
easier to accomplish, but its impact is also reduced correspondingly.

Unlike Clausewitz, Sun Tzu believes that surprise is an unquestionably practical option that should be on the military leader's mind at all
times:

[Tu Yu] They [the experts] *make it impossible for an enemy to
know where to prepare. They release the attack like a lightning
bolt from above the nine-layered heavens.*

(Sun Tzu, *The Art of War*, p. 86)

*Appear at places to which he must hasten; move swiftly where he
does not expect you.*

(Sun Tzu, *The Art of War*, p. 96)

*[Chang Yu] Take him unaware by surprise attacks where he is
unprepared. Hit him suddenly with shock troops.*

(Sun Tzu, *The Art of War*, p. 133)

Sun Tzu's faith in surprise to some extent contradicts his apparent
belief that it is possible to exert a modicum of control over events on the
battlefield, as well as his confidence in the efficacy of pre-war calculations and intelligence (which presumably could prevent the surprise
from occurring). For if one can achieve surprise, the same holds true for
the enemy. This in turn limits the potential contribution of intelligence
and calculations. It is strange that Clausewitz values intelligence so
little even though he does not believe in the possibility of being surprised, and is convinced that intelligence can often sound a timely warning. This can, again, be explained by the levels of analysis: when
Clausewitz speaks of the near-impossibility of achieving surprise,[14] he is

primarily referring to the higher operational or strategic levels, whereas Sun Tzu's high estimation of the utility of surprise is mainly in the context of the tactical level.

Clausewitz's frequent pessimistic comments regarding the value of intelligence should not be understood as a blanket dismissal of all intelligence collected in wartime. Such negative statements must be read in the context of his discussion and the level of analysis; that is, they reflect the unreliability of tactical and operational intelligence during combat in Clausewitz's time (see also Chapter 3 above and Appendix E). Since real-time communication in combat was rarely possible in his day, Clausewitz was simply giving an accurate picture of reality.

Once he moves to the higher strategic level of analysis, however, his opinion of intelligence is favorable. In *On War*, the opening statement of Chapter 6 ('Intelligence in War'), Book 1 provides the following definition of intelligence:

> **By 'Intelligence' we mean every sort of information about the enemy and his country – the basis, in short, of our own plans and operations.**
>
> (Clausewitz, *On War*, p. 117)

This indicates that he could more reliably use strategic intelligence in the pre-war planning phase as well as the initial phases of the war.

Yet immediately after Clausewitz presents this definition, he changes direction and proceeds – for the rest of the chapter – to discuss the unreliability of intelligence on the *tactical* and *operational levels*. His appreciation of strategic intelligence and its greater reliability is also evident in Chapter 9 of Book 3, where he argues that timely strategic intelligence can prevent strategic surprise. In Chapter 13, on 'The Strategic Reserve', he distinguishes between the reliability of strategic and operational intelligence as follows:

> **The movement of the enemy's columns into battle can be ascertained only by actual observation – the point at which he plans to cross a river by the few preparations he makes, which become apparent a short time in advance; but the direction from which he threatens our country will usually be announced in the press before a single shot is fired. The greater the scale of preparations, the smaller the chance of**

achieving surprise. Time and space involved are vast, the circumstances that have set the events in motion so well known and so little subject to change, that his decisions will either be apparent early enough, or can be discovered with certainty.

(Clausewitz, *On War*, pp. 210–211)

Clausewitz's observations concerning the different levels of analysis are so interwoven that the reader unacquainted with his constant shifting between them often mistakenly believes they represent contradictions. But that which holds true on one level may not necessarily be so on another.

While for Clausewitz, surprise was unusual on the strategic level but more feasible on the operational and tactical levels, today the opposite is true. In the modern world, strategic mobility, long-range delivery systems, and increased firepower have made it easier to achieve strategic surprise while the development of radars and other sensors has made operational and tactical surprise easier to prevent.

Jomini, too, concludes that surprise on the higher strategic and operational levels of war is so seldom a realistic option that it is hardly worth pursuing:

> *The surprise of an army is now next to an impossibility . . . Prearranged surprises are rare and difficult because in order to plan one it becomes necessary to have an accurate knowledge of the enemy's camp.*

(Jomini, *The Art of War*, p. 209)

> *This* [a surprise attack] *is an operation by no means to be despised in war, although it is rare, and less brilliant than a great strategic combination which renders victory certain even before the battle is fought.*

(Jomini, *The Art of War*, p. 210)

In Jomini's view, the much larger size and number of formations deployed since the French Revolution helps to explain the inability to achieve surprise on the higher levels of warfare:

> *It is certainly of great importance for a general to keep his plans secret; and Frederick the Great was right when he said that if his night-cap knew what was in his head he would throw it into the*

fire. That kind of secrecy was practicable in Frederick's time when his whole army was kept closely about him; but when maneuvers of the vastness of Napoleon's are executed, and war is waged as in our day, what concert of action can be expected from generals who are utterly ignorant of what is going on around them?

(Jomini, *The Art of War*, p. 259)

It might be argued that the lack of interest shown by Clausewitz and Jomini in deception and surprise was correct for the technological limitations of their own time, and that Sun Tzu might have exaggerated the importance of deception and surprise in the pre-technological era.[15] Strategic and operational surprise were transformed into realistic options by the Industrial Revolution, which led to previously unimaginable improvements in mobility, tremendous increases in firepower, and the development of real-time communications (which made possible the far greater coordination and control of troops separated by vast distances).[16] And once surprise had become an integral part of warfare, the value of deception grew accordingly. As a result, Sun Tzu's insistence that all warfare is based on deception suddenly became much more relevant to our own time than Clausewitz's dismissal of its worth. Once a war has begun, the achievement of surprise on the strategic and higher operational levels, which is essential for the concentration of superior force at the decisive point, now frequently hinges on the successful use of deception. In the modern industrial age, concentration of superior strength at the decisive point depends less on the number of troops and more on such elements as firepower, mobility, and technological and doctrinal surprises. As evidenced by the Allies' successful use of deception during the Second World War, the Germanic-Clausewitzian tradition – which underestimates the potential of intelligence in general, and deception in particular – has become obsolete, while Sun Tzu's positive estimation of them as indispensable remains eminently applicable.[17]

INTELLIGENCE, FRICTION AND UNCERTAINTY IN WAR

> For if many ill-conceived plans have succeeded through the still greater lack of judgment of an opponent, many more, apparently well laid, have on the contrary ended in disgrace. The confidence with which we form our schemes is never completely justified in their execution; speculation is carried on in safety, but, when it comes to action, fear causes failure.
>
> Thucydides, *The History of the Peloponnesian War*, Book 1, Section 120, p. 66

> In order not to annul our free will, I judge it true that Fortune may be mistress of one half our actions but then even she leaves the other half, or almost, under our control.
>
> Machiavelli, *The Prince*, p. 90

Intelligence is another dimension in which Sun Tzu's advice is more relevant for the contemporary military expert. Since he views intelligence as one of the most important force multipliers available to political and military leaders, Sun Tzu repeatedly emphasizes the need for meticulous intelligence-related preparations before the outbreak of war and preceding each campaign and battle. Throughout *The Art of War*, Sun Tzu reiterates that the continuous use of intelligence is essential, because it provides more accurate insights into the enemy's mind, intentions, and capabilities as well as into his estimates of one's own dispositions and plans. Thus, intelligence estimates form the basis for military plans that are best suited for exploitation of the enemy's weaknesses – plans that can be tailored to specific conditions rather than formulated in a vacuum. (Conversely, ignoring the intelligence received or neglecting to gather it in the first place courts disaster.) As mentioned earlier, Sun Tzu's insistence on obtaining the highest quality intelligence must be seen as an ideal that contributes to the educational value of his work. Even if reliable intelligence could be obtained only on rare occasions, and uncertainty never eradicated, Sun Tzu's positive attitude toward intelligence would still be important. To appreciate this, one need only

231

consider how Clausewitz's negative, if not antagonistic, opinion regarding the utility of intelligence has probably been responsible for many of the costly failures of his more dogmatic followers.[18]

Let us now turn to a more detailed examination of Sun Tzu's observations on the critical role of intelligence. *'Secret operations are essential in war; upon them the army relies to make its every move ... An army without secret agents is exactly like a man without eyes or ears'* (Sun Tzu, *The Art of War*, p. 149). It is for this reason that all important intelligence matters must be under the direct control of the leader. *'Of all those in the army close to the commander, none is more intimate than the secret agent ...'* (Sun Tzu, *The Art of War*, p. 147).

The leader must carefully select and recruit, task and control, evaluate and reward the work of his agents:

> *[Tu Mu] The first essential is to estimate the character of the spy to determine if he is sincere, truthful, and really intelligent ... Afterwards, he can be employed ... Among agents there are some whose only interest is in acquiring wealth without obtaining the true situation of the enemy, and only meet my requirements with empty words. In such a case I must be deep and subtle.*
>
> (Sun Tzu, *The Art of War*, p. 147)

Since the leader is the only one, for reasons of security, who is fully aware of his overall plans, he must personally task his agents.

> *[Mei Yao-ch'en] Secret agents receive their instructions within the tent of the general, and are intimate and close to him.*
>
> (Sun Tzu, *The Art of War*, p. 147)

Then the leader must carefully evaluate the information obtained from agents in order to avoid being deceived; this requires considerable experience and intuition on his part since, as Sun Tzu remarks, how *'Delicate indeed! Truly delicate!'* is the problem of separating truth from falsehood. *'There is no place where espionage is not used'* (Sun Tzu, *The Art of War*, p. 147). Finally, given the importance of espionage and intelligence, the leader must reward his agents generously.

> *Of all rewards none* [is] *more liberal than those given to secret agents.*
>
> (Sun Tzu, *The Art of War*, p. 147)

The Sovereign must have full knowledge of the activities of the five sorts of agents. This knowledge must come from the double agents, and therefore it is mandatory that they be treated with the utmost liberality.

(Sun Tzu, *The Art of War*, p. 149)

In fact, one of the most essential criteria for evaluating the capability of the commander is his intelligent use of intelligence.[19]

He who is not sage and wise, humane and just, cannot use secret agents. And he who is not delicate and subtle cannot get the truth out of them.

(Sun Tzu, *The Art of War*, p. 147)

And therefore only the enlightened sovereign and the worthy general who are able to use the most intelligent people as agents are certain to achieve great things.

(Sun Tzu, *The Art of War*, p. 149)

Now the reason the enlightened prince and the wise general conquer the enemy whenever they move and their achievements surpass those of ordinary men is foreknowledge.

(Sun Tzu, *The Art of War*, p. 144)

Sun Tzu's generals rely heavily on the work of spies and agents, a practice which complements his often-expressed recommendation that every effort should be made to secure victory with the least possible expense and bloodshed. This may also explain his insistence on laying the groundwork for victory before the outbreak of war:

Thus, what is of supreme importance in war is to attack the enemy's strategy ... [Li Ch'uan] Attack plans at their inception ... The supreme excellence in war is to attack the enemy's plans.

(Sun Tzu, *The Art of War*, pp. 77–78)
(see also below, Chapter 5, note 3, pp. 386–390)

This can only be accomplished through good intelligence, but there are no easy solutions here either: agents and spies are notoriously unreliable and may do more harm than good. As Sun Tzu's detailed discussion of this subject suggests, what one can do *to* the enemy can of course also be done *by* the enemy. Sun Tzu's confidence in espionage as an effective means of obtaining useful information is therefore rather exaggerated if not misplaced, and must be viewed as part of his quest for less costly, indirect methods of winning in war.

Although Sun Tzu dwells at length on the role of spies, he does not ignore other intelligence-gathering methods that largely pertain to preparations on the lower tactical level. These include basic intelligence (maps, information on climate, etc.), detailed reconnaissance, and topographical data.

> *[Tu Mu] Generally, the commander must thoroughly acquaint himself before-hand with the maps so that he knows dangerous places . . . All these facts the general must store in his mind; only then will he not lose the advantage of the ground.*
>
> (Sun Tzu, *The Art of War*, pp. 104–105)

> *Therefore, to estimate the enemy situation and to calculate distances and the degree of difficulty of the terrain so as to control victory are virtues of the superior general.*
>
> (Sun Tzu, *The Art of War*, p. 128; see also p. 64)

> *Agitate him and ascertain the pattern of his movement.*
>
> *Determine his dispositions and so ascertain the field of battle.*
>
> *Probe him and learn where his strength is abundant and where deficient.*
>
> (Sun Tzu, *The Art of War*, p. 100)

What are today called 'signals and indicators' represent another source of direct and indirect information on the enemy's situation and intentions. Sun Tzu lists the following such indicators:

> *Dust spurting upward in high straight columns indicates the approach of chariots. When it hangs low and is widespread, infantry is approaching . . .*
>
> *When the enemy's envoys speak in humble terms, but he continues his preparations, he will advance . . .* [A piece of advice that Stalin could have used in 1941 on the eve of Barbarossa.][20]
>
> *When the envoys speak in apologetic terms, he* [the enemy]

wishes a respite . . . [Which is, as Clausewitz observes, the best time to continue fighting.]

When half his force advances and half withdraws, he is attempting to decoy you.

When his troops lean on their weapons, they are famished.

When drawers of water drink before carrying it to camp, his troops are suffering from thirst.

When the enemy sees an advantage but does not seize it, he is fatigued.

When birds gather above the camp sites, they are empty . . .

When at night the enemy camp is clamorous, he is fearful.

When his flags and banners move constantly, he is in disarray.
(Sun Tzu, *The Art of War*, pp. 119–121)

Although more reliable than spies, such indicators are susceptible to deliberate manipulation by the enemy and should not be trusted without the benefit of extensive corroboration. In the process of gathering the best possible intelligence on his enemy, a successful leader must also prevent his enemy from doing likewise. This can be accomplished through two main methods: security and unpredictability. By not discussing his plans with anyone, a commander denies his adversary access to his secrets:

He should be capable of keeping his officers and men in ignorance of his plans.
(Sun Tzu, *The Art of War*, p. 136)

Set the troops to their tasks without imparting your designs.
(Sun Tzu, *The Art of War*, p. 139)

Once the troops are on the march, the effective commander can still conceal his intentions and plans through deception; he can avoid giving a clear indication of his direction of movement; improvise at the last moment (surely a contradiction to the importance Sun Tzu attaches to meticulous planning before the battle even begins . . .); make

235

himself unpredictable (through misdirection, formlessness, dissimulation, inscrutability, shapelessness); never repeat the same plan; and continuously change his military doctrine.

> *The ultimate in disposing one's troops is to be without ascertainable shape. Then the most penetrating spies cannot pry in nor can the wise lay plans against you.*
>
> *It is according to the shapes that I lay the plans for victory, but the multitude does not comprehend this. Although everyone can see the outward aspects, none understands the way in which I have created victory.*[21]
>
> *Therefore, when I have won a victory I do not repeat my tactics but respond to circumstances in an infinite variety of ways.*
>
> (Sun Tzu, *The Art of War*, p. 100)
>
> *He changes his methods and alters his plans so that people have no knowledge of what he is doing . . .*
>
> *He alters his camp-sites and marches by devious routes, and thus makes it impossible for others to anticipate his purpose.*
>
> (Sun Tzu, *The Art of War*, p. 137)

As we have seen, Clausewitz does not concern himself with the question of security because he believes that surprise is virtually impossible and that, in most cases, attempting to conceal troop movements would be futile. Furthermore, the military genius should be capable of intuitively discerning his opponent's objective despite the temporary dispersion of enemy troops. Ultimately, by keeping his troops concentrated and avoiding the temptation to disperse them, the military genius renders the enemy's efforts at security, concealment, and maneuver a waste of energy, if not a form of self-deception.

Sun Tzu, on the other hand, optimistically assumes that good intelligence makes it possible to predict the outcome of a war or battle. There is much less room in his theory on war for uncertainty, friction, and chance. His logic is simple and linear; good intelligence forms the basis for better planning, and the possibility of controlling events on the battlefield allows the implementation of those plans, culminating in the achievement of victory.

Sun Tzu's fundamental belief that the outcome of battles and wars can be predicted through careful calculation is expressed in numerous statements such as these:

I will be able to forecast which side will be victorious and which defeated.

(Sun Tzu, *The Art of War*, p. 66)

Now if the estimates made in the temple before hostilities indicate victory, it is because calculations show one's strength to be superior to that of his enemy; if they indicate defeat, it is because calculations show that one is inferior. With many calculations, one can win; with few one cannot. How much less the chance of victory has one who makes none at all! By this means I examine the situation and the outcome will be clearly apparent.

(Sun Tzu, *The Art of War*, p. 71)

It is sufficient to estimate the enemy situation correctly and to concentrate your strength to capture him. There is no more to it than this. He who lacks foresight and underestimates his enemy will surely be captured by him.

(Sun Tzu, *The Art of War*, p. 122)

Sun Tzu seems to ignore the fact emphasized by Clausewitz that even if perfect and timely intelligence were to exist in war, the pervasive effect of friction makes the accuracy of all calculations and forecasts doubtful at best.

The obvious question is: how can anyone know, in a world of secrecy, deception, and subjective perceptions, that his estimates of the enemy's strength are correct? Clausewitz comments:

The difficulty of accurate recognition constitutes one of the most serious sources of friction in war, by making things appear entirely different from what one had expected.

(Clausewitz, *On War*, p. 117)

According to Sun Tzu, the secret of victory lies in methodical, extensive pre-war calculations that include intelligence and information detailing the strengths and weaknesses of one's own troops as much as those of the enemy. In other words, he points out the importance of what is termed, in today's intelligence jargon, net assessment – that is, the comparative evaluation of the strength of both sides. Intelligence is defined here in the broadest terms, for even flawless intelligence on the enemy is of little use if the estimate of one's own strength and performance is inflated. Ironically, obtaining accurate information on one's own forces is the most challenging aspect of preparing a net assessment intelligence estimate.[22]

Sun Tzu provides us with a classical definition of net assessment:

> *Therefore I say: Know your enemy and know yourself; in a hundred battles you will never be in peril.*

> *When you are ignorant of the enemy but know yourself, your chances of winning or losing are equal.*

> *If ignorant of both your enemy and yourself, you are certain in every battle to be in peril.*

> (Sun Tzu, *The Art of War*, p. 84)

Machiavelli makes an identical observation: 'With difficulty he is beaten who can estimate his own forces and those of his enemy' (Machiavelli, *The Art of War*, p. 719). Clausewitz makes the opposite statement, however: '[the cause of inaction in war] . . . **is the imperfection of human perception and judgment which is more pronounced in war than anywhere else. We hardly know accurately our own situation at any particular moment while the enemy's, which is concealed from us, must be deduced from very little evidence**' (Clausewitz, *On War*, p. 217).

It should, however, be recognized that the sound advice to 'know one's enemy' is an ideal. Given human nature and problems of perception, ethnocentrism, and wishful thinking, to name but a few, it is impossible to understand the enemy fully (although one always needs to make the effort).[23] Often, individuals and nations are unaware of their own weaknesses and limitations, let alone those of their adversaries.

Those capable of arriving at a reasonably accurate net assessment of the situation, as Sun Tzu describes it, will never lose: '*Therefore when those experienced in war move, they make no mistakes; when they act, their resources are limitless*' (Sun Tzu, *The Art of War*, p. 129). Clausewitz, too, is aware of the need for a comparative net assessment of the strength of both sides before embarking on war:

To discover how much of our resources must be mobilized for war, we must first examine our political aim and that of the enemy. We must gauge the strength and situation of the opposite state. We must gauge the character and abilities of its government and people and do the same in regard to our own. Finally, we must evaluate the political sympathies of other states and the effect the war may have on them.

(Clausewitz, *On War*, pp. 585–586)

Once the best possible intelligence has been received and the comparative process of net assessment completed, the plans for war can be properly prepared and executed. According to Sun Tzu, the outcome can then be predicted with accuracy. This belief, which is diametrically opposed to that of Clausewitz on this issue, rests on the assumption that a successful military commander will be able to implement his plans as originally devised.

Generally, management of many is the same as management of few. It is a matter of organization.

And to control many is the same as to control few. This is a matter of formations and signals.

(Sun Tzu, *The Art of War*, p. 90)

In the tumult and uproar, the battle seems chaotic, but there is no disorder; the troops appear to be milling about in circles but cannot be defeated.

Apparent confusion is a product of good order; apparent cowardice, of courage; apparent weakness, of strength.

(Sun Tzu, *The Art of War*, p. 92)

Sun Tzu's belief that events on the battlefield can, at least to a great extent, be controlled, helps to explain his observation that '*a victorious army wins its victories before seeking battle*' (Sun Tzu, *The Art of War*, p. 87). If one side were indeed able to procure reliable intelligence on the enemy's capabilities and intentions, and then exploit this information through careful planning, and *if* these plans were carried out as originally intended, then it is possible to understand the conclusion that victory can be achieved before a shot has been fired.

Clausewitz, who would have found such statements untenable and unrealistic, remarks:

> No other human activity is so continuously or universally bound up with chance. And through the element of chance, guesswork and luck come to play a great part in war
>
> (Clausewitz, *On War*, p. 85)

> The very nature of interactions is bound to make it unpredictable.
>
> (Clausewitz, *On War*, p. 139)

> In war more than anywhere else, things do not turn out as we expect.
>
> (Clausewitz, *On War*, p. 193)

> In short, absolute, so-called mathematical, factors never find a firm basis in military calculations. From the very start, there is an interplay of possibilities, probabilities, good luck and bad, that weaves its way throughout the length and breadth of the tapestry. In the whole range of human activities, war most closely resembles a game of cards.
>
> (Clausewitz, *On War*, p. 86)

(It is interesting to note that while Clausewitz frequently compares war to a game of cards dominated by uncertainty, Jomini compares war to the more structured game of chess; Sun Tzu's theory of war, on the other hand, can be compared to the game of *go*.)

Commanders are rarely in control over events on the battlefield. The successful general is not the one who mechanically implements his original plans (as idealized by Sun Tzu), but rather the one who intuitively 'reads' the chaos on the battlefield well enough to take advantage of passing opportunities.

Clausewitz's discussion of the infinite complexity and unpredictability of war on all levels is perhaps his most original and important contribution to the study of war. War is permeated by uncertainty, friction, and chance; it involves constant change on the part of the adversaries, who act and react independently, without ever having complete information on one another.[24] Since war involves an endless chain of events whose relationship is unclear and never fixed, its sheer complexity makes any purely rational calculation or planning impossible by definition. The chaos of war poses problems 'worthy of the gifts of a Newton or an Euler' (Clausewitz, *On War*, p. 112).

> The deduction of effect from cause is often blocked by some insuperable extrinsic obstacle: the true causes may be quite unknown. Nowhere in life is this so common as in war, where the facts are seldom fully known and the underlying motives even less so.
>
> (Clausewitz, *On War*, p. 156)

Since it is impossible to weigh *all* of the relevant factors for even the simplest decisions in war, it is the military leader's intuition (his *coup d'oeil*) that must ultimately guide him in effective decision-making.

> The general unreliability of all information presents a special problem in war: all action takes place, so to speak, in the twilight, which, like fog or moonlight, often tends to make things seem grotesque and larger than they really are. Whatever is hidden from full view in this feeble light has to be guessed at by *talent*, or simply left to chance. So once again for the lack of objective knowledge, one has to trust to talent or to luck. [my emphasis]
>
> (Clausewitz, *On War*, p. 140)

> The only situation a commander can know fully is his own: his opponent's he can know only from unreliable intelligence.[25]
>
> (Clausewitz, *On War*, p. 84)

(In the heat of battle, it is doubtful that the commander has accurate information even on his own troops.)

> We must evaluate the political sympathies of other states and the effect war may have on them. To assess these things in all their ramifications and diversity is plainly a colossal task. Rapid and correct appraisal of them clearly calls for the intuition of a genius; to master all this complex mass by sheer methodical examination is obviously impossible. Bonaparte was quite right when he said that Newton himself would quail before the algebraic problems it could pose.
>
> (Clausewitz, *On War*, p. 586)

241

With this in mind. Clausewitz, not surprisingly, concludes that intelligence is untrustworthy, particularly given the nature of change on the battlefield. For Clausewitz, then, most intelligence is just another source of noise or friction, not a source of support for the military commander:

> If we consider the actual basis of this information [i.e., intelligence], how unreliable and transient it is, we soon realize that war is a flimsy structure that can easily collapse and bury us in its ruins . . . Many intelligence reports in war are contradictory; even more are false, and most are uncertain. This is true of all intelligence but even more so in the heat of battle, where such reports tend to contradict and cancel each other out. In short, most intelligence is false, and the effect of fear is to multiply lies and inaccuracies.
>
> (Clausewitz, *On War*, p. 117)

> A general in time of war is constantly bombarded by reports both true and false; by errors arising from fear or negligence or hastiness; by disobedience born of right or wrong interpretations, of ill will; of a proper or mistaken sense of duty; of laziness; or of exhaustion; and by accident that nobody could have foreseen. In short, he is exposed to countless impressions, most of them disturbing, few of them encouraging . . . If a man were to yield to these pressures, he would never complete an operation.
>
> (Clausewitz, *On War*, p. 193)

Sun Tzu, as we have seen, regards intelligence as an indispensable means of reducing uncertainty in war. Sun Tzu's commander is advised to look to *outside* information to solve his problems, whereas Clausewitz's commander turns *inward* to rely on his intuition and subjective assessment. Sun Tzu's solution is rational, Clausewitz's is heroic and romantic. Yet substituting the military genius's intuition for the systematic collection of intelligence is often a recipe for disaster, since in this situation, there is nothing to restrain the leader's temptation to indulge in wishful thinking and ignore unpleasant information.[26] (See Chapter 16 below.)

At this point, it is useful to return to the problem of the level of analysis. Unlike Sun Tzu, whose interest in intelligence spans all levels – political, strategic, operational and tactical – Clausewitz focuses almost exclusively on the lower operational and tactical levels.[27] In the pre-industrial age, the lack of real-time communications (telegraph and radio) meant that information concerning the battlefield became obsolete before it could be used. This to a large extent explains why Clausewitz thought intelligence to be of little value; yet that which is true of intelligence on the lower operational and tactical levels is not necessarily valid on the higher political and strategic levels (which Clausewitz does not discuss). Mistakenly believing that Clausewitz's poor opinion of intelligence applied to the higher levels of warfare as well as to the battlefield, many readers of *On War* agreed with his negative estimation of intelligence in general. This tendency was frequently reinforced by their earlier experiences with inaccurate intelligence (while serving on the lower operational and tactical levels), which had caused them to arrive at similarly pessimistic conclusions. By the time such military leaders had advanced through the ranks to the point where intelligence could make a much greater contribution, they were already convinced that it had little potential.

Nevertheless, even today, friction and a myriad of unpredictable events can rob real-time intelligence of its value on the lower levels of warfare. The availability of almost perfect intelligence on the operational and tactical levels is still no guarantee of success (as illustrated, for example, by the British experience in the Battle of Jutland or in the Battle of Crete).[28] Thus, it is not surprising that Clausewitz introduces the concept of friction immediately after his discussion of intelligence.

> **Everything in war is very simple, but the simplest thing is difficult. The difficulties accumulate and end by producing a kind of friction that is inconceivable unless one has experienced war . . . Countless minor incidents – the kind you can never really foresee – combine to lower the general level of performance, so that one always falls short of the intended goal . . .**
>
> **Friction is the only concept that more or less corresponds to the factors that distinguish real war from war on paper . . .**
>
> **This tremendous friction which cannot, as in mechanics, be reduced to a few points, is everywhere in contact with**

chance, and brings about effects that cannot be measured just because they are largely due to chance . . .

Action in war is like moving in a resistant element. Just as the simplest and most natural of movements, walking, cannot easily be performed in water, so in war it is difficult for normal efforts to achieve even moderate results.

(Clausewitz, *On War*, pp. 119–121)

With the predominance of uncertainty and friction in war, it is easy to see why Clausewitz put far less faith in the benefits to be derived from making and implementing detailed plans.[29]

In war, where imperfect intelligence, the threat of a catastrophe, and the number of accidents are incomparably greater than any other human endeavor, the amount of missed opportunities, so to speak, is therefore bound to be greater.

(Clausewitz, *On War*, p. 502)

War is the realm of uncertainty; three-quarters of the factors on which action in war is based are wrapped in a fog of greater or lesser uncertainty . . . war is the realm of chance. No other human activity gives it greater scope; no other has such incessant and varied dealings with this intruder. Chance makes everything more uncertain and interferes with the whole course of events.

(Clausewitz, *On War*, p. 101)

Since all information and assumptions are open to doubt, and with chance working everywhere, the commander continually finds that things are not as he expected. This is bound to influence his plans, or at least the assumptions underlying them. If this influence is sufficiently powerful to cause a change in his plans, he must usually work out new ones; but for these the necessary information may not be immediately available. During an operation, decisions have usually to be made at once: there may be no time to review the situation or even think it through. Usually, of course, new information and reevaluation are not enough to make us give up our intentions: they only call them into question. We now know more, but this makes us more, not less uncertain. The latest reports do not arrive all at once: they merely trickle in. They continually impinge on our decisions, and our mind must be permanently armed, so to speak, to deal with them.

(Clausewitz, *On War*, p. 102)

Clausewitz therefore proposes three types of solutions to compensate for the paucity of reliable intelligence. First is the intuition of the military genius as mentioned earlier; second, material strength; and third, the art of war itself.[30] Material strength is, of course, the most important factor in war, for even perfect intelligence is worthless without sufficient military force. A powerful army with a numerical advantage can win without any intelligence at all, albeit at a higher cost. Hence, Clausewitz insists that the first rule of war is to mobilize and field the largest possible force. (See Appendix F below.) Astute practitioners of the art of war can further compensate for the lack of adequate intelligence by concentrating superior force at the decisive point (despite relative inferiority), and by maintaining more than adequate reserves. While the commander may not be able to solve his own intelligence problems, his pursuit of an aggressive strategy can at least intensify the enemy's uncertainty and interfere with his ability to gather reliable intelligence. '**With uncertainty** [that is, lack of reliable intelligence] **in one scale, courage and self-confidence must be thrown into the other to correct the balance**' (Clausewitz, *On War*, p. 86). The drawback to this approach is that it is only one step removed from the complete neglect of intelligence and its potential.[31] Nevertheless, assuming that the commander's objective is to implement the principles of the art of war as effectively as possible, even the intuitive judgment of the military genius must be based on a minimum of reliable intelligence.[32]

In Book 8, on 'War Plans', Clausewitz states that no one should start '**a war . . . without first being clear in his mind what he intends to achieve by that war and how he intends to conduct it**' (Clausewitz, *On War*, p. 579). This seems simple enough until we also consider that Clausewitz believed such long-range planning to be unpredictable, given the probabilistic, uncertain, and reciprocal nature of war.

245

Mao, on the other hand, takes a somewhat more optimistic position on the possibility of making long-range plans in an uncertain environment. This can be partially explained by his involvement in a protracted, carefully planned war of attrition. In at least its first two stages, the course of this war was determined by the aggregate of many relatively small battles fought primarily on his own initiative and his own terms. Much like Sun Tzu, Mao believes in the possibility of waging war based on rational calculations and planning, which are supposed to reduce uncertainty, chance, and luck to a manageable level. For this reason, Mao *never emphasizes the role of luck and chance*.

Thus, Mao recognizes the inevitability of uncertainty in war, but he views it as a relative, not absolute, factor that can be controlled and even exploited to one's advantage through meticulous planning.

> Because of the uncertainty peculiar to war, it is much more difficult to prosecute war according to plan than the case is with other activities. Yet, since preparedness ensures success and unpreparedness spells failure, there can be no victory in war without advance planning and preparations. *There is no absolute certainty in war*, and yet it is not without some degree of relative certainty. [He continues in words echoing those of Clausewitz.] We are comparatively certain about our own situation. We are very uncertain about the enemy's, but here too there are signs for us to read, clues to follow and sequences of phenomena to ponder. These form what we call a degree of *relative certainty*, which provides an objective basis for planning in war. Modern technical developments . . . have added to the possibilities of planning in war.
>
> (Mao Tse-tung, *Selected Military Writings*, pp. 242–243)
>
> Even though future changes are difficult to foresee and the farther ahead one looks, the more blurred things seem, a general calculation is possible and an appraisal of distant prospects is necessary. In war as well as in politics, planning only one step at a time as one goes along is a harmful way of directing matters. . . . It is absolutely essential to have a long-term plan which has been thought out in its general outline and which covers an entire strategic stage or even several strategic stages . . .
>
> (Mao Tse-tung, *Selected Military Writings*, p. 131)

Uncertainty interferes with even the best-laid plans, but its effect can be overcome to some extent by flexible planning and the readiness to change plans frequently according to developing circumstances. 'Planning must change with the movement (flow or change) of the war and vary in degree according to the scale of the war' (Mao Tse-tung, *Selected Military Writings*, p. 243). The higher the level of planning, the more reliable the results are likely to be. 'A strategic plan based on the over-all situation of both belligerents is . . . more stable, but it too is applicable only in a given strategic stage and has to be changed when the war moves towards a new stage . . . [Conversely, tactical plans may] . . . have to be changed several times a day' (Mao Tse-tung, *Selected Military Writings*, p. 243).

Mao disagrees strongly with those who assert that long-range planning is impossible:

> Because of the fluidity of war, some people categorically deny that war plans or policies can be relatively stable, describing such plans or policies as 'mechanical.' This view is wrong . . . Because the circumstances of war are only *relatively certain* and the flow (movement or change) of war is rapid, war plans or policies can be only relatively stable and have to be changed or revised in good time in accordance with changing circumstances and the flow of war; otherwise we would become machinists. But one must not deny the need for war plans or policies that are relatively stable over given periods; to negate this is to negate everything, including the war itself as well as the negator himself.

> (Mao Tse-tung, *Selected Military Writings*, p. 243)

If the situation is to be assessed as a whole, clear political and strategic priorities combined with appropriate strategic plans are essential in order to prevent the 'tacticization of strategy' (see Appendix E). Mao stresses this point in his discussion on the importance of planning the first battle.

> The plan for the first battle must be the prelude to, and an organic part of, the plan for the whole campaign. Without a good plan for the whole campaign, it is absolutely impossible to fight a really good first battle . . . Hence, before fighting the first battle, one must have a general idea of how the second, third,

247

fourth, and even final battle will be fought, and consider what changes will ensue in the enemy's situation as a whole if we win, or lose, each of the succeeding battles. Although the result may not – and, in fact, definitely will not – turn out exactly as we expect, we must think out everything carefully and realistically in the light of the general situation on both sides. Without a grasp of the situation as a whole, it is impossible to make any really good move on the chessboard.

(Mao Tse-tung, *Selected Military Writings*, p. 130)

The most profound differences between Sun Tzu and Clausewitz emerge from a comparison of their observations on command and control, intelligence, surprise, and deception. For Sun Tzu, timely and reliable intelligence is essential for the rational planning of military operations and the decision to go to war. His view should not, however, be taken literally. Sun Tzu *does* mention the complexity and uncertainty of war, although he clearly believes that friction, uncertainty and chance do not merit the central role that Clausewitz would assign them.

Paradoxically, Sun Tzu's recommendation that deception be used whenever possible in essence contradicts his basic assumption that accurate intelligence can be gathered and used effectively. After all, if one's enemy is equally practised in deception, much of the intelligence received cannot be trusted. Sun Tzu's belief in the importance of relying on intelligence should therefore be understood as part of a learning process, as an ideal and not simply as a description of reality; and the search for reliable intelligence should be considered part of the *normative* desire to make the most rational decisions possible. This reminds political and military leaders to make the utmost effort to base their strategies and plans on careful preparations *before* engaging the enemy.

The fact that Sun Tzu's analysis of war is, on the whole, wider in scope than that of Clausewitz helps to explain his greater confidence in the utility of intelligence. While Clausewitz focuses on the lower levels of warfare, where the contribution of intelligence is more limited and its use more problematic, Sun Tzu extends his discussion to include the higher strategic political levels, where intelligence is generally more reliable. Most importantly, though, Sun Tzu's positive attitude toward intelligence exemplifies his fundamentally rational and calculated approach to war.

Jomini's views on intelligence fall somewhere between those of Clausewitz and Sun Tzu. By taking the *via media* between the views of intelligence as an unreliable source of disturbance and intelligence as a panacea, Jomini inevitably arrives at more realistic and balanced conclusions. Jomini's observations on this subject also merit further attention inasmuch as they may reflect Napoleon's appreciation of its utility and value. Jomini begins his analysis with the suggestion that intelligence is, at least in theory, the basis of all successful action:

> *One of the surest ways of forming good combinations in war would be to order movements only after obtaining perfect information of the enemy's proceedings. In fact, how can any man say what he should do himself, if he is ignorant what his adversary is about?*
>
> (Jomini, *The Art of War*, p. 268)

The acquisition of flawless information in wartime was, certainly in the nineteenth century, an impossibility as Jomini is quick to acknowledge. This leads him to an observation that closely resembles Clausewitz's conclusion (in *On War*, Book 1, Chapter 1, which compares war in theory and practice) that the dearth of trustworthy intelligence '*is one of the chief causes of the great difference between the theory and practice of war*' (Jomini, *The Art of War*, pp. 268–269).

Jomini also adopts a Clausewitzian approach when he suggests that the best remedy for imperfect intelligence is reliance on the intuition, or *coup d'oeil*, of the commander. He then explains in some detail what the most reliable sources of intelligence are. His five principal sources are remarkably relevant and comprehensive even for our own time:

1. A highly organized and efficient system of espionage.
2. Reconnaissance by special units.
3. The interrogation of prisoners of war.
4. 'Forming hypotheses of probabilities' [that is, a systematic analysis of courses of action open to the enemy based on information, logic, and experience].
5. Signals (see Jomini, *The Art of War*, pp. 269–270).

Like Sun Tzu, Jomini observes that spies '*enable a general to learn more surely than by any other agency what is going on in the midst of the enemy's camp*' (Jomini, *The Art of War*, p. 269). Reconnaissance cannot furnish reliable information beyond the line of the advance guard; in other words, it is primarily of immediate tactical value. And the interrogation of prisoners can yield positive results only if it is conducted by intelligence officers skilled in interrogation techniques.

In the conclusion of *Grand Military Operations*, Jomini stresses the importance of reconnaissance and intelligence (his sixth general principle):

> *6. It is most important, when we take the initiative of a decisive moment, that we should be careful to perfectly inform ourselves of the positions of the enemy and of the movements which he can make. The employment of spies is a useful means, to the consideration of which too much pains can not be given; but that which is perhaps of more use is to have the country scoured in all directions by partisans. A general should send small parties in all directions, and he must multiply the number of them with the greater care, as this system is avoided in grand operations . . . To operate without these precautions is to march in the dark, and to expose ourselves to the chance disasters which a secret movement of the enemy might produce. These things have been too much neglected; spy parties have not been organized far enough in advance, and the officers commanding light troops have not always had enough experience to conduct their detachments properly.* [33]

Jomini is also aware of the obstacles encountered in attempting to communicate intelligence in *real time* from its source in the enemy camp to the consumer; for by the time the information has reached its intended destination, it is usually obsolete.

> *But it is almost impossible to communicate with them* [one's spies in the enemy camp] *and receive the information they possess . . . Even when the general receives from his spies information of movements, he still knows nothing of those which may since have taken place, nor of what the enemy is going finally to attempt.*
> (Jomini, *The Art of War*, p. 270)

According to Jomini, the development of *well-founded* hypotheses on the enemy's possible courses of action is crucial; such hypotheses are based on the information available and complemented by a systematic, logical analysis drawn from experience, familiarity with the enemy's mindset, and a sound knowledge of the principles of war. This is as good a description as any of the modern approach to intelligence, and the bread and butter of intelligence work on all levels. '*I can*', he states, '*with great satisfaction say that this means hardly ever failed me . . . I was never more than two or three times mistaken in my hypotheses and in my manner of solving the difficulties they offered*' (Jomini, *The Art of War*, pp. 270–271).

After observing that the use of spies has been badly neglected by many of the 'modern' armies of his time (with the usual exception of the Russians), Jomini concludes his chapter on intelligence with the following set of recommendations, which are as valuable for today's military commander and intelligence expert as when they were first written:

1. *A general should neglect no means of gaining information . . .*
2. *By multiplying the means of obtaining information; for no matter how imperfect and contradictory they may be, the truth may often be sifted from them.*
3. *Perfect reliance should be placed on none of these means.*
4. *As it is impossible to obtain exact information by the methods mentioned, a general should never move without arranging several courses of action for himself, based upon probable hypotheses . . . and never losing sight of the principles of the art.*

(Jomini, *The Art of War*, pp. 273–274)

In other words, since intelligence is rarely perfect (it is probabilistic in nature), all pieces of intelligence received must be carefully corroborated, and uncertainty must be dealt with through operational contingency plans and the correct application of the principles of war.

Jomini completes his examination of intelligence most appropriately with a comprehensive analysis of the value of visual telegraph and an efficient communications system in war – as well as a strong recommendation that balloons be used for battlefield reconnaissance. His perceptive study of the role of intelligence in war thus closes on a remarkably contemporary note, providing us with a transition from pre-modern intelligence to that of the twentieth century. It is ironic that while Sun Tzu's *The Art of War* and Clausewitz's *On War* are of much greater value to modern strategists in all other respects, Jomini's *The Art of War* makes the best theoretical statement on the role of intelligence.

Table 15.1
Sun Tzu, Clausewitz, and Jomini Compared: Command and Control, the Roles of Intelligence, Surprise, Deception, and Forecasting in War

	SUN TZU	CLAUSEWITZ	JOMINI
Intelligence discussed	• On all levels of warfare	• Primarily on the operational level and on the battlefield	• On strategic but primarily on higher operational level
Attitude toward intelligence	• Positive; optimistic • Reliable intelligence can be obtained and is a major key to success in war • Very useful	• Negative, pessimistic • Intelligence is mostly unreliable, rapidly becomes obsolete, is a form of friction, makes a limited contribution to success in war • Useless	• Very positive attitude; cautiously optimistic. Intelligence can be properly analyzed, corroborated, and confirmed as a basis for planning and action • Useful
Main sources of intelligence	• Spies and observers	• Direct contact with the enemy • Commander's direct observations	• Spies, prisoners of war, logic, and systematic analysis • Balloons, special reconnaissance troops
The possibility of making rational decisions and fore-casts	• Rational, carefully calculated plans can be made on the basis of reliable intelligence • Forecasting is possible, and careful planning is an important key to victory	• War is dominated by friction, chance, and uncertainty • Therefore, although every effort should be made to make rational decisions and prepare plans, they cannot be relied upon • Forecasting in war is next to impossible • The intuition of the commander is as important as rational calculations	• Rational and successful planning can be based on good intelligence • Familiarity with the principles of war makes decisions more rational, reduces friction and makes success more likely • Friction and chance cannot be ignored • The intuition of the commander is important for the implementation of plans • Forecasts can be made and are useful even if not perfect

Command and Control	*Difficult but possible on local tactical level*	• Very difficult if not impossible on tactical and operational level	• *Difficult but not impossible on operational level if carefully prepared*
Deception and surprise	• *Deception is the basis for all successful operations* • *It is the weapon of choice* • *Surprise can be achieved and is key to success*	• **Deception is a waste of time, and of doubtful value** • **It is a weapon of the last resort** • **Surprise is impossible to achieve on the higher levels of war**	• *Deception is unimportant* • *Surprise is impossible to achieve on the higher levels of war*
Key to success in war in light of the value of intelligence	• *Make the utmost effort to obtain reliable intelligence* • *Base all planning on intelligence, and make extensive use of deception* • *Conversely, make the greatest possible effort to deny intelligence to the enemy*	• **Since intelligence is unreliable, field the largest possible force and keep your forces concentrated** • **Make use of the commander's intuition** • **By maintaining the initiative create uncertainty, (i.e., an intelligence problem for the enemy)** • **Shift the burden to the enemy**	• *Make every effort to obtain the best possible intelligence but remember that it is not perfect* • *Base your plans on the correct principles of war, always concentrate the largest possible force, and keep a force in reserve to meet unexpected situations*
Problems	• *Excessive reliance on intelligence, and deception which can become a panacea* • *Friction is underestimated, and the value of plans overestimated*	• **Ignores the possible value of intelligence and deception** • **Excessive reliance on the intuition of the commander and on brute force** • **Assumes too little control over events**	• *A modern, balanced and realistic approach* • *Relies too much on the correct identification and application of the principles of war*

16

On Military Leadership

THE ROLE OF THE MILITARY LEADER

For Clausewitz, the impossibility of procuring reliable intelligence in the heat of battle is axiomatic. It is the premise upon which much of his theoretical framework is built and from which some of his central analytical concepts are derived. The absence of accurate information constitutes one of his principal explanations (in conjunction with the role of politics and the inherent differences of the offense and defense) for the discrepancy between the ideal type of absolute war and war in practice. Thus, the shortage of reliable information on both sides forces one to forsake the theoretical concept of uninterrupted military action for the reality of paralysis and inaction. To this we must add the environment of danger and the role of friction in war as discussed by Clausewitz in Chapters 4, 5, 6, and 7 of Book 1. This section should be read as one unit in order to serve as the background for Clausewitz's explication of the military leader's role in dealing with these problems (Chapter 3). (From this point of view, the most logical arrangement of these chapters would have been to place Chapters 4–7 before, not after, Chapter 3.) All these factors make it impossible *by definition* for political and military leaders to take '*purely rational*' decisions in war (Clausewitz, *On War*, pp. 84–85). For a normal person, rational conduct amidst the danger and confusion of war is difficult, if not impossible: '. . . **here ideas are governed by other factors. [Here] the light of reason is refracted in a manner quite different from that which is normal in academic speculation. It is an exceptional man who keeps his power of quick decision intact if he has never been through this experience before**' (*On War*, p. 113). Hence, Clausewitz develops his theoretical concept of the military genius whose intuition compensates for the absence of accurate intelligence; yet this conceptually pleasing but problematic solution raises as many questions as it purports to answer. The most potentially damaging consequence of Clausewitz's reliance on the intuition of the military genius is that, if carried to extremes, it weakens one's incentive to gather the best possible intelligence and replaces the systematic search for information with intuition alone.

Sun Tzu also examines at some length the ideal character of a commander and his pivotal role, pointing out that such a leader must draw upon his experience and intuition in exercising his creative, independent judgment. Although the military leader's role in *The Art of War* does not acquire the degree of central theoretical and practical significance it is afforded in *On War*, Clausewitz's **'military genius'** and Sun Tzu's *'master of war'* or *'skillful commander'* (Sun Tzu, *The Art of War*, p. 87) actually have much in common when their superficial differences are stripped away. Still, unlike Clausewitz, Sun Tzu generally favors caution and measured calculation more than reliance on the commander's intuition.

According to Sun Tzu, the political leader's choice of a military commander might be the most critical decision he makes:

> *Now the general is the protector of the state. If this protection is all-embracing, the state will surely be strong; if defective, the state will certainly be weak ... [Chang Yu] ... A sovereign who obtains the right person prospers. One who fails to do so will be ruined.*
>
> (Sun Tzu, *The Art of War*, p. 81)

Jomini's statements on this issue echo those of Sun Tzu:

> *If the skill of a general is one of the surest elements of victory, it will be readily seen that the judicious selection of generals is one of the most delicate points in the science of government and one of the most essential parts of the military policy of a state.*
>
> (Jomini, *The Art of War*, p. 43)

> *We have already said that if the prince do [sic] not conduct his armies in person, his most important duty will be to have the position of commander well filled – which, unfortunately, is not always done.*
>
> (Jomini, *The Art of War*, p. 5)

> *The choice of generals-in-chief . . . [is] a subject worthy of the*

> *most anxious care upon the part of a wise government; for upon it often depends the safety of the nation.*
>
> (Jomini, *The Art of War*, p. 335)

Jomini goes one step further than Clausewitz and Sun Tzu, however, in his proposal of a 'modern' solution in the event that a military genius cannot be found or the wrong commander heads the army.

> *The difficulty of always selecting a good general has led to the formation of a good general staff, which being near the general may advise him, and thus exercise a beneficial influence over the operations. A well-instructed general staff is one of the most useful of organizations; but care must be observed to prevent the introduction into it of false principles, as in this case it might prove fatal.*
>
> (Jomini, *The Art of War*, p. 57)

By recognizing that this solution can generate its own problems, Jomini comes very close to discussing the pitfalls of war waged by committees or complex bureaucracies – that is, by ponderous organizations in search of consensus. To their detriment, the actions taken by such organizations often represent the lowest common denominator acceptable to all involved in the decision-making process and, as a result, seldom entail much risk – an element essential for success in war.

> *What must be the result of an operation which is but partially understood by the commander, since it is not his own conception? I have undergone a pitiable experience as prompter at head-quarters, and no one has a better appreciation of the value of such services than myself; and it is particularly in a council of war that such a part is absurd. The greater the number and the higher the rank of the military officers who compose the council, the more difficult will it be to accomplish the triumph of truth and reason, however small be the amount of dissent.*
>
> *What would have been the action of a council of war to which Napoleon proposed the movement of Arcola, the crossing of the Saint-Bernard, the maneuver at Ulm, or that at Gera and Jena? The timid would have regarded them as rash, even to madness, others would have seen a thousand difficulties of execution, and all would have concurred in rejecting them; and if, on the*

257

contrary, they had been adopted, and had been executed by any one but Napoleon, would they not certainly have proved failures?
(Jomini, *The Art of War*, p. 58)

If we again bear in mind the level of analysis, Jomini's recommendation that a general staff be assembled to support the commander, and Clausewitz's trust in the military genius are not necessarily contradictory. On the lower tactical and operational levels, where action must be taken without delay, there is no substitute for a military commander's experience and intuition. In any event, there is rarely enough time in the heat of battle for the deliberations of a council of war; for better or worse, the commander must arrive at the most logical decision under the circumstances and then execute it resolutely. In Clausewitz's words, the commander must '**stand firm like a rock**' once his decision has been made. On the higher political, strategic and even operational levels, however – where there is more time to gather information and weigh decisions carefully – a general staff or council of war serves a much more vital and constructive purpose.

Ironically, a military commander's previous experience on the battlefield – where he was accustomed to making quick, clear decisions based on his experience and intuition – is often a further impediment to effective decision-making on the higher strategic level. The same qualities that enabled Napoleon to win at Arcola or Jena were his downfall when applied to the formulation of strategy, in which sober calculations bring greater rewards than quick reactions, intuition, and guts.

The selection of a competent commander is particularly critical for Sun Tzu because he favors granting the military leader on the battlefield greater independence and discretion:

He whose generals are able and not interfered with by the sovereign will be victorious . . . To make appointments is the province of the sovereign; to decide on battle that of the general.

[Wang Hsi] . . . A sovereign of high character and intelligence must be able to know the right man, should place the responsibility on him, and expect results.
(Sun Tzu, *The Art of War*, p. 83; see also pp. 83–84, 112)

Sun Tzu's general must be able to exercise his independent, professional judgment within the general framework of the orders he has received from the political leader – but he alone can create the conditions necessary for their implementation.

> *Having paid heed to the advantages of my plans, the general must create situations which will contribute to their accomplishment.*
>
> (Sun Tzu, *The Art of War*, p. 66)

> *[Chia Lin] ... The orders of the sovereign, although they should be followed, are not to be followed if the general knows they contain the danger of harmful superintendence of affairs from the capital.*
>
> (Sun Tzu, *The Art of War*, p. 113; see also p. 112)

And if a weak sovereign with no military ability takes direct command of his army, Jomini warns that:

> His [the sovereign's] *general, interfered with and opposed in all his enterprises, will be unable to achieve success, even if he have the requisite ability. It may be said that a sovereign might accompany the army and not interfere with his general, but on the contrary, aid him with all the weight of his influence.*
>
> (Jomini, *The Art of War*, pp. 52–53)

Although Clausewitz's discussion on the ideal character of the military genius is concentrated in one of the longest chapters of *On War* (Book 1, Chapter 3) while Sun Tzu's views on this subject can be found throughout *The Art of War*, a comparison of these two texts reveals that many of their observations overlap.

THE TEMPERAMENT OF THE MILITARY LEADER

> Discipline does more in war than enthusiasm.
>
> Machiavelli, *The Art of War*, p. 718

Sun Tzu devotes much attention to the problem of selecting a military leader whose temperament lends itself to rational action under stressful conditions. Conversely, it is only natural that he also explore various ways to undermine the opponent's rational conduct and induce poorly calculated decisions at every opportunity. In his advice on the temperament of the ideal military leader, Sun Tzu basically agrees with Clausewitz, although Sun Tzu's statements are more often couched in 'negative terms', – that is, in terms of what he believes are undesirable characteristics or the best ways to exploit the foibles of the opponent's general. Sun Tzu's 'negative' approach is also demonstrated by his emphasis on pressuring one's opponent into making emotional, irrational, and poorly calculated decisions. This is recognized only indirectly by Clausewitz, perhaps because he thinks it obvious. Thus Sun Tzu advises his commander to agitate and perplex the enemy – to provoke him until he acts without thinking.

> *Anger his general and confuse him.*
>
> *[Li Ch'uan] . . . If the general is choleric, his authority can easily be upset. His character is not firm.*
>
> *[Chang Yu] If the enemy's general is obstinate and prone to anger, insult and enrage him, so that he will be irritated and confused, and without a plan will recklessly advance against you.*
>
> *Pretend inferiority and encourage his arrogance.*
> (Sun Tzu, The Art of War, p. 67)

> *If a general is unable to control his impatience and orders his troops to swarm up the wall like ants, one third of them will be killed without taking the city.*
> (Sun Tzu, The Art of War, pp. 78–79)

> *It is the business of a general to be serene and inscrutable, impartial and self-controlled.*
>
> *[Wang Hsi] . . . If serene he is not vexed; if inscrutable, unfathomable; if upright, not improper; if self-controlled, not confused.*
> (Sun Tzu, The Art of War, p. 136)

> *[Chang Yu] . . . Therefore the expert at controlling his enemy frustrates him and then moves against him. He aggravates him to confuse him and harasses him to make him fearful.*
> (Sun Tzu, The Art of War, p. 108)

According to Sun Tzu, these qualities are dangerous in a general:

> *If reckless, he can be killed . . .*

[Tu Mu] . . . A general who is stupid and courageous is a calamity . . . When people discuss a general, they always pay attention to his courage . . .

If cowardly, captured:

[Ho Yen-hsi] One who esteems life above all will be overcome with hesitancy. Hesitancy in a general is a great calamity.

If quick-tempered, you can make a fool of him:

[Tu Yu] An impulsive man can be provoked to rage and brought to his death. One easily angered is irascible, obstinate, and hasty. He does not consider the difficulties.

[Wang-Hsi] What is essential in the temperament of a general is steadiness.[1]

If he has too delicate a sense of honor, you can calumniate him.

[Mei Yao-ch'en] One anxious to defend his reputation pays no regard to anything else.

If he is of a compassionate nature, you can harass him.

[Tu Mu] He who is humanitarian and compassionate and fears only casualties cannot give up temporary advantage for long term gain and is unable to let go of this in order to seize that . . .

The ruin of the army and the death of the general are the inevitable results of these shortcomings. They must be deeply pondered.

(Sun Tzu, *The Art of War*, pp. 114–115)

Sun Tzu prizes steadiness, resolution, stability, patience, and calmness, which enable a general faced with the chaos and adversity of war to make rational, calculated decisions. Generals who react without reflection, who are courageous but easily lose control, are most susceptible to manipulation by the enemy. When untempered by rationality and driven by rash impulse, courage ends in self-destruction. The fact that courage without reflection is not revered in *The Art of War* is illustrated by the story of a courageous officer who attacked the enemy on his own initiative, '*[Tu Mu] . . . unable to control himself*', and was beheaded despite his success (Sun Tzu, *The Art of War*, p. 107).

Clausewitz's general undermines his opponent not so much by deliberately enraging him before battle and encouraging his arrogance but by applying unrelenting pressure to promote stress; by allowing him little time for calculated action; and by throwing him off balance. In this sense, it can be argued that all action on the operational level is designed to fluster the enemy, to pressure him in all possible ways.

Clausewitz does not necessarily see intelligence or sagacity as the most desirable quality for a military commander: '**Intelligence alone is not courage; we often see that the most intelligent people are irresolute**' (Clausewitz, *On War*, p. 102). Sun Tzu's comment (quoted earlier) that compassion can undermine the commander's performance also hints at this problem. Both strategists agree, however, that stability, resolution and determination are indispensable. No less than Sun Tzu, Clausewitz admires self-control, '**the gift of keeping calm even under the greatest stress**' as well as steadfastness or strength of mind, which he sees as:

> **the ability to keep one's head at times of exceptional stress and violent emotion . . . Strength of character does not consist solely in having powerful feelings, but in maintaining one's balance in spite of them. Even with the violence of emotion, judgment and principle must still function like a ship's compass . . .**
>
> (Clausewitz, *On War*, p. 107)

> **Obviously a man whose opinions are constantly changing, even though this is in response to his own reflections, would not be called a *man of character*. The term is applied only to those whose views are stable and constant.**
>
> (Clausewitz, *On War*, p. 107)

> **The commander [in battle] must trust his judgment and stand like a rock on which the waves break in vain. It is not an easy thing to do.**
>
> (Clausewitz, *On War*, p. 117)

'*[Wang Hsi said] What is essential in the temperament of a general is steadiness*' (Sun Tzu, *The Art of War*, p. 115). This quality, which might also include firmness, persistence, and maintenance of aim, is referred to by Clausewitz as the *imperative principle*. Under the conditions of battle – namely, when the commander is under great pressure, when he receives contradictory information, when friction, chance and uncertainty dominate events – Clausewitz believes that the most important quality a commander must possess is firmness and self-confidence. He must be an anchor of stability and steadiness in an environment that otherwise generates hesitation, doubts and pressure for constant change. In the following passage, Clausewitz delves at length into the logic of his recommendation that the commander 'stand like a rock':

> Only those general principles and attitudes that result from clear and deep understanding can provide a comprehensive guide to action. It is to these that opinions on specific problems should be anchored. The difficulty is to hold fast to these results in the torrent of events and new opinions. Often there is a gap between principles and actual events that cannot always be bridged by a succession of logical deductions. Then a measure of self-confidence is needed, and a degree of skepticism is also salutary. Frequently nothing short of an *imperative principle* will suffice, which is not part of the immediate thought-process, but dominates it: that principle is in all doubtful cases to stick to one's first opinion and to refuse to change unless forced to do so by a clear conviction. A strong faith in the overriding truth of tested principles is needed; the vividness of transient impressions must not make us forget that such truth as they contain is of a lesser stamp. By giving precedence, in case of doubt, to our earlier convictions, by holding to them stubbornly, our actions acquire that quality of steadiness and consistency which is termed strength of character.
>
> (Clausewitz, *On War*, p. 108; see also p. 193)

> If the mind is to emerge unscathed from this relentless struggle with the unforeseen, two qualities are indispensable: *first, an intellect that, even in the darkest hour, retains some glimmerings of the inner light which leads to truth: and second, the courage to follow this first light wherever it may lead.* The first of these qualities is described by the French term *coup d'oeil*, the second is determination.
>
> (Clausewitz, *On War*, p. 102)

These are precisely the qualities often undermined in modern times by excessively centralized command and control, increased dependence on intelligence, emphasis on 'teamwork', and intolerance of mistakes.

Like Sun Tzu, Clausewitz warns that

> **strength of character can degenerate into obstinacy. The line between the two is often hard to draw in a specific case . . . Obstinacy is not an intellectual defect; it comes from reluctance to admit that one is wrong . . . Obstinacy is a fault of temperament.**
>
> (Clausewitz, *On War*, p. 117)

Jomini selects bravery, equanimity under the most trying conditions, firmness, the ability to inspire the troops, and a sense of fairness or generosity of spirit as the most critical characteristics for a military leader.

> *The essential qualities for a general will always be as follows:*
> *First, A high moral courage, capable of great resolutions.*
> *Secondly, A physical courage which takes no account of danger. His scientific or military acquirements are secondary to the above-mentioned characteristics, though if great they will be valuable auxiliaries. It is not necessary that he should be a man of vast erudition. His knowledge may be limited, but should be thorough, and he should be perfectly grounded in the principles in the base of the art of war. Next in importance come the qualities of his personal character. A man who is gallant, just, firm, upright, capable of esteeming merit in others instead of being jealous of it, and skillful in making this merit conduce to his own glory, will always be a good general, and may even pass for a great man. Unfortunately, the disposition to do justice to merit in others is not the most common quality.*
>
> (Jomini, *The Art of War*, pp. 55–56; see also p. 59)

> *Finally, I will conclude . . . with one last truth: The first of all the requisites for a man's success as a leader is that he be perfectly brave. When a general is animated by a truly martial spirit and can communicate it to his soldiers, he may commit faults, but he will gain victories and secure deserved laurels.*
>
> (Jomini, *The Art of War*, p. 345)

THE BATTLE ENVIRONMENT AND THE INTUITION
OF THE MILITARY LEADER

Subtle and insubstantial, the expert leaves no trace; divinely mysterious, he is inaudible. Thus he is the master of his enemy's fate.
Sun Tzu, *The Art of War*, p. 97

I hope that . . . I could not be accused of wishing to make of this art a mechanism of determined wheelworks, nor of pretending on the contrary that the reading of a single chapter of principles is able to give, all at once, the talent of conducting an army. In all the arts, as in all the situations of life, knowledge and skill are two altogether different things, and if one often succeeds through the latter alone, it is never but the union of the two that constitutes a superior man and assures complete success. Meanwhile, in order not to be accused of pedantry, I hasten to avow that, by knowledge, I do not mean a vast erudition; it is not a question to know a great deal but to know well; to know especially what relates to the mission appointed to us.
Jomini, *Summary of the Art of War*, pp. 17–18

A commander-in-chief need not be a learned historian nor a pundit, but he must be familiar with the higher affairs of state and its most intimate policies . . . He

must not be an acute observer of
mankind or a subtle analyst of
human character; but he must
know the character, the habits of
thought and action, and the
special virtues and defects of the
men whom he is to command . . .
This type of knowledge cannot be
forcibly produced by an appara-
tus of scientific formulas and
mechanics; it can only be gained
through a talent for judgment
and by the application of accurate judgment to the observation
of man and matter.

Clausewitz, *On War*, p. 186

The ideal qualities for a commander in battle are set forth near the
beginning of Sun Tzu's *The Art of War*.

*By command I mean the general's qualities of wisdom, sincerity,
humanity, courage and strictness.*

*[Tu Mu] If wise, a commander is able to recognize changing
circumstances and to act expediently. If sincere, his men will
have no doubt of the certainty of rewards and punishments. If
humane, he loves mankind, sympathizes with others, and
appreciates their industry and toil. If courageous, he gains
victory by seizing opportunity without hesitation. If strict, his
troops are disciplined because they are in awe of him and are
afraid of punishment.*

*. . . If a general is not courageous, he will be unable to conquer
doubts or to create great plans.*

(Sun Tzu, *The Art of War*, p. 65)

Another description of the qualities desired in an ideal leader appears
in Chapter 4:

*[Tu Mu] . . . Now, the supreme requirements of generalship are
a clear perception, the harmony of his host, a profound strategy*

coupled with far-reaching plans, an understanding of the seasons and an ability to examine the human factors. For a general unable to estimate his capabilities or comprehend the arts of expediency and flexibility when faced with the opportunity to engage the enemy will advance in a stumbling and hesitant manner, looking anxiously first to his right and then to his left, and be unable to produce a plan. Credulous, he will place confidence in unreliable reports, believing at one moment this and at another that.

(Sun Tzu, *The Art of War*, pp. 87–88)

(The last sentence matches, almost word for word, Clausewitz's description of the dilemma of the commander faced with conflicting intelligence reports, as discussed in the chapter 'Intelligence in War', *On War*, Book 1, Chapter 6, p. 117.)

Most of these requirements for military leadership, such as clear perception, the ability to understand human factors, and proficiency in exploiting fleeting opportunities, depend largely on the experience and intuition of the master of war. Sun Tzu's insistence on the necessity of making fast decisions in order to capitalize on unique opportunities implies that the commander must rely on his 'gut feelings'; after all, he has no time to contemplate an infinite number of ever-changing variables.

According to *On War*, the commander or military genius cannot cope with the chaos on the battlefield unless he depends on his *coup d'oeil*, which Clausewitz variously refers to as: **'that superb display of divination'** (Clausewitz, *On War*, p. 112), **'the inner light'** (Clausewitz, *On War*, p. 102), **'the inward eye'** (*On War*, p. 102), **'discreet judgment'** (*On War*, p. 573), **'unerring prescience'** (*On War*, p. 573), and **'the sensitive instinct'** (*On War*, p. 213). **'It is a higher form of analysis'** (*On War*, p. 192), which Clausewitz defines as:

> **the quick recognition of a truth that the mind would ordinarily miss or would perceive only after long study and reflection.**
>
> (Clausewitz, *On War*, p. 102)

> **Action can never be based on anything firmer than instinct, a sensing of the truth.**
>
> (Clausewitz, *On War*, p. 108)

The man of action must at times trust in the sensitive

267

instinct of judgment, derived from his native intelligence and developed through reflection, which almost unconsciously hits on the right course.

(Clausewitz, *On War*, p. 213)

Circumstances vary so enormously in war, and are so indefinable, that a vast array of factors has to be appreciated – mostly in light of probabilities alone. The man responsible for evaluating the whole must bring to his task the quality of intuition that perceives the truth at every point.

Otherwise a chaos of opinions and considerations would arise, and fatally entangle judgment . . . Yet, even that superb display of divination, the sovereign eye of genius itself, would still fall short of historical significance without the qualities of character and temperament we have described.

(Clausewitz, *On War*, p. 112)[2]

In Book 8, Chapter 3B, Clausewitz defines the *coup d'oeil* with even greater precision:

. . . [The] intellectual activity [that] leaves the field of the exact sciences of logic and mathematics. It then becomes an art in the broadest meaning of the term – the faculty of using judgment to detect the most important and decisive elements in the vast array of facts and situations. Undoubtedly, this power of judgment consists to a greater or lesser degree in the intuitive comparison of all the factors and attendant circumstances; what is remote and secondary is at once dismissed while the most pressing and important points are identified with greater speed than could be done by strictly logical deduction.

(Clausewitz, *On War*, p. 585)[3]

Despite Jomini's attempt to develop a scientific theory for the conduct of war on the operational – though not the strategic – level of war, he, much like Clausewitz, repeatedly reminds us of the importance of the commander's intuition, experience, and *coup d'oeil*. His insistence that the successful commander possess such innate talent demonstrates that Jomini's aspiration to find a 'scientific' approach was impossible even on the lower operational level. (By 'scientific' Jomini seems to have meant primarily a systematic approach to be employed in teaching the art of war to the average military man; he was not referring to an exact, quantifiable, positivistic discipline as would be understood from the term today.)

A general thoroughly instructed in the theory of war, but not possessed of military coup d'oeil, coolness, and skill, may make an excellent strategic plan and be entirely unable to apply the rules of tactics in presence of an enemy . . .

(Jomini, *The Art of War*, p. 322)

It is almost always easy to determine the decisive point of a field of battle, but not so with the decisive moment; and it is precisely here that genius and experience are everything, and mere theory of little value.

(Jomini, *The Art of War*, p. 334)

I appreciate thoroughly the difference between the directing principles of combinations arranged in the quiet of the closet, and that special talent which is indispensable to the individual who has, amidst the noise and confusion of battle, to keep a hundred thousand men co-operating toward the attainment of a single object.

(Jomini, *The Art of War*, p. 344)

While Sun Tzu's discussion of intuition is more implicit and less detailed, he does, however, point out that not every good soldier makes an equally successful commander. This implies that education and experience alone are not enough; special qualities such as intuition and genius are required. Sun Tzu's master of war sees victory where the ordinary man cannot.[4] The accomplished commander relies on his own genius and unique reading of a situation to mold circumstances to his advantage.

Thus, those skilled at making the enemy move do so by creating a situation to which he must conform . . .

Therefore a skilled commander seeks victory from the situation and does not demand it of his subordinates.

[Ch'en Hao] Experts in war depend especially on opportunity and expediency. They do not place the burden of accomplishment on their men alone.

(Sun Tzu, *The Art of War*, p. 93)

At one point, Clausewitz argues that 'genius . . . needs no theory' (*On War*, p. 145):

> **Talent and genius operate outside the rules and theory conflicts with practice.**
>
> (Clausewitz, *On War*, p. 140)

> **Or again one may appeal to genius, which is above all rules; which amounts to admitting that rules are not only made for idiots, but are idiotic in themselves.**
>
> (Clausewitz, *On War*, p. 184)

In *The Art of War*, a commentator of Sun Tzu expresses the same idea in these words:

> *[Chia Lin] The general must rely on his ability to control the situation to his advantage as opportunity dictates. He is not bound by established procedures.*
>
> (Sun Tzu, *The Art of War*, p. 112)

Sun Tzu also underscores the significance of creativity (in other words, genius) in the commander, whom he urges not to repeat his tactics '*but* [to] *respond to circumstances in an infinite variety of ways*' (*The Art of War*, p. 100). On the whole, though, Sun Tzu appreciates the master of war more for his capacity to make rational calculations under stressful conditions than for his intuition.

> *[Tu Mu] . . . If I wish to take advantage of the enemy I must perceive not just the advantage in doing so but must first consider the ways he can harm me if I do.*
>
> *[Ho Yen-hsi] Advantage and disadvantage are mutually reproductive. The enlightened deliberate.*
>
> (Sun Tzu, *The Art of War*, p. 113)

Sun Tzu's general must also be an expert in a broader array of subjects than Clausewitz deems necessary:

> *Organization, control, assignment of appropriate ranks to officers, regulation of supply routes, and the provision of principal items to be used by the army.*

There is no general who has not heard of these matters. Those who master them win; those who do not are defeated.

Therefore in laying plans, compare the following elements, appraising them with utmost care.

(Sun Tzu, *The Art of War*, p. 65)

Particularly with regard to the highest levels of command, Sun Tzu's less romantic position is more relevant to the complexities of modern warfare while Clausewitz's concept remains highly problematic. How can we identify the military genius? How can such experience or talent be cultivated? Do different types of warfare and their various levels require special types of talent or genius? How do we know when the military genius has lost his inspiration? Can the experience and genius so successful in one war be as effective in the next? These and many other questions cannot be answered rationally or satisfactorily.

On the other hand, this does not mean that Clausewitz's concept of the military genius is useless. When we consider that Clausewitz's primary level of analysis is the lower level of operations, where there is little time to linger over complex decisions, no military leader can succeed without intuition – without the special ability to ask '*De quoi s'agit-il?*' (What is it all about?). The *coup d'oeil* of the military genius is not irrational; it simply reflects a different mode of rationality in which intuitive decisions can be explained rationally *ex post facto*. Yet attaching the same importance to intuition within the higher strata of politics and strategy, or relying on it to an excessive degree, may ultimately produce irrational behavior. At the highest levels of policymaking and strategy, intuition has a much smaller role to play, and can often become counter-productive.

The role of the ideal military leader is no less crucial to the people and the state in Sun Tzu's treatise than it is in that of Clausewitz. Sun Tzu refers to the master of war as the man who carries the heaviest of all responsibilities – the lives of others.

[Ho Yen-hsi] . . . the responsibility for a martial host of a million lies on one man. He is the trigger of its spirit.

(Sun Tzu, *The Art of War*, p. 108)

And therefore the general who in advancing does not seek personal fame, and in withdrawing is not concerned with avoiding punishment, but whose only purpose is to protect the people

271

*and promote the best interests of his sovereign, is the precious
jewel of the state . . . [Tu Mu] Few such are to be had.*
(Sun Tzu, *The Art of War*, p. 128)

While the model for Clausewitz's military genius might be a field
commander like Rommel, Guderian, Napoleon, Nelson or, Lee – Sun
Tzu's master of war, with his wider perspective, might be exemplified
by a Pericles, Fabius Maximus, Montgomery, or Eisenhower. Inasmuch
as no single military leader can embody all of the qualities necessary to
satisfy the demands of war, there will always be a place for both of these
valid, complementary models.[5]

Jomini adds one caveat to his analysis: he suggests that the role of
the military genius has become less important in the age of mass
mobilization. Jomini then cites the example of Napoleon, whose failure
to recognize this trend may have ultimately contributed to his downfall.

He [Napoleon] *fell from the height of his greatness because he
forgot that the mind and strength of man have their limits, and that
the more enormous the masses which are set in motion, the more
subordinate does individual genius become to the inflexible laws
of nature, and the less is the control which it exercises over events.*
(Jomini, *Grand Military Operations*, p. 462)

Unlike Jomini, Clausewitz is skeptical about the value of staff work, as
demonstrated by his critical comments in Book 8, Chapter 9:

. . . **When the usual thing occurs, and a 'trained' general
staff makes such a plan as a matter of routine . . . when the
moves themselves are made with self-styled expertise to
reach their goal by devious routes and combinations; when
modern armies have to separate in order to display 'con-
summate art' by reuniting two weeks later at the utmost
risk: then we can only say we abhor this departure from
the straight, simple, easy approach in order to plunge
deliberately into confusion. Such idiocy becomes the more
likely, the less the war is run by the commander-in-chief
himself . . . that is, as a single activity of an individual
invested with huge powers; [and] . . . the more the plan as a
whole is cooked up by an unrealistic general staff on the
recipes of a half-a-dozen amateurs.**
(Clausewitz, *On War*, p. 612)

17

Boldness and Calculation

Opportunities in war don't wait.

Pericles
Thucydides, *The History of the Peloponnesian War*, Bk 1, Section 142, p. 82

Fortune favors the bold.

Livy
In war, the power to recognize your chance and take it is of more use than anything else.

Machiavelli, *The Art of War*, p. 718

The fundamental similarities and differences between *The Art of War* and *On War* are never more evident than in their descriptions of the ideal commander's ability to manipulate risk and exploit opportunities. Both Sun Tzu and Clausewitz believe that in this most critical test of military leadership, the commander must combine courage and daring with reflectiveness, but the two strategists differ in emphasis: Clausewitz, on the whole, prefers boldness to calculation, while Sun Tzu favors what we would call calculated risks.

If courageous [a commander] *gains victory by seizing opportunity without hesitation . . .*

[Shen Pao-hsu] If a general is not courageous, he will be unable to conquer doubts or create great plans.

(Sun Tzu, *The Art of War*, p. 65)

And for this reason, the wise general in his deliberations must consider both favourable and unfavourable factors.

[Ts'ao Ts'ao] He ponders the dangers inherent in the advantages, and the advantages inherent in the danger.

By taking into account the favourable factors, he makes his plan feasible, by taking into account the unfavourable, he may resolve the difficulties.

(Sun Tzu, *The Art of War*, p. 113)

Those unable to understand the dangers inherent in employing troops are equally unable to understand the advantageous ways of doing so.

(Sun Tzu, *The Art of War*, p. 73)

Furthermore, Sun Tzu observes that there is a place, even a need, for both cautious and risk-taking commanders:

[A skilled commander] *selects his men and they exploit the situation. [Li Ch'uan] . . . Now the valiant can fight; the cautious defend, and the wise counsel. Thus there is none whose talent is wasted.*

(Sun Tzu, *The Art of War*, p. 93)

[Tu Mu] If one trusts solely to brave generals who love fighting, this will cause trouble. If one relies solely on those who are cautious, their frightened hearts will find it difficult to control the situation.

(Sun Tzu, *The Art of War*, p. 94)

Knowing when *not* to fight is as vital as knowing when to accept battle (see Sun Tzu, *The Art of War*, p. 82). Although seeking a reasonable balance between caution and courage, Sun Tzu leans toward the prudent, calculating commander rather than the one with a propensity to take greater risks. In game theory terminology, Sun Tzu concludes that the master of war should be more disposed to rely on a Montgomery-type of mini-max strategy (minimum risk and maximum gain) rather than a Rommel-type of maxi-max strategy (maximum risk and maximum gain).

By comparison, there is little doubt that Clausewitz usually prefers the daring, risk-taking general whose boldness is not necessarily circumscribed by rational calculations:

Let us admit that boldness in war even has its own prerogatives. It must be granted a certain power over and above successful calculations involving space, time, and magni-

tude of forces, for whenever it is superior, it will take advantage of its opponent's weakness. In other words, it is a genuinely creative force.

(Clausewitz, *On War*, p. 190)

Given the same amount of intelligence, timidity will do a thousand times more damage in war than audacity.

(Clausewitz, *On War*, p. 191)

In any specific action, in any measure we may undertake, we always have the choice between the most audacious and the most careful solution. Some people think that the theory of war always advises the latter. That assumption is false. If the theory does advise anything, it is the nature of war to advise the most decisive, that is, the most audacious.[1]

To Clausewitz, boldness is the trait that produces the great captains of war:

A distinguished commander without boldness is unthinkable. No man who is not born bold can play such a role, and therefore we consider this quality the first prerequisite of the great military leader.

(Clausewitz, *On War*, p. 192)

In fact, what worries Clausewitz most about the calibre of military leadership is the attenuation of boldness often experienced by commanders as they rise through the ranks:

How much of this quality [boldness] remains by the time he reaches a senior rank, after training and experience have affected and modified it, is another question.

(Clausewitz, *On War*, p. 191)

The higher the military rank, the greater the degree to which activity is governed by the mind, by the intellect, by insight. Consequently, boldness, which is a quality of temperament, will tend to be held in check. This explains why it is so rare in the higher ranks, and why it is all the more admirable when found there.

(Clausewitz, *On War*, p. 191)[2]

275

Since he believes that boldness is the most essential quality, Clausewitz prefers noble failure to inaction; and he observes that calculation without boldness is sterile and likely to fail. Consequently, boldness, which is rarest in the higher ranks, is the more decisive of the two. As he comments, '**Even foolhardiness – that is, boldness without any object – is not to be despised; basically it stems from daring, which in this case has erupted with a passion unrestrained by thought**' (Clausewitz, *On War*, p. 190).

With his greater reliance on intuition and temperament, Clausewitz's military genius can manipulate dangerous and ambiguous situations to his advantage:[3]

> **We should not habitually prefer the course that involves the least uncertainty [i.e., Sun Tzu's preference]. That would be an enormous mistake, as our theoretical arguments will show. There are times when the utmost daring is the height of wisdom.**
>
> (Clausewitz, *On War*, p. 167)

Nevertheless, since Clausewitz's foremost concern is the operational – not the strategic – level of decision-making (that is, he focuses more on the immediate outcome of a battle than on longer-range strategic policies), he would undoubtedly have recommended increased caution on the strategic level.[4]

But which general would be most effective if the two were to confront each other: the cautious-reflective, mini-max general preferred by Sun Tzu, or the risk-taking maxi-max type favored by Clausewitz? Here Clausewitz arrives at a surprising conclusion:

> **Whenever boldness encounters timidity, it is likely to be the winner, because timidity itself implies a loss of equilibrium.** *Boldness will be at a disadvantage only in an encounter with deliberate caution, which may be considered bold in its own right and is certainly just as powerful and effective; but such cases are rare.* [my emphasis]
>
> (Clausewitz, *On War*, p. 190)

18

Corbett, Clausewitz, and Sun Tzu

> He who commands the sea is at great
> liberty, and may take as much or as little of
> the war as he will.
>
> Francis Bacon

Even the most creative theories in history were not conceived in a
vacuum; one way or another, they owe something to the works of others.
To describe this intellectual and intuitive process, historian of science
I. B. Cohen develops a concept called 'the transformation of ideas',[1]
which reveals how great scientists have used the existing body of knowledge as a basis or catalyst for their own inspiration. Scientists such as
Newton and Darwin, for example, either synthesized and combined the
work of others while adding their own ideas – or were heuristically
stimulated by existing ideas to develop their own original concepts. The
same is true of those whose creative and analytical thought-processes
have 'transformed' the intricacies of strategy, in this case, naval
strategy, into an innovative theory or body of work. It is well known that
Mahan, as he himself made clear, was significantly influenced by Baron
de Jomini's work,[2] and that Sir Julian Corbett was equally influenced by
Clausewitz's *On War*.

My argument is that while Mahan integrates and synthesizes Jomini's
work with his own, Corbett uses Clausewitz's *On War* as a heuristic
point of departure. Mahan, in other words, remains loyal to Jomini's
ideas, and by extension, those of the 'continental strategists'. In contrast, Corbett, although inspired by *On War*, develops ideas different
from and sometimes contradictory to those of Clausewitz. The subtle
approach adopted by Corbett ironically resembles that of a work he had
never read – Sun Tzu's *The Art of War*.[3] In view of the limited space
available, I will focus on two of Corbett's most original ideas which also
provide excellent illustrations of the differences between naval and

land-based warfare: namely, his positions on 'the concentration of force' and 'limited war'.

Let me first, however, say a few words on what Corbett and Clausewitz *do* have in common. To begin with, Clausewitz and Corbett share a belief in the primacy of politics in war and in devising an appropriate strategy to protect the national interests. Clearly, Corbett independently understood the importance of the primacy of politics before reading *On War* in 1904, but Clausewitz's ideas did help him to clarify this idea. Corbett also believes in studying and developing the theory of war for educational purposes. His debt to Clausewitz on this score is made clear in his chapter on 'The Theoretical Study of War – Its Use and Limitations' (*Some Principles*, pp. 3–11). Herein he adds that such study will establish a 'common vehicle of expression and a common plane of thought . . . for the sake of mental solidarity between a chief and his subordinates' (Corbett, *Some Principles*, p. 8).

Corbett also agrees with Clausewitz that since even the best theory of war is 'not . . . a substitute for judgement and experience', it cannot 'systematize strategy into an exact science' (*Some Principles*, p. 10). At best, theory can ascertain what is 'normal' – but war, with its reciprocal, uncertain, and complex nature, is dominated by deviations from the norm (*Some Principles*, pp. 8–9). Friction, chance, and luck must never be discounted as well.[4] Corbett therefore resembles Clausewitz in his repeated emphasis on the importance of understanding both the value and the inherent limitations of a theory of war. 'Strategical analysis can never give exact results. It aims only at approximations, at groupings which will serve to guide but will always leave much to the judgement' (*Some Principles,* pp. 83–84). With the constantly changing nature of war (more so in Corbett's time, because of the accelerated development of new technologies and weapons at sea), the first question that either man would ask is: What is the nature of this war?[5] (Much more could be said about the similarities between the two, but let us now turn to a discussion of their differences.)

Corbett's most glaring criticism of Clausewitz, the continental strategists (i.e., Jomini), and most British naval strategists of his time concerns their 'big-battle fixation'.[6] Most of Corbett's contemporaries were content to accept this crude and highly selective version of Clausewitz's ideas because it conveniently supported their own beliefs.[7] This was a major component of the Napoleonic style of war that consisted of a 'strenuous and persistent effort – not resting to secure each minor advantage, but pressing the enemy without pause or rest till he is utterly overthrown . . .'.[8] (Corbett believes that the origin of what he terms Clausewitz's fetish for the constant search for the decisive battle could be traced back to Oliver Cromwell (*Some Principles*, pp. 22, 157, 176).) The search for the decisive battle is closely related to Clausewitz's *principle of destruction* and achievement of victory through the greatest possible *concentration of forces* at the decisive point. Clausewitz presents the idea thus:

> **Combat is the only effective force in war; its aim is to destroy the enemy's forces as a means to a further end . . . It follows that the destruction of the enemy's forces underlies all military actions; all plans are ultimately based on it, resting on it like an arch on its abutment . . . The decision by arms is for all major and minor operations in war what cash payment is in commerce . . . Thus it is evident that destruction of the enemy forces is always the superior, more effective means, with which others cannot compete.**
>
> (Clausewitz, *On War*, p. 97)

> **We . . . claim that the direct annihilation of the enemy's forces must always be the dominant consideration. We simply want to establish this dominance of the destructive principle.**
>
> (Clausewitz, *On War*, p. 228)

The maximum concentration of forces was indeed the key to winning the decisive battle and overthrowing the enemy: Clausewitz, Sun Tzu, Jomini, and all of the 'continental thinkers' would agree that this is the most important principle of war. Clausewitz puts it this way:

> **. . . As many troops as possible should be brought into the engagement at the decisive point . . . This is the first principle of strategy . . .**
>
> (Clausewitz, *On War*, pp. 194–195)

> **The best strategy is always to be very strong; first in general and then at the decisive point . . . There is no higher and**

> **simpler law of strategy than that of keeping one's forces concentrated.**
>
> (Clausewitz, *On War*, p. 204) (See also Appendix F, below.)

Corbett does not believe that the concentration of naval forces at sea is the highest and simplest law of strategy. On the contrary, he observes that the principle of concentration has become 'a kind of shibboleth' that has done more harm than good (*Some Principles*, p. 134). The *principle of concentration* is 'a truism – no one would dispute it. As a canon of practical strategy it is untrue . . .' (*Some Principles*, p. 160).

> The crude maxims as to primary objects which seem to have served well enough in continental warfare have never worked so clearly where the sea enters seriously into war. In such cases, it will not suffice to say that primary object of the army is to destroy the enemy's army, or that of the fleet to destroy the enemy's fleet. The delicate interactions of the land and sea factors produce conditions too intricate for such blunt solutions. Even the initial equations they present are too complex to be reduced by the simple application of rough-and-ready maxims.
>
> (Corbett, *Some Principles*, p. 16)

In view of his strongly held opinions, it is not surprising that Corbett expends much effort to prove his point. Indeed, his refutation of the principle of concentration at sea produces some of his most creative and original ideas in *Some Principles of Maritime Strategy*. Furthermore, the process of developing these original ideas embroiled Corbett in a vitriolic debate with some of the leading military theorists and naval experts of his time. This most assuredly did nothing to enhance his reputation, since the subtlety of his ideas destined them to be misunderstood. For example, Lord Sydenham later accused him of exerting a negative influence on the doctrine, plans, and morale of the British Navy, thereby contributing to their failure to achieve decisive results in the Battle of Jutland.[9] Many years later, Cyril Falls charged Corbett with 'minimizing the importance of combat'.[10] Despite this barrage of criticism, Corbett steadfastly refused to change his strategically 'blasphemous' conclusions.

Corbett's first argument was that superior concentration at sea cannot necessarily force a major engagement because it is easier for the enemy's fleet to avoid battle at sea than it is for an army to do so on land.

Paradoxically, the greater the concentration achieved by one's own fleet, the more likely the weaker opponent is to avoid battle. Only through dispersing or rather pretending to disperse its fleet can the stronger navy lure the enemy into battle: 'If we are too superior, or our concentration too well arranged for him to hope for victory, then our concentration has almost always had the effect of forcing him to disperse for sporadic action' (*Some Principles*, p. 138). Therefore, only less concentration (or the appearance thereof) will lead to a major battle.[11] Moreover, concentration at sea is problematic for other reasons as well. The more a navy concentrates, the fewer the sea lanes of communications and space it can secure and control. 'Concentration', Corbett notes, 'implies a continual conflict between cohesion and reach' (*Some Principles*, p. 136). A corollary of this point is Corbett's argument that complete or full concentration at sea is impossible because, from the very beginning of the conflict, a substantial number of ships must be diverted for protection of vulnerable interests such as overseas trade and other resources. 'The more you concentrate your forces and efforts to secure the desired decision, the more you will expose your trade to sporadic attacks' (*Some Principles*, p. 160; also pp. 128–152, 155–161). Superior concentration thus not only deters the weaker opponent from seeking battle, but also presents him with the opportunity to attack his enemy's exposed naval lines of communication.

Superior concentration of naval forces creates yet another serious problem. The greater the concentration of a fleet, the more difficult it is to conceal its whereabouts and movements. 'Once the mass is formed, concealment and flexibility are at an end' (*Some Principles*, pp. 131, 138). Here, Corbett is making an additional argument, much like Sun Tzu's, for the need to keep one's own dispositions 'shapeless' in order to avoid disclosing one's intentions. Sun Tzu states:

> *The ultimate in disposing one's troops is to be without ascertainable shape. Then the most penetrating spies cannot pry in nor can the wise lay plans against you. It is according to the shapes that I lay plans for victory, but the multitude does not comprehend this. Although everyone can see the outward aspects, none understands the way in which I have created victory.*
>
> (Sun Tzu, *The Art of War*, p. 100)

Corbett also believes that calculated dispersion and 'shapelessness' create unexpected combinations and surprises that bring victory.

> War has proved to the hilt that victories have not only to be won, but worked for. They must be worked for by bold strategical combinations, which as a rule entail at least apparent dispersal. They can only be achieved by taking risks, and the greatest and most effective of these is division.
>
> (Corbett, *Some Principles*, p. 134)

> The next principle is flexibility. Concentration should be so arranged that any two parts may freely cohere, and that all parts may quickly condense into a mass at any point in the area of concentration. The object of holding back from forming the mass is to deny the enemy knowledge of our actual distribution or its intention at any given moment, and at the same time to ensure that it will be adjusted to meet any dangerous movement that is open to him. Further than this our aim should be not merely to prevent any part from being overpowered by a superior force, but to regard every detached squadron as a trap to lure the enemy to destruction. The ideal concentration, in short, is an appearance of weakness that covers a reality of strength.
>
> (Corbett, *Some Principles*, p. 152; see also p. 206)

Unlike Clausewitz, and very much like Sun Tzu, Corbett underscores the value of deception in the achievement of concentration at the decisive point. For Corbett, concentration is not simply amassing the largest number of ships, as Mahan or Clausewitz would advocate; rather, it means manipulating the enemy's perceptions so that he will fight on his (Corbett's) terms. Sun Tzu describes it thus:

> *Those skilled at making the enemy move do so by creating a situation to which he must conform. They entice him with something he is certain to take, and with lures of ostensible profit they wait for him in strength.*
>
> (Sun Tzu, *The Art of War*, p. 93)

Sun Tzu's approach can be described as negative in the sense that he considers the division and distraction of the enemy to be more important than maximizing the concentration of his own forces.[12]

At this juncture, some other notable similarities between Corbett and Sun Tzu should be mentioned. Corbett develops his theoretical insights against a broad background: in other words, he is interested in the diplomatic alliance systems and coalitions formed before and during a war; he is concerned with the economic and financial dimensions of waging war, as well as with the technological and material aspects of war that are of no interest to Clausewitz. (Clausewitz wrote *On War* before the age of the Industrial Revolution, which triggered an ever-accelerating rate of technological changes.[13]) Corbett also agrees with Sun Tzu that the intelligent strategist must fight only on his own preferred terms and exploit his comparative advantage. As Sun Tzu puts it:

> *Therefore the clever combatant imposes his will on the enemy but does not allow the enemy's will to be imposed on him.*
>
> (Sun Tzu, *The Art of War*, Giles translation, p. 42)

> *And therefore those skilled in war bring the enemy to the field of battle, and are not brought by him.*
>
> (Sun Tzu, *The Art of War*, p. 96)

Corbett's preference for a limited war of a particular type in a particular place and his preference for the strategic though not operational and tactical levels are all part of his search for Britain's (or that of any other nation in similar circumstances) comparative advantage. This is a critical part of all strategic planning that Sun Tzu and Corbett emphasize, but which Clausewitz seems to ignore (see Chapter 9 above, pp. 114–115). Typically, the search for a comparative advantage is valued more by the weak, or by naval powers with limited resources to protect a vast empire or fight a formidable land power.

Another important approach shared by Corbett and Sun Tzu is their desire to win at the lowest possible cost. Since this entails taking minimum risks for maximum gains, their theories are dominated by the search for low-cost victories and force multipliers. The principal lesson Corbett draws from Britain's strategy in the Mediterranean during the War of Spanish Succession is that it reveals '. . . how an intelligent, if limited, appreciation of sea power to a tender diplomatic situation could produce results out of all proportion to its real physical potential'.[14] He learns a similar lesson from the British naval war against Napoleon, where 30,000 soldiers at the Downs forced Napoleon to tie down 300,000 men from the National Guards to defend the French coast (*Some Principles*, p. 69). Elsewhere, Corbett points out that the effect of British amphibious threats to use small contingent forces to invade the continent or to divert enemy forces to the coast '. . . was always out of all proportion to the intrinsic strength employed or the positive results it could give . . . Its value lay in its power of containing [a] force greater than its own' (*Some Principles*, p. 67).

Convinced that an economy of force was a dangerous false economy, Clausewitz instead prefers to focus on the *effectiveness* of force; that is, on the outcome, not the cost. **'In war'**, he says, **'too small an effort can result not just in failure but in positive harm** [where] **each side is driven to outdo the other . . .'** (Clausewitz, *On War*, p. 585). Clausewitz's conception of a true economy of force is not (as Sun Tzu, Corbett, or modern compilations of the principles of war would argue) to win at the lowest possible cost, but rather to make use of all available forces *regardless of the cost* (see Clausewitz, *On War*, p. 213). Corbett and Sun Tzu also share a belief in the concept of the indirect approach, which relates to the search for a comparative advantage, economy of force, surprise and deception, and limited war. (Unfortunately, a detailed comparison of Corbett, the British style of warfare, and Sun Tzu cannot be attempted here.)

Unlike Clausewitz, Jomini, and the other continental strategists, Corbett is not infatuated with the search for the decisive battle or the need for the strategic offensive. In general, he favors the strategic *defensive*, with an emphasis on the offense at the operational level. As a result, his detractors *mistakenly thought that his comments pertaining to the strategic level of war were referring to its lower levels.* Corbett's strategy is based on *rational, unsentimental calculations*, not on vaguely romantic obsessions with the brilliance of Napoleon or Nelson. Again, like Sun Tzu, Corbett is generally opposed to taking unnecessary risks in war, whereas Clausewitz believes that the military genius, led by his intuition, must be defined by his readiness to take significant risks. **'Boldness in war . . . has its own prerogatives. It must be granted a certain power over and above successful calculations . . . In other words, it is a genuinely creative force . . . A distinguished** commander without boldness is unthinkable' (Clausewitz, *On War*, pp. 190–192). Corbett certainly values boldness as an essential leadership quality, but he concludes that careful calculations and strategic creativity should govern all actions.

Since the bravado and daring inherent in bold action naturally held greater appeal for most of Corbett's critics, his sagacious observations on the strategic advantages of the defense were interpreted as signs of passivity and poor fighting spirit.[15] Upon closer examination, Corbett's strategic defensive is found to employ measures such as an intense local offensive, the projection of land forces, various types of blockades, and raids on enemy trade routes. Moreover, Corbett recognizes that once the enemy has been sufficiently weakened on sea and on land, the move over to the strategic offensive should not be delayed. Yet, as mentioned earlier, the cult of the offensive so dominated the thinking of his contemporaries that the essence of Corbett's outwardly controversial message was not really heard. As a strategist, Corbett is more concerned with the question of how to obtain certain objectives than he is with the form of a particular war.

According to Corbett, naval strategists must accept the fact that war at sea is not usually a zero-sum game, since it is rarely possible to achieve full command of the sea.

> [It is erroneous to assume] . . . that if one belligerent loses the command of the sea [that] it passes at once to the other belligerent . . . The most common situation in naval war is that neither side has the command; that the normal position is not a commanded sea, but an uncommanded sea . . . The command is normally in dispute. It is this state of dispute with which naval strategy is most nearly concerned . . .
>
> (Corbett, *Some Principles*, p. 91)

Corbett was not unduly concerned about this issue, probably because he was confident that the British Royal Navy would gain command of the sea soon enough. This 'relaxed' attitude certainly clashes with Clausewitz's concept of war as the aggressive application of force to end disputes as soon as possible. Clarity is the objective; decisive action is the means. For Clausewitz, the very idea of tolerating an ongoing dispute or a 'shared sea' would be repugnant. As one who also sought the clarity of a decisive battle, Mahan shared Clausewitz's impatience with such ambiguity.

Yet is achieving the desired concentration and winning the decisive battle worth the cost? Clausewitz, Jomini, Mahan, and the 'continental strategists' would all reply in the affirmative. Inflicting a decisive defeat allows the victor to **'compel** [the] **enemy to do** [his] **will'**. Clausewitz's own view is not, however, simplistic: he knows that even the most decisive victory is only a necessary but not a sufficient condition for accomplishing the victorious state's long-run objectives. **'In war'**, he warns, **'the result is never final'** (Clausewitz, *On War*, p. 80). By this he means that the military gains secured in battle will not last unless the political leaders and diplomats offer the vanquished side peace terms that are acceptable in the long run. This includes making a concerted effort to establish common interests between the former foes. (See Chapter 14 above.)

The search for a decisive victory does not, however, have the same allure for Corbett. As a naval strategist, he believes that

> . . . since men live upon land and not upon the sea, the great issues between nations at war have always been decided – except in the rarest of cases – either by what your army can do against your enemy's territory or national life or else by fear of what the fleet makes it possible for your army to do.
>
> (Corbett, *Some Principles*, p. 16)

In short, a decisive victory at sea is so rare that it is not normally worth the effort. When all other naval strategists of Corbett's time agreed that Nelson's victory at Trafalgar was exemplary, Corbett reasoned that such adulation was undeserved. After all, he points out, the strategic results of the great sea victory were indecisive as far as the war against Napoleon on the continent was concerned, and Nelson may have taken too great a tactical risk.

> . . . Trafalgar is ranked as one of the decisive battles of the world, and yet of all the great victories, there is not one which to all appearance was so barren of immediate result . . . It gave England finally the dominion of the seas, but it left Napoleon dictator of the continent. So incomprehensible was its apparent sterility that to fill the void a legend grew up that it saved England from invasion.[16]

Clearly, Corbett was not trying to enhance his popularity as a naval strategist when he wrote these objectively sensible words of national and naval 'heresy'. For Corbett, then, an 'open' or 'closed' blockade; the threat of a 'fleet in being'; and the naval support of land operations by transporting, supplying, and landing army troops in combined operations are the 'bread and butter' of naval operations and the essence of naval strength. As mentioned earlier, his stubborn adherence to this unpopular position in his work as well as in his lectures at the Royal Naval College later sparked accusations that his strategic theory underlay the failure of the Battle of Jutland. Surely, Corbett thought that the Battle of Jutland was unnecessary, that without a decisive victory it just confirmed British naval superiority and put the German High Seas Fleet out of the picture for the remainder of the war. Even a decisive British victory in the Battle of Jutland, as in the case of Trafalgar, was unlikely to have had more than a negligible impact on the land war.

*   *   *

Corbett's development of the concept of *limited war* provides us with another good example of his creative contribution to strategic theory in general and naval strategy in particular. The theory of war expounded by Corbett has little in common with its heuristic starting point, namely, Clausewitz's concept of limited war as set forth in *On War*. Corbett's new concept of limited war also enables us to see how the naval perspective could breathe fresh insight into a strategy that was previously ignored or misunderstood by the continental strategists.

First, a brief word on Clausewitz's concept of limited war is in place. For most of his intellectual life, Clausewitz was chiefly interested in the study of total or absolute war. This reflected his personal as well as the Prussian experience with the wars of the French Revolution and Napoleon. His ideal-type of war was indeed unlimited in scope; any lesser effort meant lost effectiveness in proportion to its deviation from the inherent, true nature of war. With the defeat of Napoleon, the restoration of the European balance of power, and the development of Prussia's strategic problems, Clausewitz gradually recognized the existence of a type of limited war that was, in reality, much more common than total war.[17] In this type of limited war, the enemy's army was no longer the center of gravity, and the optimal strategy was not a search for the decisive battle.

287

Clausewitz's 'discovery' of the prevalence of limited war in turn led to the evolution of his concept of the primacy of politics. The absolute or total war has, in theory, its own logic and momentum, which is, in reality, subject to the constraints imposed by the political interests of the state. Vital interests call for an unlimited war effort, while secondary interests justify no more than a limited investment of resources and effort. *Thus, the importance of the belligerents' stakes in a war as defined by their political leaders as well as their reciprocal interaction determines whether the war remains limited in scope.*

A second reason to limit the effort expended in war concerns *the relative strength and means available to the belligerents.* Nevertheless, if insufficient resources or strength were the only reasons for limiting a war effort, the 'operational theory of war' or other non-political factors would be enough to determine whether a war should be limited or expanded. Clausewitz's explication of the theory of limited war and the primacy of politics provides the crucial missing dimension for such determinations. If he had not made this 'discovery', Clausewitz might have begun to appreciate the prevalence of limited war anyway by viewing it as a function of insufficient means to wage all-out war. However, his later recognition of limited war was based primarily on political considerations. In a truly limited war, as defined by the political authorities, weak motivation to fight is enough to fetter the war effort of an otherwise stronger state. Thus, the degree to which a war will be limited is, in the end, determined by political and military considerations of relative strength.[18]

Clausewitz also distinguishes between defensive and offensive limited wars. Limited war normally occurs when the defending side has no incentive to go to war or when the weaker side is attacked by the stronger one. In such instances, the defense allows the passive or weaker side to wage war at the lowest possible cost while stalling until his opponent gives up, allies come to his aid, or he can move over to the attack.

If a state's objectives are confined to the acquisition of a relatively small amount of territory for annexation or bargaining purposes, it pursues a correspondingly limited war. At times, a limited offensive can take a preemptive form in order to forestall an enemy attack or secure a better forward defensive position. Clausewitz also concludes that limited offensives strengthen the attacker if the territory thereby acquired is adjacent to his own – but they can actually weaken him if the same territory is non-contiguous. In addition, Clausewitz argues that if an offensive leaves the attacker's own territory vulnerable to a counter-attack, the would-be attacker is better off preserving his territorial integrity than acquiring territory of marginal value.

Another special type of limited war identified by Clausewitz draws Corbett's interest as well: this was a situation in which one state assists another in making a limited contribution to a common cause. This involves sending

> . . . a moderately sized force [to] . . . help; but if things go wrong, the operation is pretty well written off, and one tries to withdraw at the smallest possible cost. It is traditional . . . for states to make offensive and defensive pacts for mutual support – though not to the point of fully espousing one another's interests and quarrels. Regardless of the purpose of the war or the scale of the enemy's exertions, they pledge each other in advance to contribute a fixed and usually modest force . . . It would be tidier . . . if the contingent promised . . . were placed under the ally's disposal and he were free to use it as he wished. It would then in effect be a hired force. But that is far from what really happens. The auxiliary force usually operates under its own commander; he is dependent only on his own government, and the objective the latter sets him will be as ambiguous as its aims . . . The affair is often more like a business deal. In light of what risk he expects and dividend he hopes for, each will invest about 30,000 to 40,000 men and behave as if that were all he stood to lose . . . Even when both share a major interest, action is clogged by diplomatic reservations, and as a rule the negotiations only pledge a small and limited contingent . . .
>
> (Clausewitz, *On War*, p. 603)[19]

After summarizing Clausewitz's (and Jomini's) discussion of limited war (*Some Principles*, pp. 41–51), Corbett asserts that Clausewitz 'never apprehended the full significance of his [own] brilliant theory'. His outlook 'was still purely continental and the limitations of continental warfare tend to veil the fuller meaning of the principle he had framed . . .'. Corbett then suggests that since Clausewitz's death had doomed his theory to a perpetually unfinished state, he (Corbett) would adapt Clausewitz's theory of limited war 'to modern imperial conditions . . . above all where the maritime element forcibly asserts itself . . . with its far-reaching effects for a maritime and above all an insular Power'. In the process of brilliantly adapting Clausewitz's theory to the unique circumstances of naval warfare, particularly to the needs of British strategy, Corbett actually developed his own innovative theory of limited war in maritime strategy.

Corbett undoubtedly understood intuitively the nature of this subject from his own historical research, but Clausewitz provided him, *first*, with the ideal expression 'limited war', and, *second*, with the conceptual framework for a nascent theory that did not emphasize the all-out war in search of the decisive battle. This gave Corbett the impetus to make the transition from the 'higher', continental, unlimited form of strategy to its 'lower', maritime, limited form. Corbett's original – not derivative – theory not only transcends that of Clausewitz but also adds an important new dimension to naval strategy. While Corbett was convinced that death alone had kept Clausewitz from eventually reaching the same conclusions, it is actually unlikely that Clausewitz would have progressed along these lines without direct experience in maritime warfare or familiarity with naval or imperial history (see note 18). Corbett himself mentions that although Jomini wrote a chapter on 'Principal Maritime Expeditions,' his 'entirely continental thought had failed to penetrate the subject' (*Some Principles*, p. 56).[20]

From his naval and broader imperial perspective, Corbett found Clausewitz's theory of limited war was marred by its narrow, continental focus (*Some Principles*, p. 54). He therefore constructed his own ideal paradigm of limited war by first exposing the weaknesses of Clausewitz's argument. The first of his two main points is that in wartime conditions on the continent, as opposed to those in the maritime and imperial environment, wars were fought mostly between adjacent states. This, in Corbett's opinion, made escalation almost inevitable. 'Such territory is usually an organic part of your enemy's country, or otherwise of so much importance to him that he will be willing to use unlimited effort to retain it' (*Some Principles*, p. 54). Although this critique holds true as far as it goes, Clausewitz cannot be accused of neglecting the question of escalation; in fact, he was acutely aware of the inherent tendency of war to escalate.[21] (See Appendix C, pp. 328–329.)

Corbett's second point is that in wars between contiguous continental states 'there will be no strategical obstacle to his [the enemy's] being able to use his whole force . . .' (*Some Principles*, pp. 54–55). In other words, the nature of continental war makes it difficult to limit political aims because one or both states are able to use all of the means at their disposal to protect the inevitably threatened vital interests. Maritime and imperial wars, on the other hand, are fought overseas or in remote peripheral areas that do not threaten the other belligerent's vital interests. Thus, escalation in this environment is not unavoidable because the opponent can limit his political aims or escalate according to his own discretion.

Another crucial difference between continental and maritime warfare is that in the maritime environment, the dominant naval power can isolate the theater of war to prevent the introduction of enemy reinforcements as well as secure its home defense. As Corbett demonstrates, this means that the conditions for the ideal limited war exist only in maritime warfare and can only be exploited by the preponderant naval power:

> Limited war is only permanently possible to island powers or between powers which are separated by sea, and then *only* when the power desiring limited war is able to command the sea to such a degree as to be able not only to isolate the distant object, but also to render impossible the invasion of his home territory.
>
> (Corbett, *Some Principles*, p. 57)

As long as its navy is strong enough to protect its home from invasion, an island naval power enjoys a unique advantage that Sun Tzu would have appreciated.[22] From this invulnerable position, such a navy can, at its own discretion, project its limited land power while preventing the enemy from doing the same. Even if a naval power is weaker in absolute terms, it can not only hold its own but can also use its power overseas to compete with more powerful land powers. This, in Corbett's estimation, was the secret of British power that explained how 'a small country with a weak army should have been able to gather to herself the most desirable regions of the earth, and to gather them at the expense of the greatest military powers . . . It remained for Clausewitz, unknown to himself, to discover that explanation, and he reveals it to us in the inherent strength of limited war . . .' (*Some Principles*, pp. 58–59).

In reality, Clausewitz's theory cannot claim credit for this explanation of the expansion of British power. This can be attributed solely to Corbett's own development of a new form of limited war in the unique maritime environment. Clausewitz's theory describes a defensive limited war necessitated by a state's limited ambitions or weakness, while Corbett's demonstrates how limited strength coupled with a suitable strategy and a particular set of circumstances can be used to expand the power of the state. For Clausewitz, as we know, the decision to wage a limited war is first and foremost a political decision (which can also depend on the availability of means). Corbett takes his theory of the ideal-type maritime limited war one step further as *a new method of war*. In doing so, he *moves away from political considerations* and concentrates on the most effective use of limited means by grafting his own ideal type of the true limited war onto Clausewitz's concept of **'war by limited contingency'** (Clausewitz, *On War*, p. 603). The result is an *integrated theory of combined naval and land operations* which allows a small but effective naval power (under the ideal conditions described above) to maximize the yield of the limited means at its disposal. The success of such a 'war by limited contingency' hinges upon 'the intimacy with which naval and military action can be combined to give the contingent a weight and mobility that are beyond its extrinsic power' (*Some Principles*, pp. 65, 67). This is a case where the result achieved is truly more than the sum of its parts.

Another advantage of 'war by limited contingency' in which one deploys a 'disposal force' is that, even if all fails, the possible gains outweigh the risks entailed (*Some Principles*, p. 62). When availing itself of this method, a state has the choice of fighting by either limited or unlimited means. Indeed, in the Peninsular War, which provided the perfect conditions for a 'war by limited contingency', Britain applied '. . . the limited form to an unlimited war. Our object was unlimited. It was nothing less than the overthrow of Napoleon. Complete success at sea had failed to do it, but that success had given us the power of applying the limited form, which was the most decisive form of offence within our means . . .' (*Some Principles*, p. 65). While the continental version of 'war by limited contingency' invariably escalates into an unlimited form, the maritime (British) version can remain limited (*Some Principles*, p. 66).

Obtaining 'unlimited' results with limited force – the type of force multiplier found in Corbett's paradigm of the ideal limited war – can of course be identified with the theory of Sun Tzu, who says, *'Thus the potential of troops skillfully commanded in battle may be compared to that of round boulders which roll down from the mountain heights.'* According to the commentators Chang Yu and Tu Mu, this means that *'The force applied is minute but the results are enormous'*, and *'One needs . . . but little strength to achieve much'* (Sun Tzu, *The Art of War*, p. 95).

Thus, Corbett ultimately devised a particular method of using maritime power that Clausewitz could not have considered. This method is admittedly relevant for only a small number of naval powers, but those to whom it applies can parlay their limited resources into the attainment of ambitious political objectives without risking escalation or defeat (*Some Principles*, p. 77). Corbett likens this aspect of his concept to the advantages enjoyed by the defense, which 'sometimes enable an inferior force to gain its end against a superior one'. The drawbacks of the defense do not, however, apply here. Limited war allows the naval power to maintain the initiative on both the strategic and the tactical levels, depending on the circumstances. Under the favorable conditions of Corbett's ideal limited war, the naval power can assume an offensive posture almost immediately (on the tactical or strategic levels) without exposing itself to unacceptable risks. This type of transition would take much longer to accomplish in continental warfare. Corbett then concludes that ' the limited force of war has this element of strength over and above the unlimited form . . . This point is of the highest importance, for it is a direct negation of the current doctrine that there can be but one legitimate object, the overthrow of the enemy's means of resistance and that the primary objective must always be his armed forces' (*Some Principles*, p. 74).

Having aroused the suspicion of his contemporaries with his praise of limited war and the implied passivity of equating it with the defense, Corbett makes a painfully obvious attempt to reassure his readers. To the statement that all forms of war 'demand the use of battles' he adds that achieving favorable circumstances for the ideal limited war depends first on the overthrow of the enemy's naval forces (*Some Principles*, pp. 86–87). Corbett's theory is also the answer to the chimerical search for the decisive battle because he uses the 'lower means' of war to secure the positive results necessary for an eventual move to the 'higher form' if necessary.

In *The Development of Military Thought in the Nineteenth Century*, Azar Gat describes Corbett's *Some Principles of Maritime Strategy* as 'an étude on Clausewitz'.[23] This statement underestimates Corbett's originality and contribution to strategic theory. Clausewitz's *On War* was an invaluable basis and stimulus for Corbett's theoretical work – but not its blueprint. For example, Corbett did not hesitate to take issue with Clausewitz on the importance of the search for the decisive battle and the principle of concentration. The fact that Corbett believed these factors to be far less relevant at sea was a daring departure from the accepted wisdom of his time. In developing his theory of limited war, Corbett again used *On War* as his point of departure but ended up with his own unique method of waging a limited war in a maritime environment. By inclination and the influence of the British style of warfare, Corbett actually has more in common with Sun Tzu than with Clausewitz.

As a counter-factual, we might ask whether Clausewitz would have made any changes in *On War* had he read Corbett's principles of naval strategy. The answer I believe is a qualified yes. It would have apprised him of the contribution of naval power to continental warfare, perhaps inspiring him to add a chapter on the 'pure' maritime limited war and some exceptions to the principle of concentration in naval war. Moreover, it might have provided him with some incentive to discuss the economic and financial aspects of war, including economic blockades, as part of attrition warfare.

While Mahan's theory is a good example of the theory of war at sea as influenced by the classical theory of land warfare, Corbett's theory arrives at some original insights that contradict the conventional wisdom of the continental strategists. Is Corbett's work as important or original as that of Clausewitz? Clearly not. Unlike *On War*, *Some Principles of Maritime Strategy* is repetitive and parochial, and focuses on the narrower aspects of British maritime strategy. I cannot judge Corbett's place among naval historians, but I believe that he belongs at the top of the second tier in the pantheon of classical strategic theorists.

*   *   *

As an afterthought, it is interesting to note that in the age of modern air power, Corbett's theory of limited war can acquire a degree of relevance perhaps exceeding that which its author envisioned. Today, the sustained projection of air power combined with the use of precision-guided munitions presents conditions that fit Corbett's requirements: namely, a remote overseas battlefield that can be isolated by naval and air superiority and which allows the projection, insertion, and removal of land forces at will. The sustained command of the air together with day- and night-fighting capabilities and long-range precision firepower can create the isolation necessary for a limited war in any region of the world. This scenario would, however, also require complete air superiority as well as the continuous projection of air power for a prolonged period of time. The projection of land power would, in this case, be supported by air and/or naval power (instead of by naval power alone). Modern air power can extend its reach beyond that of the old naval power concept because it depends far less on uniquely advantageous geographic conditions. The isolation of a chosen battlefield could be achieved artificially by precision fire from the air. Such use of air power could work in a conventional war (as in Korea, for example) but not in guerrilla-type warfare. Such isolation of the battlefield was almost achieved in the Korean War, although air power could not then be used to fight day and night, nor was longer-range precision-guided firepower yet available. Although such a strategy could not work in the Vietnam War because of the nature of guerrilla warfare, it performed quite well in the milieu of the Gulf War. Current and future military technologies will therefore be able to artificially isolate a battlefield for implementation of Corbett's 'limited contingency war' concept under ideal conditions.

FIGURE 18.1
CORBETT, CLAUSEWITZ, AND SUN TZU COMPARED

	CORBETT (*SOME PRINCIPLES OF MARITIME STRATEGY*)	CLAUSEWITZ (*ON WAR*)	SUN TZU (*THE ART OF WAR*)
Attitude to risk and approach to war	Avoid unnecessary risks. No maximin strategy. No strategic risks but operational and tactical risks are acceptable in general. A rational, unsentimental, and non-romantic approach to war.	Taking high risks can be the sign of a great general. Maximax strategy in battle. A balance between rational calculations and the romantic, daring, and heroic.	*Calculating, rational, unsentimental. A maxi-min strategy.*
Economy of force	Great emphasis on 'Economy of force', cheap victories if possible, a search for force multipliers, and a relative advantage.	The emphasis on effective results, not on cost or efficiency. A search for decisive results. Avoid the dangers of false economy.	*Emphasis on cheap victories, a search for a comparative advantage and force multipliers. Efficiency is as important as effectiveness.*
Limited war	The ideal limited war can only be waged in the maritime environment – not on land. It requires a remote area that can be isolated by sea; it requires the achievement of naval superiority, and the ability to extract the land forces used at will. The land forces used must act as a force multiplier and ideally pin down a much greater force. The war is limited primarily by	A war is limited first and foremost by the political objectives. War can also be limited by the available means. Limited means normally imply the need to wage a defensive war.	*Not discussed as such – but implied by the desire to win at the lowest possible cost.*

| Relevance of the theory | the means available – the political objectives may be unlimited. Fighting a limited war under ideal conditions allows the weaker side to take the initiative and be on the offensive. | Primarily for naval power | **Universal land power and strategy in general.** | *Universal land power and strategy in general.* |

19

Conclusions:
Towards a Unified Theory of War

He who considers present affairs and ancient ones readily understands that all cities and all peoples have the same desires and the same traits and that they always have had them.

Machiavelli, *Discourses*, p. 278

But war, though conditioned by the particular characteristics of states and their armed forces, must contain some more general – indeed, a universal – element with which every theorist ought above all to be concerned.

Clausewitz, *On War*, p. 593

Philosophy teaches us to recognize the relations that essential elements bear to one another, and it would indeed be rash from this to deduce universal laws governing every single case, regardless of all haphazard influences. Those people, however, who 'never rise above anecdote' as a great writer said, and who would construct all history of individual cases – starting always with the most striking feature . . . and digging only as deep as suits them, never get down to the general factors that govern the matter. Consequently their findings will never be valid for more than a single case; indeed they will consider a philosophy that encompasses the general run of cases as a mere dream.

Clausewitz, *On War*, p. 374

The extent of the cultural and historical gaps separating Sun Tzu's *The Art of War* and Clausewitz's *On War*, not to mention the apparently contradictory nature of their most well-known dicta, has encouraged the *a priori* assumption that Sun Tzu and Clausewitz espouse essentially antagonistic theories. But closer scrutiny reveals that while a number of

299

differences exist, so do many similarities and complementary ideas. The occasional selections from Jomini's *The Art of War* indicate that the differences between Jomini and Clausewitz have been overstated as well.

The main points on which Sun Tzu and Clausewitz disagree concern the value of intelligence, the utility of deception, the feasibility of surprise attack, and the possibility of reliably forecasting and controlling the course of events on the battlefield. On the qualities requisite for a military commander, though, they agree in principle but differ in emphasis: Sun Tzu relies chiefly on the master of war's skill in making calculated, rational choices, while Clausewitz considers the military genius's artistic intuition to be the critical factor. While Sun Tzu, as we have seen, is primarily concerned with *efficiency*, Clausewitz is primarily concerned with *effectiveness*. Finally, they hold similar views on the primacy of politics in war; the need to preserve the professional autonomy of the military in action; the overall importance of numerical superiority; and the folly of not securing victory as rapidly and decisively as possible once war has become inevitable.

It is on the primacy of politics issue that Jomini departs most from the ideas of Sun Tzu and Clausewitz. By insisting that the military enjoy complete freedom of action in wartime, with the ability to make any decision deemed necessary by operational requirements, Jomini resolves the tension that exists on this issue in both Sun Tzu's *The Art of War* and Clausewitz's *On War*. In other words he resolves the tension between the imperatives of military action on the one hand, and the need for political control on the other. His solution gives priority to the field commander over his civilian political masters – a position that Sun Tzu and Clausewitz would not accept.

If one were to evaluate the roles of intelligence, surprise, and deception only as outlined by Clausewitz, these three factors would appear unworthy of serious consideration. Exclusive reliance on Sun Tzu's counsel, however, would point to the opposite conclusion and probably impel a commander to overrate the value of intelligence and surprise on all levels, as well as to consider deception a panacea. But this apparent divergence of opinion should not be exaggerated, for Clausewitz draws his lessons primarily from the tactical and operational levels of warfare where uncertainty, friction, and chance are pervasive even today, while Sun Tzu analyses the same factors in the context of the higher operational and strategic levels where their effect is reduced. This naturally leads Sun Tzu to more positive conclusions. On intelligence and deception, Machiavelli's ideas are identical to those of Sun Tzu. (See detailed discussion in note 4, Chapter 15, pp. 421–423 below.) This demonstrates conclusively that there is no fundamental difference in the Eastern and Western approaches to the art of war; indeed, that which influences attitudes on these subjects has less to do with unique 'strategic cultures' and more to do with material or tactical/operational developments.

On intelligence-related issues, Jomini takes a position between Clausewitz and Sun Tzu. Like Sun Tzu, he believes in the general importance of intelligence but, like Clausewitz, he does not believe that deception and strategic and operational surprise are feasible.

At times, differences more apparent than genuine have emerged when Sun Tzu's observations have been taken too literally; that is, when his statement of an ideal has been thought to be an unrealistic prescription for practicing the art of war. For example, although Sun Tzu states that the greatest victory is that which (ideally) involves no fighting and minimal cost, this does not mean that Sun Tzu thought this feat could be accomplished frequently. Conversely, while Clausewitz declares that victory without fighting or bloodshed is rare, he nevertheless acknowledges that it is possible. One can therefore square the circle and suggest that both are correct – that each casts light on a different facet of the same issue. Rather than representing mutually exclusively paradigms, therefore, *On War* and *The Art of War* instead complement and reinforce one another.

Thus, the contradictions, or apparent contradictions, between these two treatises spring not as much from cultural, historical, or even linguistic contrasts as they do from the different levels of analysis chosen by their authors compounded by the tendency of some readers to take their statements out of context. This is not to say that cultural, linguistic, and philosophical factors are unimportant, but simply that they were not the focus of this study. For the strategist not directly concerned with Chinese or Prussian history as such, both works transcend the limitations of time and place. Strategists can, as a result, derive many valuable insights from these classics, which remain the greatest and most original studies ever written on war.

The issue is not, and never has been, a matter of which approach is superior. Both are equally relevant for the modern reader. Ultimately,

the most important rationale for such a comparative analysis is to cultivate a better understanding of war and its place as a rational political
instrument. If anything, future research will find even more common
ground between these classics.[1]

Appendix A

Contradiction and Paradox in the Theory of War

The reader's attention must be directed to the *tension* or *seeming contradiction* between Clausewitz's requirement, on the one hand, '. . . **not to take the first step without considering the last**' or his emphasis on understanding the nature of the war one is about to embark on (Clausewitz, *On War*, p. 88) and, on the other hand, his innovative discussion of the role of *friction, chance, uncertainty, luck*, and the *poor quality* of *intelligence* which reveals the near impossibility of reliably predicting the course of a war.

This contradiction is, however, more apparent than real for at least two reasons. The first is that even if attempts to understand the nature and course of a future war are unreliable, it is still better to try than to do nothing at all. Second, uncertainty, chance, luck, and friction equally affect all parties to a conflict, so the side which can, by hard thinking and careful calculations, perform even *marginally better* will gain a considerable advantage.

This is only one of the many 'internal contradictions', 'tensions', and 'paradoxical' problems that can be identified in a careful reading of *On War* and any other important theory of war. But this does not mean something is wrong with Clausewitz's thinking! *The problem lies in the contradictory nature of war itself* (i.e., an accurate study or description of war must deliberately make an effort to discuss these contradictions, tensions, and paradoxes). Discerning this is all the more difficult because Clausewitz often fails to identify these existing tensions explicitly.

Other examples of such tensions in *On War* can be mentioned very briefly in this context. The first is the apparent contradiction between Clausewitz's concepts of the *principle of continuity* and *the culminating point of victory/attack*. The *principle of continuity* suggests that success must be exploited relentlessly (i.e., once one side has gained an advantage, it must press the attack or follow through on operations to prevent the enemy from regrouping (see *On War*, pp. 82–83; Book 3, Chapter 16, 'The Suspension of Action in War', pp. 216–219; p. 265; pp. 599–600; p. 625)). At the same time, his concept of the *culminating point of victory/attack* tells us that, sooner or later, every offensive will lose momentum even as it succeeds. The commander must therefore know when to stop his advance, pursuit, or exploitation of his success and move over to the defensive. Clausewitz leaves it to the military genius, the person whose intuition will descry the best solution, to properly identify and utilize the counterforces represented by these two principles (see Chapter 13 above).

Another basic paradox of war is that a state wishing to terminate a war should not appear too eager or too weak; it must instead convey the impression that it could continue to fight indefinitely. Otherwise, the enemy will seize upon any evidence of a desire for peace as a manifestation of weakness – and as a sign that he holds the advantage. And if he feels he can win, he will refuse to negotiate or will increase his demands, thus delaying the termination of the war. As a result (particularly if both sides are afraid to disclose their desire to end the war) the pretension of strength or indifference to continued fighting becomes a self-negating prophecy that causes the war to drag on – modern examples are the First World War, the Korean War, the Vietnam War, and the Iran–Iraq War. This paradox was noted by Clausewitz in his only detailed discussion of war termination (Chapter 2 of Book 1): **'If the incentive** [to make peace] **grows on one side, it should diminish on the other'** (Clausewitz, *On War*, p. 92).[1] (See Chapter 14 above, p. 210.)

Finally, another source of tension common to both Sun Tzu and Clausewitz is their insistence on the primacy of politics in the formation of the strategy, direction, and control of war (see Chapter 6 above), for this recommendation clashes with their desire to grant the field commander operational freedom of action sufficient to capitalize on fleeting opportunities and battlefield successes. Yet neither strategist can develop criteria to delineate the roles of the civilian and military authorities. As strategists, Sun Tzu and Clausewitz insist on the primacy of politics, but as military leaders, they also want to preserve the commander's tactical and operational freedom of action. As we have seen, Jomini is the theorist who resolves this tension by proposing that once war has begun, all related decision-making authority be given to the military. This is certainly a dangerous idea that puts operational thinking ahead of strategy.

Thus, students and theorists of war should not automatically interpret war's intrinsic tensions and contradictions as theoretical weakness but rather as a reflection of war's paradoxical nature. Permeating all military activity, such unresolvable dilemmas have no simple solutions. A realistic theory of war must therefore identify and discuss its inherent paradoxes. An approach that sanctions *the intolerance of ambiguity* and endeavors to streamline the theories of war by artificially eliminating contradictions is dysfunctional, unrealistic, and counterproductive.[2]

Appendix B

The Weinberger Doctrine[1]

> *If not in the interests of the state, do not act. If you cannot succeed, do not use troops.*
>
> Sun Tzu, *The Art of War*, p. 142

The debate that gave birth to the Weinberger Doctrine is still very much alive today and in fact revolves around the same issues it did when first articulated by the Secretary of Defense on 28 November 1984 at the National Press Club in Washington DC. Many of the issues raised in this debate, which concerned the United States' use of force in world affairs, are actually relevant for every nation since they address universal problems in formulating national security policies and strategies. Though initially formulated to prevent the United States from involvement in another Vietnam War, the Weinberger Doctrine could have been applied profitably by the Soviet Union in the civil war in Afghanistan, by Israel or Syria in Lebanon, or by NATO in Bosnia.

The Weinberger Doctrine's six criteria were developed in response to two main causes – one historical and the other a policy struggle within the Reagan Administration in 1983–84. From a historical perspective, U.S. military leaders designed this set of guidelines as a distillation of the lessons learned from the Vietnam War. This failure, which they resolved must never be repeated, had alienated the U.S. military from large segments of the American people and eroded its support in Congress.[2]

The second cause was a bureaucratic 'battle royal' between Secretary of State George Shultz, the State Department, and the National Security Council (NSC), on the one hand, and Secretary of Defense Caspar Weinberger and the Pentagon, on the other, over U.S. military involvement in Lebanon and Central America.[3] While Secretary of State Shultz advocated using direct military force to support American diplomacy in both Lebanon and Central America, U.S. military leaders

– with the defeat in Vietnam still fresh in their memories – were reluctant to commit troops where the chance of achieving a quick, clear-cut or cheap victory seemed slim. Without the firm backing of the American people, taking such action would only, they feared, force the United States to subject a perpetually insufficient number of troops to a prolonged conflict; and this, in turn, would logically lead to heavy casualties, failure to achieve victory, and withdrawal or defeat. This was exactly the situation as it developed in the United States' deployment of military forces in Lebanon by the fall of 1984.

Since the summer and fall of 1982, when the suggestion of deploying U.S. troops as part of a Multinational Force (MNF) had first been made by the State Department and the NSC, the Secretary of Defense and the Joint Chiefs of Staff had strongly opposed the idea. In his memoirs, Weinberger notes the NSC's

> passionate desire to use our military . . . to send in a major force, of several American divisions and some French divisions, to 'force withdrawal' of both Syrians and Israelis. A force of that size would, of course, almost certainly become embroiled in major combat while 'peacekeeping' between Syrians and Israelis.[4]

At another point, Weinberger describes the NSC as more militant than the State Department, as spending their time thinking up

> ever more wild adventures for our troops. The NSC staff's eagerness to get into a fight somewhere – anywhere – coupled with their apparent lack of concern for the safety of our troops [was appalling].[5]

The idea of sending a major American contingent as first requested by the State Department and the NSC was rejected 'because this MNF would not have any mission that could be defined. Its objectives were stated in the fuzziest possible terms and then later when that objective was "clarified", the newly defined objective was demonstrably unobtainable.'[6] Finally, it was decided that a smaller contingent would be sent as part of the MNF, which was to interpose itself between the withdrawing armies of Israel and Syria until the Lebanese armed forces had been trained and equipped to take over the role.[7]

But the Israelis and Syrians could not agree on an Israeli withdrawal and the Lebanese army was obviously not a force to be reckoned with. Marines sent to achieve goals that were, in the first place, ambiguous and unrealistic now found themselves stranded in the Beirut airport without a mission; instead, they were a convenient target of hostile fire from a variety of primarily pro-Syrian and pro-Iranian militant groups. In meetings with the NSC, the National Security Planning Group, the Secretary of State, and the President, the Secretary of Defense and the Joint Chiefs repeatedly urged the dissolution of the MNF and the withdrawal of American troops from Lebanon. Objecting, the State Department and NSC argued this would leave the impression that the United States had 'cut and run' under pressure, that it had been 'driven out' of Lebanon.

After the suicide car-bomb attack on the Marine barracks at the Beirut airport on 23 October 1983, in which 266 U.S. Marines were killed, the terrible risks of U.S. military involvement in the chaotic Lebanese civil war came to dominate the minds of the military leaders in the Pentagon. They had to avoid being once again drawn into a costly, prolonged civil war that did not directly involve any major American interests. Weinberger characterizes Lebanon at the time as a 'powder keg' lacking a strong central government and a national consensus.

> Here was a small country torn by civil war, without strategically important resources, whose main claim to American attention was its ability to serve as a breeding ground for trouble in a very volatile region of the world.[8]

> There was little of a practical nature we could do to restore unity to this very troubled land.[9]

The worries of the U.S. military leaders were understandable. Here was another potentially demoralizing disaster, a chaotic civil war that could not be resolved by those directly involved, let alone by outsiders sent in without a clear mission and without the numbers needed to achieve meaningful results. The cost could only grow as involvement deepened, causing the loss of American public support for an undertaking it had not wanted in the first place. In the meantime, pressures to send U.S. troops to Central America to fight the communist regimes in Nicaragua and communist guerrillas in San Salvador were increasing. (These situations were replicated later on in Somalia, Bosnia, Haiti, and Rwanda, and are likely to occur again and again elsewhere.)

Unlike earlier American military experiences in the twentieth century, the war in Vietnam forced American military leaders *to become aware of the limits of their military power*. These leaders were now convinced that the practice of 'employing [their] forces almost indiscriminately and as a regular and customary part of [their] diplomatic efforts . . .'[10] would lead only to costly and dangerous entanglement in unresolvable 'gray-area conflicts'. This type of war would exact a heavy price

> without accomplishing the goal for which we committed our forces. Such policies might very well tear at the fabric of our society, endangering the single-most critical element of a successful democracy: a strong consensus of support and agreement for our basic purposes.[11]

Above all, however, the Secretary of Defense and U.S. military leaders were concerned about the morale of the U.S. military which was still fragile in the aftermath of the Vietnam War.

> Policies formed without a clear understanding of what we hope to achieve would also earn us the scorn of our troops, who would have an understandable opposition to being *used* – in every sense of the word – casually without intent to support them fully. Ultimately this course would reduce their morale and effectiveness for engagements we *must* win. [my emphasis][12]

With such concerns in mind and, more specifically, with the object of hastening the withdrawal of U.S. troops from Lebanon while avoiding similar mistakes in Central America, the Secretary of Defense established six principal tests or criteria for guidance.

Weinberger describes his six tests as follows:

WEINBERGER'S SIX TESTS [Full Text]

I have developed six major tests to be applied when we are weighing the use of U.S. combat forces abroad.

(1) FIRST, the United States should not commit forces to *combat* overseas unless the particular engagement is deemed vital to our national interest or that of our allies.

(2) SECOND, if we decide it is necessary to put *combat* troops into a given situation, we should do so wholeheartedly, and with the clear intention of winning. If we are *un*willing to commit the forces

or resources necessary to achieve our objectives, we should not commit them at all.

(3) THIRD, if we do decide to commit forces to combat overseas, we should have clearly defined political and military objectives. And we should know precisely how our forces can accomplish those clearly defined objectives. And we should have and send the forces needed to do just that. As Clausewitz wrote, '**No one starts a war – or rather, no one in his senses ought to do so – without first being clear in his mind what he intends to achieve by that war, and how he intends to conduct it.**' If we determine that a combat mission has become necessary for our vital national interests, then we must send forces capable to do the job – and not to assign a combat mission to a force configured for peace keeping.

(4) FOURTH, the relationship between our objectives and the forces we have committed – their size, composition and disposition – must be continually reassessed and adjusted if necessary. When they do change, then so must our combat requirements. We must continuously keep as beacon lights before us the basic questions: 'Is this conflict in our national interest?' 'Does our national interest require us to fight, to use force of arms?' If the answer is 'yes', then we *must* win. If the answer is 'no,' then we should not be in combat.

(5) FIFTH, before the U.S. commits combat forces abroad there must be some reasonable assurance we will have the support of the American people and their elected representatives in Congress . . . We cannot fight a battle with Congress at home while asking our troops to win a war overseas or, *as in the case of Vietnam, in effect, asking our troops not to win, just to be there.* [my emphasis]

(6) SIXTH, finally, the commitment of U.S. forces to combat should be the last resort.

* * *

Let us now examine the merits and drawbacks of these 'tests' as well as their interrelationships. As we shall see, some of the points made are not as straightforward as they appear, while others are contradictory.

In the **first test**, Weinberger calls for a policy of avoiding the commitment of troops to combat unless the *vital* interests of the United States are involved. This important test, which should be used by every nation, reflects the positions of all classical theorists of war and *raison d'état* from Sun Tzu, Thucydides, and Machiavelli to Clausewitz. Indeed, Sun Tzu states plainly, '*If not in the interests of the state, do not act*,' and Clausewitz observes, '**War is no pastime** . . . [it is] **a serious means to a serious end . . . When whole communities go to war, whole peoples, and especially civilized peoples – the reason always lies in some political situation.**'[13]

But this first test is not as simple as it seems, for there is seldom a consensus on what constitutes a vital interest. Is it sending troops to fight in Central America or avoiding intervention in that region? What about Korea or Vietnam? Perhaps it is easier to agree on what is *not* a vital U.S. interest (e.g., Bosnia, Somalia, or Rwanda). And even when there is general agreement on a vital interest, there will not necessarily be a consensus on how best to protect it. For example, should U.S. interests in the Gulf be defended militarily as in the Gulf War – or should such interests be protected, as almost half of the Senate members believed in November 1990, by other diplomatic and economic means? Should the use of force in the Gulf War be considered only as the last resort (see Weinberger's sixth test)? In fact, the Weinberger–Shultz debate reflected this problem, for it was not so much about identifying U.S. vital interests as it was about how to best protect and defend the *same* vital interests. While Weinberger and the military leaders wanted to use force only for exceptional reasons, Shultz and the State Department believed that force could be used more frequently to increase the effectiveness of U.S. diplomacy and foreign policy.

Should the United States wage war for a secondary or tertiary interest (e.g., Korea, Vietnam, Cuba) in order to protect the really vital interest? Should the British and French risk a war with Germany over the Rhineland or the Sudeten which might at a later stage affect their core interests? Should the United States risk an all-out nuclear war and a nuclear confrontation over the presence of Soviet missiles in Cuba? Or is the avoidance of a direct nuclear confrontation with the Soviet Union a higher interest than the nature of the regime in Cuba or the positioning of Soviet medium-range ballistic missiles (MRBMs) on that island? Often, the answers to such questions are provided in due course by history itself, but at other times statesmen and historians cannot agree on the advisability of a certain policy or strategy even in hindsight. Normally the criteria for forming such judgments after the fact would be the perception of success or failure, but even this can be misleading: one need only consider later debates on this subject, or the estimation of risks involved in appeasement in the 1930s and the Cuban missile crisis.

Weinberger was keenly aware of the need, at times, to fight for secondary or tertiary interests in order to enhance vital interests; or in other words, to avert a more costly involvement later on by showing readiness to fight at an earlier stage.

> We must also be farsighted enough to sense when immediate and strong reactions to apparently small events can prevent lion-like responses that may be required later. We must never forget those isolationists in Europe who shrugged that 'Danzig is not worth a war' and 'why should we fight to keep the Rhineland demilitarized'.[14]

In this way, the line between primary and secondary interests can easily become blurred. But who can agree whether the decisions to fight in Korea (1950) or Vietnam (mid-1960s) were analogous to the situations in the Rhineland (1936) or Danzig (1939)?

The history of U.S. wars and military interventions in world affairs during the Cold War is testimony to the problem: *states must often fight for secondary and even tertiary interests to protect their vital interests*; yet the first test provides no concrete advice on the identification or protection of a vital interest. Although Weinberger, in his remarks on 'The Uses of Military Power', uses the invasion of Grenada as an example of the successful implementation of his doctrine, the 'crisis in Grenada' *did not even remotely threaten vital U.S. interests*. A brief examination of the U.S. decisions to use force since Weinberger first presented his doctrine indicates that only in the Gulf War can essential U.S. interests be said to have been at stake (see Table B.1).

Finally, Weinberger mentions the need to defend the vital interests of U.S. allies. Here of course, things become even more complicated. Should the United States protect the vital interests of its allies *as they perceive them*, or only if they are also as vital for itself? The emphasis on protecting American core interests is a traditional *realpolitik* type of argument, namely, that the state should maximize and conserve its power *vis-à-vis* other states in the system. The enhancement and conservation of power is the key criterion for political and military action. In the United States, however, this approach contradicts its Wilsonian tradition of fighting for justice, freedom, and democracy, which might require the use rather than conservation of force; and it is to this tradition that both Weinberger and Shultz paid lip service in their speeches and positions.

Weinberger's readiness to use force in Grenada shows that he was more concerned with the *successful use of force*, with achieving military objectives, than with acting only to protect key U.S. interests. But in the case of Lebanon or Central America, the criterion that the United States should commit troops *only* to protect its vital interests provided him and other U.S. military leaders with a good argument against sending troops. It can be argued that whenever political and military leaders feel certain of success and are ready to commit troops to combat, they will always find a convincing explanation as to why the contemplated action protects and enhances the vital interests of their country. If anything, it is amazing how rarely – since the Second World War – the United States has resorted to the use of force to protect its truly vital interests.

Weinberger's **second test** states that once the United States decides to commit troops to action, it must do so with enough military strength to achieve its objectives. This point expresses the greatest fear of the post-Vietnam U.S. military, – namely, being sent to war with forces insufficient to accomplish their goals, with later reinforcements provided in a reluctant and piecemeal way that never rises to the level required for a quick, less costly victory. Eventually, this half-hearted approach brings only higher casualties, a prolonged war, and a decision to quit before one's goals can be attained.

Clausewitz argues that *in both theory and practice*, the most important principle of war is to concentrate the largest possible force from the start.

> **The best strategy is always to be very strong: first in general and then at the decisive point . . . The first rule, therefore, should be: put the largest possible army into the field.**[15] [See Appendix F below.]

Once again, while the second test is eminently sensible in theory, its application is more difficult in reality. Is it possible to determine what size the force should be in order to attain the objectives defined by the politicians? Furthermore, the need to concentrate a very large force in order to ensure victory may contradict Weinberger's fifth test emphasizing the advisability of mobilizing U.S. public opinion in advance. It is doubtful that U.S. public opinion would have supported the war in Korea or Vietnam if the number of troops necessary to win had been known *from the start*. It could, of course, be argued that had a large force been committed from the outset in these wars, victory could have been achieved before an even larger force became necessary.

Of course, nations usually enter a war or conflict with the desire to win, but the emphasis on victory, so noticeable in Weinberger's criteria (particularly in tests 2, 4, and 5) may be dangerous. How should victory be defined? Should wars be fought at times not so much to win as to hold out or defend a *status quo*? Is victory defined by the destruction of the enemy forces and/or the occupation of his territory or capital; or is it simply the attainment of one's objectives (which can be minimal and easy to achieve). Or is it Clausewitz's definition of '**compelling our enemy to do our will**'?[16] The United States was not able to '**compel the enemy to do its will**' in Vietnam, and was able to do so only partly in Korea and the Gulf War. Perhaps a victory can also be defined not so much as '**compelling our enemy to do *our* will**' – as much as a negative goal of preventing him from compelling us to do his will or simply from achieving his own goals. Yet such advice is mainly relevant for conventional wars involving large engagements, where it is possible to achieve a decisive victory on the battlefield. Accordingly, it is far less relevant in protracted guerrilla-type or other low-intensity conflicts in which there is no opportunity for decisive action or reaching one's goals in a short period of time.

The essence of the second test (as well as of the entire Weinberger Doctrine) is that the United States should never get involved in wars it cannot win. Yet neither the costs nor the ultimate results of war can be accurately predicted in advance; for this, as Clausewitz argues, would be '**war by algebra**'.[17] Edward Luttwak has observed that the Weinberger Doctrine is 'the equivalent of a doctor saying that he will treat the patients only if he is assured that they will recover.'[18] In the end, Clausewitz is right when he states that '**Victory alone is not everything – but is it not, after all, what really counts?**'[19] The objectives of a war and the definition of victory therefore determine the amount of resources and force to be used.

Weinberger's **third test** addresses this issue. Logically, this test should precede the second because the resources and forces required to achieve one's goals are determined by the definition of the political and military objectives. Here Weinberger insists that before committing forces to combat overseas, U.S. political and military leaders must first 'clearly define the political and military objectives.' This reflects the position of many top U.S. military leaders who primarily blamed the military failure in Vietnam on the ambiguity of their mission. Sixty-eight percent of the U.S. generals who served in Vietnam felt that the objectives of the United States were either 'not as clear as they might have been' or 'rather fuzzy and needed rethinking'.[20] We have also seen that Weinberger and the JCS were very concerned about the increased involvement in Lebanon in the absence of clearly defined objectives.

Then Weinberger cites Clausewitz directly: '**No one starts a war – or rather, no one in his senses ought to do so – without first being clear in his mind what he intends to achieve by that war and how he intends to conduct it**' (Clausewitz, *On War*, p. 579). This good advice also provides us with an excellent example of the contradictory nature of war and of the complexity of Clausewitz's thoughts, for he certainly recognized the difficulty of doing this in practice. '**In war**', he suggests, '**more than anywhere else, things do not turn out as we expect.**'[21] As he explains, war is dominated by friction, chance, and uncertainty. Therefore the expectation that the size of the forces required can be ascertained with accuracy, and that the objectives can be clearly defined without subsequent modification, is unfounded optimism. Once a war begins and opponents interact, neither the initial objectives nor the size and composition of forces can remain unchanged for long. The longer the war, the more likely it is that the initial objectives and required resources will have to be revised repeatedly. Clausewitz reminds us that '. . . **the original political objects can greatly alter during the course of the war and may finally change entirely since they are influenced by events and their probable consequences**' (Clausewitz, *On War*, p. 92). Thus, Weinberger's assumptions are more correct for military interventions/operations that can be carried out swiftly and decisively, as in Grenada or Panama, than they are for prolonged interventions or wars. The problem, of course, is that it is often very difficult to tell in advance which interventions will be short and decisive, and which will be costly and prolonged. This is precisely what happened in the 'intervention' in Kosovo, which was expected to last only a few days.

While a consistent strategy is desirable, as Weinberger points out in the third test, it is seldom possible and not always advantageous. This is recognized to some extent in the fourth test, which, as we shall see, recommends the continuous reappraisal of one's objectives and the means needed to achieve them. Weinberger's third test also conflicts with his fifth, in which he argues that before and during a war, the support of Congress and the public must be mobilized and guaranteed if possible. A measure of deliberate political ambiguity, which inevitably will also lead to greater or lesser ambiguity in the military, strategic, and operational objectives, would allow the mobilization of greater support. The more the objectives of war are defined in advance, the more difficult it may prove to mobilize the broadest possible public support, which Weinberger and the military saw as the most critical factor. In the context of the debate over the commitment of U.S. troops in Lebanon, the third test was indeed valuable in pointing to the lack of clear objectives for the U.S. miliary intervention there.

The **fourth test** may be referred to as the 'escape clause'. Since Weinberger earlier asserted that U.S. troops should only be committed with the intention of winning, or obtaining their objective, this clause calls for a continuous assessment, appraisal, and reappraisal of the situation on the battlefield; this would aid in determining whether the benefits and goals justify the use of additional troops. This test also implies that if the costs become too high, and if the objectives do *not* justify a greater investment of forces, that it is wiser to terminate the war. Weinberger argues that:

> We must continuously keep as a beacon light before us the basic questions: 'Is this conflict in our national interest? Does our national interest require us to fight, to use force of arms?' If the answers are 'yes' then we *must* win. If the answers are 'no,' then we should not be in combat.

What begins as a national interest may change with the ever-increasing costs of a war. And although winning is desirable, the dogged pursuit of victory may endanger the support of the American people – and, as in Vietnam, it may threaten an even higher interest – that of protecting the very fiber of American society. Hence, the possibility of not winning in order to protect more important vital interests must always be taken into account.

317

Weinberger's fourth test appears to be in accord with Clausewitz's *rational calculus* of war. As we have seen above, Clausewitz mentions two grounds for making peace or terminating a war which are also referred to in the Weinberger Doctrine: '. . . **the first is the *improbability of victory*, the second is its *unacceptable cost*.**'[22] (See Chapter 14 above, pp. 203–205.) This kind of calculation was clearly applied in the U.S. decision to withdraw its troops from Somalia in March 1994.

The **fifth test** represents one of the most important lessons the American military learned in Vietnam – never to go to war without the backing of the people and Congress. Once again, this is a matter of common sense that is also more difficult to achieve in practice. This test clearly agrees with Clausewitz's trinitarian analysis which emphasizes that the role of the people in supporting a war effort is critical in any period, but even more so in the age of national and total wars. Clausewitz believed that the greatest revolution in the nature of war in his time was the release of an incredible amount of energy never before tapped – namely, that of the entire French nation.[23] (See Chapter 10 above.)

When secrecy is essential for the success of an operation, a generally supportive atmosphere can be encouraged through diplomatic action, presidential speeches, and so on. In the cases of Grenada and Panama, short and quick 'victorious' operations certainly helped to make the operations popular after the fact. In prolonged wars, the problem lies not so much in obtaining the initial public and political support as it does in sustaining it for the duration. This is particularly difficult in a democracy such as the United States with its diverse political and ethnic groups. Even if the mass media, especially television reporting, remain neutral or supportive throughout a war (which was not the case in Vietnam after the Tet offensive), the daily dose of death and destruction, which has created new obstacles in the mobilization of public support, did not exist in Clausewitz's time.

For the U.S. military, one of the major explanations for the failure in Vietnam was the inability or lack of will on the parts of Presidents Johnson and Nixon to mobilize the support of the American people. While not entirely an excuse, this explanation may be inaccurate. In the first place, at least until the Tet offensive and even thereafter, U.S. public opinion generally supported the war effort in Vietnam; and had the U.S. military been able to achieve demonstrable success or convince the American people that victory was within reach, this generally favorable attitude might have continued.

Another important point pertains to leadership and the vital interests of the state. It is the duty of political leaders to lead, not be led, by public opinion. At times, public opinion might be opposed to a combat mission overseas which is, however, perceived as a vital interest by U.S. leaders. In such cases, these leaders must do their best to mobilize public opinion, educate and lead it – but, if necessary, also take action even without a clear consensus. Furthermore, public opinion can be fickle, swayed by the last success or failure on the battlefield, and lack the perseverance necessary to fight a prolonged war. As Churchill said, 'Nothing is more dangerous in wartime than to live in the temperamental atmosphere of a Gallup Poll, always feeling one's pulse and taking one's temperature.'[24]

Secretary of State Shultz's response was that when a nation has to go to war, 'there is no such thing as guaranteed public support in advance.'[25] Even if a decision to use force must be taken without the guaranteed support of public opinion, and even if it should be conducted without continuously consulting the Gallup Poll, in the long run no nation in modern times and most assuredly no democracy can persist in a prolonged war without public support.

Weinberger's **last test**, the **sixth**, states that the United States should consider the commitment of forces to combat abroad only as a last resort. While this fits in the traditional theory of *realpolitik* and *raison d'état*, it has seldom been strictly followed. In reality, the *ultima ratio* has often become the *prima ratio* in the relationships between states and other political groups or units.

The sixth test, as mentioned earlier and as immediately noticed by Secretary Shultz, seems to contradict the first by suggesting that the United States should commit troops for action only when its vital interests are threatened. By the time that these interests are genuinely threatened, however, it might already be too late to protect them. When the vital interests of a state are imperiled, immediate action intended to deter, signal resolve and commitment, or even pre-empt, might be the answer. This could simply become a semantic problem, a tautology of sorts in which a decision, for example, to pre-empt could be defined by its proponents as the last resort. The *last resort* then becomes any moment the policy maker or strategist has chosen to take action. Were the U.S. decisions to resort to force in Grenada, Panama, or the Gulf, actions of last resort? (see Table B.1). Clearly not.

This caveat is also the least related to Clausewitz's thinking. While Clausewitz, in the tradition of *raison d'état*, thought that war should not be undertaken without the most careful deliberation, he also recognized that war was commonly used as a valuable tool for achieving political ends. In addition, he would argue that not all wars are fought for *vital interests* – but that some are or should be fought for secondary or limited objectives. This, in his theory, was the primary reason to resort to limited as opposed to total war. Lesser objectives call for lesser means and resources, smaller risks, and reduced intensity and commitment. In the context of the bureaucratic debate over the commitment of U.S. troops to a dangerous and unclear mission *not* involving vital American interests, it is clear why the Secretary of Defense chose to emphasize this point. But the 'vital interest' test, as can be seen in Table B.1, was the first to be ignored by the United States (and other nations) when certain political results or actions were deemed necessary.

A strict interpretation of the Weinberger Doctrine makes it clear that force should only be employed in exceptional circumstances, only when major U.S. interests are involved and when it is a question of the last resort. This certainly does not allow for the use of military force on lesser occasions. As mentioned earlier, Weinberger's own subsequent decisions show that he was ready to interpret the six tests in a liberal way (see Table B.1).

A decision to use war as a political instrument to protect non-vital interests need not be considered as a last resort; but perhaps as the quickest, most effective – and in the longer run, perhaps also the cheapest – way for a state to fulfill its objectives. A consideration of the first and sixth tests may simply suggest that the more important the interests at stake, the less critical it is to consider war as the option of last resort.

When the Weinberger Doctrine was first made public, critics loudly proclaimed that its six tenets (particularly in conjunction with the War Powers Resolution) would make the use of force by the United States practically impossible. It was argued that if U.S. policymakers and strategists tried to implement the doctrine as phrased, the United States would be able to use its troops only 'for the Fun Wars'.[26] Unfortunately, the United States cannot choose only the wars it likes:

Americans like their military operations to be quick, cheap, and above all, clearly victorious. And it helps if the hats for the bad guys are very black indeed, and those of the good guys are alabaster white. Hold the nuances, forget the ambiguities: an Agincourt such as Grenada will do just fine.[27]

But as George Shultz points out, a great power cannot free itself so easily from the burden of choice. It must bear responsibility for the consequences of its inaction as well as for the consequences of its action.

Before the doctrine was made public, the conclusion of some such as the Lebanese diplomat, Charles Malik, was that 'Everybody knows that America does not want to fight.'[28] In *Ethics and American Power*, Molnar argued that 'Mr Weinberger's "Six Tests" seem to be spoken by the proverbial boaster in the bar: "Hold me, or I will beat him up!" Anyway, the "tests" beg the whole question of our military involvement, because they enumerate enough "ifs" and "buts" to nullify any possibility of America every going to war again.'[29] New York Congressman (D) Stephen Solarz said, 'It is a formula for national paralysis if, before we ever use force, we need a Gallup Poll showing that two-thirds of the American people are in favor of it.'[30]

Later events have shown these fears to be exaggerated. Since the Weinberger Doctrine was formulated, the United States has used force in Panama, the Gulf War, Somalia, and Kosovo (see Table B.1). This does not mean that U.S. policymakers or strategists have either ignored or followed this Doctrine. Like much else in strategy and war, the Weinberger Doctrine is based on common sense, and as we have seen, is imprecise enough to allow almost any interpretation desired. Its tenets were not applied by Weinberger himself in Grenada nor later in Panama where vital U.S. interests were *not* involved and the American people were not consulted in advance although, to some extent, they were prepared for this type of action. On the other hand, if we see the substance of the Weinberger Doctrine as giving predecence to success in war, the two interventions in Grenada and Panama can be said to have heeded its guidance.

It could be argued that the doctrine was followed almost to the letter by U.S. policymakers and military leaders in the Gulf War.[31] First, the Iraqi occupation of Kuwait and the possible threat to the stability of oil supplies and prices constituted a threat to the vital interests of the United States and its allies. Having learned the lessons of Vietnam and, following the Weinberger Doctrine, the United States *from the start* committed more than enough force necessary to win a quick and decisive victory. Moreover, the objectives of the war were on the whole well defined – the liberation of Kuwait – and achieved; other goals, such as the destruction of the Iraqi armed forces or the elimination of Saddam Hussein, may have been added later on but were never publicly admitted. Although they were not stated as part of the war's original objectives, these other objectives were pursued all the same. The first of the two was for the most part achieved while the second (the removal of Saddam Hussein from power) was not. Before and throughout the Gulf War, the United States continuously correlated means and ends while the short duration and conventional nature of the war, and the decisive victory over Iraq, saved the United States and its allies from the calculations required in a prolonged and indecisive war.

The fifth test of mobilizing U.S. (as well as Allied) public and political support was consciously followed from beginning to end, yet Congressional authorization of the use of force by the United States passed by only a very narrow margin. This raises two questions. The first is, what would President Bush have done had the vote gone otherwise? Would he have waited for yet another vote or would he have decided to launch the war in any event? The second is, what if public opinion had initially favored the operation but turned against it at a later stage? The second point is perhaps even more important inasmuch as it indicates the risks inherent in depending on the support of public opinion, which can never be taken for granted in the long run.

Had the war been more costly for the United States in terms of casualties and duration, it is very likely that public opinion, the mass media, and Congress would not have been so supportive. President Bush and the U.S. military had to take a risk here, since no one knew how quickly the war could be won and at what price. Certainly, the initial predictions of anticipated American casualties were much higher. This is the point at which leaders must make tough decisions while continuing to fight and mobilize public opinion. It could also be that the President decided to bring the war to an end at that particular time despite the opposition of the military leaders (certainly General Schwartzkopf) in order to keep public support firmly behind him.

The sixth test (i.e., that war should be the last resort) was the least relevant. Not surprising in light of their experience in Vietnam, Lebanon, and perhaps even Panama, the United States military – as represented by General Powell in his Congressional testimony before the war – urged that non-military methods be given more time to work. Thus, the war did not start as the last resort, but it wasn't the first either.

Saddam Hussein's misguided strategic decisions were apparently based on the idea that 'everybody knows America does not want to fight'. And judging from lessons learned in the Vietnam War, the requirements of the Weinberger Doctrine, numerous difficult caveats, and the narrow decision of Congress to support the war, 'everybody' was almost right. Despite its caveats, the Weinberger Doctrine did not stop the United States from later sending a large 'peacekeeping' force to Somalia. This enjoyed wide public support although it did not endanger any vital U.S. interests. But as soon as the U.S. troops started to suffer casualties, Weinberger's fourth test (or a similar type of logic) came into effect. A reevaluation of the costs and benefits and the erosion of U.S. public support led to a quick decision to withdraw U.S. troops from Somalia – a move that certainly reflected the spirit of the Weinberger Doctrine.

More recently, a similar reading of the Weinberger Doctrine by the U.S. military and politicians delayed any major U.S. involvement in the former Yugoslavia. No *direct* U.S. vital interests are at stake, the war or conflict appears to be 'unwinnable', clear objectives for U.S. policies toward the war and precise military objectives cannot be formulated, and public support for U.S. intervention is weak at best.[32] No wonder the use of force in this case has been seen as a question of last resort. When the United States decided to use its massive air-power capabilities alone to force the Serb government to withdraw from Kosovo, the operation was expected to bring rapid success. As it turned out, the operation lasted no fewer than 78 days (24 March 1999–10 June 1999). The cost of the operation was considerable financially speaking, but in terms of casualties it proved to be exceptionally cheap. It does not appear that the most vital interests of the United States were involved, although U.S. leadership and the future role of NATO were indirectly involved. On the whole, the tenets of the Weinberger Doctrine were observed, because the United States clearly defined the objectives for this operation, maintained commitment to victory, and mobilized public opinion. It is another question altogether to estimate what might have happened if the war lasted longer and the U.S. had resorted to ground operations. Fortunately, the war ended before the United States had seriously to consider the use of ground forces. In the same way, in 1994 the United States had turned down a request by the UN Secretary-General that troops be sent to Rwanda after the ethnic massacres occurred. Furthermore, the United States refused to support and authorize any large U.S. peacekeeping mission in that country given its precarious situation, the recent U.S. experience in Somalia, the antici-pated high costs, and the absence of a clear plan outlining how the UN peacekeepers would be deployed.[33] It must be remembered that the Weinberger Doctrine was written in the context of the Cold War, in which secondary and tertiary interests might have been regarded as being closer to a core interest, namely, dealing with the communist menace, than they would be today.

The Weinberger Doctrine is thus a utilitarian, realistic yardstick not much concerned with moral and ethical questions – although it has many such implications and certainly reflects the morality or ethics of the responsible use of force in a democracy. Has the Weinberger Doctrine withstood the ultimate test of time? The answer must be a qualified 'yes'. The U.S. military leaders instrumental in developing this doctrine studied it carefully and took it to heart as proven by their actions and policy or strategic recommendations preceding the Gulf War. Like any theory of strategy and war, the Weinberger Doctrine can-not furnish specific advice, since action must always be tailored to specific circumstances; but its contemplation can raise many valid ques-tions and caveats before a decision to commit forces is made. From this perspective, and given the unique nature of the American political sys-tem, the Weinberger Doctrine has made and will continue to make an important contribution to U.S. national security policy.

Since the end of the Cold War, the number of conflicts in central Africa, the Caribbean, the former Yugoslavia, and the former Soviet Union has increased dramatically. Many are bloody and intense, causing suffering that cannot be easily ignored by the rest of the world. Yet very few of these conflicts directly involve the vital interests of the United States and its allies; therefore, the issues weighed by the Weinberger Doctrine will become even more relevant in the future. Nevertheless, neither this doctrine nor any other existing theory of war is a source of concrete solutions: each crisis must be dealt with *ad hoc* according to particular moral considerations, political interests, and public attitudes. The United States and its allies will have to recognize that not all conflicts, civil wars, or otherwise chaotic, collapsing societies can be 'cured' with military solutions when the ailment is of a basically non-military nature.[34] (See also the chart and discussion in note 7 to Chapter 9 above, pp. 401–404.)

Table B.1
The Six Tests/Criteria of the Weinberger Doctrine from Vietnam to Kosovo

Test/Criterion	Vietnam	Grenada	Lebanon	Central America	Panama	War in the Gulf	Somalia	Bosnia	Kosovo
1. Are vital US interests involved?	NO	NO	NO	NO	NO	YES	NO	NO	NO
2. Commitment to victory	NO	YES	NO	NO	YES	YES	NO	NO	YES
3. Clearly defined political and military objectives	NO	YES	NO	NO	YES	YES	YES AT FIRST – NO LATER	?	YES
4. Continuous reassessment of troops/objective ratio and of costs	YES	YES	YES	YES	YES	YES	YES	YES	YES
5. U.S. government must mobilize public opinion before action	NO	NO	NO	NO	NO	YES	YES AT FIRST	YES	YES
6. Intervention/war as last resort	NO	NO	NO	NO	NO	NO	NO	NO	NO
Decision for military intervention or war	YES	YES	YES AT FIRST	NO	YES	YES	YES	YES	YES
Success or failure	FAILURE	SUCCESS	FAILURE	—	SUCCESS	SUCCESS BUT NOT COMPLETE	FAILURE	?	SUCCESS BUT NOT COMPLETE

Appendix C

Clausewitz's Ideal-Type Method Applied to Sun Tzu's *The Art of War*

> Once again we must remind the reader that, in order to lend clarity, distinction, and emphasis to our ideas, only perfect contrasts, the extremes of the spectrum, have been included in our observations. As in actual occurrence, war generally falls somewhere in between, and is influenced by these extremes only to the extent to which it approaches them.
>
> Clausewitz, *On War*, p. 517

In 'What is War?', the first chapter of *On War*, Clausewitz begins the development of his theory by using the *ideal-type* and the *dialectical* methods. The ideal-type method distills the essence of the subject under examination – war, in Clausewitz's case – while the dialectical method compares the ideal type thus developed with either another diametrically opposed ideal type or with reality.[1] The simplest and best known example of this method is Newton's conceptualization of an ideal world without gravity or friction; this enabled him to make certain assumptions about the behavior of bodies in accordance with the imaginary conditions of a frictionless world – assumptions that could then be contrasted with the real world of gravity and friction. This analytical approach led Newton to the development of his most famous laws of physics.

Clausewitz explains this process as follows:

> When two ideas form a true logical antithesis, each complementary to the other, then fundamentally each is implied in the other. If the limitations of our mind do not allow us to comprehend both simultaneously, and discover by antithesis the whole of one in the whole of the other, each will nevertheless shed enough light on the other to clarify many of its details.
>
> (Clausewitz, *On War*, p. 523)

Clausewitz first develops the ideal type of war, what war *ought to be* given its inherent nature and dynamics, which he variously refers to as 'war in theory', 'war in the abstract', 'pure theory', 'basic rigorous concept' 'a pure concept of war', 'nothing but a play of the imagination', 'a logical fantasy', 'the natural tendency of war', 'the strict law of inherent necessity' (Clausewitz, *On War*, pp. 77–79, 88, 90, 91), 'logical necessity', and 'absolute perfection' (p. 580). This ideal type consists of the three cases of interaction (or reciprocal action) that cause war in theory to escalate to the extreme. The *first case of interaction* (*Wechselwirkung*) suggests that states will use the maximum *physical* force at their disposal and that there is '**no logical limit to the application of force**'. Since each side wants to win, it will compel the enemy to follow suit; and thus the cycle of action and reaction will cause each each side to use all the force it can muster. The *second case of interaction* concerns the *objectives* of war. It states that each side will not only employ all possible force but will also try to disarm its opponent in order to avoid being disarmed. This kind of war is consequently a zero–sum game fought until one side controls the other. In theory, Clausewitz says earlier, '**the true aim of warfare is to render the enemy powerless**'. Finally, the *third case of interaction* is that as each side reaches the limits of its physical and material strength, it also devotes *all* of its *strength of will* and motivation to the pursuit of victory. A state's total strength can therefore be expressed in these terms:

TOTAL MEANS* × STRENGTH OF WILL** = 'THE MAXIMUM EXERTION OF STRENGTH'***	
* Physical and material strength	** Non-material and intangible forms of strength *** The combination of all strength and will

The theoretical interaction between these two sides, which are single-mindedly pouring all of their material strength and will into this war, can be described as follows:

THE TWO OPPONENTS' TOTAL CAPACITY TO WAGE WAR

Side A		*Side B*
MEANS × WILL	=	MEANS × WILL

War in the abstract, as premised on the three cases of interaction, is thus found to be uncontrollable and not subject to rational calculations in its inexorable drive toward the extreme. In this case, the inherent dynamics of escalation impel the participants to use all available strength – so no calculations are required! Hence, war in theory is an irrational, apolitical undertaking that is fought without interruption until one side wins. Clausewitz's war in theory can be summarized as follows:

War in the abstract, or in theory (ideal)

* War is *apolitical* and has its *own internal logic* of *escalating to the extreme*.
* War cannot be controlled.
* War is total, fought *without interruption* as a zero-sum game until one side wins.
* All resources and available strength are used without any calculations.
* War is therefore not a rational activity.

Of course, Newton knew that there was no world without friction and Clausewitz realized that war in reality was far from its ideal form.[2] Nevertheless, as Clausewitz tells us a number of times, the ferocity of the wars of the French Revolution brought war surprisingly close to its ideal type during his lifetime.

> One might wonder whether there is any truth at all in our concept of the absolute character of war were it not for the fact that with our own eyes we have seen warfare achieve this state of absolute perfection. After the short prelude of the French Revolution, Bonaparte brought it swiftly and ruthlessly to that point.
>
> (Clausewitz, *On War*, p. 580–581; see also p. 593)

> If for the moment we consider the *pure concept of war*, we should have to say that the political purpose of war has no connection with the war itself; for if war is an act of violence meant to force the enemy to do our will, its aim would *always* and *solely* be to overcome the enemy and to disarm him. That aim is derived from the theoretical concept of war; but since many wars do actually come very close to fulfilling it, let us examine this kind of war first of all.
>
> (Clausewitz, *On War*, p. 90)

> . . . The most recent series of wars does substantiate the argument. Its validity was demonstrated and its necessity was proved only too plainly by the revolutionary wars. In these wars, and even more so in the campaigns of Bonaparte, warfare attained the unlimited degree of energy that we consider to be its elementary law. We see it is possible to reach this degree of energy; and if it is possible, it is necessary.
>
> (Clausewitz, *On War*, p. 217)

> Since Bonaparte, then, war, first among the French and subsequently among their enemies, again became the concern of the people as a whole, took on an entirely different character, or rather closely approached its true character, its absolute perfection.
>
> (Clausewitz, *On War*, pp. 592–593)

Although, Clausewitz must have been 'inspired' by the new intensity of the Napoleonic wars when developing his ideal type of the absolute war, it must be emphasized that the concept itself was developed as a heuristic thought-provoking device, a logical point of reference, but *not* as a description of reality itself and certainly *not* as a recommendation to pursue the most violent or destructive type of war.

Having established this analytical approach, Clausewitz dedicates the remainder of Chapter 1, Book 1 to an explanation of how and why war in the real world differs from the idealized version with which he began his discussion. (See also Book 8, Chapter 2, pp. 579–581, where Clausewitz repeats his explanation of how and why the absolute war in theory is different from war in reality.) And it is this comparison that leads him to the development of some of his most profound and innovative ideas. These include the following: all of the available strength does not need to be used, since something is always known of the enemy's strength (Section 7, p. 78); also, even if the maximum strength is desired for the war effort, it can never be mobilized simultaneously, and even if this were possible, such a force could never be concentrated in one place at one time (Section 8, p. 79). In addition, a decisive military victory does not last forever, so the motivation to expend all strength and resources to win all can never be total (Section 9, p. 80). As a result, political and diplomatic means must be employed in addition to the use of force. Clausewitz then introduces the element of political or rational calculations, which shows that war is normally a rational cost/benefit activity, not an apolitical juggernaut. (Section 11, pp. 80–81). War in reality is never fought on a continuous and uninterrupted basis as its logic suggests (Sections 12–14, pp. 81–83). In reality, war is interrupted for a variety of reasons such as the asymmetry in strength between the offense and defense. At times, this creates a situation in which even the stronger side lacks sufficient strength to overcome the advantage conferred by the stronger mode of war (i.e., the defense) (Sections 15–17, pp. 83–84). Imperfect intelligence often prevents a stronger side from attacking because it does not know that it holds the advantage (Section 18). The resulting uncertainty, chance, and friction make all actions probabilistic or to some degree a gamble (Sections 19–22). (Sections 12–17 are explained in greater depth and detail in Book 3, Chapter 16, pp. 216–219.[3]) And given the aversion to risk inherent in human nature – with its tendency to favor worst-case analysis – inaction and delays inevitably follow (Section 22, p. 86). In reality, therefore, careful calculations make war a political or policy-making issue rather than, as in theory, a senseless act of escalation to the extreme driven by its own logic and momentum (Sections 23–24, pp. 86–87).

The principal difficulty encountered in understanding the first chapter, 'What is War?', stems from its complex, abstract, and incremental explanation of the difference between war in theory and war in reality, in which Clausewitz gradually begins to construct his ideal type of war in reality (*as distinct from war in the abstract and war in practice*). The *ideal type of war in reality* can be described as follows:

The *ideal type of war in reality* is, in a way, the mirror-image of war in the abstract, and should therefore not be confused with *war in practice*. In real life, war is not always guided by clear political objectives, and cost/benefit calculations are either entirely neglected or incomplete.

War in reality (ideal)

* The objectives of war are determined by the political leaders of state, who also determine and calculate the costs and benefits involved.
* The political leaders/authorities are in full control of the military.
* Only the minimum necessary amount of resources and strength needed to win are used.
* War is not always fought until one side wins.
* War is frequently interrupted and not waged continuously.
* War is essentially a rational activity.

Often, political leaders are not in control of events or military leaders, while resources are squandered.

A comment made by Clausewitz near the end of *On War* may hint that he saw his description of war in reality as another ideal type and *not* as *actual* war in practice:

> **Just as absolute war has never in fact been achieved, so we will never find a war in which the second concept [*war in reality*] is so prevalent that the first can be disregarded altogether.**

> (Clausewitz, *On War*, p. 582)

Had Clausewitz never written more than the 15-odd pages of this chapter, his place as the greatest theorist and teacher on war would remain unchallenged. His methodology is so creative and powerful that this short, complex chapter incorporates most of the concepts developed in the rest of *On War*. This transition from the ideal to the real world of war can be depicted as shown in Figure C.1.

As argued here in Chapters 2 ('Comparing Sun Tzu and Clausewitz') and 11 ('The Ideal and the Real'), Sun Tzu at least tacitly uses the ideal-type method when he asserts that the '. . . *best policy is to take the state intact*' (Sun Tzu, *The Art of War*, p. 77) and that '*to subdue the enemy without fighting is the acme of skill*' (Sun Tzu, *The Art of War*, pp. 77, 79). '*Your aim must be to take all-under-heaven intact. Thus your*

FIGURE C.1
WAR IN THEORY AND REALITY COMPARED

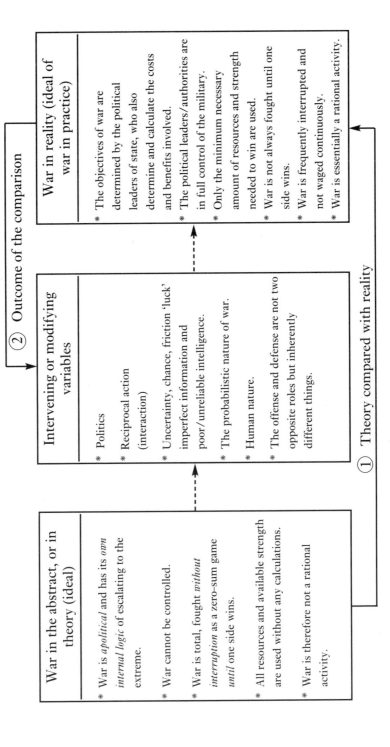

② Outcome of the comparison

War in the abstract, or in theory (ideal)

* War is *apolitical* and has its *own internal logic* of escalating to the extreme.

* War cannot be controlled.

* War is total, fought *without interruption* as a zero-sum game *until* one side wins.

* All resources and available strength are used without any calculations.

* War is therefore not a rational activity.

Intervening or modifying variables

* Politics

* Reciprocal action (interaction)

* Uncertainty, chance, friction 'luck' imperfect information and poor/unreliable intelligence.

* The probabilistic nature of war.

* Human nature.

* The offense and defense are not two opposite roles but inherently different things.

War in reality (ideal of war in practice)

* The objectives of war are determined by the political leaders of state, who also determine and calculate the costs and benefits involved.

* The political leaders/authorities are in full control of the military.

* Only the minimum necessary amount of resources and strength needed to win are used.

* War is not always fought until one side wins.

* War is frequently interrupted and not waged continuously.

* War is essentially a rational activity.

① Theory compared with reality

troops are not worn out and your gains will be complete. This is the art of offensive strategy' (Sun Tzu, *The Art of War*, p. 79). *One needs little to achieve much'* (Sun Tzu, *The Art of War*, p. 95). This cannot be taken literally, as advice that can be implemented under normal circumstances in war. As Sun Tzu knew only too well from the Chinese experience, violence and bloodshed in war and conflict are inevitable.[4] (See Chapter 11 above, 'The Ideal and the Real'.)

In Chapter 11 I have also shown how Clausewitz demolishes in principle the idea that 'winning without fighting' is sound advice although he does concede that it can become possible under *exceptional circumstances*. Many of Sun Tzu's other statements represent idealized norms as well. His point that war should be brought to an end as quickly as possible is certainly a universal idea that would make sense to any commander or theorist, but actually doing so can be extremely difficult. Clausewitz's recommendation that all available forces be concentrated at the decisive point and his emphasis on the *principle of destruction* as he calls it (i.e., that all other things being equal the quickest and surest way of winning a war is by destroying the enemy's forces) also point to the desirability of making war as short and 'economical' as possible.[5]

The fact that *all* military commanders want to win as quickly as possible by concentrating superior force explains why that which might be true if only one side were to apply the principles of war is rarely true when both sides subscribe to the same logic. As explained above, the weakness of Sun Tzu's argument is the premise that only one side will be privy to these principles. For example, his characterization of deception as the key to victory (or to use modern terminology, as the most important force multiplier) must be understood as an ideal concept. Deception alone is no panacea or guarantee of victory, and its use by both sides can easily cancel out a hoped-for advantage. In principle, all nations are aware that 'to know the enemy and to know oneself', or to use the enemy's own weight against him, makes eminent sense, but putting this into practice is a more challenging proposition. Likewise, Sun Tzu's idea that victory can be secured by making *rational decisions based on accurate and reliable information* under commanders who are in full control of their troops can seldom exist in reality (see Chapter 7 above, 'The Rational Calculus of War'). The recommendation that war should be waged as a purely rational and controlled activity can therefore be understood only as a normative idealized principle.

Clausewitz uses the ideal-type method as a methodological point of departure, as a heuristic device to explore the nature of war through comparison with reality. Sun Tzu, on the other hand, remains in his *idealized-normative world*. Above all, he fails to sufficiently emphasize the *reciprocal* and *dialectical* nature of war in which the constant action and reaction of the warring parties forecloses the possibility of a *monopoly on wisdom for either*. In contrast, the interactive and reciprocal nature of war is Clausewitz's most important postulate on the conditions of war and is, needless to say, a more realistic one.

If, on the other hand, we understand Sun Tzu's insights into the art of war *not* as an attempt to establish a unilateral monopoly on wisdom but instead as an *ideal type*, his arguments make much more sense. We can summarize Sun Tzu's ideal type of war or normative model for the master of war as follows:

The Ideal Way of Winning

* Winning without bloodshed or the use of force. Otherwise the minimum necessary use of violence.
* Once a war breaks out it should be brought to an end as quickly as possible.
* Make rational decisions on the basis of knowing the enemy's strengths and weaknesses (good intelligence) as well as one's own strengths and weaknesses (introspection).
* Extensive use of deception as a force multiplier.
* Use the enemy's weaknesses and assets against him.

At this point, an interesting question comes to mind. What if Sun Tzu had used Clausewitz's dialectical method and compared his ideal type of war with war in actuality? If Sun Tzu had posed the Clausewitzian questions of why and how war in theory differs from war in reality, the process of explaining the inevitable discrepancies would have produced additional insight into the nature of war and, ultimately, an even more refined and realistic theory.

As Clausewitz tells us, one ideal type implies the existence of the other. In addition, the observation of war in reality as well would allow us to develop the ideal type of war in reality that represents the antithesis of Sun Tzu's ideal type of war in the abstract. This ideal type of war in reality would include the following observations: war is not normally bloodless but involves the extensive use of concentrated force; violence and bloodshed are inevitable; 'little' force will *not* normally bring success in war; many, if not most, wars are prolonged and indecisive; it is very difficult in the real world of deception and contradictions to obtain reliable intelligence; and therefore it is difficult to wage war on a rational basis since the unfolding of events cannot be controlled by the masters of war. Sun Tzu's war in reality would look like this:

War in reality

* Extensive use of force and violence cannot be avoided.
* Little force cannot achieve much.
* Wars are often prolonged and indecisive.
* Intelligence is often unreliable.
* It is extremely difficult to perceive and understand one's own weaknesses and strengths.

In the next phase, the comparison of Sun Tzu's ideal type of war in the abstract with the ideal type of war in reality would lead Sun Tzu and his disciples to refine some of the observations made in *The Art of War*. This kind of comparison would direct far more attention to the reciprocal nature of war; it would also emphasize that no one side has a monopoly on the principles of war, that deception by itself can never be a panacea, that Sun Tzu's opponents are as capable of using deception as he is, and that even the most assiduous effort to wage war on the basis of rational calculations and careful planning is bound to be undermined by uncertainty, friction, and chance. When approximating Clausewitz's analytical method, Sun Tzu's modifying or intervening variables between war in the abstract and war in reality would appear as shown in Figure C.2.

Such a comparison would not transform *The Art of War* into *On War*. While still assigning greater importance to intelligence and deception than *On War*, Sun Tzu's 'Clausewitzian' analysis would more realistically delineate both their potential contribution and their *limits*. *The Art of War* would still recommend rational planning, but would further explore the limits of rationality in war and the role of friction and

FIGURE C.2
THE IDEAL WAY OF WAGING WAR COMPARED WITH THE REALITIES
(SUN TZU – *THE ART OF WAR*)
Outcome of the Comparison

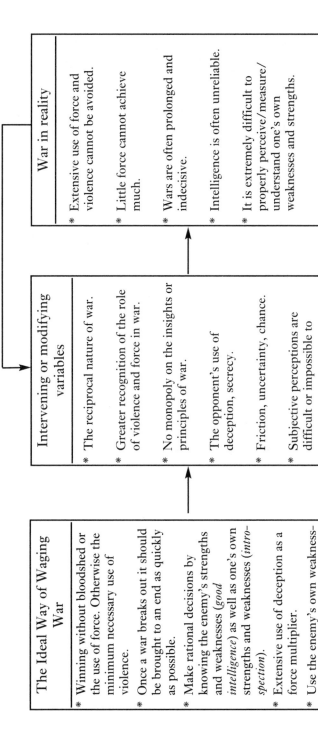

The Ideal of War Compared with War in Reality

The Ideal Way of Waging War

* Winning without bloodshed or the use of force. Otherwise the minimum necessary use of violence.
* Once a war breaks out it should be brought to an end as quickly as possible.
* Make rational decisions by knowing the enemy's strengths and weaknesses (*good intelligence*) as well as one's own strengths and weaknesses (*introspection*).
* Extensive use of deception as a force multiplier.
* Use the enemy's own weaknesses and weight against him.

Intervening or modifying variables

* The reciprocal nature of war.
* Greater recognition of the role of violence and force in war.
* No monopoly on the insights or principles of war.
* The opponent's use of deception, secrecy.
* Friction, uncertainty, chance.
* Subjective perceptions are difficult or impossible to overcome.

War in reality

* Extensive use of force and violence cannot be avoided.
* Little force cannot achieve much.
* Wars are often prolonged and indecisive.
* Intelligence is often unreliable.
* It is extremely difficult to properly perceive/measure/understand one's own weaknesses and strengths.

uncertainty. A greater emphasis on the *reciprocal nature of war* and the fact that no side has a monopoly on the principles of war should create more respect for, and appreciation of, the enemy.

Finally, the recognition of the inevitable use of force and violence in war as well as a greater emphasis on the role of material factors would disabuse all of the notion that war can be reduced to an intellectual exercise, to a battle of wits in which violence, force, and bloodshed are secondary or minor. A more realistic recognition of the role of violence in war does not mean, however, that the masters of war should forsake all efforts to win their wars as quickly and cheaply as possible. This is a corrective or approach from which Clausewitz and other Western military theorists could have benefited.

Once again, the artificial methodological exercise (a *Gedanken* experiment) as described above indicates how much the comparative reading of *The Art of War* and *On War* allows each to facilitate a deeper understanding of the other.

SUN TZU AND CLAUSEWITZ AS SEEN FROM EACH OTHER'S PERSPECTIVE

These tables include a brief summary of some of the most important concepts, assumptions, or approaches to war propounded by Sun Tzu and Clausewitz. By having each hypothetically criticize the other we can highlight their principal differences and better perceive the ways in which *On War* and *The Art of War* complement one another. The wisdom of both can thereby be synthesized into a higher theoretical level that benefits from the best of two worlds.

Table C.1
Sun Tzu contra Clausewitz

<u>Clausewitz's observations/assumptions</u>	<u>Sun Tzu's critique</u>
The principle of destruction – 'It is evident that the destruction of the enemy forces is always the superior, more effective means with which others cannot compete' (all other things being equal) (*On War*, p. 97). Clausewitz makes it clear however that he means 'the killing of the enemy's spirit' as much as his physical destruction (*On War*, pp. 259–297).	*An emphasis on the destruction of the enemy forces in battle can lead to the neglect of other non-violent possibilities that might prevent bloodshed. Instead of destroying the enemy's forces, do your best to convince them to surrender and move over to your side; thus, instead of destroying them, add them to your own power.*
'The best strategy is always to be very strong; first in general and then at the decisive point.'	*While true in general, the principle of the superior concentration of force is not a panacea. It can stifle the imagination and lead to a reluctance to separate/disperse troops for deception, which may attain decisive results without concentration. It could be more important to disperse the enemy troops than to concentrate your own! The superior concentration of troops may become an obsession emphasizing simplistic 'quantitative' solutions. The achievement of surprise by numerically inferior troops can be more important than numerical superiority achieved by the concentration of forces.*
'Most intelligence reports in war are contradictory, even more are false and most are uncertain.' The master of war cannot usually trust the reliability of his intelligence.	*This observation is true more on the tactical and operational levels than on the strategic level. Acceptance of this observation causes reliable intelligence to be ignored and discourages efforts to obtain better*

339

Clausewitz's observations/assumptions	Sun Tzu's critique
	information. A negative attitude toward intelligence on the tactical and operational levels translates into its neglect on the strategic level. The search for better intelligence is not a search for perfectly reliable intelligence but only for relatively better intelligence than the enemy has. (The balance of intelligence.) The side which has access to relatively better intelligence can reduce (though not eliminate) friction and uncertainty thus gaining the advantage.
'Surprise is a tactical device ... cases in which surprises led to major results are very rare ... surprise can rarely be *outstandingly* successful.'	*Not so. The master of war must always try to secure an advantage over his enemy by achieving surprise on all the levels of warfare including the strategic. As Clausewitz himself suggests –* 'Surprise ... becomes the means of gaining superiority' (*On War*, p. 198). *Surprise is a more important force multiplier than superior concentration. The master of war must always try to surprise his opponent.*
Deception 'should not be considered as a significant intelligence field of action at the disposal of the commander' (*On War*, p. 203). 'Diversions can be useful ... but not invariably so. Sometimes they can actually do harm ... the value of large-scale diversion is very doubtful ...' (*On War*, pp. 562–563).	*'All warfare is based on deception.' Deception is cheap, difficult to counter and therefore the most cost-effective force multiplier. Deception is one of the best ways to achieve surprise, which in turn facilitates success in war.*

Table C.2
Clausewitz contra Sun Tzu

Sun Tzu's advice or assumptions	Clausewitz's possible counter-argument
Sun Tzu's own side is assumed to be smarter and more subtle; that is, to have a monopoly on a superior understanding of war and the principles of war. Optimistic best case analysis, ethnocentric? Hubristic?	Both sides are assumed to be equally intelligent and subtle. Always assume that your enemy is as good as you are. This is a pessimistic, worst-case analysis. All sides are assumed to have equal access to and insights into the art, principles, and logic of war. A greater emphasis on war as a dialectical and reciprocal interaction.
Sun Tzu emphasizes psychological factors; special operations; using the enemy's weight against himself; the indirect approach; and deception. Represents a more subtle approach to war.	Nothing in Western tradition implies that psychological factors, the indirect approach, or deception are less important. Deception has always been part of the western tradition of war as can be seen from the Trojan Horse, the Bible, Byzantine strategic thinking, Machiavelli, or the British Double Cross system in the Second World War. But it is dangerous to overestimate the role of deception in modern times. Special operations are marginally important in support of major operations and can only have a tactical and operational – *not strategic* – value. Too much emphasis on subtlety, indirect approach, etc., may encourage false hope in 'miracle' solutions and cause neglect of physical, material, and other, more *direct* aspects of war.

Sun Tzu's advice or assumptions

The ideal strategy/plan in war is to win without fighting or violence. 'Generally in war the best policy is to take a state intact'; 'to subdue the enemy without fighting is the acme of skill', 'your aim is to take all under heaven intact', 'one needs but little to achieve much'.

Clausewitz's possible counter-argument

In the first place Clausewitz agrees that if possible one should try to win without fighting, and recognizes at least three possible ways of doing so:

A. War by algebra, mainly in theory (i.e., by demonstrating such overwhelming strength that the enemy will yield without fighting).

B. By maneuvering on the battle-field in such a way so as to convince the opponent that he has no chance to win. ('Checkmate').

C. By other non-military means (i.e., diplomacy, economic pressure, etc.) Although winning without fighting is commendable – in reality it is the exception!

If such a bloodless victory is achieved – as in A or C above – it is *not* war by definition – but something else.

The possibility of winning by other (non-violent, subtle) means is viable *only* if the enemy plays by the same rules (i.e., he is also ready to renounce the use of force and not to escalate the war if he is about to be defeated). Clausewitz emphasizes that the reluctance to use force, or the use of too little military force in war can be counter-productive and self-defeating, and will most likely backfire. In war, *effectiveness* is more important than *efficiency*. The desire to win a cheap victory is a false economy that can be more costly in the end. 'The principle of destruction' suggests that whenever possible

Sun Tzu's advice or assumptions	Clausewitz's possible counter-argument
	the quickest, most effective and ultimately the cheapest way of achieving one's goals *in war* is to destroy the enemy's forces.
Some specific examples of Sun Tzu's advice/principles of war: *'Engage in battle only when odds are overwhelmingly in your favor.'* *Always identify and exploit your comparative advantage.*	Clausewitz's actual or most likely counter-argument: A worthy opponent will attack you by his own initiative when the odds are in his favor (i.e., avoiding battle in inferior circumstances does not depend on you alone). War is a reciprocal affair. How can you be sure that you have *overwhelming* superiority? Can you trust your intelligence in a world of deception and uncertainty? While you are trying to make the enemy fight on your own preferred terms, the enemy in turn will try to make you fight on his own preferred terms. Why should you succeed more than he does? But identifying your comparative advantage and fighting on your best terms is always a good idea.
'Attack the enemy's strategy.' (See note 3, Chapter 5, pp. 386–390 below.)	He can attack your strategy as much as you can attack his. It is the strategic *interaction* that matters the most. How can you be sure that you have properly identified the enemy's strategy to begin with; and in the next phase how will it interact with yours?
Deceive the enemy. 'All warfare is based on deception.'	Deception is to be used whenever possible, but it is not a panacea. If you can deceive the enemy, he can also deceive you.

343

Sun Tzu's advice or assumptions	Clausewitz's possible counter-argument
Acquire better and more reliable intelligence. 'Know the enemy and know yourself; in a hundred battles you will never be in peril.'	Very good advice, but how often can one obtain reliable intelligence on the enemy and even on one's own troops. Intelligence acquired on the strategic level can often be reliable, but on the operational and tactical levels reliable intelligence is very difficult to obtain. Therefore, even though every effort should be made to obtain the best possible intelligence, the master of war cannot afford to place too much reliance on intelligence but must depend instead on the art of war itself, i.e., the maximum concentration of his troops, the maintaining of reserves, the experience and intuition of the leader, and the maintenance of aim.
	If deception is as important and effective as Sun Tzu claims, and if both sides can use it equally well, how can one rely on the intelligence obtained?

Appendix D

Clausewitz's *On War* as a *Gestalt* or a Systemic Theory[1]

> Its scientific character consists in an attempt to investigate the essence of the phenomena of war and to indicate the links between these phenomena and the nature of their component parts.
>
> Clausewitz, *On War*, p. 61 (Clausewitz's preface to an unpublished manuscript on the theory of war, written between 1816 and 1818.)

> The essential interconnections that genius has divined, the critic has to reduce to factual knowledge.
>
> Clausewitz, *On War*, p. 165

The opening statement of *On War* makes it clear that war can only be studied as a whole, as a *Gestalt* or *system* rather than as an exact or positive science. Clausewitz reminds the reader from the outset that true isolation of individual variables – normally a basic requirement for the development of a theory in the exact sciences – is impossible in the study of war. Other prerequisites of the exact sciences that do not exist in war include the ability to quantify variables and repeat experiments under controlled conditions. This, then, is Clausewitz's often-overlooked opening statement:

> I propose to consider first the various *elements* of the subject, next its various [or individual or separate] *parts* or *sections* and finally the *whole* [*das Ganze*] in its internal structure. In other words, I shall proceed from the simple to

the complex. *But in war more than in any other subject, we must begin by looking at the nature of the whole; for here more than elsewhere, the part and the whole must always be thought of together.* [italics in the last sentence are mine]

(Clausewitz, *On War*, p. 75; the same statement also appears in an abbreviated form on p. 484)

Clausewitz's reiteration of such statements throughout the text indicates how central this observation was to his theory of war. In Chapter 5 of Book 2, he states:

But in war as in life generally all parts of a whole are interconnected and thus the effects produced, however small their cause, must influence all subsequent military operations and modify their final outcome to some degree, however slight. In the same way, every means must influence even the ultimate purpose.

(Clausewitz, *On War*, p. 158)

In Book 3, Chapter 2, he stresses the importance of grasping the essential nature of a war without becoming lost in the analysis of artificially isolated details.

It would, however, be disastrous to try to develop our understanding of strategy [i.e., the operational art of war] by emphasizing these factors *in isolation, since they are interconnected in each military action in manifold and intricate ways.* A clearly analytical labyrinth would result, a nightmare in which one tried in vain to bridge the gulf between this abstract basis and the facts of life. Heaven protect the theorist from such an undertaking! For our part, we shall continue to examine the picture as a *whole*, and take our analysis no further than is necessary in each case to elucidate the idea we wish to convey, which will always have its origins in the impressions made *by the sum total* of the phenomena of war rather than in speculative study. [my emphasis]

(Clausewitz, *On War*, p. 183)

He returns to this theme in the first chapter of Book 8, where he argues that one of the most important functions of a general theory of war is to create a systematic framework for studying the complexity of war as a whole. The result is 'pure strategy'. Clausewitz then switches suddenly from what we would consider pure strategy today to the 'purely operational' level of war, where he discusses how generals cope with the infinite complexities of battle. This is another good example of his ambiguous use of the word 'strategy'. He continues as follows:

> ... **We can see how many factors are involved** [i.e., in battle] **and have to be weighed against each other; the vast, the almost infinite distance there can be between a cause and its effect, and the countless ways in which these elements can be combined.** *The function of theory is to put all this in systematic order,* **clearly and comprehensively, and to trace each action to an adequate, compelling cause ...** [Theory] *should show how one thing is related to another ...* [my emphasis]
>
> (Clausewitz, *On War*, pp. 577–578)

In fact, Clausewitz describes strategic theory as dealing with **'planning; or rather, its attempts to shed light on the components of war and their interrelationships ...'** (Clausewitz, *On War*, p. 177).

Interestingly, Mao Tse-tung places the same emphasis on the need to study war as a whole; but this is not surprising since, as a communist who believed in dialectical materialism, he would naturally view war in a broader social and economic context. Mao and Clausewitz thus arrive at similar conclusions for somewhat different reasons. (For Mao, this is a clear reason for the primacy of politics and strategy and the subordinate position of tactics.)

> Wherever there is war, there is a war situation. As a whole ... any war situation which acquires a comprehensive consideration of its various aspects and stages forms a war situation as a whole ... The task of the science of strategy is to study those laws for directing war that govern a war situation as a whole ... An understanding of the whole facilitates the handling of the part, and because the part is subordinate to the whole. The view that strategic victory is determined by tactical successes alone is wrong because it overlooks the fact that victory or defeat in war is first and foremost a question of whether the situation as

a whole and its various stages are properly taken into account
. . . But the situation as a whole cannot be detached from its
parts and become independent of them, for it is made up of all
its parts . . . All this explains the importance of taking into
account the situation as a whole. What is most important for the
person in over-all command is to concentrate on attending to
the war situation as a whole . . . The relationship between the
whole and the part holds not only for the relationship between
strategy and campaign but also for that between the campaign
and tactics . . . The only way to study the laws governing a war
situation as a whole is to do some hard thinking. For what pertains to the situation as a whole is not visible to the eye, and we
can understand it only by hard thinking; there is no other way.
[Compare this with Clausewitz's statement: **'That is why we
think it is useful to emphasize that all strategic planning
rests on tactical success alone'** (Clausewitz, *On War*, p. 386; see
also Appendix E below).]

(Mao Tse-tung, *Selected Military Writings*,
pp. 81-83; see also p. 119)

This emphasis on the need to study war as a *Gestalt* or a *system* rather
than through the attempted isolation of variables is particularly important when examining the role of moral factors on the course of war.[2]
(See Chapter 8, pp. 81–89.) According to Clausewitz, the synergism of
physical and psychological, material and intangible factors is far too
complex to be neatly quantified by simple formulas.

**The effects of physical and psychological factors form an
organic whole, which unlike a metal alloy, is inseparable by
chemical processes.**

(Clausewitz, *On War*, p. 184;
for a similar discussion, see also p. 77)

That which is true of the inseparable connection between the physical
and moral factors in Clausewitz's study of war also holds true for his
entire theory. Despite the numerous tensions and contradictions
between various concepts developed in *On War*, it is clear that they are
all logically interconnected. *Clausewitz's thinking is not only systematic,
but also systemic.* Often writing in a stream-of-consciousness style,
Clausewitz has created a consistent and coherent system of interrelated

concepts that makes it easier for us not only to better comprehend his ideas but also to infer his ideas on subjects that he does not address explicitly or in detail (e.g., such as war termination; see Chapter 14 above). One can also extrapolate from this what his ideas would be on problems that he did not discuss at all or which emerged long after his death (e.g., the role of economics, technology, and public opinion in war).

Because of its infinite complexity and 'non-linear' nature, war can only be understood as an organic *whole* not as a mere compendium of various separate elements. Clausewitz tried to simplify the theory of war by constructing a basic analytical framework from its lowest common denominators. The greatness of *On War* is that it comes as close as possible to achieving this goal. Yet in his pioneering, original work, Clausewitz first had to develop many of the concepts separately and in detail before he could combine them in one coherent summary. In his note on the genesis of his early manuscript, written around 1818, he comments:

> **My original intention was to set down my conclusions on the principal elements of this topic in short, precise, compact statements, without concern for system or formal connection. The manner in which Montesquieu dealt with the subject was vaguely on my mind.** [Had Clausewitz written *On War* as he originally intended, his work would have looked more like Sun Tzu's *The Art of War*.] **. . . But . . . my nature, which always drives me to develop and systematize, at last asserted itself here as well . . . Eventually my tendency completely ran away with me; I elaborated as much as I could . . . The more I wrote and surrendered to the spirit of analysis,** *the more I reverted to a systematic approach,* **and one chapter after another was added . . .** [my emphasis]
>
> (Clausewitz, *On War*, p. 63)

As he continues, Clausewitz makes it clear that he initially planned to develop a tighter and more comprehensive framework.

> **In the end I intended to revise it all again, strengthen the casual connections . . . draw together several analyses into a single conclusion and produce a reasonable whole.**
>
> (Clausewitz, *On War*, p. 63)

As it turned out, Clausewitz was never able to produce a new 'whole' by revising the book. His obsession with detailed analysis led him farther and farther away from the forest of high theory into the trees of the lower-level operational and tactical theory of war. The more he explored operational issues, the further he strayed from his goal of developing a comprehensive framework for the analysis of war. Some of the links between important aspects of war are highlighted by Clausewitz's occasional cross-references between various concepts or chapters, but many remain fragmented and incomplete. Clausewitz's 'digression' into a detailed discussion of operational matters was inevitable because of his interest in writing a practical book about fighting wars more effectively. Furthermore, it is impossible to understand the higher levels of war without studying its nature and uncertainties on the lower levels. In the process of doing so, however, Clausewitz ran out of time to return to the development of a final comprehensive conceptual framework.

Although this overall framework has never been fully articulated, all of the elements necessary for its construction are present in the text.[3] This may be a weakness as far as the final editing of the book was concerned, but it is otherwise a blessing in disguise that forces each reader to develop his own comprehensive understanding (i.e., his own framework) of the 'Clausewitzian system', or his 'system of concepts'. Given the richness, complexity, and subtlety of *On War*, reconstruction of 'the Clausewitzian system' requires careful and repeated reading of the book. As a result, the typical reader, instead of grasping the Clausewitzian system as a whole, concentrates on particular independent concepts, such as the center of gravity, friction, the trinitarian analysis, limited war, the military genius, economy of force, or the culminating point of victory. This is a mechanical, at times counter-productive, exercise in which the total of the work seems to be *less than the sum of its parts*.

The 'Clausewitzian system' is not dogmatic, static, or finite. On the contrary, the relationship of its parts is variable, dynamic, and adaptable. Different readers interpret the interactions, connections, and relative significance of the various parts of the 'system' in different ways. What is important is to understand how the various concepts *can relate to and influence each other*. This is why the analysis of war on all of its levels must always encompass such a wide variety of factors (some of which can be only partly identified; not identified in time; or identified after the event) and relate them to one another.[4]

These two 'flow charts' represent a first experimental attempt to connect Clausewitz's ideas in a simplified visual way. This is by no means the only possible version, since other combinations or sets of interconnections are equally possible. Although the connections are clear, this does not mean that such clear or simple connections always exist in reality or in Clausewitz's theory. The chart is therefore intended only as a heuristic device to enhance the reader's understanding of a complicated text and help him to arrive at his own insightful interpretation of the 'Clausewitzian system'. Above all, the reader must avoid the temptation to reduce Clausewitz's systematic and 'organic' theory of war to a rigid mechanical formula. Even though Clausewitz never revised *On War* to his satisfaction, his disclaimers not withstanding, he did develop a coherent and systematic theory of war comprehensive enough to connect its diverse constituents into the desired whole.

Appendix E

The Problem of the Level of Analysis and the 'Tacticization of Strategy'

> Without a good plan for the whole campaign, it is absolutely impossible to fight a really good first battle. That is to say, even though victory is won in the first battle, if the battle harms rather than helps the campaign as a whole, such a victory can only be reckoned a defeat. . . . Hence, before the first battle one must have a general idea of how the second, third, fourth, and even the final battle will be fought. . . . It is absolutely essential to have a long-term plan.
>
> Mao Tse-tung, *Selected Military Writings*, pp. 130–131

In theory, the relationship between the three levels of analysis is hierarchical. Traditionally depicted as a pyramid in which strategy is at the top and the operational and tactical levels are subordinate, this simplistic model does not reflect the dynamic relationship between the three levels in the real world.

A strictly hierarchical structure is also authoritarian, and normally suggests that orders and decisions flow only from top to bottom with a monopoly on all decisions at the highest, strategic level. In the real world, however, operational or tactical considerations can and do influence strategic decisions often as much as they are influenced *by* them. For example, the United States' reluctance to incur heavy casualties or lose soldiers as POWs, which is at least a partially tactical or operational problem, can affect the choice of strategy or the country's position at the bargaining table. In the First World War, the combina-

FIGURE E.1
THE TRADITIONAL HIERARCHY OF
INFLUENCE AND DECISION-MAKING IN WAR

tion of trenches, barbed wire, and machine guns – a relatively low-level technical-tactical problem – exerted a decisive influence on the strategies employed. Often, the mere availability of a certain weapons system rather than political, economic, or long-range military considerations will dictate the choice of strategy. For example, the invention of submarines before the First World War created inexorable pressures to use the U-boats as a weapon against Britain despite the risk of drawing the United States into the war.[1]

In other instances, outstanding performance on the tactical or operational level causes political and military leaders to emphasize short-run success on the battlefield while neglecting the development of a coherent long-range strategy. Yet when a strategy is not consciously formulated, it emerges by default. Instead of being the driving force in war, strategy becomes a mere by-product or afterthought. In prolonged wars, this is a recipe for disaster, since even extraordinary tactical and operational successes may not add up to a winning strategy. During the Second Punic War Hannibal never lost a major battle in Italy – yet his tactical prowess was not enough to secure final strategic victory. This was also the weakness of Napoleon, whose tactical brilliance was greatly admired by Clausewitz.

A general such as Bonaparte could ruthlessly cut through all his enemies' strategic plans in search of battle, because he seldom doubted the battle's outcome. So, whenever the strategists did not endeavor with all their might to crush him in battle with superior force, whenever they engaged in

> **subtler (and weaker) machinations, their schemes were swept away like cobwebs . . . Bonaparte was well aware that everything turned on tactical results . . . That is why we think it is useful to emphasize that all strategic planning rests on tactical success alone . . .**
>
> (Clausewitz, *On War*, p. 386; see also p. 615)[2]

This is an excellent example of what can be called the 'tacticization of strategy' (i.e., lower-level operational considerations defining the strategy in war). In most cases, taking this approach is a grave mistake. (Other examples of reliance on operational success as a substitute for a comprehensive, calculated strategy are Ludendorff's 'last offensive' of March 1918, or Rommel's campaign in North Africa.)

The aforementioned quotation from *On War* runs counter to Clausewitz's emphasis on the primacy of politics, the need to understand the nature of the war, and the importance of not taking 'the first step without thinking about the last'. It must therefore be examined in the broader context of his work, where higher-level considerations are unquestionably more important. This apparent contradiction can be at least partially explained by the fact that (1) most of *On War* is actually concerned with operational rather than strategic problems; and (2) Clausewitz admired military geniuses such as Napoleon who often succeeded by taking high risks on the operational level.

Clausewitz's preoccupation with operational problems also caused him to overestimate the importance of battles and all military aspects of war. As Ho Chi Minh and Mao Tse-tung realized, constant military activity and patience, even without 'military victories', can be enough to compel the enemy to do one's will. Although Clausewitz did not completely ignore such possibilities, he believed that, on the whole, military victories *were a necessary condition* for imposing one's will on the enemy. (see in particular Book 1, Chapter 2, on 'The Purpose and Means in War').

The problem of the 'tacticization of strategy' (i.e., the operational or military tail wagging the political-strategic dog) was of the greatest concern for Mao Tse-tung and for Marxist strategists in general. Mao's thoughts on, as he calls it, the relationship of *the part to the whole situation* in war is more cautious and reasonable. In this case, one could say he was more Clausewitzian than Clausewitz, since Mao's Party always controls the barrel of the gun.

In contrast to Napoleon, and to Clausewitz's admiration of Napoleon's operational brilliance, Mao consistently *warns of the danger* of the 'tacticization of strategy':

> The view that strategic victory is determined by tactical successes alone is wrong because it overlooks the fact that victory or defeat in war is first and foremost a question of whether the situation as a whole and its various stages are properly taken into account.
>
> (Mao Tse-tung, *Selected Military Writings*, pp. 81–82)

Mao's insistence that we consider the 'situation as a whole' is of course the essence of strategic thinking. Mao's approach, which is calculating and rational without a shred of sentimental or romantic influence, causes him to stand out as a strategic leader when compared with others such as Napoleon, Hitler, and the various high commands of the First World War.

> If there are serious defects or mistakes in taking the situation as a whole and its various stages into account, the war is sure to be lost. 'One careless move loses the whole game' refers to a move affecting the situation as a whole, a move decisive for the whole situation and not to a move of a partial nature, a move which is not decisive for the whole situation. As in chess so in war. But the situation as a whole cannot be detached from its parts and become independent of them, for it is made up of all its parts.
>
> (Mao Tse-tung, *Selected Military Writings*, p. 82)

This discussion demonstrates why the dynamic relationship among the different levels of war is best depicted by the following diagram, in which the relative importance of each level in the direction and control of war is signified by the size of the box representing it. Moreover, this diagram emphasizes the actual reciprocal relationships among the various levels of waging war, regardless of their ranking in the formal hierarchy of its decision-making processes.

FIGURE E.2
THE THREE LEVELS OF WAR
AS A COMPLEX MODEL OF INTERACTION

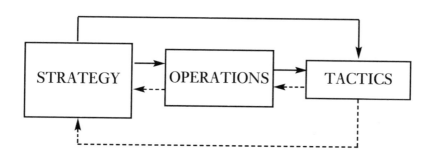

FIGURE E.3
THE RELATIVE IMPORTANCE OF EACH LEVEL
FOR POLITICAL CONTROL AND THE
DIRECTION OF WAR

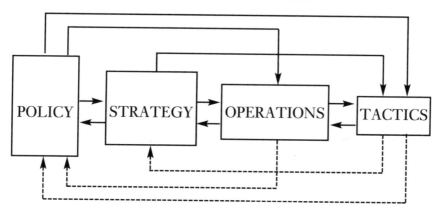

Throughout history the principal cause of the tacticization of strategy has been the uncontrolled ambition of military field commanders or the tactically and operationally oriented thinking of political leaders. In the twentieth century, particularly after the Second World War, an additional cause emerged in the form of military-technological developments (i.e., new military means that instead of serving strategy in fact determined the logic underlying major strategic choices). Increasingly, technological means have started to wag the strategic dog. This is especially true of the new third dimension of war – air war.

This trend, which can be identified clearly in the Second World War and later in the Korean and Vietnam Wars, became even more obvious in the Gulf War and the war in Kosovo. The greatly enhanced capabilities of modern air-delivered precision-guided munitions can destroy almost any physical/material target that can be identified. This technological trend, combined with the reluctance of Western political leaders to take or inflict unnecessary casualties for non-vital secondary or tertiary national interests, has created a situation in which targeting has *de facto* become a substitute for proper strategic planning.

Indeed, the latest doctrinal developments in the U.S. military vision (Joint Vision 2010, 2020) of the future of conventional war suggest the gradual blurring of the traditional distinctions between the strategic and lower operational and tactical levels of war. In other words, the expected quality of new wartime intelligence (i.e., 'information dominance', 'information superiority', 'battlefield or battlespace transparency') – and accurate target acquisition in real time – will allow a faster paced 'sensor-to-shooter' war, in which there will be less time to consult the higher strategic and operational commands. These doctrines therefore envision a much faster pace of war, with more effective and widespread destruction of enemy forces once the war begins. In this scenario, there would be no need for continuous strategic decision-making – all that would be necessary to break the enemy's will would be to destroy his military forces and other targets through relentless military action. With the overlapping of strategy and operations, there will be less need for the middle command echelon – fast action defined by 'targeteers', sensors, and delivery platforms will become the strategy. Once the order to begin the war has been given, the outcome of the war will depend on the ability of air power of all types to identify and destroy enemy targets at will – rather than on a detailed, long-range strategic plan.

The war in Kosovo has already demonstrated this trend. Accurate bombing from the air became the strategy of choice because technological developments made it possible and because it was politically acceptable: after all, it minimized casualties on all sides. Yet, despite the success achieved, the war lasted much longer than expected: moreover, it is not clear that the war was guided by a clear long-range strategy or that such strategic objectives (if defined) were achieved in the long run. Destruction of targets at will does not add up to a clear or coherent strategy; nor does crippling the enemy's military and economic infrastructure automatically bring political and strategic success. Revolutionary improvements in military intelligence and target acquisition on all levels as well as the ever-greater sophistication of precision-guided munitions will further increase the pressures as well as opportunities for the 'tacticization of strategy'.

Neither victorious and ambitious field commanders nor impressive military technologies – the means available to political leaders and the state – should define the strategy of any war whether by preference or by default. Military success alone, the destruction of the enemy's military might or economic infrastructure, does not in the long run necessarily ensure the achievement of one's political aims.

The long-term success of every war can be achieved only by first identifying its political objectives. This is not always, as is often thought, either self-evident or simple. Instead of first defining clear objectives and strategies, political leaders now decide to take action on the basis of the promise of air power to destroy targets at will, at a much lower cost in casualties and collateral damage. But the best and most suitable means should be decided only *after* the political objectives and purpose of the war have been identified. Even then, there is a need continuously and carefully to examine whether such military success is leading to the desired political results and to a policy of war termination that can translate military success into corresponding political success. Doing that which is politically acceptable or militarily possible does not automatically add up to the development of an adequate strategy. Targeting, destruction, and attrition are only *one* aspect of strategic planning.

Recent events have shown that while enormous strides have been made in perfecting and developing the means of war, the same cannot be said of the ability to understand the nature, purpose, and political direction of war, or the ability to translate military success into political achievements. The Gulf War and the war in Kosovo were successful in military terms, but not as much in political and strategic terms; after all, the political opponents of the United States are still in power, the United States and its allies still have to maintain considerable forces in the regions involved, and in many ways, the political environment is hardly more stable or favorable. This is precisely why it has become even more important, in the age of high-tech wars, to study the political and strategic dimensions that might otherwise by overshadowed by the attractions of modern technology. The most remarkable military/ technological successes are barren without the guidance of a coherent long-range strategy. One need only consider the fact that U.S. technological superiority was ultimately of no avail in the Vietnam War. Since even the most advanced targeting systems do not win wars, they are at best a necessary but never sufficient condition.

A few points need to be mentioned in this context.

1 Not all wars will provide the best environment for the newly developed technologies (i.e., such technologies are the most effective in a conventional high-tech war against a technologically inferior enemy, but not in low-intensity wars against guerrilla tactics or terrorism; nor will they be as effective against equally sophisticated opponents.) (See Note 1 to the Introduction, pp. 369–370.)

2 The promise of much faster-paced war may not be realized in a political environment where leaders want *more* not *less* political control in order to minimize the costs of war, particularly in wars fought for secondary interests. They are likely to have more layers of command, which will slow down the pace of war. In other words, the gap between what technology can deliver and what the political leaders will allow may grow wider not narrower.

3 Our opponents may surrender or yield to military pressure even while they succeed in avoiding the political consequences.

The promise of quick and cheap victories will increasingly tempt strategic decision-makers to take action because they can, thus weakening the longer-range strategic planning that is so critical for real success in war. This is not to suggest that modern military-technological developments are unimportant, simply that even the best technology must be used in a political and strategic context that will ultimately define its longer-range effectiveness.

Appendix F

Clausewitz and the Principle of Concentration

There is an ancient rule of war that cannot be repeated often enough: hold your own forces together, make no detachments, and, when you are ready to fight the enemy, assemble all your forces and seize every advantage to make sure of success. The rule is so certain that most of the generals who have neglected it have been punished promptly.

Frederick The Great, *Instructions for His Generals*, trans. Brigadier General Thomas R. Phillips

It thus follows that as many troops as possible should be brought into the engagement at the decisive point . . . This is the first principle of strategy. In the general terms in which it is expressed here it would hold true for Greeks and Persians, for Englishmen and Maharattas, for Frenchmen and Germans.

(Clausewitz, *On War*, p. 195)

If a single principle of war can be identified as the linchpin of Clausewitz's entire operational theory of war, it is his *principle of concentration*. This principle is so central to the intricate relationships of his concepts and insights that Clausewitz uses uncharacteristically emphatic language to ensure that its role is properly understood; indeed, 'the maximum concentration of force' or 'the principle of concentration' is, in his view, 'the first', 'the highest', 'the simplest', and 'the most elementary' law of strategy (Clausewitz, *On War*, pp. 204–205).[1] (In this context and throughout *On War*, the word 'strategy' primarily means what we now refer to as the operational or even tactical level of war, although Clausewitz also uses it to connote the highest level of war as we understand it today.)

On the strategic level, the *principle of concentration* indicates mobilization of a nation's entire war potential (see Section 5, p. 77 in *On War* and the quotations cited immediately below). But when discussing the *principle of concentration* in *On War*, Clausewitz is, however, generally referring to the operational and even tactical levels of war, where he mentions the commander's concentration of all available troops at the 'decisive point' for battle. Such concentration, *all other things being equal*, enables the better concentrated and thus the stronger force to quickly overwhelm and destroy (physically and/or morally) its weaker opponent.

> **The best strategy is always to be very strong; first in general [i.e., the mobilization of the total war potential of the state] and then at the decisive point [i.e., the operational level]. Apart from the effort needed to create military strength which does not always emanate from the general [i.e., full national mobilization, which is a political decision], there is no higher and simpler law of strategy [here used as the operational level!] than that of *keeping one's forces concentrated*. No force should ever be detached from the main body unless the need is definite and urgent. We hold fast to this *principle* and regard it as a reliable guide.**
>
> (Clausewitz, *On War*, p. 204)

> **The simultaneous use of all means intended for a given action appears as an elementary law of war.**
>
> (Clausewitz, *On War*, p. 205)

> **The rule then . . . is this: all forces intended and available for a strategic purpose [i.e., primarily meant in this context as the operational level] should be applied simultaneously; their employment will be the more effective the more everything can be concentrated in a single action at a single moment.**
>
> (Clausewitz, *On War*, p. 209)

In tactics, as in strategy, superiority of numbers is the most common element in victory . . . strategy decides the time when, the place where, and the forces with which the engagement is to be fought . . . [here, strategy clearly means the operational level] . . . We are left with the bare concept of the engagement . . . in which the only distinguishing factor is the number of troops on either side. These numbers, therefore, will determine victory . . . This is the first principle of strategy . . . In modern Europe even the most talented general will find it very difficult to defeat an opponent twice his strength . . . A significant superiority in numbers (it does not have to be more than double) will suffice to assure victory, however adverse the other circumstances . . . A main factor is the possession of strength at the really vital point. *Usually it is actually the most important factor.* To achieve strength at the decisive point depends on the strength of the army and on the skill with which this strength is employed [i.e., identifying the 'decisive point' depends to a large extent on the intuition and experience of the commander].

The first rule, therefore, should be: put the largest possible army into the field. This may sound a platitude but in reality it is not.

(Clausewitz, On War, pp. 194–195)

In the discussion of each of his 'principles of war' and ideas, though, Clausewitz *is always careful to point out the exceptions.*[2] Thinking along the same lines, Jomini states that *'every maxim has its exceptions'* (Jomini, *The Art of War*, p. 84) while Moltke the Elder takes note of the 'relative validity' of all of the principles of war. In fact, by pondering these exceptions, he sheds more light on his idea and explores the principle in further depth. Above all he makes the didactic point that no principle of war should be mechanically applied: the intelligent commander must always use his own judgment and must not hesitate to break the rules when he can profit from doing so.[3]

The principle of concentration is, in turn, closely related to the concepts of the *economy of force*,[4] *the center of gravity*, and *the principle of destruction* (for the interaction or interconnection of these concepts, see Chart 4 above, opposite p. 350). The idea of the economy of force suggests that no part of the available forces should remain idle or unused (Clausewitz, *On War*, p. 213). The greatest possible number of troops can thus be concentrated at the decisive point, so that when the critical moment of battle has arrived (which can be judged by the experience and intuition of the master of war) no reserves will be held back.

> **When the decisive stage of the battle has been reached . . . all forces must be used to achieve it [victory] and any idea of reserves, of available combat units that are not meant to be used until after this decision is an absurdity.**
>
> (Clausewitz, *On War*, p. 211)

The concept of the center of gravity in turn indicates where and against what objective the concentrated forces should be unleashed. Identification of the enemy's center of gravity is thus an essential step in properly implementing the principle of concentration. Clausewitz is adamant on this point:

> **The ultimate substance of enemy strength must be traced back to the fewest possible sources, and ideally to one alone [i.e., the enemy's center of gravity]. The attack on these sources must be compressed into the fewest possible actions – again ideally, into one. Finally, all minor operations must be subordinated as much as possible. In short, the first principle is: act with the utmost concentration.**
>
> (Clausewitz, *On War*, p. 617)

> **. . . A stroke at the center of gravity of the enemy's forces, tends, in some degree, to keep [the fighting forces] concentrated.**
>
> (Clausewitz, *On War*, p. 486)

All efforts must be directed at the enemy's center of gravity, and secondary objectives ignored, as Clausewitz explains in detail (Clausewitz, *On War*, pp. 617ff.). It is when the center of gravity has been identified, and all forces concentrated against it, that victory (i.e., the destruction of the enemy forces) is most likely to be achieved.

Jomini also classifies the principle of concentration as one of the four fundamental principles of war (Jomini, *The Art of War*, p. 70) and observes its relationship to the concept of the center of gravity (or the 'decisive point' as he calls it).

(1) To throw by strategic [i.e. the operational level] *movement the mass of an army, successively, upon the decisive points of a theater of war . . .*

(2) To maneuver to engage fractions of the hostile army with the bulk of one's forces.

(3) On the battle-field, to throw the mass of the forces upon the decisive point, or upon that portion of the hostile line which it is of the first importance to overthrow [i.e., to concentrate superior forces against the enemy's center of gravity].

(4) To arrange that these masses shall not only be thrown upon the decisive point, but that they shall engage at the proper time and with energy.

(Jomini, *The Art of War*, p. 70)

Jomini then wisely adds an escape clause:

This principle [meaning the four maxims] *has too much simplicity to escape criticism. One objection is that it is easy to recommend throwing the mass of the force upon the decisive points, but that the difficulty lies in recognizing those points.*

(Jomini, *The Art of War*, pp. 70–71)

It is interesting to note that three of Jomini's four fundamental principles of war convey the same idea in different words.

Finally, the principle of concentration is also closely related to the *principle of destruction*, which states that when all other things are held equal, the destruction of the enemy forces *is the most effective* (even if not the least costly) way 'to compel him to do our will' thus achieving our own political objectives (see Chapter 11 above).[5] This is the case because the superior concentration of forces is the simplest and safest approach (all other things being equal) to destroying the enemy forces.

Like Clausewitz, Mao repeatedly emphasizes the importance of troop concentration for success in battle and war. Mao also makes a point of distinguishing between the problems related to concentrating forces on the strategic level as opposed to the lower operational and tactical levels. At the highest strategic level, Mao's long-term guerrilla strategy could depend on strategic dispersal and on deliberately *avoiding* the concentration of troops as long as the strategic balance favors the enemy. By contrast, concentration on the lower tactical and operational levels is always essential even in his theory of guerrilla warfare.

On the strategic level, and when retreating, Mao also underscores the military as well as psychological importance of focusing on one enemy at a time, one front at a time. It is imperative to avoid 'striking with two "fists" and splitting the main force of the Red Army in two, to seek victories simultaneously in two strategic directions' (Mao Tse-tung, *Selected Military Writings*, p. 134). 'Oppose the strategy of striking with two "fists" in one direction at one time' (Mao Tse-tung, *Selected Military Writings*, p. 97). Avoiding wars on more than one front and thus maintaining strategic concentration is a valuable lesson from which Napoleon, the Germans in the First World War, Hitler in the Second World War, or the Athenians opening a new front in Sicily would certainly have profited.

On the tactical and operational level, the maximum possible concentration is always recommended. '. . . [Of the conditions necessary to defeat the enemy, the] concentration of troops is the first and most essential' (Mao Tse-tung, *Selected Military Writings*, p. 132). 'The kind of concentration we advocate is based on the principle of guaranteeing absolute or relative superiority on the battlefield' (Mao Tse-tung, *Selected Military Writings*, p. 136; see also pp. 144, 145, 162–163).

Mao explains the difference between concentrating on the strategic and lower levels as follows:

> The Chinese Red Army, which entered the arena of the civil war as a small, weak force, has since repeatedly defeated its powerful antagonist and won victories that have astonished the world and it has done so by relying largely on the employment of concentrated strength. Any one of its great victories can prove this point. When we say 'Pit one against ten, pit ten against a hundred' we are speaking of strategy, of the whole war and the overall balance of forces, and in the strategic sense that is just what we have been doing. However, we are not speaking of campaigns and tactics in which we must never do so. Whether in counter-offensive or offensive, we should always concentrate . . . Our strategy is to 'pit one against ten' and our tactics to 'pit ten against one' – this is one of our fundamental principles for gaining mastery over the enemy.
>
> (Mao Tse-tung, *Selected Military Writings*, p. 134–135)

Although strategic dispersion at the beginning of a war is dictated by a position of weakness, not of choice – the successive concentration of forces each time on the lower tactical and operational level ultimately yields an aggregate of successes: this eventually tips the strategic balance of power in favor of the formerly weaker side. As illustrated by the experience of the Red Army during the final phase of the Chinese Civil War, the previous 'underdog' is now in a position to make the long-awaited transition to the 'higher level' of conventional war and achieve victory through the maximum concentration of troops. (Mao dedicates an entire section of his essay on 'Strategy in China's Revolutionary War' to the question of concentration of troops (Mao Tse-tung, *Selected Military Writings*, pp. 131–137).)

Notes

INTRODUCTION

1. There are at least four possible types of war (and numerous variations), which differ according to the belligerents' level of technological sophistication.

A TYPOLOGY OF FOUR TYPES OF POSSIBLE WARS ACCORDING
TO THE LEVEL OF TECHNOLOGICAL DEVELOPMENT

| | | *SIDE A* | |
		HIGH-TECH	LOW-TECH
SIDE B HIGH-TECH		HIGH-TECH AGAINST HIGH-TECH ①	LOW-TECH AGAINST HIGH-TECH ②
LOW-TECH		③ HIGH-TECH AGAINST LOW-TECH	④ LOW-TECH AGAINST LOW-TECH

The first type of war occurs between enemies with equally advanced levels of technological sophistication. In this case, neither side possesses a particular advantage, but the pace of war is likely to be faster and the rates of attrition higher, while collateral damage may be reduced on both sides (e.g., a conventional 'central front' type of war).

The second type takes place between a less technologically advanced belligerent and a technologically sophisticated opponent (what is referred to in the current jargon as an 'asymmetrical war'). Here, we must assume that the technologically disadvantaged side will seek a variety of ways to neutralize the technological superiority of his opponent. The 'underdog' can, for example, maximize his own comparative advantages by resorting to guerrilla warfare, terrorism, passive resistance, or any other combination of low-intensity warfare, possibly even the threat to use low-tech weapons of mass destruction (good examples of this type of war would be the Vietnam War, the Soviet Union's war in Afghanistan, or that of Russia in Chechnya).

A third type of war takes place between a technologically advanced state and its low-tech opponent, who chooses, or is obliged, to fight a conventional war on the technologically sophisticated enemy's terms. In such a one-sided war, the weaker state will suffer a sort of paralysis brought on by the paucity of military options at its disposal (e.g., the Israeli air war against Syria in 1982; the Gulf War against Iraq; and the war in Kosovo).

The fourth type is any war between low-tech opponents that rely on few, if any, advanced technologies. This would include belligerents who physically possess sophisticated military equipment but cannot use it effectively (e.g., some African or Asian civil wars, or wars between less developed countries).

Most of the recent military literature on war published in the United States and the West addresses the third type of war. This, not surprisingly, reflects the military success of the United States and its allies in the Gulf War and in Kosovo, fascination with computer-age technologies, and shrinking military budgets, which fuel the incentive to find new force multipliers. Seldom, though, has history shown us wars that can be fought on the preferred terms of only one of the belligerents.

2. We now have strong circumstantial evidence (from his diary) that Mao read at least the first book of Clausewitz's *On War* in Chinese translation and may have participated in a seminar session that he initiated on Clausewitz (spring 1938). This is probably not enough to explain some of the striking similarities between Clausewitz's *On War* and Mao's ideas in 'Problems of Strategy in China's Revolutionary War' (December 1935), 'Problems of Strategy in the Guerrilla War against Japan' (May 1938), and 'On Protracted War' (May 1938). My assumption is that, although Mao may have been familiar with *some* of Clausewitz's ideas, his theoretical work on war is largely original. (Of course, there are other more important influences on Mao's intellectual process, or his *'transformation of ideas'*, which include Sun Tzu's *The Art of War*, traditional Chinese military history and folklore, Marxist theory, and Mao's personal experience of directing war.) Some of the similarities to Clausewitz's work and methodology, as well as to Western strategy, can undoubtedly be attributed to Marxist-Leninist analysis. The evidence that Mao read at least the first book of Clausewitz's *On War* can be found in Zhang Yuan-Lin, 'Mao Zedong und Carl von Clausewitz: Theorien des Krieges. Beziehung, Darstellung und Vergleich' (PhD dissertation, University of Mannheim, 1995). For the concept of the transformation of ideas, see I. Bernard Cohen, *The Newtonian Revolution* (Cambridge: Cambridge University Press, 1980).

CHAPTER 1: STRATEGY: PAST THEORIES,
MODERN PRACTICE

1. Sun Tzu (trans. Samuel B. Griffith), *Sun Tzu, The Art of War* (New York: Oxford University Press, 1971). All quotations in the text (referred to as Sun Tzu, *The Art of War*) are from this edition, which is the most readily accessible to the modern English-speaking reader. The first translation into English – a rather poor and incomplete rendering – was Sun Tzu (trans. Captain E. F. Calthorpe), *The Book of War: The Military Classic of the Far East* (London: John Murray, 1908). Other translations that might be of interest are: Sun Tzu (trans. Thomas Cleary), *The Art*

of War (Boston: Shambhala, 1988); Sun Tzu (trans. Chang Lin), *The Art of War: Military Manual* (Hong Kong: Far East Book Press, 1969); Sun Tzu (trans. A. and G. Chen), *The Art of War* (Singapore: Graham Brash (PTE) Ltd, 1982); and Sun Tzu (trans. Lionel Giles), *The Art of War* (London: Luzac, 1910), now available in the following reprint: Sun Tzu (ed. James Clavell), *The Art of War* (New York: Delacorte, 1983). Another reprint of the Giles translation was published by Graham Brash (Singapore, 1989). Giles's translation of the text (without his comments and notes) was also published in a series by the Military Service Publishing Company of Harrisburg, Pennsylvania in 1944, with an introduction and notes by Brigadier General Thomas R. Phillips. Two other interesting translations are one by Tai Mien-Leng, *The Art of War* (n.p., Taipei & Taileron, 1954), which is based on Giles; and an original and very useful translation by Tang Zi-Chang, *Principles of Conflict: Recompilation and New English Translation with Annotation of Sun Tzu's 'Art of War'* (San Rafael, CA: T.C. Press, 1969). This also includes a survey of the Chinese art of war in Sun Tzu's time. (See also the bibliography.)

None of the currently available translations of *Sun Tzu* (the title *The Art of War* was added later – the original title was simply *Sun Tzu*) is entirely accurate. Each translator has employed at least a few contemporary Western phrases or words that do not exist in the original, and has inevitably, even if unintentionally, contributed some of his own ideas. This is particularly true of General Samuel B. Griffith's readable translation and less so of the Giles translation. The modern translator and editor of *Sun Tzu* must not only grapple with the problem of translating from Chinese to English, but must also establish the meaning of classical Chinese characters that have fallen into disuse or acquired new, varied meanings and nuances in different dialects of modern Chinese. Avoiding the imposition of modern strategic concepts and terminology is perhaps the most difficult task of all, particularly when one's objective is to make the translation understandable to the reader on his own terms. For the problems involved in translating *The Art of War* into English see Arthur Waldron, 'More Than Just Semantics', *Naval War College Review* (Autumn 1994), pp. 113–114.

Scholarly interest in this subject is, despite these obstacles, on the increase. In 1993 alone, the following three translations and reinterpretations were published: Sun Tzu (trans. R. Ames), *Sun Tzu, The Art of Warfare* (New York: Ballantine Books, 1993); Sun Tzu (trans. J. H. Huang), *Sun Tzu: The New Translation* (New York: William Morrow, 1993); R. D. Sawyer (trans.), *The Seven Military Classics of Ancient China* (Boulder, CO: Westview Press, 1993). Published in 1994, another translation by Ralph D. Sawyer, entitled *Sun Tzu: The Art of War* (New York: Barnes & Noble, 1994), includes an extensive introduction, commentaries, and a bibliography. On the various translations of Sun Tzu's *The Art of War* into other languages see Tang Zi-Chang, *Principles of Conflict* (San Rafael, CA: T. C. Press, 1969), pp. 171–178; this is an outstanding translation and survey of Sun Tzu's *Art of War*.

Of these, the first two translations are based on the Yin–ch'üeh–shan texts discovered in a Han tomb excavation in 1972. Written on bamboo slats a little more than two millennia ago, this copy is now the earliest known text of this classical work. Of great interest are the five previously unknown partial chapters included in this version and the additional material discovered in later excavations.

For the sake of brevity, statements attributed directly to Sun Tzu as well as to the traditional commentators in his text are all referred to in my discussion as Sun Tzu; but each citation from commentators other than Sun Tzu is preceded by the name of the specific authority (such as Tu Mu, Ts'ao Ts'ao, Chang Yu, Mei Yao-ch'en, and Ho Yen-hsi, to name a few). In addition, all references are made to Sun Tzu rather than to *the* Sun Tzu, a term arising from the assumption that *The Art of War* is a compilation of the wisdom of at least several authors over many generations. On this, see Edward O'Dowd and Arthur Waldron, 'Sun Tzu for Strategists', *Comparative Strategy*, vol. 10 (1991), pp. 25–36.

All quotations from *On War* are from Carl von Clausewitz (ed. and trans. Sir Michael Howard and Peter Paret), *On War* (Princeton, NJ: Princeton University Press, 1984), which is referred to throughout as *On War*. On the translations of *On War* to English, see C. Bassford, *Clausewitz in English: The Reception of Clausewitz in Britain and America 1815–1945* (New York: Oxford University Press, 1994).

2. In his introductory chapter to the *Summary of the Art of War*, Jomini makes a similar comment:

> *For a general officer, after having assisted in a dozen campaigns, ought to know that war is a great drama, in which a thousand physical or moral causes operate more or less powerfully and which cannot be reduced to mathematical calculations.*
>
> (Jomini, *The Summary of The Art of War*, pp. 17–18)

(Clausewitz makes comments to the same effect throughout *On War* – for example, see p. 134; p. 148; pp. 577–578; and pp. 585–586.) This quotation is from the introduction to the first and more obscure translation (1854) of Jomini's *Summary of The Art of War*. The omission of this introduction – 'Notice to the present theory of war, and of its utility' (pp. 9–21) – from the better known and currently the only available translation of 1862, explains why readers thought Jomini believed in the study of war as science. The preface to the earlier translation, however, explicitly states that Jomini *did not* consider war to be an exact science. And while a careful reading of the subsequent edition should have made his opinion on this matter clear enough, his frequent use of the word 'science' might have been the source of confusion. Contemporary readers understand 'science' to mean 'exact science', but Jomini was employing this word as it was often used in the nineteenth century to connote 'a systematic approach to a subject'. The first translation, from which the two preceding quotations are taken, is Baron de Jomini (trans. Major O. F. Winship and Lt. E. E. McLean), *Summary of the Art of War or a New Analytical Compend of the Principal Combinations of Strategy, of Grand Tactics and of Military Policy* (New York: G. P. Putnam, 1854). Since the second translation is the only one still in print, it was therefore used as the standard reference in this book: it is Baron de Jomini (trans. Captain G. H. Mendell and W. Craighill), *The Art of War* (Philadelphia: J. B. Lippincott, 1862), currently reprinted by the Greenwood Press of Westport, Connecticut. This second translation is referred to here as Jomini, *The Art of War;* the older version is referred to as Jomini, *The Summary of the Art of War.*

These two translations are alike except for an introductory chapter in the rare first translation that was omitted in the second. This introductory chapter includes an interesting critical survey of the literature that Jomini consulted and used as a point of departure for his own work. Most intriguing are his critical comments concerning Clausewitz's *On War.* The amount of negative attention that Jomini lavishes on Clausewitz's work betrays his professional jealousy and reluctant respect. These excerpts illustrate Jomini's ambivalent attitude towards Clausewitz:

> *One cannot deny to General Clausewitz great learning and a facile pen; but this pen, at times a little vagrant, is above all too pretentious for a didactic discussion, the simplicity and clearness of which ought to be its first merit. Besides that, the author shows himself by far too skeptical in point of military science; his first volume is but a declamation against all theory of war, whilst the two succeeding volumes, full of theoretic maxims, prove that the author believes in the efficacy of his own doctrines, if he does not believe those of others.*

> *As of myself, I own that I have been able to find in this learned labyrinth but a small number of luminous ideas and remarkable articles; and far from having shared the skepticism of the author, no work would have contributed more than his to make me feel the necessity and utility of good theories, if I had ever been able to call them in question; it is important simply to agree well as to the limits which ought to be assigned to them in order not to fall into a pedantry worse than ignorance . . .* [In a hit below the belt, Jomini can't resist adding in a note that] *An ignorant man endowed with a natural genius . . . can do great things; but the same man* [presumably like Clausewitz] *stuffed with false doctrines studied at school, and crammed with pedantic systems, will do nothing good unless he forget what he had learned. It is necessary above all to distinguish the difference which exists between a theory of principles and a theory of systems . . .*

> [Clausewitz] . . . *seemed thus to apply himself to sapping the basis of the science* [of war] . . .

> (Jomini, *Summary of the Art of War,* pp. 14–15)

Jomini's introductory chapter indicates (as I show throughout this book) that his theoretical assumptions on the nature of war are not as different from those of Clausewitz as he would have us believe. (See in particular pp. 15 and 17–18 of the introductory chapter.) He cannot resist one final bitter comment in which he accuses Clausewitz of plagiarizing the work of other authors, above all his own.

> *The works of Clausewitz have been incontestably useful, although it is often less by the ideas of the author, than by the contrary ideas to which he gives birth. They would have been more useful still, if a pretentious and pedantic style did not frequently render them unintelligible.* [Note that in a quotation cited earlier, Jomini actually said . . . *'One cannot deny to General Clausewitz great learning and a facile pen . . .'*] *But if, as a didactic author he has raised more doubts than*

he has discovered truths, as a critical historian, he has been an unscrupulous plagiarist, pillaging his predecessors, copying their reflections, and saying evil afterwards of their works, after having travestied them under other forms. Those who shall have read my campaign of 1799, published ten years before his, will not deny my assertion, for there is not one of my reflections which he has not repeated.

(Jomini, *Summary of the Art of War*, p. 21)

From a psychological standpoint, these quotations make fascinating reading. Jomini appears to be on the defensive against Clausewitz's repeated assertion that war cannot be studied as an exact science in the final analysis. Clausewitz has challenged the theoretical foundation of much of Jomini's work; and stung by the critical comments of someone for whom he had grudging respect, Jomini could not conceal his profound disappointment (see Clausewitz, *On War*, pp. 215 and 516, and the comments of Peter Paret in 'The Genius of *On War*', in Clausewitz, *On War*, pp. 10–12. In addition, see Peter Paret, *Clausewitz and the State* (Oxford: Clarendon Press, 1976), in particular pp. 71, 148, 152–153, 202, 339, 357).

The reader forms the impression that had Clausewitz referred to Jomini's work more favorably, Jomini would have readily acknowledged the importance of *On War*. A clear indication of this ambivalent love–hate attitude is found in his introductory chapter where he expresses his sorrow that Clausewitz could not read his latest work (*Summary of the Art of War*): '. . . *For my part, I regret that it* [i.e., Clausewitz's *On War*] *was written before the author was acquainted with my* Summary of the Art of War, *persuaded that he would have rendered to it some justice*' (p. 14). These words evince Jomini's perpetual desire to be recognized as an equal by Clausewitz.

3. In order to further enhance my argument that the logic of strategy and the study of war are universal rather than exclusively bound to a specific culture or time, I have decided to add references to Machiavelli's and Mao Tse-tung's studies and observations on war in this edition. Machiavelli is ideal for this purpose inasmuch as he wrote before the emergence of the modern national European state with which Clausewitz is identified. All quotations from Machiavelli (unless otherwise noted) are taken from Niccolò Machiavelli (trans. Allan Gilbert), *Machiavelli: The Chief Works and Others*, 3 vols (Durham, NC: Duke University Press, 1965), cited here as *Machiavelli: Works*.

4. Clausewitz repeatedly refers to the immense political changes in the nature of war that took place during his lifetime. See also Clausewitz, *On War*, pp. 217–218, 220, 246, 265, 266, 313, 479, 583, 590–594. For Clausewitz's view that all European armies of his time were on the same level of material and technological development (supporting his concept of the static nature of material and technological factors) see, for example, *On War*, pp. 186, 226.

5. See Michael I. Handel, *War, Strategy and Intelligence* (London: Cass, 1989), Chapter 2, 'Quantity vs. Quality: Numbers Do Count', pp. 95–130.

6. Reluctant, because there was (and still is) a vociferous minority of 'blood and guts' military officers and instructors which persists in the belief that *On War* is nothing

but 'deep kraut', or an anachronism that only confuses those attempting to apply it to the real world. Ever on the hunt for manual-style answers, they present every ambiguity or contradiction as incontrovertible evidence of the entire text's irrelevance. See Joel Achenbach, 'War and the Cult of Clausewitz: How a Long-Dead Prussian Shaped U.S. Thinking on the Persian Gulf', *Washington Post* (6 December 1990) – in particular the section entitled 'Theory vs. Reality'. If anything, this article shows that there was no cult of Clausewitz, that he has no influence, and that he is consistently misunderstood! See also Lloyd J. Matthews, 'On Clausewitz', *Army*, vol. 38 (Feb. 1988), pp. 20–24; also J. E. Shepard, '*On War*: Is Clausewitz Still Relevant?' *Parameters*, vol. 20, no. 3 (Sept. 1990), pp. 85–99. Here, two major problems are evident: the first is intolerance of ambiguity as expressed in the assumption that the existence of contradictions renders a book useless (see Appendix A on this); the second is an attempt to apply poor Carl's writings to every new problem from the war against drugs to nuclear war, and then to dismiss his work if he has nothing to say on these topics. This is akin to rejecting the Bible because it has nothing specific to say on morality and ethics in the stock exchange or because it does not discuss computers or women's liberation. Should one reject the insights of Thucydides or Machiavelli merely because they did not comment on the mass media or nuclear weapons?

Since the U.S. military was never defeated in a major battle during the Vietnam War, it is not surprising that a few officers blamed the political leadership (as well as the mass media and anti-war demonstrators) for losing the war instead of blaming the U.S. military's failure to understand how to fight and win, despite the unique constraints imposed by the U.S. political environment. (On the political environment in which the Vietnam War was fought and its influence on the formation of U.S. strategy on the highest level, see Leslie Gelb and Richard K. Betts, *The Irony of Vietnam: The System Worked* (Washington, DC: The Brookings Institution, 1979).)

Fortunately, this version of the 'stab in the back' myth did not fall on fertile ground in the U.S. military. Much is owed to the important and timely work of Colonel Harry G. Summers on the lessons of the Vietnam War. Through the (then) recently published edition of *On War* translated by Sir Michael Howard and Peter Paret, Colonel Summers rediscovered that a successful strategy depends not only upon the military, but also on the government and the people, and that it is possible to win a war militarily while losing it politically. And since any rationally conducted war is intended to achieve political goals, the proper consideration of its political dimensions is essential. This book had a very positive influence on the development of the U.S. military's thinking on strategy in the early 1980s and (albeit indirectly) on the formulation of the Weinberger Doctrine. See Harry G. Summers Jr., *On Strategy: A Critical Analysis of the War in Vietnam* (Novato, CA: Presidio Press, 1982). (*On Strategy* first appeared as a publication of the Strategic Studies Institute (SSI) at the U.S. Army War College, Carlisle Barracks, PA, 1981.)

The problem with the Prussian/German military leadership in the Franco-Prussian War of 1870, and even more so during the First World War and its aftermath, was that the German generals became involved in politics in order to shape their nation's military and political strategies. In contrast, the U.S. military in Vietnam experienced the opposite problem – that of considering any involvement in politics as unprofessional or even 'dirty'. This produced a Jominian type of separation between the political leadership and military strategy, which were viewed as independent fields of activity. In a doctrinal manual entitled *The Principles of Strategy for An Independent Corps or Army In a Theater of Operations*, published by the Command and General Staff School at Fort Leavenworth, Kansas, in 1936, one finds the following statement (p. 19):

> 26. POLITICS AND THE CONDUCT OF WAR. Politics and strategy are radically and fundamentally things apart. Strategy begins where politics ends. All that soldiers ask is that once the policy is settled, strategy and command shall be regarded as being in a sphere apart from politics.

This was also the position of General MacArthur, the most political of all U.S. generals, who claimed – after fighting to implement his own alternative policies during the Korean War – that in war, operational considerations must take precedence over political ones: 'I do unquestionably state that when men become locked in battle there should be no artifice under the names of politics, which should handicap your own men' (quoted in David Rees, *Korea: The Limited War* (London: Macmillan, 1964), p. 267). Truman's dismissal of General MacArthur in April 1951 brought this 'Jominian' position to an end insofar as the U.S. military was concerned. (The JCS consistently supported President Truman in his confrontation with General MacArthur.) From then on, if anything, the U.S. military became increasingly detached from the formulation of policy in times of war.

Thus, it appears that either too much or too little involvement in politics can create serious problems. No military organization on the highest levels can avoid becoming involved in, or trying to influence, political affairs as they pertain to the conduct of war. The only problem is to strike the proper balance in this endeavor. It is to Colonel Summers' credit that his measured analysis of the role of politics in shaping military strategy has made the military more aware of the crucial part it plays in the highest-level formulation of strategy. Moreover, the trust and reciprocal respect that existed between President Reagan and the military (and which continued under President Bush) undoubtedly led to the U.S. military's interest in and trust of politics.

7. 'On the Use of Military Power', Pentagon News Release, 28 October 1984.
8. See Richard K. Betts, *Soldiers, Statesmen and the Cold War Crises* (Cambridge, MA: Harvard University Press, 1977). On the cautious approach of the U.S. military in the crisis preceding the Gulf War, see Bob Woodward, *The Commanders* (New York: Simon and Schuster, 1991).
9. The American intelligence community's gross overestimation of Iraqi strength before the war can be partially explained by the following factors:
   (1) Like all other military organizations, the U.S. military, whether subconsciously or not, tends to rely on worst-case analysis in most circumstances. This justifies the concentration of more power and allows the achievement of

more decisive results when war breaks out. If the war does not proceed according to plan, a failure or lack of progress can then always be explained by pointing to the 'fact' that the enemy possessed overwhelming strength. On the other hand, a victory is all the more impressive when the enemy is thought to have presented a formidable threat. From a military point of view, therefore, it almost always pays to overestimate the opponent. In the Gulf War, over-estimating the Iraqis actually had a positive effect, for it caused the United States to concentrate more than enough troops, which then brought about a more decisive, less costly victory.

(2) U.S. intelligence, especially military intelligence, tends to concentrate more on the measurable, quantitative dimensions (e.g., hardware in general, numbers of tanks and aircraft, and air defenses) and less on the more elusive dimensions (e.g., morale, motivation, and level of training). On paper, the Iraqi military was impressive in sheer quantitative terms. In addition, U.S. human intelligence assets (HUMINT) in Iraq are said to have been weak, while satellite intelligence could not provide the type of intelligence required for estimating Iraq's non-material strength, nor could it provide direct infor-mation on the intentions of the Iraqi leadership.

(3) The United States underestimated its own strength partially because its state-of-the-art weaponry, designed for a hypothetical war against the U.S.S.R. in central Europe, had not been tested in action.

(4) The U.S. underestimated the force multiplier shock effect of launching the war, through which it achieved strategic and operational surprise, maintained the initiative, undermined the entire Iraqi command and control system, and threw the Iraqis off balance.

(5) Iraqi deception also made a major contribution to the overestimation of Iraqi strength. Towards the end of the Iran–Iraq war, American visitors briefed by the Iraqi military uncritically accepted the Iraqis' exaggerated view of their own strength. Having no access to the Iranian side of the story, some of these Americans unknowingly became the prime conduits in an Iraqi disinforma-tion campaign. See Stephen C. Pelletiere, Douglas V. Johnson and Leif R. Rosenberger, *Iraqi Power and U.S. Security in the Middle East* (Carlisle Barracks, PA: Strategic Studies Institute, 1990) and by the same authors, *Lessons Learned: The Iran–Iraq War* (Carlisle Barracks, PA: Strategic Studies Institute, January, 1991). The latter publications discuss the mobilization of a million-man Iraqi army and call Iraq 'a superpower in the Persian Gulf'. It is also noted that Iraq is superb (or 'formidable' as the author puts it elsewhere) on the defense and that the Iraqi army is well equipped and trained to carry out mobile operations. This publication warns that a possible war with Iraq that is not quickly decided would be expensive in terms of both lives and resources (p. 67). Relatively speaking, Iraq seemed to be a great military power compared with Iran, but this was not, however, a good indicator to use in assessing its potential performance *vis-à-vis* the United States.

10. The works of Sun Tzu and Clausewitz (and Jomini to a lesser extent) have also directly influenced, and are extensively quoted in, the U.S. Army's doctrinal

manual, *Operations FM 100–5* (Washington, DC: Headquarters, Department of the Army, May 1986) as well as in the Marine Corps manual, *Warfighting FMFM1* (Washington DC: Department of the Navy, Headquarters, United States Marine Corps, March 1989).

11. General Sir Archibald Wavell, *Speaking Generally* (London: Macmillan, 1946), p. 79.

CHAPTER 2: COMPARING SUN TZU AND CLAUSEWITZ

1. The best introduction to this subject is still Hans J. Morgenthau, *Politics Among Nations* (5th edition, New York: Alfred A. Knopf, 1973).
2. Quoted from B. H. Liddell Hart's foreword to Sun Tzu, *The Art of War*, pp. v–vi.
3. See John K. Fairbank, 'Introduction: Varieties of the Chinese Military Experience', in John K. Fairbank and Frank A. Kierman Jr. (eds.), *Chinese Ways in Warfare* (Cambridge, MA: Harvard University Press, 1974), p. 25.
4. This is closer to Carl von Clausewitz (ed. and trans. H. W. Gatzke), *Principles of War* (Harrisburg, PA: Military Service Publishing Company, 1943), which Clause-witz wrote for the Prussian Crown Prince Frederick William while serving as his instructor. The text of *Principles of War* can also be found in the third volume of Colonel Graham's 1873 translation of *On War* – see Carl von Clausewitz (trans. Colonel T. T. Graham) (London: Kegan, Paul, Trench, Trubner, 1940), vol. 3, pp. 178–229.
5. On the role of theory in Clausewitz's work, see also Peter Paret, *Clausewitz and the State* (Oxford: Oxford University Press, 1976), in particular pp. 147–168; and pp. 198–199.
6.

> One might wonder whether there is any truth at all in our concept of the absolute character of war were it not for the fact that with our own eyes we have seen warfare achieve this state of absolute perfection . . . Bonaparte brought it swiftly and ruthlessly to that point. War, in his hands, was waged without respite until the enemy succumbed, and the counterblows were struck with almost equal energy. Surely it is both natural and inescapable that this phenomenon should cause us to turn again to the pure concept of war with all its rigorous implications.
>
> (Clausewitz, *On War*, p. 580)

But this argument is followed by a qualifying statement:

> War is dependent on the interplay of possibilities and probabilities, of good and bad luck, conditions in which strictly logical reasoning often plays no part at all and is always apt to be a most unsuitable and awkward intellectual tool. It follows too that war can be a matter of degree.
>
> Theory must concede all this; but it has the duty to give priority to the absolute form of war and to make that form a general point of reference,

so that he who wants to learn from theory becomes accustomed to keeping that point in view constantly, to measuring all his hopes and fears by it, and to approximating it when he can or when he must.

(Clausewitz, *On War*, p. 581; pp. 590 ff.)

7. See Michael I. Handel, (ed.), *Clausewitz and Modern Strategy* (London: Cass, 1986), Introduction, pp. 4–10.
8. Sun Tzu (trans. S. B. Griffith), *The Art of War*, Foreword, p. vi.
9. In General Gunther von Blumentritt, *A Collection of the Military Essays of Gunther Blumentritt*, MS C-096, Historical Division, European Command, Foreign Military Studies Branch, U.S. Army Europe (mimeographed, in German, no date), '*Was kann uns Clausewitz noch heute bedeuten?*', pp. 453–467.
10. This was the view of the elder Moltke, see Hajo Holborn, 'The Prusso-German School: Moltke and the Rise of the General Staff', Chapter 10 in Peter Paret (ed.), *Makers of Modern Strategy* (Princeton, NJ: Princeton University Press, 1986), p. 289.
11. Clausewitz's observations on the theory of war very closely resemble those made a century later by A. E. Housman on the subject of textual analysis:

> Textual criticism is not a branch of mathematics, nor indeed an exact science at all. It deals with a matter not rigid and constant, like lines and numbers, but fluid and variable . . . It is therefore not susceptible of hard-and-fast rules. It would be much easier if it were; and that is why people try to pretend that it is, or at least behave as if they thought so. Of course you can have hard-and-fast rules if you like, but then you will have false rules, and they will lead you wrong; because their simplicity will render them inapplicable to problems which are not simple . . . A textual critic [a strategist or military leader] engaged upon his business is not at all like Newton investigating the motions of the planets; he is much more like a dog hunting for fleas. If a dog hunts for fleas on mathematical principles, basing his researches on statistics of area and population, he would never catch a flea except by accident. They require to be treated as individuals; and every problem which presents itself to the textual critic [or military leader] must be regarded as possibly unique (A. E. Housman, 'The Application of Thought to Textual Criticism', in J. Carter (ed.), *A. E. Housman: Selected Prose* (Cambridge: Cambridge University Press, 1961), p. 132.)

I would like to thank Sir David Hunt for drawing my attention to Housman's essay and its similarity to Clausewitz's discussion of the theory of war.

12. For brief biographical sketches of the various Chinese commentators on Sun Tzu's work, see Appendix 4 in Samuel Griffith's translation of *The Art of War*, pp. 184–186. The advice of the better-known commentators on Sun Tzu's original text of the *Art of War* will be treated here as *an organic integral part of the text.*
13. Jomini, *The Art of War*, pp. 325, 327 and 323. See also Baron de Jomini, *Summary of the Art of War or a New Analytical Compend of the Principal Combinations of Strategy, of Grand Tactics and of Military Policy.*
For additional literature on Jomini, see:

Alger, John, *Antoine-Henri Jomini: A Bibliographical Survey*. New York: West Point, 1975, pp. 77–92.

Brinton, Crane, Craig, Gordon A. and Gilbert, Felix. 'Jomini'. In E. M. Earle, ed. *Makers of Modern Strategy*. New York: Atheneum, 1966.

von Caemmerer, Lt.-General. *The Development of Stragetical Science during the 19th Century*. London: Hugh Rees, 1905, pp. 11–22.

Gat, Azar. *The Development of Military Thought: The Nineteenth Century*. Oxford: Oxford University Press, 1992.

Gat, Azar. *The Origins of Military Thought: From the Enlightenment to Clausewitz*. Oxford: Oxford University Press, 1989, pp. 106–135.

Howard, Michael. 'Jomini and the Classical Tradition in Military Thought'. In *The Theory and Practice of War*, edited by Michael Howard, pp. 3–21. London: Cassell, 1965.

Shy, John. 'Jomini'. In Peter Paret, ed. *Makers of Modern Strategy: From Machiavelli to the Nuclear Age*, pp. 143–186; and pp. 886–887. Princeton, NJ: Princeton University Press, 1986.

Strachan, Hew. *European Armies and the Conduct of War*. London: George Allen & Unwin, 1983, pp. 60–75.

14. See Baron A.-H. de Jomini (trans. Colonel S. B. Holabird), *Treatise on Grand Military Operations: or a Critical and Military History of the Wars of Frederick The Great, As Contrasted With the Modern System. Together with a Few of the Most Important Principles of the Art of War*, 2 (New York: Van Nostrand, 1865), vol. II, p. 446. To be quoted below as Jomini, *Grand Military Operations*.

15. Jomini, *Summary of the Art of War*, p. 18. See also note 2 above.

CHAPTER 3: THE DEFINITION OF WAR:
A QUESTION OF THE LEVEL OF ANALYSIS

1. This is Clausewitz's famous definition of war, which makes it clear that war, by its very nature, involves the use of violence or force. The original German word '*Gewalt*', loosely translated here as 'force', actually has a much stronger connotation of 'violence' or 'violent force'. Without the use of violence or force, we cannot speak of war. Furthermore, this definition firmly establishes that war is a means to an end – it serves the instrumental purpose of compelling the enemy to do something he would not otherwise do. Such 'compellence' can be either *positive* or *negative*. It is positive when force is used to make the enemy concede something against his will; and negative when force is used to *prevent* him from forcing *us* to make concessions.

Ironically, the only flaw in this definition is that it does not mention the *reciprocal nature of war* (i.e., that war is a clash of at least two belligerents trying to impose their wills on each other). One side's attempt to impose his will on his adversary without a similar response on the adversary's part cannot be considered war. Clausewitz notes this in his seemingly paradoxical, provocative statement that war begins only when the defender (not the attacker) decides to defend himself actively (Clausewitz, *On War*, p. 377) (see also pp. 146–147 above). I would therefore modify Clausewitz's definition to read: 'War is thus an act of force to compel our enemy to do our will, while he tries to do the same to us.'

2. Although Clausewitz confines his discussion to the art of war itself in *On War*, his other works evince his interest in subjects such as the diplomacy of building and maintaining alliances, and in the diplomatic preparations preceding a war. See for example: 'From Observations on Prussia in Her Great Catastrophe (1823–1825)', in Peter Paret and Daniel Moran (eds.), *Carl von Clausewitz: Historical and Political Writings* (Princeton: Princeton University Press, 1992), pp. 30–85. An earlier, little known translation into English is Colonel Conrad H. Lanza's *Notes on Prussia During the Grand Catastrophe of 1806 by Clausewitz*, The General Staff School, *The Jena Campaign Source Book* (Fort Leavenworth, KS: General Service Schools Press, 1922).

3. In addition to remembering that Clausewitz generally uses the word 'strategy' to describe what we would refer to today as the operational level of war, readers of *On War* should note that Clausewitz's analysis often makes a transition from the strategic to the operational or even tactical levels of war without warning. For example, he begins Book 1, Chapter 6 on 'Intelligence in War' with a definition of intelligence on the strategic level but follows it immediately with a discussion of intelligence on the lower tactical level. Yet the nature and reliability of intelligence is completely different on these two levels. In his introductory chapter to Book 8 on War Plans, Clausewitz tells us that he will be considering the problem of war as a whole, as '**pure strategy**', but then he turns directly to a discussion of the nature of great generalship on the tactical level. This is a bit perplexing, since planning for war and tactical military leadership are plainly two distinct issues requiring particular if not contradictory talents.

4. See also Jomini, *Grand Military Operations*, pp. 277 and 460. A contemporary definition of strategy is provided by the U.S. Joint Chiefs of Staff (JCS):

> Strategy is the art and science of developing and using political, economic, psychological, and military forces as necessary during peace and war, to afford the maximum support to policies, in order to increase the probabilities and favorable consequences of victory and lessen the chances of defeat.

Somewhat obscured by its verbosity, the meaning of this definition would benefit from the application of Occam's razor – the principle that the fewest possible assumptions should be used in explaining something. After being shaved with this philosophic rule, the shortened version could read: 'strategy is the development and use of all resources in peace and war in support of national policies to secure victory'. For the JCS, strategy is therefore an activity that takes place in peace time as much as during war – an activity that includes building up forces, the use of threats for deterrence, and the use of diplomatic and economic pressure in conjunction with military force. In contrast, Clausewitz's and Jomini's conceptions of strategy do not include coercive diplomacy or peacetime strategy but are instead related directly and exclusively to the operational conduct of war. (*Department of Defense Dictionary of Military and Associated Terms*, Dec. 1989 (Joint Pub. 1–02, Washington, DC) p. 350.)

5. Jomini emphasized the importance of making the proper preparations for war, and saw logistics as an integral part of the study of war and the art of command. Jomini defined logistics (a term he invented) as '*the art of moving armies . . . which brings the troops to the point of engagement . . . the means and arrangements which work out the plans of strategy and tactics*' (see Jomini, *The Art of War*, p. 69; see also pp. 43–51, and 252–268). For a historical perspective on 'logistics' in war, see Martin van Creveld, *Supplying War* (Cambridge: Cambridge University Press, 1977).

CHAPTER 4: CLAUSEWITZ AND MAO TSE-TUNG ON THEORY AND PRACTICE IN WAR

1. German distinguishes between two types of knowledge: *Wissen*, which refers to theoretical knowledge and understanding, and *Können*, which refers to practical widsom or applied knowledge.
2. See Robert Jervis, *The Logic of Images in International Relations* (Princeton, NJ: Princeton University Press, 1970); Robert Jervis, *Perception and Misperception in International Politics* (Princeton, NJ: Princeton University Press, 1976); Charles Perrow, *Normal Accidents: Living with High-Risk Technologies* (New York: Basic Books, 1984).
3. See also Peter Paret, *Clausewitz and the State* (Oxford: Clarendon, 1976), pp. 147–168.

CHAPTER 5: 'ATTACKING THE ENEMY'S PLANS' AND THE CONCEPT OF 'THE CENTER OF GRAVITY': EASTERN PSYCHOLOGY AND WESTERN MECHANICS

1. Many scholars studying Clausewitz's *On War* have traced his methodology or 'methodological style' to Kant's philosophy as taught by J. G. C. Kiesewetter in lectures that Clausewitz attended in Berlin in 1803 (see Peter Paret, *Clausewitz and the State*, pp. 160–161; W. B. Gallie, *Philosophers of Peace and War*, pp. 52–53), or the philosophers of the Enlightenment and of German idealism in general (Paret, *Clausewitz and the State*, p. 84). Yet strangely enough, no one has directly tied Clausewitz's 'methodological style' to that of Newton's scientific method. (On Newton's style, see I. Bernard Cohen, *The Newtonian Revolution* (Cambridge: Cambridge University Press, 1980)). Although Clausewitz's 'methodological style' contains elements of more than one source, the strongest influence, as evidenced by the text of *On War*, can be attributed to Newton.

   Newton made extensive use of the ideal-type method (well known to German philosophers). This consisted of 'a purely mathematical construct or imagined system – not merely a case of nature simplified but a wholly invented system of the sort that does not exist in the real world at all . . . In phase two, Newton compares his mental construct with the real world' (Cohen, *The*

Newtonian Revolution, p. 166; see also I. B. Cohen, *Revolution in Science* (Cambridge, MA: Harvard University Press, 1985), pp. 161–175). This is precisely the method used by Clausewitz.

> In order to lend clarity, distinction, and emphasis to our ideas, only perfect contrasts, the extremes of the spectrum, have been included in our observations. As an actual occurrence, war generally falls somewhere in between, and is influenced by these extremes only to the extent to which it approaches them.
>
> (Clausewitz, *On War*, p. 517)

While Clausewitz makes no mention of Kant, Kiesewetter, or any other German philosopher of his time in *On War*, he refers to Newton more than several times. (among others, see pp. 112, 146, 586). Even more importantly, Clausewitz directly borrows many of Newton's concepts from the world of physics and applies them to the study of war, as illustrated by the following excerpts:

Time, Motion and Energy

> Every physical force requires time to become effective. A force that, if gently and gradually applied would suffice to arrest a body in motion, will be overcome by it if there is not enough time for it to operate. The laws of physics provide a pertinent image of many features of our psychology . . .
>
> (Clausewitz, *On War*, p. 572)

Clausewitz uses a similar creative example from the theory of physics to show how other military theorists arrive at poor theoretical insights on military operations and make incorrect use of the theory of physics:

> When the strength and capability of armed forces are being calculated, *time* is apt to be treated as a factor in total strength on the analogy of dynamics. It is assumed in consequence that half the effort or half the total forces could achieve as much in two years as the whole could do in one. This assumption, which rests, sometimes explicitly, sometimes implicitly, at the basis of military planning, is entirely wrong. Like everything else in life, a military operation takes time. No one, obviously, can march from Vilna to Moscow in a week; but here there is no trace of that reciprocal relationship between time and energy that we would find in dynamics.
>
> (Clausewitz, *On War*, p. 597)

The Concept of the Center of Gravity

> A center of gravity is always found where the mass is concentrated most densely . . .
>
> (Clausewitz, *On War*, p. 485)

Clausewitz's definition of a major battle sounds as though it were taken from Newtonian physics in more than one way:

A major battle in a theater of operations is a collision between two centers of gravity.

(Clausewitz, *On War*, p. 489)

The same can be said for his definition of a center of gravity:

. . . One must keep the dominant characteristics of both belligerents in mind. Out of these characteristics a certain center of gravity develops, the hub of all power and movement, on which everything depends. That is the point against which all our energies should be directed.

(Clausewitz, *On War*, pp. 595–596)

Conservation of Energy

Every reduction in the strength on one side can be considered an increase on the other.

(Clausewitz, *On War*, p. 566)

Machines, Inertia and Friction

. . . Once conditions become difficult, as they must when much is at stake, things no longer run like a well-oiled machine. The machine itself begins to resist, and the commander needs tremendous willpower to overcome this resistance. The machine's resistance need not consist of disobedience and argument . . . As each man's strength gives out, as he no longer responds to his will, the inertia of the whole generally comes to rest on the commander's will alone.

(Clausewitz, *On War*, p. 104; see also p. 122 on the role of general friction in war)

Clausewitz's application of the concept of friction to war is perhaps the concept most obviously borrowed from Newtonian physics. As in Newton's theory, friction is one of the principal factors explaining the difference between war in theory and war in practice. As Clausewitz tells us, friction 'is the only concept that more or less corresponds to the factors that distinguish real war from war on paper' (Clausewitz, *On War*, p. 119). But unlike the world of physical science, 'the tremendous friction [in war] . . . cannot, as in mechanics, be reduced to a few points, is everywhere in contact with chance, and brings about effects that cannot be measured, just because they are largely due to chance' (Clausewitz, *On War*, p. 120).

Friction in war (and in human affairs in general) is far more difficult to deal with because it cannot be defined or measured, or dealt with in a systematic way. Unlike the world of physics in which situations and experiments can be repeated and studied under controlled conditions, '. . . every war is rich in unique episodes' (Clausewitz, *On War*, p. 120). This of course limits the observer's capacity to formulate reliable general laws or to make accurate predictions.

This small sample of Clausewitz's use of concepts from Newtonian physics demonstrates the heuristic value that Newton's theoretical world and the scientific and mathematical theories of his time had on the development of Clausewitz's theory of war. Clausewitz's use of concepts such as friction, center of gravity, momentum and inertia, and conservation of energy as well as his use of examples drawn from optics, statistical analysis (probability), and so on, clearly link him to the world of scientific methods and the methodologies of the natural sciences.

Other concepts such as the collision of opposing bodies in motion (**'War is the impact of opposing forces'**, Clausewitz, *On War*, p. 205), the use of power, the culminating point of victory, the principle of continuity, and others are also either directly or indirectly related to Newtonian physics. It is interesting to note that Clausewitz used metaphors from the inanimate world of physics not only to develop his own original concepts, but no less importantly, to show how collision, energy and movement in the inanimate world of physics *differ* from the nature of collision, action, interaction, and counter-action in the human environment. To Clausewitz's credit, while he borrowed extensively from Newtonian mechanics, he did not do so mechanically; he consistently resisted any temptation to reduce war to scientific formulas or to claim that war could be studied as an exact science. He never tired of making it clear that war **'is not the action of a living force upon a lifeless mass . . . but always the collision of two living forces'** (Clausewitz, *On War*, p. 77). **'War is not an exercise of the will directed at inanimate matter, as is the case with the mechanical arts . . . In war, the will is directed at an animate object that reacts . . . It is clear that continued striving after laws analogous to those appropriate to the realm of inanimate matter was bound to lead to one mistake after another. Yet it was precisely the mechanical arts that the art of war was supposed to imitate'** (Clausewitz, *On War*, p. 149).

He attacks those theorists of war who **'usually exclude all moral qualities from strategic theory, and only examine material factors. They reduce everything to a few mathematical formulas of equilibrium and superiority, or time and space, limited by a few angles and lines. If that were really all, it would hardly provide a scientific problem for a school boy'** (Clausewitz, *On War*, p. 178; see also p. 215). The temptation to reduce war to a few simple 'scientific' or 'mechanical' formulas in now even greater in the age of computers and high-tech war. Clausewitz's warning that war is a collision between living forces that can learn, adapt, and develop various material and non-material counter-moves is as valid today as it was in his time. His discussion of the differences between the inanimate world of science and the animate world of war and human interaction is a strong reminder that any theory of war has its limitations: it cannot therefore be expected to provide a full or comprehensive answer to the dynamic nature of interaction and reciprocal action in war.

It has occasionally been argued that the Western attitude to war represents a 'mechanistic' approach; in other words, a view of war as a simple collision between concentrated masses.

The Napoleonic model of conflict – momentum equals mass times velocity, victory equals maximal momentum concentrated at the decisive point – may be

385

taken as representative of an entire school of Western conflict theory, from the reduction of war by Vegetius to the organization of the legion, through the Newtonian revolution in mechanics . . .

(Howard L. Boorman and Scott A. Boorman,
'Strategy and National Psychology in China', p. 152)

This critical view of the Western approach to war is compared with the more sophisticated Chinese psychological approach to war. Whatever the merits of this view, it stands in clear contrast to Clausewitz's theory of war. Clausewitz's reliance on the Newtonian theory of physics does not in any way prevent him from giving equal emphasis to the role of psychological, moral, and creative factors in his theory of war. While Clausewitz used the language and methods of the exact sciences in the development of his theory of war, he always used them as a point of departure, not as a dogma or model to be emulated.

2. Another interesting discussion of the concept of the center of gravity on the operational level is found in Friedrich von Bernhardi, *On War of To-Day*, 2 vols. (London: Hugh Rees, 1912), vol. 2, Chapter 5: 'Space and the decisive direction', pp. 243–284. This book, which includes numerous references to Clausewitz's *On War*, is an excellent example of the turn-of-the-century interpretation and criticism of Clausewitz in the German military. On this subject see also A. J. Echevarria, 'Neo-Clausewitzianism: Freytag-Loringhoven and the Militarization of Clausewitz in German Military Literature Before the First World War' (unpublished Ph.D. dissertation, Princeton, 1994).

3. A closer examination of Sun Tzu's statement that 'what is of supreme importance in war is to attack the enemy's strategy' will help to clarify his meaning. A better understanding of this phrase can be gained by (a) comparing Griffith's translation with a number of others; and (b) viewing the statement and the phrase following it in the context of Sun Tzu's discussion.

GILES: *Thus, the highest form of generalship is to baulk the enemy's plans; the next best is to prevent the junction of the enemy's forces . . .* (pp. 17–18).

Interestingly, all of the translators except Giles agree that the second of Sun Tzu's recommendations is to use diplomatic means to undermine the enemy's alliances. In contrast, Giles renders the meaning *operational* (i.e., the enemy should be prevented from concentrating his forces or combining them with those of his allies).

CLEARY: *Therefore the superior militarist strikes while schemes are being laid, the next best thing is to attack alliances* (pp. 68–69).

In another book, Cleary translates the same sentence differently: '*The superior military artist strikes while schemes are being laid*' (Cleary, ed. and trans., *Mastering the Art of War: Zhuge Liang's and Liu Ji's Commentaries on the Classic by Sun Tzu* (Boston: Shambhala, 1989), p. 76.

HUANG: *So, the best military strategy is to crush their plans; following this is to crush their diplomatic relations* (p. 49).

CHEN: *The highest form of military leadership is to overcome the enemy by strategy. The next best way is to absorb the enemy through an alliance* (p. 17).

AMES: *Therefore, the best military policy is to attack strategies; the next best to attack alliances* (p. 111).

SAWYER: *Thus the highest realization of warfare is to attack the enemy's plans; next best is to attack their alliances* (p. 177).

TANG: *Therefore, the first order of strategy is to win by policy, the next is by use of diplomacy* (p. 192).

CHENG: *The highest form of generalship is to conquer the enemy by strategy. The next highest form of generalship is to conquer the enemy by alliance* (p. 5).

TAI: *Thus the best commandership is to frustrate the enemy's plans and schemes (with powerful armed forces to back you up); the next is to sever his diplomatic relations with his allies* (p. 10).

In the various versions, some of the translators prefer the word 'plans' to the word 'strategy'. 'Plans' seems to be more specific and connotes more precise knowledge or better intelligence regarding the enemy's intentions; and while the Griffith translation suggests that this is the best course of action *in war* and Sawyer terms it *the highest realization of warfare*, most of the others indicate that this advice should be implemented either *before* the outbreak of war or as the opening move. Finally, all of these versions use the expression *military* strategy or *military* leaders although it seems that the policy or strategy recommended by Sun Tzu favors the use of diplomacy and other non-violent approaches – not just military action. In other words, the strategy recommended as the first and best course of action by Sun Tzu does not involve the use of force; in the West, this would not be considered the highest form of generalship or of military skills, but instead as an act of statesmanship or political acumen. Thus, Tang Zi Chang's translation states that the first order of strategy is winning by *policy*. (See Chart 5, opposite p. 389.) (See also Figure 5.1.)

The simplest interpretation may indeed be that Sun Tzu is referring to a purely military activity. If reliable information on the enemy's intention to launch a war can be obtained, the wisest military move would be to preempt by attacking the enemy first, while he is preoccupied with his own preparations. This is the interpretation of Ho Shih as quoted by Giles: *'When the enemy has made a plan of attack against us, we must anticipate him by delivering our own attack first'* (Giles translation, p. 18).

In this case, the side that attacks the enemy's strategy or plans is seizing the initiative and in fact making the first move in the war. A variation on this is an *interceptive attack* in which the enemy's opening moves are foiled by a carefully prepared countermove.

On a more general level, this type of strategy need not be purely reactive – that

FIGURE 5.1
A POSSIBLE ORGANIZING CONCEPT FOR SUN TZU'S THEORY OF WAR

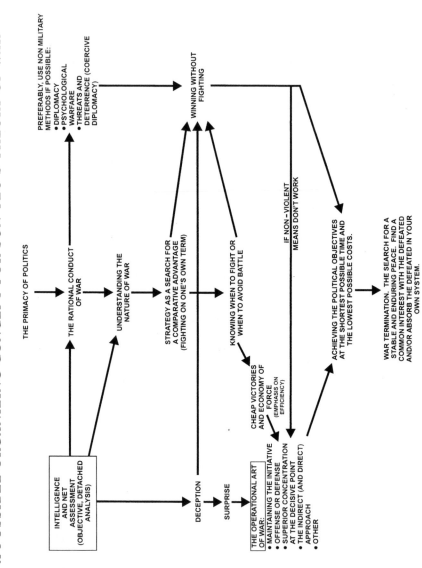

INTELLIGENCE AND NET ASSESSMENT (OBJECTIVE, DETACHED ANALYSIS)

THE PRIMACY OF POLITICS

THE RATIONAL CONDUCT OF WAR

PREFERABLY, USE NON MILITARY METHODS IF POSSIBLE:
• DIPLOMACY
• PSYCHOLOGICAL WARFARE
• THREATS AND DETERRENCE (COERCIVE DIPLOMACY)

UNDERSTANDING THE NATURE OF WAR

STRATEGY AS A SEARCH FOR A COMPARATIVE ADVANTAGE (FIGHTING ON ONE'S OWN TERM)

WINNING WITHOUT FIGHTING

KNOWING WHEN TO FIGHT OR WHEN TO AVOID BATTLE

CHEAP VICTORIES AND ECONOMY OF FORCE (EMPHASIS ON EFFICIENCY)

IF NON-VIOLENT MEANS DON'T WORK

DECEPTION

SURPRISE

THE OPERATIONAL ART OF WAR:
• MAINTAINING THE INITIATIVE
• OFFENSE OR DEFENSE
• SUPERIOR CONCENTRATION AT THE DECISIVE POINT
• THE INDIRECT (AND DIRECT) APPROACH
• OTHER

ACHIEVING THE POLITICAL OBJECTIVES AT THE SHORTEST POSSIBLE TIME AND THE LOWEST POSSIBLE COSTS.

WAR TERMINATION. THE SEARCH FOR A STABLE AND ENDURING PEACE. FIND A COMMON INTEREST WITH THE DEFEATED AND/OR ABSORB THE DEFEATED IN YOUR OWN SYSTEM.

is, trying to thwart or preempt the enemy's intended actions. It can also be an *initiated strategy* in a conflict over power, resources, or hegemony in which the side heeding Sun Tzu's advice takes the offensive after considering the enemy's intentions. (This concept is most directly expressed in Cleary's translation and Giles's commentary.)

Another more common interpretation would imply a policy of attacking the enemy's strategy, plans, or intentions by *non-military means*. This would occur in peacetime before the enemy could achieve a military advantage.

In Chapter 3 on 'Planning an Offensive', Sun Tzu's argument begins with a general statement extolling the ability to win *without* fighting or bloodshed.

> *Generally in war the best policy is to take a state intact; . . . to capture the enemy's army is better than to destroy it. . . . To subdue the enemy without fighting is the acme of skill.*

> (*The Art of War*, p. 77)

After this opening statement, Sun Tzu presents a *progression* or *sequence*, a continuum of action from peace to war, from non-violent means to the use of force and from the most cost-effective to the least cost-effective military methods of attaining one's objectives. The progression is as follows:

Pre-war peaceful moves	1. Thus, what is of supreme importance is to attack the enemy's strategy (plans). 2. Next best is to disrupt his alliances.
War	3. The next best is to attack his army. 4. The worst policy is to attack cities.

Viewed in this way, the recommendation to attack the enemy's strategy or plans is the first of four possible strategies which explores how to win at the lowest possible cost. This strategy could – but ideally should not – lead to war (see Chart 5).

Influencing the enemy's intentions before resorting to military means can be achieved, for example, through projection of an actual or deceptive superior military posture (i.e., deterrence). In this way, the opponent should be convinced that he is not strong enough to compel us to do his will or to begin a war. On the defensive/reactive side, we can convince him to abandon his intentions; on the offensive level, we can compel him to yield to our demands without having to resort to the use of force. In this and the next phase we can use diplomacy to disrupt the enemy's alliances and isolate him; conversely, we can also build a more powerful alliance of our own (as indicated by Cheng Lin's translation).

In the context of Sun Tzu's four-stage progressive argument, 'attacking the enemy's strategy or plans' refers to a *pre-war* phase in which non-violent methods of achieving the state's goals are given precedence.

This interpretation once again illustrates the broader context and higher level of analysis that Sun Tzu considers in achieving the goals of the state. It also provides a clear example of the blending of diplomatic (and other) means with military methods. While Clausewitz wrote a book exclusively on war, Sun Tzu wrote one on the art of diplomacy or statecraft, *and* war. If Clausewitz is concerned only with actual war between states, Sun Tzu explores war *and* other types of conflict between states, in which the line between war and peace is not as evident. Clausewitz and other Western strategists would not consider such activities part of war or part of the military leader's tasks. (Clausewitz does, however, mention that the military commander ought to be familiar with such non-military methods and the overall situation in order to obtain a sense of how his actions fit into the overall policy.) Winning without bloodshed, Sun Tzu's concept of the highest attainment of strategic success, is not considered part of war as such in the West – this is *an artificial distinction for which Western states have paid a considerable price when confronting Asian states such as North Korea or North Vietnam.* The translation of Sun Tzu's recommendation to attack the enemy's strategy as the best *military* strategy (Huang) or highest form of *military* leadership (Cheng) or the highest form of *generalship* (Giles) is misleading inasmuch as Sun Tzu's advice transcends what is considered military activity in the West. In the West, such pre-war policies and the use of non-military means would be considered grand strategy or statesmanship.

The translations considered here also fail to agree on the best title for Chapter or Section 3 of *The Art of War* from which the quotation is taken. The most common translation associates this section with the attack or offense. Griffith's title is 'Offensive Strategy'; Huang's is 'Planning an Offense'; Ames' is 'Planning the Attack'; and Sawyer's 'Planning Offensives'. The last three also agree that this section deals with planning. The title of Giles and Tai Mien-leng is 'Attack by Stratagem' which emphasizes the deceptive element of the attack (or the preemptive attack). Cleary's title, 'Planning a Siege' emphasizes only one aspect of Sun Tzu's discussion, while Cheng's title, 'Strategy' appears to be too broad. The title that makes the most sense in light of the preceding discussion is, however, that of Tang Zi-Chang – namely, 'Political Offensive – Winning by Policy'.

Just as the different commentators on *The Art of War* cannot agree on the precise meaning of some of Sun Tzu's most important ideas, there is no consensus on some of Clausewitz's key concepts, particularly the content of Book 1, Chapter 1, and Book 8. (See, for example, Robert Hepp, 'Der Harmlose Clausewitz', *Zeitschrift für Politik* 3 (September and December, 1978), pp. 303–318, 390–429, which is a critique of Raymond Aron's interpretation of *On War* in *Penser La Guerre*.) In this sense, there is not and cannot be a final agreement on some of the most important issues in both books. Ultimately, this must be left to the reader.

4. For Machiavelli, as much as for Clausewitz, the enemy's army (i.e., military strength) is the center of gravity. As the most fundamental factor in the well-being of the state, military strength is the guarantor of the ruler's ability to stay in power

and maintain control over his state. Therefore, a prince who loses his army clearly cannot survive.

> Men, steel, money, and bread are the sinews of war; but of these four, the most necessary are the first two, because men and steel find money and bread, but bread and money do not find men and steel.
>
> (Machiavelli, *The Art of War*, pp. 719–720)

> I conclude, thus, that without its own arms, no principality is secure, indeed it is wholly obliged to fortune, since it does not have virtue to defend itself in adversity. And it has always been the opinion and judgment of wise men 'that nothing is so infirm and unstable as fame or power not sustained by one's own force.'
>
> (Machiavelli, *The Prince* (Harvey C. Mansfield trans.),
> Chicago, IL: University of Chicago Press, 2nd edn, p. 57)

> It is necessary for a prince to have good foundations for himself: otherwise he must of necessity be ruined. The principal foundations that all states have, new ones as well as old or mixed, are good laws and good arms. And because there cannot be good laws where there are not good arms, and where there are good arms there must be good laws, I shall leave out the reasoning on laws and shall speak of arms.
>
> (Machiavelli, *The Prince*, Mansfield trans., p. 48)

It is not surprising, therefore, to find that Machiavelli would agree with Sun Tzu's admonition to those who neglect the study of war: *'War is of vital importance to the state; the province of life or death; the road to survival and ruin. It is mandatory that it be thoroughly studied'* (Sun Tzu, *The Art of War*, p. 63). Machiavelli cautions the reader thus:

> A prince should have no other object, nor any other thought, nor take anything else as his art but the art of war and its orders and discipline; for that is the only art which is of concern to one who commands . . . One sees that when princes have thought more of amenities than of arms, they have lost their states. And the first cause that makes you lose it is the neglect of this art; and the cause that enables you to acquire it is to be a professional in this art . . . Therefore, he [the prince] should never lift his thoughts from the exercise of war, and in peace he should exercise it more than in war.
>
> (Machiavelli, *The Prince*, Mansfield trans., pp. 58–59)

5. In *On War of To-Day*, Bernhardi stresses that after the enemy's armed forces, the most important 'center of gravity' is the enemy's capital:

> It may therefore indeed be imperative to select the hostile capital as the object of the attack. If it is threatened, it may be anticipated that the hostile main force must stand at bay to protect the capital. And if we succeed in pushing the hostile forces away from the capital, or more than that, in occupying that place itself, the whole administration of the hostile State is upset, and thus also the army most seriously damaged.

Nevertheless, as he observes, occupation of the enemy's capital does not always lead to the desired results:

> Military history always shows anew, by its examples, the importance of the capital for the conduct of war. The fact that Hannibal was unable to capture Rome deprived him of the palm of ultimate victory; and Napoleon chose nearly always the hostile capital as the main point of his strategic attack, which had for its object crushing the hostile State by its capture. His career, more than anything else, makes it also plain how this calculation may sometimes deceive. Neither in Spain nor in Russia did the conquest of the capital decide the war. It is therefore, in our time, especially imperative not to overrate the importance of the capital. The more the war partakes of a national character, and the more the population passionately participates in it, the more will the capital lose its decisive importance.

But like so many other strategists, Bernhardi cannot quite make up his mind. He continues:

> But it will always be of the highest importance to capture it, or for the defender to maintain it. Especially in France is the importance of the capital as the centre of military power still obvious.
>
> (Bernhardi, vol. 2, *On War of To-Day*, p. 269)

6. Machiavelli makes the same comment: 'Victory in the field is more profitable than siege' (*Discourses*, p. 416). 'Therefore they [the Romans] believed it better and more profitable to subjugate cities by any other methods than by blockading them' (*Discourses*, p. 413).

CHAPTER 6: THE PRIMACY OF POLITICS AND THE MILITARY COMMANDER

1. In the tradition of *raison d'état*, Machiavelli makes an almost identical statement in a chapter entitled 'A Prince's Duty about Military Affairs':

> ... A wise prince, then, has no other object and no other interest and takes as his profession nothing else than war and its laws and discipline; that is the only profession fitting one who commands ... The chief cause that makes you lose your princedom is neglect of this profession, and the cause that makes you gain it is expertness in this profession.
>
> (Machiavelli, *Works*, vol. 1, *The Prince*, p. 55)

2. From this point of view, the wars conducted by Hitler and Saddam Hussein as well as most of Napoleon's wars cannot be considered as serving a rational purpose, only a personal one.

3. On this see, for example, Chen-Ya Tien, *Chinese Military Theory: Ancient and Modern* (Oakville, Ontario, Canada: Mosaic Press, 1992), pp. 31–33.

4. In the *Discourses on the First Decade of Titus Livius*, Machiavelli praises the Romans for giving their generals plenary power:

Among the matters deserving consideration is the sort of authority with which they [the Romans] sent out their consuls, dictators and other army leaders; their authority was very great and the Senate reserved nothing except authority to start new wars and make treaties. Everything else they handed over to the judgment and power of the consul . . . he could fight a battle or not fight one, and attack this city or the other, as he thought best.

(Machiavelli, *Works*, vol. 1, p. 417)

5. 'Its [war's] grammar, indeed, may be its own, but not its logic' (Clausewitz, *On War*, p. 605).

6. Samuel P. Huntington, *The Soldier and the State* (New York: Vintage Books, 1964), part 1, pp. 1–143. See also Samuel P. Huntington, 'Civilian Control of the Military: a Theoretical Statement', in Heinz Eulau, S. J. Eldersveld, and Morris Janowitz, *Political Behavior: A Reader in Theory and Research* (Glencoe, IL: The Free Press, 1956), pp. 380–385.

7. *'Panem et Circenses.'*

Recently, John Keegan, in *A History of Warfare* (New York: Alfred A. Knopf, 1993) (to be cited as HOW), and Martin van Creveld, in *The Transformation of War* (to be cited as TOW) (New York: The Free Press, 1991), have argued that throughout most of history, until the wars of the French Revolution and Clausewitz's time to be precise, wars were not fought for political purposes and were not a continuation of politics or policy by other means. Both have convinced themselves that war never served, and can never serve, a rational political purpose. Based on highly selective case studies, their arguments are logically and historically unconvincing and furthermore contain a number of internal contradictions.

Martin van Creveld argues that '. . . War as a continuation of *politik*, let alone *realpolitik*, is in some ways a modern invention. Even if we substitute "rulers" for the "state", the view still does not date further back than the Renaissance' (TOW, p. 126). He then asserts that most premodern wars, as well as many modern wars, fought for justice, religion, or existence, are not political wars. This is at best a dubious argument that omits a careful consideration of what politics is all about. After all, there is no reason why wars fought for freedom, independence and self-determination, justice, or religion cannot *also* be considered political! Religious leaders or those fighting for justice, for example, can also be political leaders. Keegan would undoubtedly agree with van Creveld's statement that '. . . the contemporary strategic premise that sees wars as making sense only when they are fought for reasons of policy or interest represents a point of view that is both Eurocentric and modern' (TOW, p. 155).

Sun Tzu was clearly not European and he lived more than two thousand years before Clausewitz, the French Revolution, and the modern European state; nevertheless, he thought that wars are fought for the interests of the state (or any other group). In a time close to that of Sun Tzu, Thucydides also believed that the states or the Greek city-states fought for what they perceived to be their vital political interests. Van Creveld argues that '. . . war has not always been waged for "interest." In fact, the term "interest" as herein used is a sixteenth-century neologism . . .'

(TOW, p. 212). '. . . To say that people go to war for their "interests", and that "interest" comprises whatever any society considers good and useful for itself, is as self-evident as it is trite' (TOW, p. 217). This argument is akin to suggesting that gravity did not exist before Newton! Perhaps the term 'interest' is a neologism, but men and states still fought for their interests long before the term was invented.

Van Creveld then develops what he probably considers to be his decisive logical argument: 'At bottom, the reason why fighting can never be a question of interest is – to put it bluntly – that dead men have no interests' (TOW, p. 158). But this is not a very convincing argument because people fight or have fought not only for their personal interests but also for those of their families, clans, tribes, city-states, or modern states. 'The state', he continues, 'is a cold monster. Sending men to die in the interests of somebody or something else is not war but murder of the most obscene kind' (TOW, p. 188). Needless to say, men often agree to fight and risk their lives because they identify themselves (rightly or wrongly) with an interest or cause they share with that of somebody or something else. This represents an important interest they can only achieve for themselves and their dependents by cooperating with others.

So, what do men and states fight for which is not political and not trivial? Here van Creveld gives an astounding answer:

> . . . War, far from being merely a means, has very often been considered an end – a highly attractive activity for which no other can provide an adequate substitute . . .' (TOW, p. 218, also p. 221). '. . . While war's usefulness as a servant of power, interest, and profit may be questioned, the inherent fascination it has held for men at all times and places is a matter of historical fact. When all is said and done, the only way to account for this fascination is to regard war as the game with the highest stakes of all.
>
> (van Creveld, TOW, p. 218)

'War', van Creveld concludes, '. . . is the continuation not of politics but of sport' (sic!) (TOW, p. 191). 'War, in short, is grand theater' (TOW, p. 171). 'While the usefulness of war as a means for gaining practical ends may well be questioned, its ability to entertain, to inspire, and to fascinate has never been in doubt' (TOW, p. 226). The absurdity of this proposition becomes obvious if one imagines the President of the United States declaring war on Canada, Mexico, or Cuba to provide the American public with 'panem et circenses' to substitute for a strike in the baseball league. (Furthermore, sport, like most other human activities, can also involve politics or even be dominated by politics! Sport is not necessarily an apolitical activity.)

This argument is also contradictory – for if men refuse to die for the interests of that 'cold monster', the state, why should they agree to do so for sport? After all, dead men cannot continue to participate in the thrill of sport either.

John Keegan reaches similar conclusions, although for other reasons. On the basis of utopian idealism, he deems war a bloody, costly, and irrational activity that must be abolished. 'Politics,' he maintains, 'must continue; war cannot' (HOW, p. 391). 'Despite confusion and uncertainty, it seems just possible to glimpse the emerging outline of a world without war' (HOW, p. 58). 'I am impressed by the evidence . . . [war] may well be ceasing to commend itself to human beings as desirable or productive, let alone rational, means of reconciling their discontents. This is not mere idealism . . . War truly has become a scourge, as was disease throughout most of human history.' He next makes clear the purpose of his book: 'Charting the course of human culture through its undoubtedly warlike past towards its potentially peaceful future is the theme of this book' (HOW, pp. 59–60). Similar sentiments and hopes were expressed more than two millennia ago by Isaiah, and over two hundred years ago by Kant, yet the brutal realities of war continued to dominate human affairs and the swords were not beaten into plowshares.

It is curious, to say the least, that Keegan envisions a future world without war after presenting a 392-page discussion of different wars supposedly fought for non-rational and non-political reasons. If this is the case, *why should human beings suddenly cease fighting if war has never been a rational, purposeful activity?* What will cause the human race to so rapidly become more rational and peaceful? *If anything might possibly moderate or reduce the incentive to resort to war, it would probably be political calculations as Clausewitz suggested and not something inherent in human nature.*

In order to make the case that war should be abolished in the future, Keegan pursues two main lines of argument. The first endeavors to show that war is not and never has been rational – therefore it must be abolished. The second asserts that the concept of war as rational or instrumental (i.e., as serving a political purpose) is somehow Clausewitz's evil invention.

Keegan therefore selects a number of case studies from the history of conflict which ostensibly prove that war has not been waged for rational reasons (i.e., the Maoris, the Aztecs, the Assyrians, the Mamelukes and Arabs, the Mongols, the Easter Island tribes, and so on). None of these cases as discussed proves his point. In each instance, a very rational, instrumental, hence also a political explanation can be found to demonstrate why such wars or conflicts took place. For example, Keegan does not consider the conflict/war in the former Yugoslavia to be political or rational. Yet the desire of each group involved – the Serbs, Bosnians, Croats, Macedonians, Albanians, or Slovenes – is to achieve self-determination, political independence, and statehood, which would allow each to take better care of their own national interests. *What wars could be more political than these?* The fact that such wars become too costly to be worth the expected benefits does not mean that they were not initiated for what were, at the outset, perceived as rational objectives. In fact it is Clausewitz who recognizes in a most constructive way the *non-rational* dimensions of war when he argues that once war begins it can acquire a momentum of its own in which the politicians lose control. *If anything, politics, according to what Clausewitz actually says, moderates war and should make it less violent and less costly.* As he argues in Chapter 2 of Book 1, once the cost of war exceeds any benefit it should be brought to a quick end (*On War*, pp. 90–92). Clearly, the tribes annihilating each other on Easter Island were battling over the allocation of scarce resources and therefore represent an early example of ecological disaster on an isolated island. A powerful argument that even primitive war is rational and instrumental, and hence political, is provided, for instance, in R. Brian Ferguson, *Explaining War* (Cambridge: Cambridge University Press, 1990), pp. 26–55, and others in Jonathan Haas, *The Anthropology of War* (Cambridge: Cambridge University Press, 1990). See also Arthur Waldron's letter to the *Times Literary Supplement* of 26 February 1993.

(In the introduction to his book, Keegan argues that British Regiments fight for the honor of their Regiments; while this may or may not be the case, *the United Kingdom never went to war for Regimental honour* (see pp. xiv–xv).)

In his second line of argument, Keegan sets up a strawman of Clausewitz's ideas in *On War*. Unfortunately, his 'summary' of Clausewitz has nothing to do with what Clausewitz actually said. Clausewitz's ideas are either misunderstood or quoted out of context. (For an understated critique of the case, see Christopher Bassford's article, 'John Keegan and the Grand Tradition of Trashing Clausewitz: A Polemic', in *War in History*, vol. 1, no. 3, November 1994, pp. 319–336.)

Keegan's *ad hominem* argument portrays Clausewitz as the incarnation of evil, the Anti-Christ. Keegan's argument certainly has a tone of religious fervor to it. It is, he avers, Clausewitz who invented the political nature of war, who suggested that war can serve rational and political ends. (By the way, Jomini – who for a long while had even more influence than Clausewitz – also insists that wars are fought for political reasons.) It is therefore, according to Keegan, Clausewitz's *influence* which led to the atrocities and bloodshed of the First and Second World Wars. 'And although this catastrophic outcome must not be laid at the door of Clausewitz's study, we are nevertheless right to see Clausewitz as the ideological father of the First World War . . .' (HOW, p. 22). '. . . The objects of the First World War were determined in great measure by the thoughts that were Clausewitz's . . . His ideas undoubtedly bore heavily on the assumptions made by generals before 1914 . . .' (HOW, p. 354). In other words, had Clausewitz not existed, war would not be political and the atrocities of modern war could have been avoided. *Post hoc ergo propter hoc.* Of course, with or without Clausewitz, we can see that the wars of the twentieth century would have taken a similar course. Can there be a more blatant case of the messenger or observer being blamed for the bad news, *and in fact for a message he never even delivered?* Clausewitz had very little if any direct influence on anyone simply because very few soldiers, statesmen, or scholars have ever gone to the trouble of actually reading his work. As Keegan himself so aptly puts it, 'My real difficulty with Clausewitz began when I realized that, of the thousands of soldiers, high and low, I have known in a working lifetime, not one of them has ever volunteered that Clausewitz had been any influence on him at all' (John Keegan, 'Peace by Other Means?: War, Popular Opinion and Politically Incorrect Clausewitz', *Times Literary Supplement*, 11 December 1992, pp. 3–4). What remains a mystery is that *if no soldiers ever read Clausewitz, as Keegan claims* (and he is not entirely wrong!), *how is it that Clausewitz had so much influence on modern war?*

To be sure, Keegan argues that 'war is not the continuation of politics by other means' (HOW, p. 3). He contends that the idea that war is the continuation of politics is parochial (p. 24) whereas in fact Clausewitz's idea of the political logic or foundation of war is universal. By the time Keegan reaches page 391, without noticing, he finally argues that the military do after all serve a political purpose, when he states: 'The world community needs, more than it has ever done, skilful and disciplined warriors who are ready to put themselves *at the service of its authority*' (HOW, p. 391, my emphasis). Any authority directing the military is of course political, and the military serving or fighting on behalf of any authority does so not for regimental honor or as a game, but for political reasons only.

The basic contradiction in Keegan's argument is that if indeed war has always been non-rational and non-political, why should it suddenly come to an end if human nature has not changed and environmental and ecological pressures will probably create *more, not fewer,* causes of conflict? Keegan's argument that wars are not rational thus defeats his own desire to bring wars to an end.

The ideas advanced by Keegan and van Creveld, whose books appeared at roughly the same time, reflect the growing confusion created by the end of the Cold War and the increase in low-intensity conflict. The legitimate questions they have asked need to be addressed, but unfortunately neither develops a convincing frame-work for understanding contemporary war. They have by no means replaced the Clausewitzian paradigm. Both fail to distinguish between war and *other types of conflict*, and both fail to understand or discuss the nature of politics. Politics exists not only in modern states but in all types of human groups.

Oddly enough, neither of these authors refers in any detail to Sun Tzu (although van Creveld remarks that *The Art of War* is the best work ever written on the subject), Machiavelli, and Thucydides. Long before the French Revolution, each of these strategists presented arguments very similar to those of Clausewitz and, in particular, recognized the political nature of war. (On Machiavelli's view of war as a political activity, see, for example, F. L. Taylor, *The Art of War in Italy* 1494–1529 (Cambridge: Cambridge University Press, 1921), esp. Ch. 8, pp. 157–158 and 167–169. See also Neal Wood's introduction to *The Art of War*, p. xxvi.) Whether conventional or low-intensity, whether between or within states, war and conflict almost always, in one way or another, serve a political purpose. While Clausewitz's *On War* may not explain all types of modern conflicts, his work still represents, in general, the most powerful analysis of the political nature of war. In this sense, van Creveld was certainly right when, in another article, he referred to the Clausewitzian framework for the study of war as *eternal* (Martin van Creveld, 'The Eternal Clausewitz', in Michael I. Handel, *Clausewitz and Modern Strategy* (London: Cass, 1986), pp. 35–50).

Mao Tse-tung puts an end to all such arguments very simply by stating: 'In a word, war cannot for a single moment be separated from politics' (Mao Tse-tung, *Selected Military Writings*, p. 227).

Finally, when all is said and done, the importance of Clausewitz's *On War* is not confined to his ideas on the primacy of politics or the trinitarian analysis, but is also based on many other creative concepts and ideas that have become part of the language used by every strategist. Among those concepts are the role of friction in war, the probabilistic nature of war, the importance of understanding the nature of war, the role of moral forces in war, his methodological observations and insights, the complexity of war, the culminating point of victory, to mention but a few.

CHAPTER 7: THE RATIONAL CALCULUS OF WAR: CORRELATING ENDS AND MEANS

1. For a good summary of the purely rational decision-making model, see Yehezkel Dror, *Policymaking Reexamined* (San Francisco, CA: Chandler, 1968).

2. Machiavelli, once again more like Sun Tzu, believed in the importance of rationality in waging war (Felix Gilbert, 'Machiavelli: The Renaissance of the Art of War', in Peter Paret (ed.), *Makers of Modern Strategy* (Princeton, NJ: Princeton University Press, 1986), p. 30). As Felix Gilbert shows, Machiavelli's belief that wars could be fought on the basis of *rational laws* may have formed the basis for another mistaken conclusion, namely that performing rational calculations on the outcome of possible engagements might render battle and bloodshed unnecessary:

> When war is seen as determined by rational laws, it is only logical *to leave nothing to chance* and to expect that the adversary will throw his hand in when he has been brought into position where the game is rationally lost. The result of considering war as a mere science or at least of overvaluing the rational element in military affairs leads easily to the view that war can be decided quite as well on paper as on the battlefield. [my emphasis]
>
> (Gilbert, 'Machiavelli: The Renaissance of the Art of War', p. 30)
> (This is a somewhat puzzling observation in light of Machiavelli's emphasis on the role of Fortune in war.)

Gilbert could very well have made the same observations about Sun Tzu. Yet as much as Clausewitz thought that war was *essentially* (but *not* exclusively) a rational activity or *that the non-rational dimensions of war could be rationally and systematically analysed*, he would have considered such a statement unrealistic if not absurd:

> **It would be an obvious fallacy to imagine war between civilized peoples as resulting merely from a rational act on the part of their governments and to conceive of war as gradually ridding itself of passion . . . comparative figures of their strength would be enough. That would be a kind of war by algebra . . . If war is an act of force, the emotions cannot fail to be involved.**
>
> (Clausewitz, *On War*, p. 76)

> **Theorists are apt to look on fighting in the abstract as a trial of strength without emotion entering into it. This is one of a thousand errors which they quite consciously commit because they have no idea of its implications.**
>
> (Clausewitz, *On War*, p. 138)

Although Clausewitz would be the first to agree that war should be fought as rationally as possible, he knew that it was naive and dangerous to believe that war could be conducted as a purely rational activity. On Clausewitz's general agreement with Machiavelli's ideas, see Gilbert, 'Machiavelli: The Renaissance of the Art of War', p. 31; Paret, *Clausewitz and the State*, pp. 169–179; and Peter Paret and Daniel

Moran, *Clausewitz: Historical and Political Writings* (Princeton, NJ: Princeton University Press, 1992), pp. 268–269; and 279–282 (see also note 25, Chapter 15, p. 428 below).

3. For Clausewitz's adherence to the principles of *raison d'état*, see Paret, *Clausewitz and the State*, pp. 94–95, 130, 169–179. On the problem of assuming that the '**government transforms psychological energy into rational policy, which the army helps carry out**', see pp. 369–370. See also Azar Gat, *The Origins of Military Thought* (Oxford: Oxford University Press, 1989), Part 2, Chapter 7, pp. 215–250.

CHAPTER 8: CLAUSEWITZ ON THE ROLE OF 'MORAL FORCES' IN WAR

1. See, for example, the interesting interpretation of Clausewitz's *On War* by Charles Reynolds in *The Politics of War: A Study of the Rationality of Violence in Inter-State Relationships* (New York: St. Martin's Press, 1989).
2. In recent years, 'politically correct' strategists and theorists of 'information war', 'cyber-war,' and the 'revolution in military affairs' (RMA) have suggested that future and current wars could become much cheaper in terms of human costs and casualties through the use of long-range stand-off precision-guided munitions, in particular, cruise missiles. Labeling this new era the age of 'post-heroic warfare', Edward Luttwak has argued in two lengthy articles that the United States should reduce the number of conventional troops, tanks, and ground forces in general and replace them with cruise missiles. He contends that since the U.S. government and public opinion clearly have no stomach for taking casualties, ground forces have become useless for them from a political perspective. Hence his promotion of cruise missiles, which seem, on the other hand, to constitute a cheap, effective, and *politically acceptable* weapon. (See Edward N. Luttwak, 'Toward Post-Heroic War', *Foreign Affairs*, May/June 1995, vol. 74, no. 3, pp. 109–122; and 'A Post-Heroic Military Policy', *Foreign Affairs*, July/August 1996, vol. 75, no. 4, pp. 33–34.)

While Luttwak's first assumption may or may not be correct, depending on the interests involved and shifting public opinion, the second assumption – that high-tech weapons can replace ground troops or for that matter, all types of forces that would involve taking casualties – proved to be clearly wrong. The desire to win wars with minimal cost and greatest speed is as old as war itself, but unfortunately, this cannot be achieved under normal circumstances. In Chapter 11 of this book ('The Ideal and the Real: Victory without Bloodshed and the Search for the Decisive Battle', pp. 135–154), I argue that Sun Tzu's aspiration to win war without bloodshed or at a very low cost is only a normative ideal – not a realistic proposition. I have also shown how Clausewitz indirectly demolishes this supposition.

Nevertheless, the perennial but unrealistic desire to avoid casualties and win cheaply has persisted throughout history. A recent example is the ineffective American attempt to compel Saddam Hussein to disarm and allow thorough weapons inspections. The United States failed to accomplish these goals despite the firing of cruise missiles and the selective use of air power against Iraqi military and other targets. Such half-measures may only cost the United States and the rest of the world more in the end. The clearly announced reluctance of the United States and its NATO allies to use ground troops or to take any casualties in their war with Serbia led only to disastrous consequences and probably to *much higher costs in the end*. So much for post-heroic war.

Here once again, the classical theory of strategy, particularly Clausewitz's theory of war, can serve as a valuable corrective and realistic guide. Clausewitz himself had to argue strenuously against some of the trendy theories of his own time; namely, the idea that wars can be won without bloodshed. In the opening page of *On War*, he makes a point of debunking such naïve ideas:

> **Kind-hearted people might of course think that there was some ingenious way to disarm or defeat an enemy without too much bloodshed, and might imagine this is the true goal of the art of war. Pleasant as it sounds, it is a fallacy that must be exposed: war is such a dangerous business that mistakes which come from kindness are the worst.**
>
> (Clausewitz, *On War*, p. 75; see also p. 259)

Clausewitz believed that attempts to win cheaply without fighting end in what he called 'half-and-half' affairs that often '**deteriorate into downright make-believe**' (Clausewitz, *On War*, p. 609). His conclusion, then, was that '**fighting is the only possible means**' to attain the political object; that '**everything is governed by a supreme law, the decision by force of arms**' (Clausewitz, *On War*, p. 99). In other words, all other things being equal, '**the destruction of the enemy forces is the superior, more effective means with which others cannot compete**' (Clausewitz, *On War*, p. 97). He further adds that although destruction of the enemy forces is expensive in the short run, it is often cheaper and more effective in the long run. '**In war too small an effort can result not just in failure but in positive harm . . .**' (Clausewitz, *On War*, p. 585).

CHAPTER 9: THE SUPREME ACT OF JUDGMENT: UNDERSTANDING THE 'NATURE OF WAR' AND THE 'TRINITARIAN ANALYSIS'

1. In the early edition of the Howard and Paret translation of *On War*, the phrase *eine Wunderliche Dreifaltikeit* was translated as 'a paradoxical trinity'. In subsequent editions, it was replaced by the phrase, 'a remarkable trinity' (*On War*, p. 89). The Graham translation interprets this expression as 'a wonderful trinity', which, according to Raymond Aron, actually corresponds more with the German word *wunderbar* than with *wunderliche*. The Jolles translation chose the words 'strange trinity' to express the idea. Perhaps the best way to translate this phrase would be 'an amazing trinity'.

2. See also Clausewitz's brief discussion of the nature of war at the end of Chapter 2

of Book 1, where he argues that the nature of war must always be interpreted in 'the manner in which war in practice deviates in varying degrees from its basic, rigorous concept [i.e., the absolute war] . . .War [can take] this form or that, but [it always remains] subject to that basic concept, as to a supreme law' (Clausewitz, *On War*, p. 99). The difference between the nature of war in theory and in practice is defined by its political nature.

3. Corbett is also very interested in what he calls the *primordial question* of understanding the nature of each war. Like Clausewitz, he also finds the key in political factors:

> When a Chief of Staff is asked for a war plan . . . he will ask what is the political object of the war, what are the political conditions, and how much . . . the question at issue means respectively to us and to our adversary. *It is these considerations which determine the nature of the war.* This [is the] primordial question . . .
>
> > (Julian S. Corbett, *Some Principles of Maritime Strategy* (Annapolis, MD: Naval Institute Press, 1988), p. 27. Corbett discusses the nature of war throughout Part 1, pp. 3–87.)

The first strategist to discuss how to determine the nature of a war is Frontinus in *Stratagems and Aqueducts* (Loeb Classical Library), trans. C. E. Bennett (Cambridge, MA: Harvard University Press, 1969), pp. 23–27.

4. Mao Tse-tung, 'Strategy in China's Revolutionary War', in *Selected Military Writings of Mao Tse-tung*, pp. 86–87. Recently, much has been made of Mao's personal study of Clausewitz's *On War* through various less than accurate Chinese translations. His diary indicates that he read at least Book 1 of *On War*, and may have even led a one-time seminar session on it. (See Zhang Yuang-Lin, *Mao Zedong und Carl von Clausewitz: Theoriend des Krieges Beziehung, Darstellung und Vergleich*, Mannheim: Ph.D. dissertation: University of Mannheim, 1995.)

Although many of Mao's ideas resemble and even expand upon some of Clausewitz's ideas, it appears that Mao nevertheless developed these ideas independently. It stands to reason that Mao was not all that familiar with *On War* and must therefore be seen as a truly original student of war.

5. Herman Khan, *On Escalation* (New York: Praeger, 1965).

6. Harry G. Summers, Jr., 'Defense Without Purpose', *Society*, November/December (1983), pp. 4–17.

7. In his book *The Transformation of War*, Martin van Creveld argues that the Clausewitzian 'trinitarian war' (as he refers to it) does not describe – and is in fact irrelevant to – premodern war as well as to future low-intensity conflict. 'Trinitarian war . . . was unknown to most societies during most history'. Martin van Creveld, *The Transformation of War* (New York: The Free Press, 1991). One could just as easily declare that prose did not exist before its discovery by Molière's Tartuffe.

Van Creveld's argument is not convincing, though, for the role of the people, the military, and the government can be identified (or, to be more exact, passions and emotions, creative leadership and intuition, and rational calculations) – even if in a rudimentary form – in every state, society, or group. Without explicitly referring to his analysis of society and war as trinitarian, I have already shown that Machiavelli's analysis specifically addresses all three elements and their intricate interrelationship; and, as shown in Chapter 10, this could also be said of Sun Tzu more than 2,000 years ago.

In every conflict or war, *some* of the people do the fighting while the rest provide other forms of active and passive support. *All* of the people cannot fight, even if they so desire, because of such reasons as age, relative strength, or skill. Consequently, the distinction between *the people* (or society) and *the military* (or warriors) is universal as well as eternal.

In the same way, a political or governmental function cannot be absent, although it may exist only in an embryonic form. Someone (the political leader) must decide the purpose or objectives of the conflict or war, since all of the warriors cannot usually issue orders simultaneously or decide to fight only when they see fit; a leader or select group must make the coordinated decisions for the rest. And this, by definition, is the function of the political authority or government, whether or not it is explicitly identified as such. At times, the political and military leadership may overlap or even be identical (e.g., Pericles, Frederick the Great, or Napoleon), with the warrior king leading his troops in battle, but the two functions are still not the same.

Although van Creveld does not consider Clausewitz's trinitarian analysis (that is, Clausewitz's entire theoretical framework for the analysis of war) to be relevant to, for example, the Greek *polis*, the Peloponnesian wars, and pre-modern war in general, we can see that Clausewitz himself 'applied' this framework quite convincingly to such earlier periods (*On War*, Book 8, Chapter 3B). For example, according to Pericles' funeral oration, the soldiers who died (the military) made 'the most glorious contribution' that can be made for those left behind (the people) to preserve a free and democratic way of life (a government selected by the people). Pericles clearly suggests that only the Athenian democratic system justified such dedication and that the people living in other political systems with less freedom would not be as motivated (Thucydides, *The History of the Peloponnesian War*, Book 2, Sections 34–56; see also W. Robert Connor, *Thucydides* (Princeton, NJ: Princeton University Press, 1985), p. 68). As Connor has commented: '. . . The Funeral Oration develops an image of a society that sustains individual freedom and fulfillment and is in turn sustained by its citizens' willingness to fight and die for it' (*ibid.*, p. 68). This readiness to sacrifice for the common good, of course, represents the basis for Machiavelli's argument in favor of a citizen-army.

A trinitarian type of analysis can also be applied to Pericles' (the political leader/government) decision *not* to leave the walls of Athens and *not* to fight the Spartans outside the city. Although the political and strategic decision to wage a war of attrition makes sense, it is unpopular with the Athenian people, whose innately restless character and active temperament chafes at the idea of remaining passive. This makes it doubly difficult for them to stand by while their property outside the city walls is destroyed. Thus, the Periclean strategy does not match the temperament of the Athenian people and the divisive nature of their democratic system. Here also the three elements of Clausewitz's trinity are alive and well, for not all Athenians are part of the military (i.e., not all Athenians participated in the Sicilian expedition). Hans Delbrück, *History of the Art of War*, vol. 1, *Antiquity* (Westport, CT: Greenwood Press, 1975), pp. 135–143; Donald Kagan, *The Archidamian* War (Cornell, NY: Cornell University Press, 1991).

Van Creveld claims that Clausewitz's trinitarian analysis does not apply to low-intensity conflict, yet the trinity is certainly represented in Mao's treatise on guerrilla warfare: the Communist party ('the government' or political authority) is in control of the gun (the military element), while the military (the fish) hide in the sea of the general population.

The trinitarian analysis is even applicable to *chaotic situations* such as the *Intifada* and the wars in Lebanon, Bosnia, Somalia, and Rwanda – all *internal conflicts* that Clausewitz did not have in mind. While situations of utter chaos often lack, at least initially, a locus of political control or a decision-making authority, such a center sooner or later emerges. Even if the *Intifada* begins as a leaderless, spontaneous uprising, the entire population is not involved. At first the active, tire-burning warriors, the young '*shabab*', do most of the fighting on their own, but at some point a leader (a *Ra'is*) emerges. After all, the *Intifada* is ultimately nothing but an attempt to establish an independent Palestinian state – an entity in which *the people*, their *political leaders* (the government), and their *armed force* (the military) will be able to operate. The same can be said of chaotic situations in Lebanon or Somalia, where the absence of a strong central political authority spawns numerous groups of warriors with their own supporters and leaders. The is nothing new in history about *chaotic situations* or *stasis* as it is referred to in Thucydides.

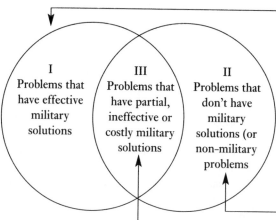

I. Problems that have military solutions. Defense against an invading force, the occupation of territory, a war between two armed nations, other. Sun Tzu and Clausewitz are always relevant.

II. Problems that do not have military solutions and are not military by nature. Lack of political culture, fighting political corruption, demographic problems, pollution and ecological problems, political and social chaos, etc.

III. Problems that have partial military solutions or ineffective military solutions or much too costly solutions. The use of force to gain time for other action (as II) Vietnam, Malaya, the Philippines, where a military solution or the use of force have a transitory effect only.

403

Although Clausewitz's 'trinitarian analysis' can be applied to most instances involving conflict and civil strife, the examples brought by van Creveld – including chaos, civil strife, civil wars, and low-intensity wars – are primarily types of *internal conflict* better classified as problems of political order and internal stability. These problems are more the concern of the works of political theorists, ranging from Thomas Hobbes' *The Leviathan* to Samuel P. Huntington's *Political Order in Changing Societies*. Clausewitz's analysis does not pretend to address the topic of conflict *within* states, but rather examines conflict *between* states. Clausewitz would probably classify the issues cited by van Creveld as problems for the police, perhaps supported by the military, and would then go on to recommend political reform, political education, or another form of government as the solution, with political theory furnishing the necessary insight.

Clausewitz's theories and insights are hardly being discredited as we approach the twenty-first century. A theory cannot be applied to problems that it was never intended to explain, and military theories on war cannot replace a political theory on the evolution of societies and disorder or harmony within the state. These two types of theory can, however, be related or overlapping, but they are *not* substitutes for each other.

In this context it is worthwhile mentioning Stanislav Andreski's definition of what is war and what it is not: 'We can define war as organised fighting between groups of individuals belonging to the same species but occupying distinct territories, thus distinguishing war from fights between isolated individuals as well as from struggles between groups living intermingled within the same territory, which can be classified as rebellions, revolutions, riots and so on.' Stanislav Andreski, *Wars, Revolutions, Dictatorships* (London: Cass, 1992), p. 1.

Finally, if we consider Clausewitz's trinitarian analysis, as we should, to represent not so much the *people*, the *military*, and the *government*, but the *passions and emotions, leadership, intuition* and *creativity,* and *rational calculations,* then van Creveld's dismissal of Clausewitz's trinitarian analysis becomes even less plausible. After all, passions, leadership, creative genius, and rational calculations, have always existed in all wars.

 8. Plutarch, *Lives*, Dryden translation (New York: Modern Library, 1992), p. 572.
 9. Lincoln's letter quoted in Stephen W. Sears, 'Lincoln and McClellan', p. 24 in Gabor S. Boritt (ed.), *Lincoln's Generals* (New York: Oxford University Press, 1994), pp. 2–50.
10. 'The German Army of the early 1940s was quite simply the best in the world. At small-scale ground action it had no peer . . . No one who met them *on their own terms* ever beat them, and to have fought them in France in 1942 [as the American military wanted to in the Spring of 1942] would have been on their own terms. The trick of it, to which the Russians and we under British tutelage later gave much thought *was to meet them on other terms than their own . . .*' (Eric Larrabee, *Commander in Chief: Franklin Delano Roosevelt, His Lieutenants, and their War* (New York: Touchstone, 1988), pp. 137–138).
11. John Lewis Gaddis, *Strategies of Containment* (New York: Oxford University Press, 1982), p. 56.
12. *Ibid.*, p. 61.

CHAPTER 10: THE FIRST ELEMENT OF THE
REMARKABLE TRINITY: THE PEOPLE IN ARMS

1. Jomini, *The Art of War*, Chapter 1, Article 8, pp. 29–35; and Clausewitz, *On War*, Book 6, Chapter 26, pp. 479–483.
2. See Mao Tse-tung, *Selected Writings of Mao Tse-tung* (Peking: Foreign Languages Press, 1963).
3. For an outstanding case study on this process, see Alistair Horne, *A Savage War of Peace: Algeria 1954–1962* (New York: Viking Penguin, revised edition, 1987).
4. See Michael R. Gordon and General Bernard E. Trainor, *The General's War* (Boston: Little, Brown, 1995), pp. 324–329.
5. See Gordon A. Craig, *The Politics of the Prussian Army, 1640–1945* (New York: Oxford University Press, 1955), Chapter 2, pp. 37–81; William O. Shanahan, *Prussian Military Reforms, 1786–1813* (New York: Columbia University Press, 1945); Walter M. Simon, *The Failure of the Prussian Reform Movement, 1807–1819* (Cornell, NY: Cornell University Press, 1955).
6. See the introduction to Richard D. Challener, *The French Theory of the Nation in Arms* (New York: Columbia University Press, 1955), pp. 3–4. See also John A. Lynn, *The Bayonets of the Republic: Motivation and Tactics in the Army of Revolutionary France 1791–1794* (Urbana: University of Illinois Press, 1984).
7. Jean-Jacques Rousseau (trans. W. Kendal), *The Government of Poland*, (Indianapolis: Bobbs-Merrill, 1972), p. 81. Chapter 12, 'The Military System', contains many excellent insights into people's or guerrilla warfare and includes a brilliant analysis of how to best defend Poland in view of its unique geographical situation. After identifying Poland's strategic weaknesses and assets, Rousseau develops a 'mobile' defense strategy emphasizing its comparative advantages (pp. 79–88).
8. *On War*, Book 8, Chapter 3B, pp. 585–594.

CHAPTER 11: THE IDEAL AND THE REAL:
VICTORY WITHOUT BLOODSHED AND THE
SEARCH FOR THE DECISIVE BATTLE

1. See Frank Kierman Jr., 'Phases and Modes of Combat in Early China', in Fairbank and Kierman (eds.), *Chinese Ways in Warfare*, pp. 27–67. See also Chen-Ya Tien, *Chinese Military Theory: Ancient and New* (Oakville, Ontario, Canada: Mosaic Press, 1992), Chapter 2, 'Survey of Ancient Chinese Military Theories', pp. 21–66; and E. E. Bahnforth, *A Chinese Military Strategist of the Warring States: Sun Pin*, unpublished Ph.D. dissertation (New Brunswick, NJ: Rutgers University, 1979).
2. Fairbank, 'Introduction: Varieties of the Chinese Military Experience', Fairbank and Kierman (eds.), *Chinese Ways in Warfare*, pp. 27–67.
3. *Ibid.*, p. 7.
4. *Ibid.*
5. *Ibid.*

6. *Ibid.*, p. 10.
7. *Ibid.*, p. 11.
8. As Fairbank puts it, 'Much of China's military experience is directly comparable with experience elsewhere . . . Comparative studies will no doubt show up the sinological fallacy as to China's alleged uniqueness. But still there remains the imprint of a specific geography and history that produced in China specific habits of mind and action' (*ibid.*, p. 25). To Fairbank, that which differentiates the Chinese approach to war includes '(1) A tendency to disesteem heroism and violence, not to glorify it . . .; (2) A tradition of land warfare that prefers defense to offense and stresses the exhausting of an attacker or the pacification of a rebel as less costly than their extermination . . .; [and] (3) A tie-up between militarism and bureaucracy, rather than commercial expansion, least of all overseas' (*ibid.*, pp. 25–26). All of these qualities have also been exhibited by various Western societies throughout history (even if not all simultaneously in a single country).
9. In this context, what Clausewitz means by *economy of force* (Ökonomie der Kräfte) is the opposite of this term's definition in twentieth-century British and American doctrine manuals (see Robert Crowley and Geoffrey Parker, eds., *The Reader's Companion to Military History* (Boston: Houghton Mifflin, 1996), pp. 146–147). Modern military manuals have typically defined economy of force as the desire to use the minimum number of troops necessary to achieve a given objective. While the British and American doctrines and also, one suspects, Sun Tzu are concerned with efficiency and economy (in the sense of conserving resources) – Clausewitz defines economy of force as making use of all forces available in battle:

> **The man of action [i.e. the commander] must at times support his decision by certain rules, or established routines. One of these simplified features, or aids to analysis, is always to make sure that *all* forces are involved – always to ensure that *no part of the whole force is idle*. If a segment of one's force is located where it is not sufficiently busy with the enemy, or if troops are on the march – that is, idle – while the enemy is fighting, then these forces are being managed uneconomically. In this sense, they are wasted, which is even worse than using them inappropriately. When the time for action comes, the first requirement should be that all parts must act . . .**
>
> (Clausewitz, *On War*, p. 213; see also pp. 206–207)
>
> **This is even more true on the higher strategic level! The rule, then, that we have developed is this: all forces intended and available for a strategic purpose should be applied simultaneously; their employment will be the more effective the more everything can be concentrated in a single action at a single moment.**
>
> (Clausewitz, *On War*, p. 209)

10. See also Clausewitz, *On War*, pp. 194–197, and this book, Chapter 12.
11. See Michael I. Handel, *War, Strategy and Intelligence* (London: Cass, 1989), p. 4, for the value of truisms concerning war.

Basil H. Liddell Hart describes his strategy of the indirect approach as follows:

> Thus a move round the enemy's front against his rear has the aim not only of avoiding resistance on its way but in its issue. In the profoundest sense, it takes the line of least resistance. The equivalent in the psychological sphere is the line of least expectation. They are the two faces of the same coin, and to appreciate this is to widen our understanding of strategy [which is the operational level according to today's definition]. For if we merely take what obviously appears the line of least resistance, its obviousness will appeal to the opponent also; and this line may no longer be that of least resistance.
>
> (B. H. Liddell Hart, *Strategy* (New York: New American Library, 1974), p. 327)

12. Machiavelli expresses the same idea in *The Art of War* in a section entitled 'The Folly of Making an Enemy Desperate' (Machiavelli, *The Art of War*, in *Works*, vol. 2, pp. 700–701).

13. Seemingly unaware of this statement by Clausewitz, Liddell Hart makes essentially the same point: 'A more profound appreciation of how the psychological permeates and dominates the physical sphere has an indirect value' (Liddell Hart, *Strategy*, p. 328). Liddell Hart then sharply criticizes Clausewitz's emphasis on the quantitative over the qualitative dimensions of war as well as his emphasis on the concentration of superior force and his failure to 'penetrate fully [into the deeper truth] that in war every problem, and every principle, is a duality' (*ibid.*, pp. 328–329). This statement reveals Liddell Hart's lack of familiarity with Clausewitz's methodology and ideas. It is ironic that despite his warning against trying to couch strategic theories in mathematical terms, Liddell Hart ultimately gives the reader a series of shallow if not mathematical formulas that add nothing new to that which Sun Tzu and Clausewitz had stated long before.

Liddell Hart summarizes his opinion of Clausewitz thus:

> The theory of human mass dominated the military mind from Waterloo to the World War. This monster was the child of the French Revolution by Napoleon. The midwife who brought it into the military world was the Prussian philosopher of war, Clausewitz, cloudily profound. He unfortunately died while his own thought was still fermenting – leaving his papers in sealed packets, with a significant note: 'Should this work be interrupted by my death, then what is found can only be called a mass of formless conceptions . . . open to endless misconceptions.' So they proved.
>
> (B. H. Liddell Hart, *Thoughts On War* (London: Faber & Faber, 1944), p. 33)

On Liddell Hart's misinterpretation of Clausewitz see, for example, Huntington, *The Soldier and the State*, pp. 55–58; Jay Luvaas, 'Clausewitz, Fuller and Liddell Hart', in Handel (ed.), *Clausewitz and Modern Strategy*, pp. 197–212; Christopher Bassford, 'John Keegan and the Grand Tradition of Trashing Clausewitz: A Polemic', *War in History*, 1, No. 3, 1994, pp. 319–336.

14. Although Clausewitz views the destruction of the enemy's forces in battle as the

quickest, most effective method of achieving a state's political objectives in war, he does *not* see this destruction only in physical terms but also – and with equal emphasis – *in moral terms*! For his definition of the 'principle of destruction' and his discussion of the destruction of the enemy's forces '**as the superior, more effective means with which others cannot compete**', see *On War*, p. 97, and Book 4, 'The Engagement', Chapters 3–5 and 11, pp. 227–237, 258–262 as well as p. 529.

On the surface, it appears that Clausewitz's stress on the 'principle of destruction' as the key to victory is the opposite of Sun Tzu's emphasis on winning without fighting and on minimizing violence. I do not, however, believe that this is the case. Sun Tzu would probably agree that once a state's political objectives cannot be achieved through non-violent means, Clausewitz's *principle of destruction* (i.e., the physical *and* moral destruction of the enemy's forces) makes sense because it would prevent the unnecessary prolongation of a war. Clausewitz's *principle of destruction* and his *principle of continuity* are in harmony with Sun Tzu's idea that once wars break out, they should be terminated as quickly as possible (see Chapter 13 above).

15. See Machiavelli, *Works: The Discourses*, Chapter 12, 'A prudent general lays every necessity for fighting on his own soldiers and takes it away from those of the enemy', p. 459.

16. The same type of idea can be found in Thucydides' *The History of the Peloponnesian War*:

> And we are wise, because we are educated with too little learning to despise the laws, and with too severe a self-control to disobey them, and we are brought up not to be too knowing in useless matters – such as the knowledge which can give a specious criticism of an enemy's plans in theory, but fails to assail them with equal success in practice – but are taught to consider that the schemes of our enemies are not dissimilar to our own, and that the freaks of chance are not determinable by calculation. In practice we always base our preparations against an enemy on the assumption that his plans are good; indeed, it is right to rest our hopes not on a belief in his blunders, but on the soundness of our provisions. Nor ought we to believe that there is much difference between man and man, but to think that the superiority lies with him who is reared in the severest school.
>
> (*The Landmark Thucydides: A Comprehensive Guide to the Peloponnesian War* (a newly revised edn of the R. Crawley trans.), ed. Robert B. Strassler (New York: Touchstone, 1996), Book 1, Section 84, p. 47)
> (hereafter cited as Thucydides, *The History of the Peloponnesian War*)

Jomini also remarks that '*military science rests upon principles which can never be safely violated in the presence of an active and skillful enemy . . .*' (Jomini, *The Art of War*, pp. 17–18).

Sun Tzu's relatively one-sided analysis of war has also been noted by Scott A. Boorman. 'This emphasis [on a one-sided, non-probabilistic analysis of war] leads to paradoxes when the text [*The Art of War*] grows more concrete in the later chapters; the fixed interpretations of enemy behaviors given there are likely to make a commander who literally followed them himself vulnerable to stratagem.' Scott A. Boorman, 'Deception in Chinese Strategy', Chapter 16 in William W. Whitson (ed.), *The Military and Political Power in China in the 1970s* (New York: Praeger 1972), pp. 313–337, 328.

17. Kierman, 'Phases and Modes of Combat in Early China', in Fairbank and Kierman, *Chinese Ways in Warfare*, p. 65.

18. Clausewitz, *On War*, pp. 96–99, 218–219, 265, 313, 592–593.

19. Clausewitz recognizes yet another possibility of achieving a bloodless victory. Such a victory can be attained when the attacker overextends himself against a weaker, retreating opponent who chooses a Fabian strategy of deliberately avoiding battle.

> **All campaigns that are known for their so-called temporizing, like those of the famous Fabius Cunctator, were calculated primarily to destroy the enemy by making him exhaust himself.** [Such a strategy leads the attacker to] . . . **be worn out largely by his own efforts** . . . [The attacker will perish by] . . . **his own exertions.**
>
> (Clausewitz, *On War*, p. 385)

20. Lenin thought that Clausewitz's analysis on the defender's role in deciding the outbreak of a war was very clever. See Donald E. Davis and Walter S. G. Kohn, 'Lenin's "Notebook on Clausewitz"', in David R. Jones, ed., *Soviet Armed Forces Review Annual*, vol. 1, 1977 (Gulf Breeze, FL: Academic International Press, 1997), p. 200.

21. Clausewitz hated bombastic theories, pretentious military and academic writers, and those whom he referred to as 'pedants'. Unfortunately, such theories and writers are certainly as evident today as they were in the nineteenth century. The proliferation of word-processing and exchanges on the Internet will certainly not alleviate the problem. It is therefore worthwhile quoting Clausewitz at length on this matter, which he discusses at the end of Chapter 5 in Book 2 on Critical Analysis (pp. 168–169):

> **We therefore consider it essential that the language of criticism should have the same character as thinking must have in wars. Otherwise it loses its practical value and criticism would have contact with its subjects** . . . **We will thus avoid using an arcane and obscure language, and express ourselves in plain speech. The complex forms of cognition should be used as little as possible, and one should never use elaborate scientific guidelines as if they were a kind of truth machine** . . . **However, this pious aspiration, if we may call it that, has rarely prevailed in critical studies; on the contrary, a kind of vanity has impelled most of them to an ostentatious exhibition of ideas. The first common error is an awkward and quite impermissible use of certain narrow systems of formal bodies of laws. It is never difficult to demonstrate the one-sidedness of such systems** . . .
>
> **A** . . . **far more serious menace is the retinue of jargon, technicalities, and metaphors that attends these systems. They swarm everywhere – a lawless rabble of camp followers. . . Mere technical expressions and metaphors – are sometimes nothing more than ornamental flourishes of the critical narrative.**

Thus it has come about that our theoretical and critical literature, instead of giving plain, straightforward arguments, in which the author at least always knows what he saying and the reader what he is reading, is crammed with jargon, ending at obscure crossroads where the author loses his readers. Sometimes these books are even worse: they are just hollow shells. The author himself no longer knows just what he is thinking and soothes himself with obscure ideas which would not satisfy him if expressed in plain speech.

Critics have yet a third failing: showing off their erudition and misuse of historical examples. . . . A fact that is cited in passing may be used to support *the most contradictory views*; and three or four examples from distant times and places, dragged and piled up from the widest range of circumstances, tend to distract and confuse one's judgment without proving anything. The light of day usually reveals them to be mere trash, with which the author intends to show off his learning. What is the practical value of these obscure, partially false, confused and arbitrary notions? Very little – so little that they have made theory, from its beginnings, the very opposite of practice, and not infrequently the laughing-stock of men whose military competence is beyond dispute.

This could never have happened if by means of simple terms and straightforward observation of the conduct of war, theory had sought to determine all that was determinable; if, without spurious claims, with no unseemly display of scientific formulae and historical compendia, it had stuck to the point and never parted company with those who have to manage things in battle by the light of their native wit.

(Clausewitz, *On War*, pp. 168–169)

Clausewitz's insistence on common sense and clear language will surely ring true for every reader who has despaired of such obfuscation in some modern theories of war.

22. The last quotations from Clausewitz stand as a warning against overreliance on the indirect approach and the use of stratagem and deception as a panacea in war. After every successful indirect approach and surprise achieved through stratagem and deception, there is still the need for hard fighting.

23. Machiavelli makes a similar statement: 'A general cannot avoid a battle when the enemy is resolved upon it at all hazards' (Machiavelli, *The Discourses*, pp. 443–448).

24. In fact, Clausewitz makes an earlier reference to this important observation on the first page of *On War* where he states:

If one side uses force without compunction, undeterred by the bloodshed it involves, while the other side refrains, the first will gain the upper hand. That side will force the other to follow suit; each will drive its opponent toward the extreme, and the only limiting factors are the counterpoises inherent in war.

(Clausewitz, *On War*, pp. 75–76)

Clausewitz then returns to an in-depth examination of this subject at the end of Chapter 2 of Book 1, pp. 96–100.

25. Machiavelli reaches very similar conclusions:

> When these lazy princes and effeminate republics send out one of their generals, the wisest command they think they can give him is that he shall by no means come to battle, but rather above everything else, shall refrain from combat. Yet though they believe that in this they imitate the prudence of Fabius Maximus, who, by deferring combat, saved their state for the Romans, they do not understand that in most instances their command is worthless or damaging. We have to accept this conclusion: a general who decides to remain in the field cannot escape battle whenever his adversary intends to engage in it no matter what. So an order not to fight amounts to saying: 'Fight the battle when the enemy wishes to, not when you do'.
>
> (Machiavelli, *Works: Discourses*, pp. 454–455)

26. Mao Tse-tung's definition of war echoes that of Clausewitz: '. . . the elementary object of war as "politics with bloodshed", as mutual slaughter by opposing armies' (Mao Tse-tung, *Selected Military Writings*, pp. 229–230). The sentence goes on in words similar to those used by Clausewitz. The object of war is specifically 'to preserve oneself and destroy the enemy' (to destroy the enemy means to disarm him or 'deprive him of the power to resist', and does not mean to destroy every member of his forces physically, *ibid.*, pp. 230–231).

CHAPTER 12: SPEED, NUMERICAL SUPERIORITY, AND VICTORY

1. The first principle mentioned in this context is to identify the enemy's *center of gravity* and to concentrate all one's forces against it. Both principles are the most important element in preparing a plan of war designed for the total defeat of the enemy (see Clausewitz, *On War*, pp. 617–637).

2. For similar ideas, see Machiavelli, *Discourses*, p. 342:

> The first of all was to make their [the Romans'] wars, as the French say, short and big. Coming into the field with large armies, they finished in a very short time their war with the Latins, Sammites, and Tuscans.

3. Jomini reaches the same conclusion: '. . . *the art of war consists of bringing into action upon the decisive point of the theater of operations the greatest possible force . . .*' (Jomini, *The Art of War*, p. 114).

   Mahan's entire theory of naval warfare rests on the same premise – that of maximum concentration. Max von Hoffmann, one of the most successful practitioners of the art of war in the twentieth century, reaches the same conclusion '. . . One of the chief principles of military science is that in a decisive action one can never be strong enough.' Von Hoffmann, *The War of Lost Opportunities* (New York: International Publishers, 1925), p. 61.

4. See also Jomini, *Grand Military Operations*, p. 457.
5. Machiavelli, who is as interested in deception as Sun Tzu, also devotes consider-able attention to finding ways of dividing the enemy's strength. Much of what he has to say about deception is directed to accomplishing this end (see in particular Book 6 of *The Art of War*): 'A general ought to strive with all his skill to divide the forces of the enemy, either by making him suspicious of men in whom he trusts, or by giving him some cause for dividing his forces and in that way become weaker . . . there is no more certain way to divide hostile soldiers than to have the country of part of them attacked, so that they abandon the war to go to defend it' (*The Art of War*, p. 697). (See note 4, Chapter 15, pp. 421–423 below.)
6. See Michael I. Handel (ed.), *Strategic and Operational Deception in the Second World War* (London: Cass, 1987), pp. 1–91.
7. For an illuminating discussion on the relationship between the offense and defense in Clausewitz's *On War*, see Lieut.-General von Caemmerer, *The Development of Strategical Science during the Nineteenth Century*, pp. 28–50.
8. These quotations from Clausewitz refute Liddell Hart's assertion that Clausewitz overemphasized the importance of numerical superiority and the superior concen-tration of force.

   Jomini agrees with both Sun Tzu and Clausewitz on this point: '*Experience has constantly proved that a mere multitude of brave men armed to the teeth make neither a good army nor a national defense*' (Jomini, *The Art of War*, p. 40).

   Thucydides addresses the question of numerical superiority in Phormio's eloquent speech to the Athenian sailors before the naval battle of Naupactus (429 BC). These sailors, who are about to face a numerically superior Peloponnesian fleet, are told that courage, motivation, skill, experience and morale are all more important factors than numerical superiority (Thucydides, *The History of the Peloponnesian War*, Book 2, Sections 88–89, pp. 145–146).

   In *The Art of War*, Machiavelli also emphasizes that 'the *virtu* of our soldiers is of more consequence than their numbers' (Machiavelli, *The Art of War*, p. 203).

CHAPTER 13: THE PRINCIPLE OF CONTINUITY AND THE CULMINATING POINT OF VICTORY: THE CONTRADICTORY NATURE OF WAR

1. See Brigadier-General Reginald Clare Hart, *Reflections on the Art of War* (London: William Clowes & Sons, 1897), second edition, pp. 191–201; also Baron Colmar von der Goltz, *The Nation in Arms*, pp. 362–374.
2. See Robert Rhodes James, *Gallipoli* (London: Batsford, 1965); and Brig.-General C. F. Aspinall-Oglander, *Gallipoli*, 4 vols. (London: William Heinemann 1929–32).
3. On this, see Delbrück, *History of the Art of War*, vol. 1, *Antiquity*, pp. 337–338.
4. *Ibid.*, p. 337.
5. Machiavelli, *Discourses*, 2.27 on p. 402, and 2.30 on p. 411.

6. *On War*, pp. 379, 385.
7. Clausewitz, *On War*, p. 83.
8. *On War*, p. 83. See also Book 6 on 'The Defense', in particular Chapters 1–8, pp. 357–389; and Book 7 on 'The Attack', in particular Chapters 1–5, pp. 523–528.
9. See also *On War*, p. 370.
10. See *On War*, pp. 83–84 and pp. 217–218.
11. Especially in modern times, the inherent advantage of the defense – or its force multiplying effect – is often an unknown quantity that varies according to changes in terrain, the development of new weapons technologies, and so on. Estimating the relative strength of the defense to the offense before the outbreak of a war is now even more difficult than in Clausewitz's time. The best example of this was the inability of all armies in Europe before the First World War to assess properly the greatly increased strength of the defense. See, for example, Jack Snyder, *The Ideology of the Offensive: Military Decision Making and the Disasters of 1914* (Ithaca: Cornell University Press, 1984).
12. 'In the absolute form of war, where everything results from *necessary causes and one action rapidly affects another, there is, if we may use the phrase, no intervening neutral void*' (Clausewitz, *On War*, p. 582).
13. For a detailed look at the consequences of forgetting the principle of continuity in the Korean War, see David Rees, *Korea: The Limited War*, and Bernard Brodie, *War and Politics* (New York: Macmillan, 1973), Chapter 3, pp. 57–112.
14. Pierre Renouvin (trans. R. I. Hall), *War and Aftermath* (New York: Harper and Row, 1968) pp. 105–114; Martin Kitchen, *The Silent Dictatorship* (New York: Holmes and Meier, 1976) pp. 247–271; John Wheeler-Bennett, *Hindenburg: The Wooden Titan* (New York: Macmillan, 1967); Harry Rudin, *Armistice 1918* (New Haven, CT: Yale University Press 1944).
15. *On War*, Book 7, 'The Attack', Chapters 4–5, pp. 527–528; and Chapter 22, pp. 566–573.
16. On the transition from guerrilla warfare (or mobile warfare, as Mao refers to it), see Chapter 8, 'Problems of Strategy in Guerrilla War', in *Selected Military Writings*, pp. 181–183.

CHAPTER 14: CLAUSEWITZ ON WAR TERMINATION

1. In the first chapter of *The Strategy of Conflict*, Thomas C. Schelling discusses the importance of recognizing common interests in war:

> In taking conflict for granted, and working with an image of participants who try to 'win,' a theory of strategy does not deny that there are common as well as conflicting interests among the participants. In fact, the richness of the subject arises from the fact that, in international affairs, there is mutual dependence as well as opposition. Pure conflict, in which the interests of two antagonists are completely opposed, is a special case: it would arise in a war of complete

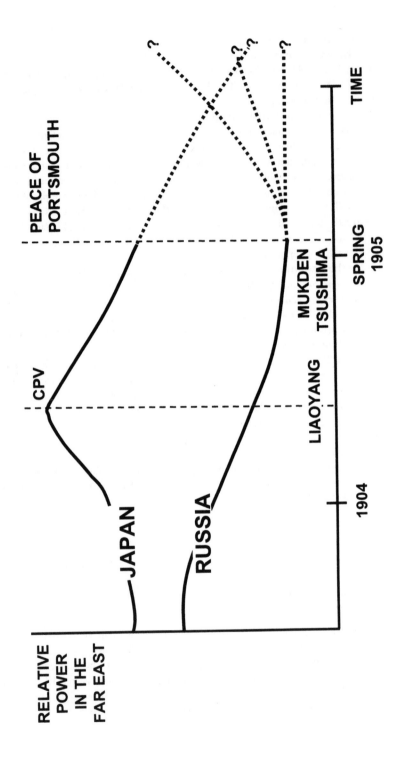

FIGURE 14.5
WAR TERMINATION IN THE RUSSO-JAPANESE WAR

extermination, otherwise not even in war. For this reason, 'winning' in a conflict does not have a strictly competitive meaning; it is not winning relative to one's adversary. It means gaining relative to one's own value system; and this may be done by bargaining, by mutual accommodation, and by the avoidance of mutually damaging behavior. If war to the finish has become inevitable, there is nothing left but pure conflict; but if there is any possibility of avoiding a mutually damaging war, if conducting warfare in a way that minimizes damage, or of coercing an adversary by threatening war rather than waging it, the possibility of mutual accommodation is as important and dramatic as the element of conflict. Concepts like deterrence, limited war, and disarmament, as well as negotiation, are concerned with the common interest and mutual dependence that can exist between participants in a conflict.

(Thomas C. Schelling, *The Strategy of Conflict* (Cambridge, MA: Harvard University Press, 1976), pp. 4–5)

2. As described in the epigraph to Churchill's six-volume *History of the Second World War*, magnanimity and good will are part of the lesson to be learned. It is interesting to note that two of the four morals distilled from Churchill's lifetime experience have to do with war termination and represent perhaps the most important lesson of the First and Second World Wars. Machiavelli quotes Scipio in a telling observation resembling Churchill's 'moral': 'The Romans, if they are defeated, are not depressed in spirit, nor, if they conquer, do they grow arrogant' (Machiavelli, *The Discourses*, p. 499).

3. See Thucydides, *The History of the Peloponnesian War*, pp. 190–207. For a perceptive commentary, see W. Robert Connor, *Thucydides* (Princeton, NJ: Princeton University Press, 1985), pp. 79–91.

4. Napoleon's enemies in Spain and Russia were the great exception. They refused to negotiate even after they had been defeated and their territory occupied.

5. To the very end of the First World War, Ludendorff aspired to terminate the war through a decisive German victory as required by Clausewitz's theory of absolute war. As Ludendorff states in his memoirs, his aim was to concentrate '. . . all our resources . . . using them to the utmost in order to achieve peace on the battlefield as the very nature of war demands' (quoted in Azar Gat, *The Development of Military Thought: The Nineteenth Century* (Oxford: Oxford University Press, 1992), p. 109).

6. Japan at the end of the Russo-Japanese War (1904–05) and Germany toward the end of the First World War provide instructive lessons about two very different approaches to war termination.

By the time the Japanese had added the Battle of Mukden (summer 1905) to their unbroken string of important victories over Russia, they appeared poised to press on toward final victory. Yet this apparently strong position was achieved at such a high cost that the Battle of Mukden actually marked their culminating point of victory. At this juncture, the Japanese government and military realized that continuing the war would become increasingly difficult, given Japanese casualties and economic woes. Although clearly victorious on land and sea, the Japanese were

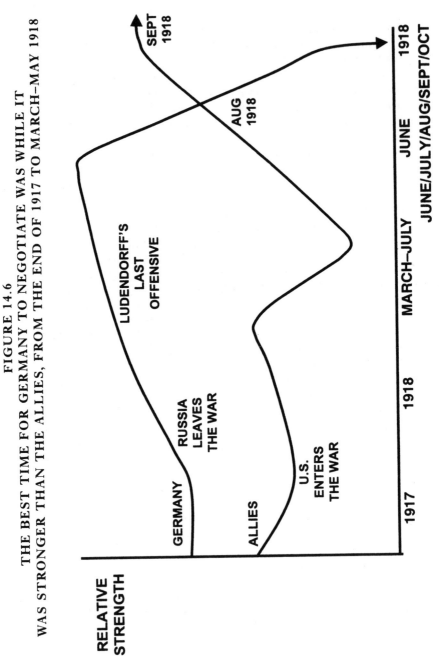

FIGURE 14.6

THE BEST TIME FOR GERMANY TO NEGOTIATE WAS WHILE IT
WAS STRONGER THAN THE ALLIES, FROM THE END OF 1917 TO MARCH–MAY 1918

concerned about the future power trends in the conflict: namely, that Russia would find it relatively easier to go on fighting and dramatically increase its war effort in the Far East. As a result, the Japanese decided to use the good offices of the United States to open peace negotiations with the Russian government while they still had the upper hand. The Japanese government *did* have to accept less than it had originally wanted, but nevertheless improved its overall territorial, political, and military position in the Far East. The concessions made by the Japanese government as part of its relatively moderate position provided sufficient incentive for the Russians to sign the Peace of Portsmouth (5 September 1905), despite their failure to defend their position and possessions in Manchuria and Korea.

The timing of the war termination process initiated by the Japanese in the late summer of 1905 provides a positive – even though unusual – example of exploiting victories on the battlefield while avoiding the long-term pitfalls of intoxication with success on the battlefield. Inasmuch as it took the possible negative consequences of continuing the war into account, the Japanese strategy of war termination appears in hindsight as a rare example of a wise policy of 'moderation' and enabled Japan to consolidate its gains in Manchuria and Korea.

The German General Staff decisions in late 1917–early 1918 provide an excellent example of the failure to consider the adverse consequences of continuing a war – though Germany appeared to be ahead militarily. By the end of 1917, the Germans had won the war in the east against Russia. The military collapse of Russia and the political turmoil it was experiencing (i.e., the Russian Revolution) allowed the German High Command to move considerable forces from the Eastern to the Western Front, where the Germans had achieved numerical superiority for the first time. The German defensive line (the Hindenburg Line) was in good shape, Allied tanks were not yet ready in sufficient numbers, and American troops had not yet appeared in numbers large enough to pose a serious threat. In other words, Germany was in a very strong position to initiate peace negotiations; but to do so meant that the Germans would have to make the Allies a generous offer that included relinquishing most, if not all, of their territorial objectives. This they were not prepared to do. Instead, the Germans never stopped insisting that Poland and Belgium belonged within the German sphere of influence.

Rather than trying to initiate peace negotiations, the German High Command under Ludendorff and Hindenburg (the so-called 'silent dictatorship') decided to use the forces released from the east to launch a highly risky final attack in the west. Although this all-or-nothing move at first achieved a number of major operational successes (March–May 1918) in the west, it gradually lost momentum. After extending further and further past the culminating point of victory, the attack had collapsed under the Allied counter-blows by late summer 1918. Following the Allied breakthrough on the Bulgarian front and the resulting armistice with Bulgaria, the German High Command lost its will to continue fighting and at that point wanted to bring the war to a quick conclusion. Within half a year, the Germans had fallen from a superior military position in the west into a state of utter despair. By the time the military situation had *forced* the Germans to negotiate, they had no bargaining chips left. Thus, Germany's unwillingness to make any concessions to the Allies from late 1917 to early 1918 (while it still enjoyed an advantageous position), as well as its continuous search for purely military solutions, merely hastened its final defeat. The penalty for this lack of foresight was severe: the destruction of Wilhelmine Germany and the humiliating signing of the Versailles Treaty as dictated by the Allies. Unlike the Japanese in 1905, the Germans had to accept a war termination under the worst possible conditions because they did not begin negotiations while they were still ahead.

For the Russo-Japanese War see: David Walder, *The Short Victorious War: The Russo-Japanese Conflict 1904–5* (London: Hutchinson, 1973); Dennis and Peggy Warner, *The Tide at Sunrise: A History of the Russo-Japanese War 1904–1905* (New York: Charterhouse, 1974); Raymond A. Esthus, *Double Eagle and Rising Sun: The Russians and the Japanese at Portsmouth in 1905* (Durham, NC: Duke University Press, 1988); Eugene P. Trani, *The Treaty of Portsmouth* (Lexington: University of Kentucky Press, 1969); Shumpei Okamoto, *The Japanese Oligarchy and the Russo-Japanese War* (New York: Columbia University Press, 1970). For Germany in 1918, see: Harry R. Rudin, *Armistice 1918* (New Haven, CT: Yale University Press, 1944); Martin Kitchen, *The Silent Dictatorship* (New York: Holmes and Meier, 1976); Fritz Fischer, *Germany's War Aims in the First World War* (New York: W. W. Norton, 1967); John W. Wheeler-Bennett, *The Forgotten Peace: Brest-Litovsk, March 1918* (New York: William Morrow, 1939); Alan Palmer, *Victory 1918* (London: Weidenfeld and Nicolson, 1998).

7. See Paul Pillar, *Negotiating Peace: War Termination as a Bargaining Process* (Princeton, NJ: Princeton University Press, 1983), particularly pp. 53–58; also Michael I. Handel, 'The Problem of War Termination', in *War, Strategy and Intelligence* (London: Cass, 1989), pp. 455–485; in particular, pp. 470–481.

A word is in place on correlating the culminating point of victory and the optimal point of war termination. The graphic analysis of these two points is essentially the same, since they both concern the estimation of current and future power trends of adversaries in war. In the case of the culminating point of victory, the question is, how does the attacker recognize the point at which the waning strength of the attack requires him to make the transition from the offense to the defense? With the correct timing, the erstwhile attacker can switch over to the defense while he is still strong enough to maintain and consolidate his gains. At the same time, the former defender becomes stronger and moves over to the attack, possibly retaking that which he had lost earlier in the war.

Identifying the optimum point of war termination poses a similar problem: How does one make the transition from war to peace while preserving the gains made until that point? Should the transition from war to peace be delayed, the previously stronger or more successful side might find itself in a weaker bargaining position because the formerly weaker enemy, possibly backed by new allies, has become a force to be reckoned with on the battlefield.

Identification of either the culminating point of victory or the optimum point of war termination is, in any case, a formidable task. It requires an accurate understanding of a complex and dynamic situation and the projection of trends into an uncertain future. Of the two, the culminating point of victory is a bit easier to

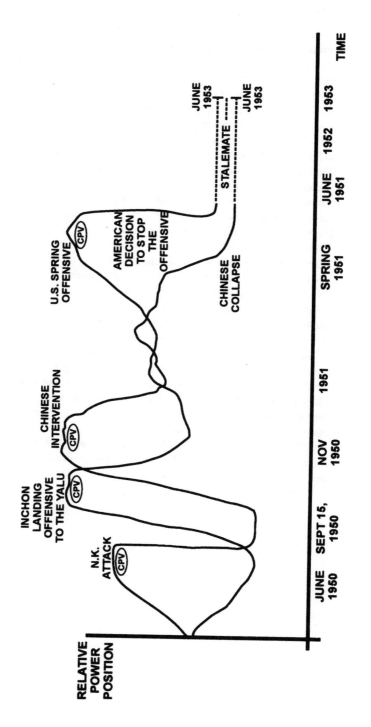

FIGURE 14.7

REVERSALS OF POWER ON THE KOREAN BATTLEFIELD (JUNE 1950–JUNE 1951) AND THE STALEMATE ON THE MAIN LINE OF RESISTANCE AFTER SUMMER 1941

ascertain because the transition from the offense to the defense is ultimately the attacker's decision alone. He can unilaterally halt his offensive without depending on a direct dialogue or negotiations with his opponent. By contrast, mutual co-operation is critical for war termination.

Another connection between these two types of problems is that correct identification of the culminating point of victory should also put the attacker in the strongest possible bargaining position vis-à-vis the defender. Logically speaking, this is the point at which he should make an offer to begin peace negotiations. But as we have seen, the situation is not as simple as it first seems because the attacker might be oblivious to the slowing momentum of his attack. If he suffers from the 'victory disease', his unjustified confidence will propel him well beyond the culminating point of victory into a possibly perilous situation. At best he will forfeit the gains that he once thought secure; at worst he will suffer ignominious defeat. On the other hand, even if the attacker stops at the culminating point of victory, the weaker side will be reluctant to enter into negotiations from his disadvantageous position. He will therefore prefer to wait for outside help or for some other development that will bring him success on the battlefield. In this type of situation, both sides could pass through several 'cycles' of victory and defeat, or offense and defense, without being able to identify the best timing for peace negotiations. In the Korean War, for example, the North Koreans won the initial phase of the war when, between June and September, they occupied most of Korea. They did, however, extend themselves beyond their culminating point of victory, a fact that became evident with the success of MacArthur's landing at Inchon. MacArthur then marched to the Yalu until he overshot his culminating point of victory when the Chinese intervened in November 1950. The Chinese counter-attack carried them once again beyond Seoul and their culminating point of victory. Finally, Ridgeway's counter-attack in the winter and spring of 1951 pushed the Chinese north of the 38th Parallel. At this point, with the Chinese defeated and the United States careful not to go once again beyond the culminating point of victory, both sides were finally ready to negotiate (see Figure 14.7).

CHAPTER 15: DECEPTION, SURPRISE, AND INTELLIGENCE

1. John Ferris and Michael I. Handel, 'Clausewitz, Intelligence and Uncertainty in the Art of Command and Military Operations', *Intelligence and National Security*, vol. 10, no. 1 (January 1995), pp. 1–58.
2. This is precisely Machiavelli's idea of deception. See Machiavelli, *Works, The Art of War*, 'How to distract the enemy and divide his forces', pp. 696–698.
3. On the Chinese attitude to deception see Howard L. Boorman and Scott A. Boorman, 'Strategy and National Psychology in China', *The Annals*, vol. 370, (1967), pp. 143–155; and Scott A. Boorman, 'Deception in Chinese Strategy', in *The Military and Political Power in China in the 1970s*, ed. W. W. Whitson (New York: Praeger, 1972), pp. 313–337.
4. Machiavelli, in his extensive, sophisticated discussion of wartime deception, emphasizes its importance no less than Sun Tzu. Machiavelli distinguishes between *private morality* – the ethics of individual behavior – and *raison d'état* – the morality of public responsibility in acting for the good of the state.

> Although to use fraud in all one's actions is detestable, nevertheless in carrying on war it is praiseworthy and brings fame: he who conquers the enemy by fraud is praised as much as he who conquers them by force.
>
> (Machiavelli, *Discourses* 3.40, p. 518)

> No expedient whatever for saving . . . [the] country [is] to be rejected . . . When it is absolutely a question of the safety of one's country, there must be no consideration of just or unjust, merciful or cruel, of praiseworthy or disgraceful; instead, setting aside every scruple, one must follow to the utmost any plan that will save her life and keep her liberty.
>
> (Machiavelli, *Discourses*, 3.41, p. 519)

Thus, for Machiavelli as for Sun Tzu (though not Clausewitz), deception is one of the most important requirements for success in war: '. . . a prince who wishes to do great things must learn to deceive.' Great leaders like Cyrus come to power by the judicious use of deception, not by the use of force. Machiavelli makes the cynical observation that no

> – man originally placed in humble fortune has come to great authority only by open force and honesty, but I firmly believe they have done it by fraud alone . . . [While] force alone will [never] be enough . . . fraud alone certainly will be enough.
>
> (Machiavelli, *Discourses*, 2.13, p. 357)

In his discussion of deception and stratagem in *The Prince*, *The Discourses*, and *The Art of War*, Machiavelli outlines how the use of deception is intended to facilitate the achievement of surprise. He considers surprise to be a key element for success, an element that shortens a war's duration while avoiding unnecessary attrition and costs. (Machiavelli, *The Art of War*, pp. 653–654, 673–674, p. 712).

Deception for Machiavelli, as for Sun Tzu, is above all a method for causing the enemy to disperse, to divert his troops. Preventing the enemy from concentrating his forces thus assists one's commander in marshalling superior strength against his opponent at the decisive point. (See, for example, Machiavelli, *The Art of War*, pp. 696–697, 650–651; and throughout *The Discourses* and *The Prince* as well.)

More specifically, Machiavelli stresses the use of *acclimatization* (i.e., conditioning the enemy to a certain repetitive pattern of behavior that one changes at the critical moment). Conversely, he warns the commander not to base his own plans and expectations on his enemy's repetitive behavior (see Machiavelli, *The Art of War*, pp. 700, 712, and throughout).

Like Sun Tzu, he also frequently discusses the use of agents and double agents. When a spy is caught, he argues, it is best not to expose him or execute him but rather to exploit the opportunity to use him as a channel for passing deceptive information to the enemy (as in the British double-cross system of the Second World War). Machiavelli explains:

> When you suspect that there is in your army someone who keeps your enemy informed of your plans, you cannot do better, if you wish to profit from his evil intention, than to inform him about things you do not intend to do, but about things that you do intend to do, you will keep him silent, and you will say that you fear things that you do not fear, and those that you do fear you will conceal. This will lead the enemy, in the belief that he knows your plans, to undertake various actions in which you can easily deceive and defeat him.
>
> (Machiavelli, *The Art of War*, p. 695)

Machiavelli also echoes Sun Tzu in his advice on how to counter deception; but, as the case always is, such suggestions are not of much help (see Machiavelli *Discourses*, 3.48, pp. 526–527; Machiavelli, *The Art of War*, 712–713).

Although Sun Tzu and Machiavelli certainly have nothing in common in terms of culture or historical periods, their emphasis on the role of deception in war transcends all.

Machiavelli resembles Sun Tzu in the considerable amount of attention he devotes to the problem of avoiding deception as well as in the fact that his advice is only generally helpful.

> [As to the second case], that of being drawn into one [a trap or ambush] . . . you must be shrewd about not believing easily things not in accord with reason. For example, if the enemy puts some booty before you, you ought to believe that within it there is a hook and that it conceals some trick. If many of the enemy are put to flight by your few, if a few of the enemy assail your many, if the enemy turn in sudden flight, and one not reasonable – invariably . . . you ought to fear a trick. And you should never believe that the enemy does not know how to carry on his affairs; rather, if you hope to be less deceived . . . and . . . run less risk, in proportion as your enemy is weaker, in proportion as he is less cautious, you should the more respect him.
>
> (Machiavelli, *The Art of War*, trans. Allan Gilbert, vol. 2, pp. 673–674;
> also pp. 712–714)

Like that of Sun Tzu, Machiavelli's faith in the value of deception stands in contrast to some of his other insights. For example, in his general rules of warfare, which are presented as a set of military aphorisms, he gives this advice: 'In war the power to recognize your chance and take it is of more use than anything else' (Machiavelli, *The Art of War*, p. 718). But how should a commander in the heat of battle know whether what appears to be an opportunity actually offers a chance for victory or is just part of the enemy's attempt to deceive him? Should one heed Machiavelli's caveat that a situation which looks too good to be true probably is, or should one follow his advice to take calculated risks and exploit fleeting opportunities? Even the best theory cannot provide an answer to this dilemma.

5. These are some of the more useful works that can serve as an introduction to the study of deception:

Boorman, Scott A. 'Deception in Chinese Strategy'. In William W. Whitson, ed. *The Military and Political Power in China in the 1970's*, pp. 313–337. New York: Praeger, 1972.

Daniel, Donald C. and Herbig, Katherine, eds. *Strategic Military Deception*. New York: Pergamon Press, 1982.

Deception Research Program. *Misperception Literature Survey*. Princeton, NJ: Mathtech, Inc. and ORD/CIA Analytic Methodology Research Division, March 1979.

Deception Research Program. *Thoughts on the Cost-Effectiveness of Deception and Related Tactics in the Air War, 1939 to 1945*. Princeton, NJ: Mathtech, Inc. and ORD/CIA Analytic Methodology Research Division, March 1979

Gooch, John and Perlmutter, Amos, eds. *Military Deception and Strategic Surprise*. London: Cass, 1982. Also a special issue of the *Journal of Strategic Studies*, 5 March 1982.

Handel, Michael I., ed. *Military Deception in Peace and War*. Jerusalem: Papers on Peace Problems, The Leonard Davis Institute, The Hebrew University, 1985.

Handel, Michael I., ed. *Strategic and Operational Deception in the Second World War*. London: Cass, 1987.

Howard, Sir Michael. *British Intelligence in the Second World War*, vol. 5. *Strategic Deception*. London: HMSO, 1990.

Jones, R. V. 'Intelligence and Deception'. In R. Pfaltzgraff and Warren H. Milberg, eds. *Intelligence Policy and National Security*, pp. 3–22. London: Macmillan, 1981.

Jones, R. V. *Reflections On Intelligence*. London: Heinemann, 1989.

Masterman, J. C. *The Double-Cross System*. New Haven, CT: Yale University Press, 1972.

Montagu, Ewen. *The Man Who Never Was*. Philadephia, PA: J. B. Lippincott, 1954.

Mure, David. *Master of Deception*. London: William Kimber, 1980.

von Senger, Hans, ed. and trans. M. B. Gutitz. *The Book of Stratagems: Tactics for Triumph and Survival*. New York: Viking, 1991.

Sun Haichen, ed. and trans. *The Wiles of War: 36 Military Strategies From Ancient China*. Beijing: Beijing Foreign Languages Press, 1991.

Whaley, Barton. *Stratagem: Deception and Surprise in War*. Cambridge, MA: Center for International Studies, MIT, 1969.

6. In *The Discourses*, Machiavelli states:

> When an enemy seems to be making a great mistake, we should believe it hides a trick . . . It is fitting to observe here that the general of an army should put no faith in a mistake the enemy makes openly; it always hides some stratagem, since it is unreasonable for men to be so incautious. But often the desire for victory so blinds men's perceptions that they see nothing except what appears to their advantage.
>
> (Machiavelli, *Works: The Discourses*, p. 526)

On this type of advice Clausewitz comments:

> **The textbooks agree, of course, that we should only believe reliable intelligence and should never cease to be suspicious, but what is the use of such feeble maxims? They belong to that wisdom which for want of anything better scribblers of systems and compendia resort to when they run out of ideas.**
>
> (Clausewitz, *On War*, p. 117)

7. The difficulties inherent in correctly understanding the meaning of classical Chinese writings such as *The Art of War* are reflected in the widely varying translations of the title of Chapter 5. This title has been translated as *Energy* (Giles and Griffith); *Strategic Advantage* (Sawyer); *Combat Power* (Huang); *Force* (Cleary); *Organization* (Chen); *Formation* (Cheng Lin); and *Principles of Initiative* (Tang Zichang); *Directing* (Wing). Indeed, these titles seem to have little in common with each other.

8. For a succinct explanation of the *chi* and *cheng* maneuver, see also the Giles translation of the *Art of War*, pp. 34–35.

9. For a detailed discussion, see Michael I. Handel, *Strategic and Operational Deception in the Second World War* (London: Cass, 1987), pp. 1–91.

10. *Ibid.*

11. See Michael I. Handel (ed.), *Strategic and Operational Deception in the Second World War* (London: Cass, 1990), p. 1.

12. But in *Grand Military Operations*, Jomini notes the value of diversions as a means of inducing the enemy to disperse or divide his troops (Principle number five, p. 452). For a detailed criticism of Jomini's lack of appreciation of deception and surprise, see Basil H. Liddell Hart, *The Ghost of Napoleon* (London: Faber & Faber, 1993) pp. 105.

13. Frederick the Great quoted by Von der Goltz in *The Nation In Arms*, p. 198.

14. In contrast to the conclusions of Jomini and Clausewitz on this issue, modern literature on surprise stresses (1) the desirability of strategic and operational surprise and (2) the near-impossibility of avoiding it despite the tremendous sophistication of modern intelligence (and the far greater amount of resources invested to this end):

Betts, Richard K. *Surprise Attack*. Washington DC: The Brookings Institution, 1982.

Handel, Michael I. *War, Strategy and Intelligence*. London: Cass, 1989.

Kam, Ephraim. *Surprise Attack*. Cambridge, MA: Harvard University Press, 1988.

Wohlstetter, Roberta. *Pearl Harbor: Warning and Decision*. Stanford: Stanford University Press, 1962.

15. By this statement I do not mean that deception was unimportant in earlier periods of history. On the contrary, when, in earlier times, military organizations resembled one another more closely, deception actually played a relatively more important role; indeed, it was one of the few elements that could give one side the advantage. What I am arguing is that deception in the pre-technological era was mainly *improvised* on the tactical and lower operational levels and that it was much more difficult to implement on the higher operational and strategic levels. There are, to be sure, excellent examples of successful deception operations (and the achievement of surprise) on the higher levels as well. During the Napoleonic Wars, with their emphasis on the importance of numerical superiority at the point of engagement and their obsession with the principle of quantity, deception was viewed with skepticism; and since the prevailing wisdom was that deception had little chance of success, using troops for diversionary operations was considered a waste when such troops (it was believed) could otherwise be used more profitably at the point of engagement. For a detailed discussion, see Michael I. Handel (ed.), *Strategic and Operational Deception in the Second World War* (London: Cass, 1987), Introductory essay; see also Michael I. Handel, 'Intelligence in Historical Perspective', in Keith Neilson and B. J. C. McKercher (eds.), *Go By The Land: Military Intelligence in History* (New York: Praeger, 1992).

16. See Michael I. Handel (ed.), *Intelligence and Military Operations* (London: Cass, 1990), pp. 13–15.

17. See Handel (ed.), *Strategic and Operational Deception in the Second World War*, pp. 1–92.

18. For an in-depth discussion of Clausewitz's evaluation of the role of intelligence, see Handel (ed.), *Intelligence and Military Operations*, Chapter 1; also Handel (ed.), *Clausewitz and Modern Strategy*, pp. 66–69. See also John Ferris and Michael I. Handel, 'Clausewitz, Intelligence, Uncertainty and the Art of Command in Military Operations', *Intelligence and National Security*, vol. 10, no. 1 (January 1995), pp. 1–58.

19. See Michael I. Handel (ed.), *Leaders and Intelligence* (London: Cass, 1989). Of all modern leaders, Winston S. Churchill – by virtue of his personal interest in, and his management and use of intelligence – comes closest to Sun Tzu's model of the ideal leader. See David Stafford, *Churchill and the Secret Service* (New York: Overlook Press, 1997).

20. *On War*, Book 1, Chapter 1, Section 13. For the paradoxical nature of war termination, see also Handel, *War, Strategy and Intelligence*, pp. 43–44.

21. In *Some Principles of Maritime Strategy*, Sir Julian Corbett expresses very similar ideas on the value of shapelessness, deception, concentration, and surprise in naval warfare (see also Chapter 18 above, pp. 281–282). Bismarck's diplomacy before the

wars against Denmark in 1864, Austria in 1867, and France in 1870 constitutes an excellent example of the secrecy that kept his immediate and longer-run aims shapeless. In each instance, Bismarck knew exactly why and when he needed a crisis to lead to war as well as the part to be played by each war in the progression toward his long-term objective (i.e., the unification of Germany under Prussia). For a long time, his opponents failed to perceive any pattern or clear direction in each of his wars – and by the time they did (1870–71), the balance of power had already changed. Bismarck's opponents either reluctantly supported him in each war or remained neutral. Had they been able to discern his long-range plans earlier, they would have been able to cooperate effectively to prevent him from achieving his goals.

22. See Handel (ed.), *Intelligence and Military Operations*, p. 59.

23. On the problems of perception (of which ethnocentrism is one) and of knowing oneself and the enemy, see Ken Booth, *Strategy and Ethnocentrism* (New York: Holmes and Meier, 1979); Robert Jervis, *The Logic of Images in International Relations* (Princeton, NJ: Princeton University Press, 1970); Robert Jervis, *Perception and Misperception in International Politics* (Princeton, NJ: Princeton University Press, 1976); Herbert Goldhamer (ed. Joan Goldhamer), *Reality and Belief in Military Affairs* (Santa Monica: The Rand Corporation, R-2448-NA, February 1979). See also John W. Dower, *War Without Mercy* (New York: Pantheon Books, 1986).

24. For a detailed look at Clausewitz's views on uncertainty as a dominant factor in war, see Handel (ed.), *Intelligence and Military Operations*, pp. 13–21.

In *The History of the Peloponnesian War*, Thucydides takes a position that is somewhere between those of Sun Tzu and Clausewitz. Like Clausewitz, he states that war is always unpredictable and that most plans are doomed to fall through in practice; but like Sun Tzu, he nevertheless believes that extensive, careful preparations for war can, to a point, mitigate the uncertainties encountered.

> The course of war cannot be foreseen, and its attacks are generally dictated by the impulse of the moment; and where overweening self-confidence has despised preparation, a wise apprehension has often been able to make headway against superior numbers.
>
> (Thucydides, *The History of the Peloponnesian War*, Book 2,
> Section 11, p. 97; see also the comments of Pericles in Book 1,
> Section 140, p. 80)

Chance, uncertainty, and the inability to control future events provide a powerful motive to seek peace while one has the advantage:

> Indeed, sensible men are prudent enough to treat their gains as precarious . . . and think that war, so far from staying within the limits to which a combatant may wish to confine it, will run the course that its chances prescribe; and thus, not being puffed up by confidence in military success, they are less likely to come to grief, and most ready to make peace. This, Athenians, you have a good opportunity to do now with us [the Spartans] and thus to escape the possible disasters

which may follow upon your refusal, and the consequent imputation of having owed to accident even your present advantage . . .

> (Thucydides, *The History of the Peloponnesian War*,
> Book 4, Section 18, p. 233)

But consider the vast influence of accident in war, before you are engaged in it. As it continues, it generally becomes an affair of chances, chances from which neither of us is exempt, and whose events we must risk in the dark.

> (Thucydides, *The History of the Peloponnesian War*,
> Book 1, Section 78, p. 44)

See also Lowell Edmund's *Chance and Intelligence in Thucydides* (Cambridge, MA: Harvard University Press, 1975).

Machiavelli also makes extensive reference to the idea of *Fortune*:

We are unable to change for two reasons: one, that we cannot counteract that to which nature inclines us; the other, that when with one way of doing a man has prospered greatly, he cannot be persuaded that he can profit by doing otherwise. That is why Fortune varies for the same man; she varies the times, but he does not vary his ways. This also brings about the ruin of cities, because republics do not vary their methods with the times . . . but they are slower, since it is more trouble for them to vary, because variation must result from times that agitate the entire state. To make the state vary, one man alone who varies his own mode of action is not enough.

> (Machiavelli, *Works: The Discourses*, vol. 1, p. 453)

[*Fortune shows her power when men are weak*]

We see, therefore . . . how much . . . present republics differ from ancient ones. We also see, for this reason, every day miraculous losses and miraculous gains. Because, where men have little ability, Fortune shows her power much, and because she is variable, republics and states often vary, and vary they always will until some one arises who is so great a lover of antiquity that he will rule Fortune in such a way that she will not have cause to show in every revolution of the sun how much she can do.

> (Machiavelli, *Works: The Discourses*, vol. 1, pp. 411–412)

[*Men can assist Fortune; they cannot thwart her*]

I assert . . . once more . . . according to what we see in all the histories, that men are able to assist Fortune but not to thwart her. They can weave her designs but cannot destroy them. They ought, then, never to give up as beaten, because, since they do not know her purpose and she goes through crooked and unknown roads, they can always hope, and hoping are not to give up, in whatever fortune and whatever affliction they may be.

> (Machiavelli, *Works: The Discourses*, vol. 1, p. 408. See also Chapter 25 in
> *The Prince*, 'Fortune's Power in Human Affairs and How She Can Be
> Forestalled', Machiavelli, *Works: The Prince*, vol. 1, pp. 89–92)

Field Marshal Lord Wavell depicts the role of uncertainty in war in these words:

War is a muddle; it is bound to be. There are so many incalculable accidents in this uncertain business – a turn of the weather that could not be foreseen, a message gone astray, a leader struck down at the critical moment – that it is very rarely that even the best laid plans go smoothly. The lesson is to realise and provide as far as possible against the uncertainties of war, but not to be discouraged if they happen; it is extraordinary how, if you carry on steadily with your job and use common sense, the worst-looking muddles will straighten themselves out.

(Wavell, *Speaking Generally* (London: Macmillan, 1946), p. 79)

In the works of Thucydides, Machiavelli, and Clausewitz, *chance*, *luck*, and *fortune* occupy an important, even central, role in explaining the unique nature of war. While none of these strategists eschews careful planning to the greatest possible extent, each recognizes the limits of rational calculations and control over events in war. In elaborating on such inevitable limitations, Clausewitz advances his concepts of *uncertainty*, *probability*, and *friction*.

Nevertheless, the role of friction and uncertainty in war – although always significant – began to diminish in modern wars with the advent of real-time communications, in which more reliable intelligence and information can be transmitted and received, as well as with the occurrence of wars that increasingly tap a nation's entire war potential. It has been said that when a successful officer was recommended to Napoleon for promotion to the rank of general, Napoleon always asked first if he was a lucky man. Today, the more pertinent questions would be: is he a good staff officer, can he work with others, will he be able to make rational decisions under pressure based on available information? Thus, although luck, fortune, and chance are still valuable concepts, their place in the theory of war is bound to decline relative to that of other explanations.

25. In his commentary on Sun Tzu, Mei Yao Ch'en makes the same type of observation: '*That which depends on me, I can do; that which depends on the enemy cannot be certain*' (Sun Tzu, *The Art of War*, p. 85).
26. Handel (ed.), *Intelligence and Military Operations*, pp. 15–21.
27. For Clausewitz's own perception of the level of analysis, see *On War*, p. 159, where he states: '**That which seems correct when looked at from one level may, when viewed from a higher one, appear objectionable.**'
28. Handel (ed.), *Intelligence and Military Operations*, pp. 40–49.
29. For Machiavelli, Fortune (especially if negative) can play a role comparable to that of friction or accident. Machiavelli certainly recognizes the role of friction or accident in war. 'Things new and sudden dismay armies . . .' (*The Art of War*, p. 719). 'It is better to overcome the enemy with hunger than with steel, for in victory with the latter Fortune is much more powerful than ability' (p. 718).
30. Handel (ed.), *Intelligence and Military Operations*, pp. 11–21.
31. *Ibid.*, pp. 20–21.

In *On War of To-Day*, Bernhardi has further elaborated on Clausewitz's idea that maintaining the initiative and creating uncertainty for the enemy is more important than the effort expended in obtaining notoriously unreliable intelligence:

There is only one means of making the decisions easier in all these elements of doubt, and to preserve unity of action: the will of using this means unswervingly must therefore constantly dominate a commander. It consists always, and under any circumstances, even after a defeat and in retreat, of *preserving the initiative and acting in compliance with the preponderance of one's own intentions* instead of submitting to those of the enemy. He who always tries to learn first what the enemy intends doing, in order to make up his mind, will always be dictated to by the opponent. Ever to remain active, ever to be undertaking something; never, without urgent necessity, to sit still and wait – that is what is required of a commander. But this injunction gains more particular significance under modern conditions. [emphasis in the original]

(Bernhardi, *On War of To-Day*, vol. 2, p. 343)

Indeed, Bernhardi may inadvertently encourage the attitude that intelligence is not all that important. Yet, at the same time, his comment ought to serve as a caveat for modern commanders who have come to expect too much from intelligence. In an age of abundant rather than scarce information, this warning can at least serve the cause of moderating unwarranted faith in its powers.

32. Handel (ed.), *Intelligence and Military Operations*, pp. 15–21.
33. Jomini, *Grand Military Operations*, pp. 452–453.

CHAPTER 16: ON MILITARY LEADERSHIP

1. Note the emphasis on self-control in Sun Tzu's text. Thucydides makes the following statement along the same lines:

For war of all things proceeds least upon definite rules, but draws principally upon itself for contrivances to meet an emergency; and in such cases the party who faces the struggle and keeps his temper best meets with most security, and he who loses his temper about it, with correspondent disaster.

(Thucydides, *The History of the Peloponnesian War*, Book 1, Section 122, p. 67)

2. Compare Clausewitz's characterization of the military genius' *coup d'oeil* with Thucydides' description of Themistocles:

For Themistocles was a man who exhibited the most indubitable signs of genius; indeed, in this particular he has a claim on our admiration quite extraordinary and unparalleled. By his own native capacity, alike unformed and unsupplemented by study, he was at once the best in those sudden crises which admit little or no deliberation . . . This extraordinary man must be allowed to have surpassed all others in the faculty of intuitively meeting an emergency.

(Thucydides, *The History of the Peloponnesian War*, Book 1, Section 138, p. 79)

3. In his essay on guerrilla warfare in the *Encyclopedia Britannica* (1926 edn), T. E. Lawrence presents a wonderful definition of the *coup d'oeil*: 'There is a "felt" element in troops, not expressible in figures, and the greatest commander is he

whose intuitions most nearly happen. Nine-tenths of tactics are certain, and taught in books: but the irrational tenth is like the kingfisher flashing across the pool and that is the test of generals. It can only be ensued by instinct, sharpened by thought practising the stroke so often that at the crisis it is as natural as a reflex' (p. 951). See also 'The Formation of a Revolt' (p. 115) in T. E. Lawrence, *Oriental Assembly* (London: Williams and Norgate, 1939).

4. Thucydides calls attention to the military genius's ability to exploit opportunities on the battlefield by sensing the spreading panic on the enemy's side:

> Let us not shrink from the risk, but let us remember that this is just the occasion for one of the baseless panics common in war; and that to be able to guard against these in one's own case, and to detect the moment when an attack will find an enemy at this disadvantage, is what makes a successful general.
>
> (Thucydides, *The History of the Peloponnesian War*, Book 3, Section 30, p. 172)

5. Some other works of interest on military leadership are:

Freytag-Loringhoven, Major-General Baron Hugo von. *The Power of Personality in War*. Harrisburg, PA: The Military Service Publishing Company, 1955.

Fuller, J. F. C. *Generalship: Its Diseases and Their Cure: A Study of the Personal Factor in Command*. London: Faber & Faber, 1933, and Harrisburg, PA: Military Service Publishing Co., 1936.

Goltz, Colmar von der. *The Nation in Arms*. London: Hugh Rees, 1913.

Hart, Brigadier-General R. C. *Reflections on the Art of War*. London: William Clowes, 1897; 2nd edition, Chapter 1, 'The High Qualifications of Great Generals', pp. 1–55.

Holland-Rose, J. H. 'The Prophetic Instinct in Nelson.' In J. H. Holland-Rose, *The Indecisiveness of Modern War*. London: S Bell, 1927.

Liddell Hart, B. H. *Greater than Napoleon: Scipio Africanus*. London: William Blackwood, 1930.

Montgomery, Field-Marshal. *The Path to Leadership*. London: Collins, 1964.

Moran, Lord D. *The Anatomy of Courage*. London: Constable, 1945.

The Kermit Roosevelt Lecture. Field-Marshal Sir William Slim, 'Higher Command in War'. U.S. Army Command and General Staff College, mimeo, no date.

Roskill, Captain S. W. *The Art of Leadership*. London: Collins, 1964. Includes a useful bibliography.

Wavell, Field Marshal Lord A. P. *Generals and Generalship*. The Lee Knowles Lectures, Cambridge, 1939. Harmondsworth: Penguin, 1941.

Wavell, Field Marshal Lord A. P. 'A Note on Command'. In Field Marshal Lord A. P. Wavell, *Speaking Generally*. London: Macmillan, 1946, pp. 74–77.

CHAPTER 17: BOLDNESS AND CALCULATION

1. Clausewitz, *Principles of War*, pp. 13–14.
2. Machiavelli, like Clausewitz, believes that fortune favors those who are impetuous and ready to take risks. See Machiavelli, *The Prince*, p. 92.
3. For a detailed analysis of this idea, see John Ferris and Michael I. Handel, 'Clausewitz, Intelligence, Uncertainty and the Art of Command in Military Operations', *Intelligence and National Security*, vol. 10, no. 1 (January 1995), pp. 1–58.
4. For a discussion of Clausewitz's alternating praise of audacity and prudence, see also R. Aron, 'Reason, Passion and Power in the Thought of Clausewitz', in *Social Research* (Winter 1972), pp. 599–621.

CHAPTER 18: CORBETT, CLAUSEWITZ, AND SUN TZU

1. I. B. Cohen, *The Newtonian Revolution* (Cambridge: Cambridge University Press, 1980), Chapter 4, pp. 157–221.
2. See, for example, Azar Gat, *The Development of Military Thought: The Nineteenth Century* (Oxford: Clarendon Press, 1992), p. 190; and Captain A. T. Mahan, *Naval Strategy Compared and Contrasted with the Principles and Practice of Military Operations on Land* (Boston, MA: Little, Brown, 1911), p. 17.
3. The first good English translation of Sun Tzu's *The Art of War*, by Lionel Giles, was published in 1910, while most of Corbett's ideas in *Some Principles of Maritime Strategy* (London: Longmans, 1911), had been developed much earlier. (See also 'The Green Pamphlet' of 1909 as reprinted in Julian S. Corbett, *Some Principles of Maritime Strategy*, ed. Eric J. Grove (Annapolis, MD: Naval Institute Press, 1988), pp. 305–345.
4. See D. M. Schurman, *The Education of a Navy* (London: Cassell, 1965), on Corbett's conclusions in *England in the Seven Years' War*, 2 vols. (London: Longmans, Green 1907), p. 168.
5. See Clausewitz, *On War*, pp. 88–89; and Corbett, *Some Principles* (paraphrasing Clausewitz), pp. 5–6; 17–18; 27–28; and Chapter 2, p. 31ff.
6. Schurman, *The Education of a Navy*, p. 164.
7. Although Clausewitz indeed emphasizes the importance of the decisive battle, all other things being equal, he also points (as does Corbett) to the great risks and costs involved and mentions alternative methods. However, when Clausewitz *does* emphasize the destruction of the enemy, he is not always referring to physical destruction alone but also to psychological and moral destruction as well. (See Clausewitz, *On War*, p. 97.)
8. This is Clausewitz's 'principle of continuity'. See Chapter 13 above.
9. See Donald M. Schurman, *Julian S. Corbett, 1854–1922* (London: Royal Historical Society, 1981), pp. 168–169; 194.
10. Schurman, *The Education of a Navy*, p. 174n (referring to Cyril Falls, *The Art of War* (London: Oxford University Press, 1961), p. 44).

11. In *On War*, Clausewitz recognizes a similar phenomenon on at least one major occasion. Napoleon concentrated such a formidable invasion force against Russia in 1812 that he caused the Russians to withdraw rather than fight. Had he concentrated a small, less obviously superior force at the outset, the Russians might have accepted battle on or close to the border, thus enabling Napoleon to win through superior generalship.

12. See Chapter 12 above; in particular, pp. 159–160.

13. See Michael I. Handel, ed., *Clausewitz and Modern Strategy* (London: Cass, 1986).

14. Schurman, *The Education of a Navy*, p. 161n.

15. In the conclusion of his study of the Russo-Japanese War (1904–05), Corbett notes that the Japanese navy never lost its offensive spirit despite its predominantly defensive role. His last sentence reads: 'It is here, then, if anywhere, in this enduring capacity to withstand the demoralizing influence of a prolonged defensive, that the Japanese showed upon the sea, at any rate, a distinctly higher genius for war than their enemy' (Julian S. Corbett, *Maritime Operations in the Russo-Japanese War, 1904–1905*, vol. 2 (Annapolis, MD: Naval Institute Press, 1994), p. 398).

16. Julian S. Corbett, *The Campaign of Trafalgar* (London: Longmans, 1910), p. 408.

17. For an excellent discussion, see Azar Gat, *The Origins of Military Thought from the Enlightenment to Clausewitz* (Oxford: Clarendon Press, 1989), pp. 217–226.

18. Clausewitz's analysis of limited war as defined by its *political objectives* (or national interests) on the one hand and by the available means (or limitation of resources) on the other, can be described by the matrix in Figure 18.2.

FIGURE 18.2
THE LIMITATION OF WAR ACCORDING TO POLITICAL OBJECTIVES AND THE SCALE OF THE MEANS USED

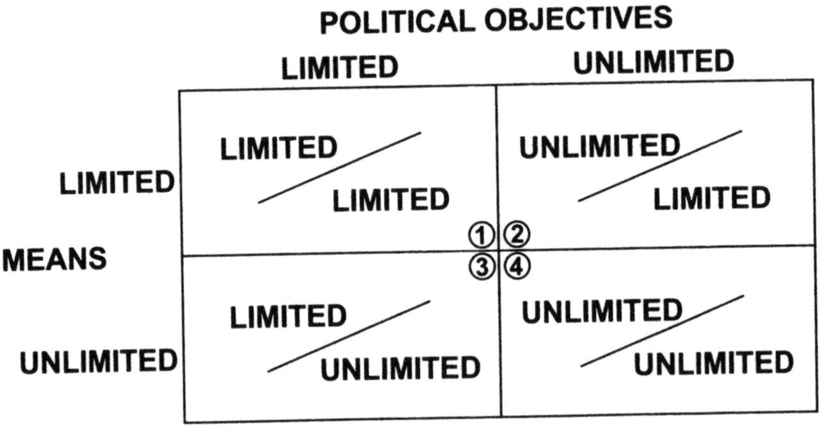

This matrix shows four possible combinations. The *first* (Box 1), which is limited in terms of both politics and resources, indicates that it does not involve any major interests and is fought either defensively or to gain some minor bargaining advantages. It follows, then, that only very limited means would be dedicated to its execution.

The *second* type of war (Box 2) although unlimited in its political objectives, is subject to the constraints imposed by limited resources. This could be a weaker state fighting for vital interests or a war on a particular front that is part of a larger unlimited war (e.g., Wellington's campaign in Spain, in which a limited British contingent fought for an unlimited objective – the overthrow of Napoleon and the restoration of the European balance of power).

The *third* type (Box 3) is limited by its political objectives. Although the war might involve the vital interests of one state, it does not involve the vital interests of the other. None of the belligerents intends to win a decisive/total victory. Yet, despite these limited political objectives, such a war can often involve the expenditure of unlimited resources. The Russo-Japanese War of 1904–05 and the Vietnam War are good examples. With its limited and well-defined political objectives, Japan did not intend nor expect to overthrow Russia, yet by the end of the war, Japan had nearly exhausted its human, financial, and material resources. In the Vietnam War, the United States never intended to overthrow North Vietnam, but ended up expending vast amounts of resources on the war effort anyway.

The *fourth* type (Box 4) represents the ideal of an unlimited or total war. This involves attaining unlimited objectives such as the overthrow of the enemy and the corresponding use of all available resources. Although this kind of war might be waged initially by one side alone, its nature would normally force all other participants to employ a similar strategy. Typical of Napoleonic strategy, this 'higher form' of war reached its most extreme manifestation in the First and Second World Wars. As Clausewitz points out, the frequently occurring transitions from one type of war to another reflect the reciprocal nature of war and the way in which one belligerent's decisions affect those of his opponent. While the decision to wage a limited war of one type or another would often require a tacit or explicit agreement by both sides, the escalation from a limited to an unlimited war can be dictated by one side alone.

19. For a direct discussion of limited war in *On War*, see: Note of 27 July 1827, pp. 69–71; Book 1, Chapter 1, pp. 87–88; Book 6, Chapter 30, pp. 501–521; Book 7, Chapter 16, pp. 548–550; and Book 8. The issue of limited war as limited by means is, by implication, discussed throughout the book. Corbett summarizes Clausewitz's theory of limited war in *Some Principles of Maritime Strategy*, pp. 41–51.

20. See Baron de Jomini, *The Art of War* (Westport, CT: Greenwood Press, 1977), pp. 361–390.

21. Clausewitz makes it clear that **'transitions from one type to the other** [i.e., from limited to unlimited war] **are likely'** (*On War*, Note of 27 July 1827, p. 69).

22. *'It follows that those skilled in war can make themselves invincible . . .'* (Sun Tzu, *The Art of War* (New York: Oxford University Press, 1963), p. 85 and Chapter 4 in general).

23. Gat, *The Development of Military Thought in the Nineteenth Century*, p. 218.

CHAPTER 19: CONCLUSIONS:
TOWARDS A UNIFIED THEORY OF WAR

1. The inclusion of Mao Tse-tung's theories in this edition confirms, if anything, the universal logic of the theory of war, which transcends culture, geography, and time. Although Mao is indisputably the product of Chinese culture and history, his theory of war resembles that of Clausewitz more than that of Sun Tzu. This is particularly true of his discussion of protracted war, which closely resembles Clausewitz's analysis of 'The People in Arms' (Chapter 26, Book 6 of *On War*) as well as his discussion of the primacy of politics in war, the nature of war, its theory and practice, and the study of war as a whole (as a *Gestalt*). Unlike Sun Tzu, and more like Clausewitz, Mao would have viewed 'shortcuts', such as trying to win a major war without fighting, as unrealistic.

Nevertheless, Mao *does* share Sun Tzu's belief that waging war according to carefully made, objective calculations while minimizing unnecessary risks brings the greatest success. Like Sun Tzu, Mao also puts much greater emphasis than Clausewitz on the reliability and importance of intelligence and deception. Consequently, Mao would agree with Sun Tzu that chance, friction, and luck play a less significant role in war than Clausewitz believed.

Thus, where Clausewitz emphasizes the importance of the creative military genius in war as the only solution for inaccurate intelligence and the uncertainties produced by friction, Sun Tzu and Mao place their confidence in the less rarefied solution of rational calculations based on reliable intelligence and meticulous planning. Indeed, Mao's theories were accepted around the world as an appealing strategic paradigm not because he was Chinese or a Marxist, but because they held universal appeal for those engaged in wars of the weak against the strong.

FIGURE 19.1
A COMPARISON OF CLAUSEWITZ AND MAO TSE-TUNG'S THEORIES OF WAR, ON A NUMBER OF KEY ISSUES

	MAO TSE-TUNG	CLAUSEWITZ
The primacy of politics	War is controlled and directed by the political authorities.	War is controlled and directed by the political authorities.
Understanding the nature of war	Developing and maintaining a correct understanding of the nature of war is a crucial process that calls for continuous adaptation of all strategic and operational plans. This is therefore an ongoing assessment that begins *before* the outbreak of the war and *continues* throughout its duration.	Understanding the nature of the war is the most important question that needs to be answered *before* the outbreak of war. (There is no explicit discussion of understanding of the nature of the war as an ongoing process.)
The study of war (war as a 'whole')	War can be understood only as a '*Gestalt*' – as a whole. It is both impossible and undesirable to examine factors influencing the course of war in *isolation* from each other and from the general political and social context.	War can only be studied as a whole. Factors/variables cannot analytically be separated from each other. Therefore war can never be waged or studied as an exact science.
Rational calculations	War should be waged on the basis of rational and accurate calculations ('scientific Marxist analysis'). This requires a detached *objective analysis*, which, if correctly performed, minimizes the possible role of chance and luck. Moreover, unnecessary risks should be avoided. (In this, Mao is close to Sun Tzu.)	Ideally war ought to be waged as rationally as possible – but in reality non-rational forces (e.g. human nature, chance, luck, and friction, the reciprocal nature of war, etc.) make it impossible to wage war as a purely rational activity, since calculations can only go so far. Taking creatively high-risk decisions defies linear rational calculations and poses unsolvable dilemmas to an opponent who expects rational behaviour.
The military genius	The military genius does *not* play an important role in Mao's military theory. The intuition of the military genius is replaced by rational calculations, staff work, and an objective analysis of the situation.	Since fully rational decisions are impossible in the real world and decisions must be made quickly on the basis of incomplete information, the intuition of the military genius plays a key role in Clausewitz's theoretical framework.

APPENDIX A: CONTRADICTION AND PARADOX IN THE THEORY OF WAR

1. For a general discussion of the paradoxical nature of the war termination process, see Michael I. Handel, *War, Strategy and Intelligence* (London: Cass, 1989), Chapter 9, pp. 455–484; and Paul R. Pillar, *Negotiating Peace: War Termination as a Bargaining Process* (Princeton, NJ: Princeton University Press, 1983). See also Fred Charles Ikle, *Every War Must End* (New York: Columbia University Press, 1971). Clausewitz addresses the problem of war termination in Book 1, Chapter 2, pp. 90–92 of *On War*. On Clausewitz and war termination, see also Paul Kecskemeti, *Strategic Surrender: The Politics of Victory and Defeat* (Stanford, CA: Stanford University Press, 1958); and Paul Kecskemeti, 'Political Rationality in Ending War', in an excellent collection edited by William T. R. Fox, *How Wars End, The Annals of the American Academy of Political and Social Science*, vol. 392, November 1970, pp. 105–115.) (See also Chapter 14 above.)
2. For a discussion of the paradoxical nature of war, see also Handel, *War, Strategy and Intelligence* (London: Cass, 1989), pp. 32–33 and Chapter 5. For a different approach, see Zeev Maoz, *Paradoxes of War* (Boston, MA: Unwin Hyman, 1990).

APPENDIX B: THE WEINBERGER DOCTRINE

1. The Weinberger Doctrine has been reprinted in many different publications and official documents. I used the full text as published in Weinberger, *Fighting for Peace: Seven Critical Years in the Pentagon* (New York: Warner Books, 1990), Appendix 'The Uses of Military Power,' text of remarks by Secretary of Defense Caspar W. Weinberger to the National Press Club, 28 November 1984, pp. 433–445. See also Weinberger, 'U.S. Defense Strategy', *Foreign Affairs* (Spring 1986), pp. 675–697.
2. On the Weinberger Doctrine and the war in Vietnam, see Eric P. Alterman, 'Thinking Twice: the Weinberger Doctrine and the Lessons of Vietnam', *The Fletcher Forum*, vol. 10 and 10.1, Winter 1986, pp. 93–109; 'Lessons from a Lost War', *Time* (15 April 1985), pp. 40–45; Paul Seabury, 'Taking Necessary Risks', in Ernest Lefever (ed.), *Ethics and American Power* (Washington, DC: Ethics and Public Policy Center, 1985), p. 44.
3. For Secretary of State Shultz's position see George P. Shultz, *Turmoil and Defeat: My Years as Secretary of State* (New York: Charles Scribner & Sons, 1993), pp. 645–651. Shultz's counter-statement to the Weinberger Doctrine was delivered on 9 December 1984 in a speech at Yeshiva University in New York.
4. Weinberger, *Fighting for Peace*, p. 151.
5. *Ibid.*, p. 159. See also p. 161.
6. *Ibid.*, pp. 151–152.
7. *Ibid.*, p. 152.
8. *Ibid.*, p. 147.

9. *Ibid.*, p. 138.
10. *Ibid.*, p. 437.
11. *Ibid.*, p. 437.
12. *Ibid.*, p. 437.
13. Sun Tzu, *The Art of War*, p. 142; Clausewitz, *On War*, p. 86.
14. *Ibid.*, p. 443.
15. Clausewitz, *On War*, pp. 204, 104.
16. Clausewitz, *On War*, p. 75.
17. Clausewitz, *On War*, p. 76.
18. 'Lessons from a Lost War', *Time*, April 15, 1985, p. 42.
19. Clausewitz, *On War*, p. 291.
20. Alterman, *Thinking Twice*, p. 99.
21. Clausewitz, *On War*, p. 193.
22. *Ibid.*, p. 91.
23. On the role of the people in *On War*, see in particular p. 89; and pp. 585–594.
24. Quoted in B. Adler, *The Churchill Wit* (New York: Coward-McCann, 1965), p. 59.
25. George P. Shultz, 'The Ethics of Power', in Lefever (ed.), *Ethics and American Power*, p. 15.
26. William Safire, *New York Times* (3 December 1984) p. A23.
27. Hempstones, 'The Weinberger–Shultz Debate is Beneficial', in Lefever (ed.), *Ethics and American Power*, p. 22.
28. Quoted in Thomas Molnar, 'Rules That Paralyze Action', in Lefever (ed.), *Ethics and American Power*, p. 30.
29. *Ibid.*, p. 30.
30. Quoted in 'Lessons From a Lost War', *Time* (15 April 1985), p. 42.
31. See Thomas R. Dubois, 'The Weinberger Doctrine and the Liberation of Kuwait', *Parameters* (Winter 1991–1992), pp. 24–38.
32. General Colin Powell, 'Why Generals Get Nervous', *The New York Times* (8 October 1992).
33. See 'U.S. is Showing a New Caution on UN Peacekeeping Missions', *New York Times* (18 May 1994), pp. 1, A6.
34. See Powell, 'Why Generals Get Nervous'.

APPENDIX C: CLAUSEWITZ'S IDEAL-TYPE METHOD APPLIED TO SUN TZU'S *THE ART OF WAR*

1. See also Raymond Aron, 'Clausewitz's Conceptual System', *Armed Forces and Society*, vol. 1, no. 1 (November 1974), pp. 49–59; and Raymond Aron, 'Reason, Passion and Power in the Thought of Clausewitz', *Social Research* (Winter 1972).
2. Clausewitz never recommended (despite John Keegan's assertions to the contrary) that war be pursued in its absolute form. 'He was struggling', Keegan argues, 'to advance a universal theory of what war *ought* to be, rather than what it actually was

and had been' (Keegan, *A History of Warfare* (New York: Alfred A. Knopf, 1993)), p. 6. Keegan continues:

> Could he but find the language to persuade the Prussian army that warfare was indeed a form of political activity, that the more nearly it could approximate to 'true war', the better it served a state's political ends and that any gap remaining between true war and the imperfect form of 'real war' should be recognized simply as the deference that strategy paid to political necessity . . .
>
> (Keegan, *A History of Warfare*, p. 17)

> Clausewitz argued by reduction that in war the worse the better, because the worse is nearer to 'true' rather than 'real' war.
>
> (Keegan, *A History of Warfare*, p. 17)

But Clausewitz never makes any such assertions – in fact, he argues the opposite, as this appendix shows. Keegan appears to confuse Clausewitz's methodology with a recommendation for waging a 'true', 'absolute' war. See also Christopher Bassford, 'John Keegan and the Grand Tradition of Trashing Clausewitz: A Polemic', *War in History*, vol. 1, no. 3 (November 1994), pp. 319–336.

3. Mao Tse-tung also describes the probabilistic nature of war: 'We admit that the phenomenon of war is more elusive and is characterized by greater uncertainty than any other social phenomenon; in other words, that it is more a matter of "probability" ' (Mao Tse-tung, *Selected Military Writings*, p. 238).

4. See the preface and introduction by Ralph D. Sawyer to *The Art of War* (New York: Barnes and Noble, 1994), pp. 13–162; A. I. Johnson, 'The Role of Violence in Traditional Chinese Strategic Thought' (unpublished mimeo); and Kierman, Jr., 'Phases and Modes of Combat in Early China', in Fairbank and Kierman (eds) *Chinese Ways in Warfare*. See also Bassford, 'John Keegan and the Grand Tradition of Trashing Clausewitz: A Polemic'.

5. For the *principle of destruction*, see *On War*, pp. 90–92; 96–97; 229–230; 236; 258; 526; 529; 560; 579; 595; 601.

> **The grand objective of all military action is to throw the enemy – which means destroying his armed forces. It was therefore possible to show . . . that battle is the one and only means that warfare can employ.**
>
> (Clausewitz, *On War*, p. 577)

> **[Destruction is] . . . reduction of the strength relatively larger than our own.**
>
> (Clausewitz, *On War*, p. 230)

> **The destruction of the enemy forces is always the superior, more effective means, with which others cannot compete.**
>
> (Clausewitz, *On War*, p. 97. See also Chapter 11 above.)

APPENDIX D: CLAUSEWITZ'S *ON WAR* AS A *GESTALT* OR A SYSTEMIC THEORY

1. The new shorter *Oxford Dictionary* defines *Gestalt* as 'An integrated perceptual structure of unity conceived as functionally more than the sum of its parts.' The Webster's *Third International Dictionary* defines *Gestalt* as 'A structure of configuration of physical, biological, or psychological phenomena so integrated as to constitute a functional unity with properties not derivable from its parts in summation.'

   A *system* is defined by the *Oxford Dictionary* as a 'group or set of related or associated material or immaterial things forming a unity or a complex whole'. Webster's defines a *system* as 'a complex unity formed of many often diverse parts subject to a common plan or serving a common purpose. An aggregation or assemblage of objects joined in a regular interaction or interdependence.'

   In both cases, a *Gestalt* or a system produces a new whole that is more than the sum of its parts. The difference between a *Gestalt* and a *system* is that it is easier to define and identify the parts of a system and predict their interaction. In this sense, the concept of a *Gestalt* is better suited for describing the nature of war than a system.

   Another related concept is that of *synergy*, which the Oxford Dictionary defines as '[a] combined or correlated action of a group of parts . . . A combined effect greater than the sum of their separate effects'. *Synergism* is defined as 'a combined activity of two drugs [or any other elements, units, factors, etc.] when this is greater than the sum of the effects of each one separately'. Webster's defines *synergy* simply as 'combined action or operation' and *synergism* as 'cooperative action of discrete agencies such that the total effect is greater than the sum of the two or more effects [than] taken independently'.

   A system, unlike a *Gestalt*, usually has well-defined borders and clear, predetermined connections between its parts. Having observed this distinction, Clausewitz states more than once that war cannot be compared to a mechanical system: '. . . **Friction cannot, as in mechanics, be reduced to a few points. [It] is everywhere in contact with chance, and brings about effect that cannot be measured'** (Clausewitz, *On War*, p. 120). Clausewitz also mentions the futility of unsuccessful attempts to **'transform formation and orders to battle into automata, designed to discharge their activity like pieces of clockwork set by a mere word of command'** (Clausewitz, *On War*, p. 133). He then criticizes many earlier theorists for trying to reduce war to 'systems'. This, he reasons, stems from their failure to see that **'war branches out in almost all directions and has no definite limits while any system, any model has the final nature of a synthesis . . . Mechanical and optical structures are not subject to dispute'** (Clausewitz, *On War*, pp. 134, 136). A *Gestalt*, on the other hand, more closely resembles war because it acknowledges the synergistic linkage of diverse variables whose unpredictable interaction takes place within an open, indefinite, and constantly changing environment.

2. For an outstanding discussion of the nature of complex systems, which to some

extent also describes Clausewitz's complex theory of war, see Charles Perrow, *Normal Accidents* (New York: Basic Books, 1986). Perrow's study, which has great heuristic value for any student of war, reveals two types of possible inter-actions in a high risk environment – *linear interactions* and *complex interactions*. He defines linear interactions as 'those in expected and familiar production or maintenance sequence . . . [that] are quite visible even if unplanned'. Complex interactions, on the other hand, are 'those of unfamiliar sequence . . . either not visible or not immediately comprehensible' (p. 78). For a detailed analysis, see Perrow, *Normal Accidents*, particularly pp. 72–100. Needless to say, Clause-witz's theory of war deals with a high-risk environment far more complicated than that of the high-risk technological system discussed by Perrow. Unlike nuclear reactors, large chemical plants, or air traffic systems, war is a reciprocal activity in which each side deliberately (not accidentally) interferes with his opponent's performance. Such a system of conflict and reciprocity can be viewed as a hyper-complex or super-complex system. See also Robert Jervis, *System Effects: Complexity in Political and Social Life* (Princeton, NJ: Princeton University Press, 1997).

3. As Clausewitz explains, '**There is no need today to labor the point that a scientific approach does not consist solely, or even mainly, in a complete system and a comprehensive analysis doctrine . . . In the formal sense, the present work contains no such system; instead of a complete theory it offers only material for one**' (from a note to an unpublished manuscript on the theory of war, written between 1816 and 1818; *On War*, p. 61).

4. In *Clausewitz and the State*, Peter Paret elegantly summarized the value and limits of Clausewitz's search for links between the past and the whole in the development of a comprehensive theory of war: '. . . laws which identify the relationships between parts of a whole are necessary and valid in the analytic, cognitive process. They lose much of their validity in the realm of action, since specific actions do not follow laws, or rules derived from them. This distinction is central to Clause-witz's theoretical work. The analysis of means and purpose, however, does permit generalizations of some practical value' (p. 165).

APPENDIX E: THE PROBLEM OF THE LEVEL OF ANALYSIS AND THE 'TACTICIZATION OF STRATEGY'

1. On this see, for example, A. Offer, *The First World War: An Agrarian Interpretation* (Oxford: Oxford University Press, 1988), Chapter 24, 'A Second Decision for War: the U-boat Campaign', pp. 354–367.

The German decision to resort to unrestricted U-boat warfare in February 1917 is a classical example of a decision based on faulty *operational calculations* and wish-ful thinking that led to negative strategic consequences and ultimately to defeat (*ibid.*, p. 364). *Major* decisions taken by the German High Command during the First World War (e.g., the Schlieffen Plan, the decision to launch an unrestricted

U-Boat campaign, and Ludendorff's last offensive of March 1918) were of this type. In each case, operational planning based on 'purely military considerations', wishful thinking, *and best-case, static*, short-range analyses gambled against the odds and lost. The resulting strategic disasters illustrate why policy and strategic decision making should never be the exclusive domain of military leaders.

2. French Field Marshal Foch expressed the same idea in words reminiscent of Clausewitz: 'Only tactical results bring advantages in war . . . There is no longer any strategy to be compared with the strategy which aims at tactical results, at victory by battle. And since strategy has no existence in itself, since it has value only by tactics . . . tactical results are everything . . .' Foch thus carries the primacy of tactical results *ad absurdum*. The disastrous results produced by French strategy during the First World War bear sad testimony to the folly of the tacticization of strategy. Quoted in Lorenzo M. Corwell, 'The Illusion of the Decisive Napoleonic Victory', *Defense Analysis*, vol. 4, no. 4 (1988), pp. 329–346. Quoting Marshal Foch, *The Principles of War*, trans. J. De Mornini (New York: H. K. Fly, 1918, pp. 40–43). A different translation is Ferdinand Foch, *The Principles of War*, trans. Hilaire Belloc (London: Chapman and Hall, 1921), Chapter 2, 'Primal Characteristics of Modern War'.

APPENDIX F: CLAUSEWITZ AND THE PRINCIPLE OF CONCENTRATION

1. The principle of concentration is the basis for Lanchester's famous *n-square* law which laid the foundation for modern military operations research – the mathematical study of conventional combat. In Chapter 12 ('Unification of Forces In Time'), Book 3, of *On War*, Clausewitz's intuitive understanding of the *n-square* law's mathematical logic is evidenced by the fact that his language and examples closely resemble those employed by Lanchester in Chapter 5 ('The Principle of Concentration: The N-Square Law') of *Aircraft in War: The Dawn of the Fourth Arm*. See F. W. Lanchester, *Aircraft in War: The Dawn of the Fourth Arm* (London: Constable and Co., 1916), pp. 39–53. See also John W. R. Lepingwell, 'The Laws of Combat? Lanchester Reexamined', *International Security*, 12 (Summer 1987), pp. 89–134; and Thomas F. Homer-Dixon, 'A Common Misapplication of the Lanchester Square Law: A Research Note', *International Security*, 12 (Summer 1987), pp. 135–139.

2. On this point, see also Gallie, *Philosophers of Peace and War* (Cambridge: Cambridge University Press, 1979), p. 44.

3. On the importance of the principle of concentration, see also for example, Bernhardi, *On War of To-Day*, vol. 2, Chapters 8–9, pp. 336–381; Goltz, *The Nation in Arms*, pp. 169–183. For a detailed discussion of the concept of concentration in Sun Tzu, see *The Art of War*, Chapter 6.

4. Clausewitz's definition of *economy of force* is very different from the modern understanding of what it means. Today's manuals usually define *economy of force* as the

use of the minimum number of troops or resources necessary to attain one's objective. To Clausewitz, *economy of force* has the opposite meaning; that is, the commander must always concentrate *all* available troops and resources to achieve his goals. In Clausewitz's view, it is uneconomical to maintain troops which remain idle. Accordingly, the principle of the economy of force relates directly to the even more important principle of maximum concentration. (See Appendix D, pp. 345–352; also the second 'flow chart' opposite p. 350. See Robert Cowley and Geoffrey Parker, eds., *Military History* (Boston, MA: Houghton Mifflin, 1996), pp. 146–147.)

5. In the final quarter of the nineteenth century, Mahan further developed and applied the *principle of concentration* (in conjunction with the principle of destruction) to naval warfare. In his first book, *The Influence of Sea Power upon History 1660–1783*, as well as in his numerous subsequent works, Mahan identified the principle of concentration as the key to achieving a decisive victory over the enemy's main battle fleet and thereby gaining command of the sea. Although he bases many of his insights on Jomini's works, his emphasis on 'strategic concentration of force and tactical boldness [as] the leading principles of naval operations' also agrees with Clausewitz's observations in *On War* (a work with which he was not familiar, although a copy of the first English translation of *On War* was acquired by the library of the U.S. Naval War College in March 1892). For an excellent discussion of Mahan's work and his application of the early nineteenth century theories of land warfare to war ar sea, see Azar Gat, *The Development of Military Thought: The Nineteenth Century* (Oxford: Oxford University Press, 1992), Chapter 4, pp. 174–204. The quotation is from p. 190.

Bibliography

Achenbach, Joel. 'War and the Cult of Clausewitz: How a Long-Dead Prussian Shaped U.S. Thinking on the Persian Gulf.' *Washington Post*, 6 December 1990.

Adcock, F. E. *The Greek and Macedonian Art of War*. Berkeley: University of California Press, 1957.

Adler, Bill. *The Churchill Wit*. New York: Coward-McCann, 1965.

Agar-Hamilton, J. A. I. and Turner, L. C. F. *Crisis in the Desert*. Capetown: Oxford University Press, 1952.

Agar-Hamilton, J. A. I. and Turner, L. C. F. *The Sidi Rezeg Battles 1941*. Capetown: Oxford University Press, 1957.

Alger, John I. *Antoine-Henri Jomini: A Bibliographical Survey*. New York: West Point, 1975.

Alger, John I. *The Quest for Victory: The History of the Principles of War*. Westport, Conn.: Greenwood Press, 1982.

Alterman, Eric R. 'Lessons From a Lost War.' *Time*, 15 April 1985, pp. 40–45.

Alterman, Eric R. 'Thinking Twice: The Weinberger Doctrine and the Lessons of Vietnam.' *The Fletcher Forum* 10 and 10.1 (Winter 1986): 93–109.

Alterman, Eric R. 'The Uses and Abuses of Clausewitz.' *Parameters* 27 (Summer 1987): 18–32.

Ames, Roger T. and Lau D. C. *Sun Pin: The Art of Warfare*. New York: Ballantine Books, 1996.

Ancona, Clemente. 'Der Einfluss Clausewitz "Vom Kriege" auf das marxistische Denken von Marx bis Lenin.' In *Clausewitz in Perspektive*, edited by Günther Dill, pp. 560–592. Frankfurt: Ullstein, 1980.

Andreski, Stanislav. *Military Organization and Society*. Berkeley: University of California Press, 1968.

Andreski, Stanislav. *Wars, Revolutions, Dictatorships*. London: Cass, 1992.

Anglo, Sydney. *Machiavelli: A Dissection*. New York: Harcourt Brace and World, 1969.

Aron, Raymond. *Peace and War*. New York: Doubleday, 1966.

Aron, Raymond. 'Reason, Passion and Power in the Thought of Clausewitz.' *Social Research* (Winter 1972): 599–621.

Aron, Raymond. 'Clausewitz's Conceptual System.' *Armed Forces and Society*, 1 (November 1974): 49–59.

Aron, Raymond. *Clausewitz: Philosopher of War*. London: Routledge and Kegan Paul, 1976. This is an abbreviated translation of *Penser la guerre, Clausewitz*. 2 vols. Paris: Editions Gallimard, 1976.

Aron, Raymond. *Sur Clausewitz*. Brussels: Editions Complexe, 1987.

Aron, Raymond. 'Thucydides and the Historical Narrative.' In *Politics and History*, edited by Raymond Aron. New York: The Free Press, 1988.

Aron, Raymond. *Memoirs*. New York: Holmes and Meier, 1990.

Aspinall-Oglander, C. F. *Gallipoli*. London: William Heinemann, 1932.

Bahnemann, Jörg. 'Der Begriff der Strategie bei Clausewitz, Moltke und Liddell Hart: Eine Untersuchung der Beziehungen zwischen politischer und militärischer Führung.' *Wehrwissenschaftliche Rundschau* 18 (1968): 33–57.

Baldwin, P. M. 'Clausewitz in Nazi Germany.' In *The Second World War*, edited by Walter Laqueur, pp. 778–799. Beverly Hills: Sage, 1982.

Baqué, Jean-François. *L'Homme Qui Devinait Napoléon: Jomini*. Paris: Perrin, 1994.

Barnett, Correlli. 'Clausewitz: How Not to Win a War.' *Horizon* 13 (Summer, 1971): 48–53.

Bassford, Christopher. *Clausewitz in English: The Reception of Clausewitz in Britain and America 1815–1845*. New York: Oxford University Press, 1994.

Bassford, Christopher. 'John Keegan and the Grand Tradition of Trashing Clausewitz: A Polemic.' *War in History*, 1 (November 1994): 319–336.

Bassford, Christopher and Villacres, Edward J. 'Reclaiming the Clausewitzian Trinity.' *Parameters* 25 (Autumn 1995): 9–20.

Baucom, Lt.-Col. (Ret.) Donald R. *Clausewitz On Space War*. Maxwell Air Force Base, AL: June 1992, Center for Aerospace Doctrine, Research, and Education, Report Number AU-ARI-CPSS-91-B.

Behrens, C. B. A. 'Which Side was Clausewitz On?' *New York Review of Books*, 14 October 1976, pp. 41–43.

Belasius, Dirk. 'Carl von Clausewitz und die Hauptdenker des Marxismus.' *Wehrwissenschaftliche Rundschau* 16 (1966): 278–294; 335–354.

Belloc, Hilaire. *The Tactics and Strategy of the Great Duke of Marlborough*. London: Arrowsmith, 1933.

von Bernhardi, Friedrich. 'Clausewitz über Angriff und Verteidigung. Versuch einer Widerlegung.' *Beihefte zum Militär-Wochenblatt* 12 (1911): 399–412.

von Bernhardi, Friedrich. *On War of To-day*. 2 vols. London: Hugh Rees, 1912.

Betts, Richard K. *Soldiers, Statesmen and the Cold War Crises*. Cambridge, MA: Harvard University Press, 1977.

Betts, Richard K. *Surprise Attack*. Washington, DC: The Brookings Institution, 1982.

Beyerchen, Alan. 'Clausewitz, Nonlinearity and the Unpredictability of War.' *International Security* 17 (Winter 1992/93): 59–90.

Blumenson, Martin. 'A Deaf Ear to Clausewitz: Allied Operational Objectives in World War II.' *Parameters* 23 (Summer 1993): 16–29.

Blumentritt, Günther. 'Was kann uns Clausewitz noch heute Bedeuten?', pp. 453–466; and 'Theorie und Praxis,' pp. 467–479. In *A Collection of Military Essays of Günther Blumentritt*. Historical Division, HQ. United States Army,

Europe. MS# C–096. Mimeograph in German (no date). These essays were written in December 1947.

von Boetticher, Friedrich. *The Art of War: A Military Testament.* Historical Division, HQ, US. Army, Europe. MS#P–100. (May 1951).

Booth, Ken. *Strategy and Ethnocentrism.* New York: Holmes and Meier, 1979.

Boorman, Howard L. and Boorman Scott, A. 'Strategy and National Psychology in China', *The Annals*, Vol. 370 (1967): 143–155. (Special issue edited by Don Martindale on national character in the perspective of the social sciences.)

Boorman, Scott A. *The Protracted Game.* New York: Oxford University Press, 1969.

Boorman, Scott A. 'Deception in Chinese Strategy.' In *The Military and Political Power in China in the 1970s*, edited by W. W. Whitson, pp. 313–337. New York: Praeger, 1972.

Brinton, Crane, Craig, Gordon A. and Gilbert, Felix. 'Jomini.' In *Makers of Modern Strategy*, edited by Edward Mead Earle. New York: Atheneum, 1966.

Brodie, Bernard. *War and Politics.* New York: Macmillan, 1973.

Brodie, Bernard. 'Clausewitz: A Passion for War.' *World Politics* 25 (January 1973): 288–308.

von Caemmerer, R. *Clausewitz.* Berlin: B. Behr's Verlag, 1905.

von Caemmerer, R. *The Development of Strategical Science during the Nineteenth Century.* London: Hugh Rees, 1905.

Camon, Col. H. *Clausewitz.* Paris: R. Chapelot, 1911.

Carlyle, Robert. *Clausewitz's Contemporary Relevance.* Camberley, UK: Strategic and Combat Studies Institute, 1995. (Occasional Paper No. 16.)

Challener, Richard D. *The French Theory of the Nation in Arms.* New York: Columbia University Press, 1955.

Chen, Chiao. 'Chinese Strategic Behaviour.' In C. A. Syeschab, and A. Sievres and S. Szywkiewicz (eds), *Society, Culture, and Patterns of Behavior*, pp. 71–95. Bad Honef: Hore Lemann, 1990.

Chen-Ya Tien. *Chinese Military Theory: Ancient and Modern.* Oakville, Ontario, Canada: Mosaic Press, 1992.

Clark, Marc T. 'The Continuing Relevance of Clausewitz.' *Strategic Review*, Winter (1998): 54–61.

Clarke, Duncan L. *Strategy and Policy: Their Theoretical Relationship.* Ph.D. dissertation, University of Virginia, June 1971.

von Clausewitz, Carl. 'On War.' *Military and Naval Magazine of the United States* 5–6 (August and September 1835). (The first comprehensive review of the German edition of *On War.* Originally published in *The London Metropolitan*, June 1834.)

von Clausewitz, Carl. *Notes on Prussia During the Grand Catastrophe of 1806.* Translated by Colonel C. H. Lanza in *The Jena Campaign.* Fort Leavenworth, KS: The General Service Schools Press, 1922.

von Clausewitz, Carl. *On War*, 3 vols. (trans. J. J. Graham, introduction and notes by Colonel F. N. Maude. London: Kegan Paul, French, Trübner, 1940. (The third volume also includes a full translation of Clausewitz's 'Summary of the Instruction to His Royal Highness the Crown Prince in the years 1810, 1811, and 1812'. The Graham translation first appeared in London in 3 vols. N. Trübner, 1873.)

von Clausewitz, Carl. Translated and edited by H. W. Gatzke. *Principles of War*. Harrisburg, PA: Military Service Publishing Company, 1943.

von Clausewitz, Carl. Edited by Lt.-Col. J. I. Greene. Introduction by J. F. C. Fuller. *The Living Thoughts of Clausewitz*. London: Cassell, 1945.

von Clausewitz, Carl. *On War*. Translated by O. S. Matthijs Jolles. New York: Random House, 1943, and Washington, DC: Infantry Journal Press, 1950.

von Clausewitz, Carl. Edited by E. M. Collins. *War, Politics and Power*. Chicago: Gateway, 1962.

von Clausewitz, Carl. Edited by R. A. Leonard. Preface by Michael Howard. *A Short Guide to Clausewitz*. London: Weidenfeld and Nicolson, 1967.

von Clausewitz, Carl. *On War*. Edited with an introduction by Anatol Rapoport. Harmondsworth: Penguin, 1968. (This edition is based on the J. J. Graham translation.)

von Clausewitz, Carl. *The Campaign of 1812 in Russia*. Translated by Lord Ellesmere (1843). Hattiesburg, MI: Academic International Press, 1970.

von Clausewitz, Carl. Translated and edited by Sir Michael Howard and Peter Paret. *On War*. Princeton, NJ: Princeton University Press, 1976.

von Clausewitz, Carl. Edited with an introduction by Werner Hahlweg. *Verstreute kleine Schriften*. Osnabrück: Biblio, 1979.

von Clausewitz, Carl. *Vom Kriege*, 19th edn. Introduction by Werner Hahlweg. Bonn: Dummler, 1980.

von Clausewitz, Carl. *Two Letters on Strategy*, ed. and trans. Peter Paret and Daniel Moran. Carlisle, PA: U.S. Army War College, 1984.

von Clausewitz, Carl. *Historical and Political Writings*. Translated and edited by Peter Paret and Daniel Moran. Princeton, NJ: Princeton University Press, 1992.

von Clausewitz, Carl. *The Campaign of 1812 in Russia*. Translated by Lord Ellesmere (1843). Introduction by G. F. Nafziger. Novato, CA: Presidio Press, 1992.

www.clausewitz.com/CWZHOME/Wordndx.htm

Cleary, Tom, ed. and trans. *Mastering the Art of War: Zhuge Liang's and Liu Ki's Commentaries on the Classic by Sun Tzu*. Boston, MA: Shambhala, 1989.

Coats, Wendell J. 'Clausewitz's Theory of War: An Alternative View.' *Comparative Strategy* 5 (1986): 351–373.

Collins, Edward M. 'Clausewitz and Democracy's Modern Wars.' *Military Affairs* 19 (1955): 15–20.

Connor, W. Robert. *Thucydides*. Princeton, NJ: Princeton University Press, 1985.

Corbett, Julian S. *Some Principles of Maritime Strategy*. London: Longmans, Green and Co., 1911.

Corbett, Julian, S. *The Campaign of Trafalgar*. London: Longmans, 1910.

Craig, Gordon A. 'Delbrück: The Military Historian.' In *Makers of Modern Strategy*, edited by E. M. Earle, pp. 260–283. Princeton, NJ: Princeton University Press, 1943.

Craig, Gordon A. *The Politics of the Prussian Army 1640–1945*. New York: Oxford University Press, 1956.

van Creveld, Martin. 'The Eternal Clausewitz.' In *Clausewitz and Modern Strategy*, edited by Michael I. Handel. London: Cass, 1986.

van Creveld, Martin. *Supplying War*. Cambridge: Cambridge University Press, 1977.

van Creveld, Martin. *The Transformation of War*. New York: The Free Press, 1991.

van Creveld, Martin. *The Art of War: War in Military Thought* (London: Cassell, 2000).

Croce, Benedetto. 'Action, succès et jugement dans le *Vom Kriege* de Clausewitz.' *Revue de métaphysique et de morale* 42 (1935): 247–258. Also translated into German: 'Handeln, Erfolg und Urteil in Clausewitz "Vom Kriege."'. In *Clausewitz in Perspektive*, edited by Günther Dill, pp. 407–418. Frankfurt: Ullstein, 1980.

Crowell, Lorenzo M. 'The Illusion of Decisive Napoleonic Victory', *Defense Analysis*, vol. 4, no. 4 (1988): 329–346.

Däniker, Gustav. 'General Antoine Henri Jomini.' In *Klassiker der Kriegskunst*, edited by Werner Hahlweg, pp. 267–284. Darmstadt: Wehr und Wissen, 1960.

Daniel, Donald C. and Herbig, Katherine L., eds. *Strategic Military Deception*. New York: Pergamon Press, 1982.

Davis, Donald E. and Kohn, Walter S. G. '"Lenin's" Notebook on Clausewitz.' In *Soviet Armed Forces Review Annual*, vol. 1. Edited by David R. Jones, pp. 188–229. Gulf Breeze, FL: Academic International Press, 1977.

Davis, Donald E. and Kohn, Walter S. G. 'Lenin as a Disciple of Clausewitz.' *Military Review* 51 (September 1971): 49–55.

Deception Research Program. *Misperception Literature Survey*. Princeton, NJ: Mathtec Inc. and ORD/CIA Analytic Methodology Research Division, 1979.

Deception Research Program. *Thoughts on the Cost-Effectiveness of Deception and Related Tactics in the Air War, 1939 to 1945*. Princeton, NJ: Mathtec Inc. and ORD/CIA Analytic Methodology Research Division, 1979.

Delbrück, Hans. *Die Strategie des Perikles erläutert durch die Strategie Friedrichs des Grossen*. Berlin: Georg Reiner, 1890.

Delbrück, Hans. 'General von Clausewitz.' In *Historische und Politische Aufsatze*, pp. 205–222. Berlin: Georg Stilke, 1908.

Delbrück, Hans. *The Modern Era. History of the Art of War*, vol. 4. Westport, CT: Greenwood Press, 1985.

Delbrück, Hans. 'General von Clausewitz'. In Hans Delbrück, *Historische und Politische Aufsatze*. Berlin: Walther und Apolant 1887.

Department of Defense Dictionary of Military and Associated Terms. Washington, DC: Joint Publication 1–02, 1989.

Dexter, Byron. 'Clausewitz and Soviet Strategy.' *Foreign Affairs*, 29 (October 1950): 41–55.

Dill, Günther., ed. *Clausewitz in Perspektive*. Frankfurt: Ullstein, 1980.

Dixit, Avinash K. and Nalebuff, Barry J. *Thinking Strategically: The Competitive Edge in Business, Politics and Everyday Life*. New York: W. W. Norton, 1991.

Dower, John W. *War Without Mercy*. New York: Pantheon Books, 1986.

Dubois, T. R. 'The Weinberger Doctrine and the Liberation of Kuwait.' *Parameters* (Winter 1991–92): 24–38.

Echevarria, Antulio Josep. 'Neo-Clausewitzianism: Freytag-Loringhoven and the Militarization of Clausewitz in German Military Literature before the First World War.' Ph.D. dissertation, Princeton, 1994.

Echevarria, Antulio Josep. 'Borrowing From the Master: Uses of Clausewitz in German Military Literature Before the Great War.' *War in History*, Vol. 3, No. 3 (July, 1996): 274–292.

Edmund, Lowell. *Chance and Intelligence in Thucydides*. Cambridge, MA: Harvard University Press, 1975.

Elffers, Joost and Greene, Robert. *The 48 Laws of Power*. New York: Viking Press, 1998.

Elting, John R. 'Jomini: Disciple of Napoleon.' *Military Affairs* 27 (1967): 17–26.

Elting, John R. 'Jomini and Berthier.' In *The Consortium of Revolutionary Europe, 1750–1850: Proceedings 1989 to Commemorate the Bicentennial of the French Revolution*, pp. 247–251. Tallahassee, FL: Florida State University, 1990.

Esteves, Luis Raul. *438 Notes on Clausewitz' 'On War'*. San Juan, Puerto Rico: La Primavera, 1952.

Etzold, T. H. 'Clausewitzian Lessons for Modern Strategists.' *Air University Review* 4 (May–June 1980): 24–28.

Fairbank, John K. and Kierman, Frank A. Jr., eds. *Chinese Ways in Warfare*. Cambridge, MA: Harvard University Press, 1974.

Falls, Cyril. *Ordeal By Battle*. New York: Oxford University Press, 1943.

Ferris, John and Handel, Michael I. 'Clausewitz, Intelligence, Uncertainty and the Art of Command in Military Operations.' *Intelligence and National Security* 1 (January 1995): 1–58.

Foch, Marshal. *The Principles of War*. London: Chapman and Hall, 1921.

Franklin, W. D. 'Clausewitz on Limited War.' *Military Review* 6 (1967): 23–29.

Frederick The Great. *Instructions for His Generals*. Harrisburg, PA: Military Publishing Co., 1944.

von Freytag-Loringhoven, Hugo Baron. *The Power of Personality in War*. Harrisburg, PA: The Military Service Publishing Co., 1955.

Frontinus. *Stratagems and Aqueducts*. (Trans. C. E. Bennett) Loeb Classical Library, Cambridge, MA: Harvard University Press, 1969.

Fuller, J. F. C. *The Generalship of Ulysses S. Grant*. London: J. Murray, 1929.

Fuller, J. F. C. *Armament and History*. London: Eyre and Spottiswoode, 1946.

Fuller, J. F. C. *The Conduct of War 1789–1961*. New Brunswick, NJ: Rutgers University Press, 1961.

Fuller, William C, Jr. *Strategy and Power in Russia 1600–1914*. New York: The Free Press, 1992.

Furlong, Raymond B. '*On War*, Political Objectives, and Military Strategy.' *Parameters* 13 (December 1983): 2–10.

Gabriel, Jurg Martin. 'Clausewitz Revisited: A Study of his Writings and of the Debate over their Relevance to Deterrence Theory.' Ph.D. dissertation. Washington, DC: American University, 1971.

Gallie, W. B. 'Clausewitz Today.' *European Journal of Sociology* 19 (1978): 143–167.

Gallie, W. B. *Philosophers of Peace and War: Kant, Clausewitz, Marx, Engels and Tolstoy*. Cambridge: Cambridge University Press, 1978.

Gallie, W. B. 'Power Politics and War Cultures.' *Review of International Studies*, 14 (January 1988): 17–27.

Gallie, W. B. *Understanding War*. London: Routledge, 1991.

Gat, Azar. 'Clausewitz on the Defense and Attack.' *Journal of Strategic Studies*, 11 (March 1988): 20–26.

Gat, Azar. 'Machiavelli and the Decline of the Classical Notion of the Lessons of History in the Study of War.' *Military Affairs* 52 (October 1988): 203–205.

Gat, Azar. 'Clausewitz's Final Notes.' *Militärgechichtliche Mitteilungen* 1 (1989): 45–51.

Gat, Azar. *The Origins of Military Thought: From the Enlightenment to Clausewitz*. Oxford: Oxford University Press, 1989.

Gat, Azar. 'Clausewitz's Political and Ethical World View.' *Political Studies* 37 (1989): 97–106.

Gat, Azar. 'Clausewitz and the Marxists: Yet Another Look.' *Journal of Contemporary History* 27 (1992): 363–382.

Gat, Azar. *The Development of Military Thought: The Nineteenth Century*. Oxford: Oxford University Press, 1992.

Gelb, Leslie and Betts, Richard K. *The Irony of Vietnam: The System Worked*. Washington, DC: The Brookings Institution, 1979.

Gembruch, Werner. 'Zu Clausewitz' Gedanken über das Verhältnis von Krieg und Politik.' *Wehrwissenschaftliche Rundschau* 9 (1959): 619–633.

Geoffrey-Woodhead, A. *Thucydides on the Nature of Power*. Cambridge, MA: Harvard University Press, 1970.

Gibbs, Norman H. 'Clausewitz on the Moral Forces in War.' *Naval War College Review* (January/February 1975): 15–21.

Gilbert, Felix. 'From Clausewitz to Delbrück and Hintze: Achievements and Failures of Military History.' *Journal of Strategic Studies* 3 (1981).

Gilbert, Felix. 'Machiavelli: The Renaissance of the Art of War.' In *Makers of Modern Strategy*, edited by Peter Paret. Princeton, NJ: Princeton University Press, 1986.

Goldhamer, Herbert (ed. J. Goldhamer). *Reality and Belief in Military Affairs*. Santa Monica: The Rand Corporation, 1979.

von der Goltz, Colmar. *The Conduct of War*. London: Kegan Paul, Trench, Trübner. 1908.

von der Goltz, Colmar. *The Nation in Arms*. London: Hugh Rees, 1913.

Gooch, John and Perlmutter, Amos, eds. *Military Deception and Strategic Surprise*. London: Cass, 1982.

Gourville, Xavier Comte de. *Jomini*. Berlin: Gustav Kiepenheuer, 1938.

Gray, Colin S. *War, Peace and Victory*. New York: Simon and Schuster, 1990.

Gray, Colin S. *Modern Strategy*. Oxford: Oxford University Press, 1999.

Gregory, Donna U. *Clausewitz: A Mind Under Arms*. La Jolla, CA: University of California, Institute on Global Conflict and Cooperation, 1988.

Guss, Kurt. *Krieg als Gestalt: Psychologie und Pädagogik bei Carl von Clausewitz*. Munich: Verlag für Wehrwissenschaften, 1990.

Haas, Jonathan. *The Anthropology of War*. Cambridge: Cambridge University Press, 1990.

Haffner, Sebastian. 'Mao und Clausewitz.' In *Clausewitz in Perspektive*, edited by Günther Dill, pp. 652–663. Frankfurt: Ullstein, 1980.

Hagemann, Ernest. *Die deutsche Lehre Vom Kriege Vol. 1 von Bernhorst zu Clausewitz*. Berlin: Mittler und Sohn, 1990.

Hahlweg, Werner. 'Lenin und Clausewitz.' *Archiv für Kulturgeschichte* 36 (1954): 30–59, part 1; 357–387, part 2; also reprinted in *Clausewitz in Perspektive*, edited by Günther Dill, pp. 592–651. Frankfurt, Ullstein, 1980.

Hahlweg, Werner. 'Clausewitz, Lenin and Communist Military Attitudes Today.' *Royal United Services Institute*, 618 (May 1960): 221–225.

Hahlweg, Werner. *Clausewitz: Soldat – Politiker – Denker*. Göttingen: Musterschmidt, 1969.

Hahlweg, Werner. 'Clausewitz und die Französische Revolution.' *Zeitschrift für Religions und Geistesgechichte*, 3 (1975): 240–251.

Hahlweg, Werner, ed. *Carl von Clausewitz: Schriften-Aufsätze-Studien-Briefe*, vol. 2, parts 1 and 2. Gottingen: Vandenhoeck und Ruprecht, 1990.

Handel, Michael I., ed. *Military Deception in Peace and War*. Papers on Peace

Problems. Jerusalem: The Leonard Davis Institute, The Hebrew University, 1985.

Handel, Michael I., ed. *Clausewitz and Modern Strategy*. London: Cass, 1986.

Handel, Michael I., ed. *Strategic and Operational Deception in the Second World War*. London: Cass, 1987.

Handel, Michael I., ed. *Leaders and Intelligence*. London: Cass, 1989.

Handel, Michael I. *War, Strategy and Intelligence*. London: Cass, 1989.

Handel, Michael I., ed. *Intelligence and Military Operations*. London: Cass, 1990.

Hanzhang, General T. *Sun Tzu's Art of War: The Modern Chinese Interpretation*. New York: Sterling, 1987.

Harsch, Joseph. 'Battlesword and Rapier: Clausewitz, Jomini and the American Civil War.' *Military Affairs* 38 (December 1974): 133–138.

Hart, Brigadier-General R. C. *Reflections on the Art of War*. William Clowes & Sons, 1897.

Hartl, Maria. *Carl von Clausewitz: Persönlichkeit und Stil*. Emden: Kunst und Leben, 1956.

Hartmann, Uwe. *Carl von Clausewitz: Erkentniss Bildung, Generalstabausbildung*. Munich: Olozg, 1998.

Hempstone, S. 'The Weinberger–Shultz Debate is Beneficial.' In *Ethics and American Power*, edited by E. Lefever. Washington, DC: Ethics and Public Policy Center, 1985.

Henderson, Bernard W. *The Great War Between Athens and Sparta: A Companion to the Military History of Thucydides*. London: Macmillan, 1927.

Hepp, Robert. 'Der harmlose Clausewitz.' *Zeitschrift für Politik* 3 (September 1978): 303–318; 25 (December 1978): 390–429.

Hesketh, Roger. *Fortitude: The D-Day Deception Campaign*. London: St. Ermins Press, 1999.

Hetzler, Hans Wilhelm. '"Bewegung im erschwerenden Mittel" Handlungstheoretische Elemente bei Carl von Clausewitz.' In *Institution und Technische Zivilisation*, edited by Eckart Pankoke, pp. 199–214. Berlin: Duncker and Humblot, 1990.

Hintze, Otto. 'Clausewitz und die Strategie Friedrichs des Grossen.' *Forschungen zur Brandenburgischen und Preussichen Geschichte* 33 (1920): 131–177.

Hobohm, Martin. 'Delbrück, Clausewitz und die Kritik des Weltkrieges.' *Preussische Jahrbücher* 181 (1920): 202–232.

von Hoffmann, General Max. *The War of Lost Opportunities*. New York: International Publishers, 1925.

Hoffmann, Stanley. 'The Sword and the Pen.' A review of Raymond Aron's *Clausewitz, Philosopher of War*. *The New Republic*, 4 November 1985, pp. 38–41.

Homer-Dixon, Thomas F. 'A Common Misapplication of the Lanchester

Square Law: A Research Note.' *International Security* 12 (Summer 1987): 135–139.

Horne, Alistair. *A Savage War of Peace: Algeria 1954–62,* 2nd rev. edn. New York: Viking Penguin, 1987.

Housman, A. E. 'The Application of Thought to Textual Criticism.' In *A. E. Housman: Selected Prose*, edited by J. Carter. Cambridge: Cambridge University Press, 1961.

Hou-Wee, Chow, Sheang-Lee, Khai, and Hidajat, Bambang Walujo. *Sun-Tzu: War and Management.* Reading, MA: Addison-Wesley, 1996.

Howard, Michael. 'Clausewitz and His Misinterpreters.' *The Listener*, 22 March 1956, pp. 279–280.

Howard, Michael. 'Jomini and the Classical Tradition in Military Thought.' In *The Theory and Practice of War*, edited by Michael Howard. London: Cassell, 1965.

Howard, Michael. 'War as an Instrument of Policy.' In *Diplomatic Investigations*, edited by H. Butterfield and M. Wight, pp. 193–201. Cambridge, MA: Harvard University Press, 1968.

Howard, Michael. 'The Military Philosopher.' *Times Literary Supplement*, 25 June 1976, pp. 754–755.

Howard, Michael. *War in European History*. Oxford: Oxford University Press, 1977.

Howard, Michael. *Clausewitz*. New York: Oxford University Press, 1988.

Howard, Michael. *British Intelligence in the Second World War,* Volume 5: *Strategic Deception*. London: HMSO, 1990.

Howard, Michael. *Clausewitz on War*. (A Bradley Lecture Series Publication.) Washington, DC: Library of Congress, 1998.

Huntington, Samuel P. 'Civilian Control of the Military: A Theoretical Statement.' In *Political Behavior: A Reader in Theory and Research*, edited by Samuel J. Eldersveld and Eulau Heinz, pp. 380–385. Glencoe, IL: The Free Press, 1956.

Huntington, Samuel P. *The Soldier and the State*. New York: Vintage Books, 1964.

Ikle, Fred Charles. *Every War Must End*. New York: Columbia University Press, 1971.

Irvine, D. D. 'The French Discovery of Clausewitz and Napoleon.' In *Studies on War*. Washington, DC: The Infantry Journal, 1943.

Izzo, Lawrence L. 'The Center of Gravity is not an Achilles' Heel.' *Military Review* 68 (January 1988): 72–77.

James, Robert Rhodes. *Gallipoli*. London: Batsford, 1965.

Jervis, Robert. *The Logic of Images in International Relations*. Princeton, NJ: Princeton University Press, 1970.

Jervis, Robert. *Perception and Misperception in International Politics*. Princeton, NJ: Princeton University Press, 1976.

Jervis, Robert. *System Effects: Complexity in Political and Social Life.* Princeton, NJ: Princeton University Press, 1997.

Jianxiang, Bi. 'The Impact of Clausewitz on Mao: War and Politics.' MA. Thesis, Edmunton University of Alberta, Spring 1989.

Jomini, Baron Antoine-Henri de. *Summary of the Art of War or a New Analytical Compend of the Principal Combinations of Strategy, of Grand Tactics and of Military Policy.* Translated by Major O. F. Winship and Lt. E. E. McLean. New York: G. P. Putnam, 1854.

Jomini, Baron Antoine-Henri de. *The Art of War.* Philadelphia, PA: J. B. Lippincott, 1862.

Jomini, Baron Antoine-Henri de. *Treatise on Grand Military Operations: or a Critical and Military History of the Wars of Frederick the Great, as Contrasted with the Modern System. Together with a Few of the most Important Principles of the Art of War.* Translated by Colonel S. B. Holabird. New York: Van Nostrand, 1865.

Jomini, Baron Antoine-Henri de. *Jomini and His Art of War.* Edited with an introduction by Lt.-Col. J. D. Hittle. Harrisburg, PA: Military Service, 1947.

Jones, Archer. 'Jomini and the Strategy of the American Civil War, A Reinterpretation.' *Military Affairs* 34 (December 1970): 127–131.

Jones, J. R. *Marlborough.* Cambridge: Cambridge University Press, 1993.

Jones, R. V. 'Irony as a Phenomenon in Natural Science and Human Affairs.' *Chemistry and Industry* (13 April 1968): 470–477.

Jones, R. V. 'Intelligence and Deception.' In *Intelligence, Policy and National Security.* Edited by R. Pfaltzgraff and Warren H. Milberg. London: Macmillan, 1981.

Jones, R. V. *Reflections on Intelligence.* London: Heinemann, 1989.

Jones, R. V. *Future Conflict and New Technology.* The Washington Papers, No. 88. Washington DC, The Center for Strategic and International Studies. Beverly Hills, Sage Publications, 1981.

Johnston, R. M. *Clausewitz To Date.* Cambridge: The Military Historian and Economist, 1917.

Judson, Horace Freeland. *The Search For Solutions.* New York: Holt, Rinehart, & Winston, 1980.

Kaegi, Jr., W. I. 'On War.' *Armed Forces and Society*, 1 (Fall, 1978): 123–132.

Kaegi, W. E. *Some Thoughts on Byzantine Military Strategy.* Brookline, MA: Hellenic College Press, 1983.

Kagan, Donald. *The Archidamian War.* Cornell: Cornell University Press, 1991.

Kahn, David. 'Clausewitz at Carlisle.' *Military Affairs* (October 1985): 191.

Kam, Ephraim. *Surprise Attack.* Cambridge, MA: Harvard University Press, 1988.

Kecskemeti, Paul. *Strategic Surrender: The Politics of Victory and Defeat.* Stanford: Stanford University Press, 1958.

Kecskemeti, Paul. 'Political Rationality in Ending Wars.' In *How Wars End,* edited by W. Hart, *The Annals of the American Academy of Political and Social Science*, 392 (November 1970): 105–116.

Keegan, John. 'Peace by Other Means? War, Popular Opinion and Politically Incorrect Clausewitz.' *Times Literary Supplement*, 11 December 1992, pp. 3–4.

Keegan, John. *A History of Warfare*. New York: Alfred A. Knopf, 1993.

Kelley, Lawrence H. *War Before Civilization*. New York: Oxford University Press, 1996.

Kessel, Eberhard. 'Doppelpolige Strategie: Eine Studie zu Clausewitz, Delbrück und Friedrich d. Gr.' *Wissen und Wehr* 12 (1931): 622–631.

Kessel, Eberhard. 'Zur Entstehungsgechichte von Clausewitz' Werk *Vom Kriege*.' *Historische Zeitschrift* 151 (1935): 97–100.

Kessel, Eberhard. 'Zur Genesis der modernen Kriegslehre.' *Wehrwissentschaftliche Rundschau* 3 (1953): 405–433.

Kessel, Eberhard. 'Die doppelte Art des Krieges.' *Wehrwissenschaftliche Rundschau*, 4 (1954): 298–310.

Kheng-Hor, Khoo. *Sun-Tzu and Management*. Selangor Darnl Ehsan, Malaysia Pelandnk Publication, 1996.

King, James E. 'On Clausewitz: Master Theorist of War.' *Naval War College Review* 30 (Fall 1977): 3–36.

Kipp, Jacob W. 'Lenin and Clausewitz: The Militarization of Marxism 1914–1921.' *Military Affairs* (October 1985): 184–191.

Kitchen, Martin. 'The Political History of Clausewitz.' *Journal of Strategic Studies* 11 (March 1988): 27–50.

Kondylis, Panajotis. *Theorie des Krieges: Clausewitz–Marx–Engels–Lenin*. Stuttgart: Klett-Cotta, 1988.

Krause, Donald G. *The Art of War for Executives*. New York: Perigee, 1995.

Krause, Donald G. *Sun-Tzu: The Art of War for Executives*. London: Nicholas Brealey, 1996.

Krüger, Norbert. 'Adolf Hitlers Clausewitzkenntnis.' *Wehrwissenschaftliche Rundschau* 18 (1968): 467–471.

Lanchester, F. W. *Aircraft in War: The Dawn of the Fourth Arm*. London: Constable & Co., 1916.

Lange, Sven. *Hans Delbruck und der Strategiestreit*. Freiburg: Rombach, 1995.

Larabee, Eric. *Commander in Chief: Franklin Delano Roosevelt, His Lieutenants, and Their War*. New York: Touchstone, 1988.

Lau, D. C. 'Some Notes on the Sun-Tzu.' *Bulletin of the School of Oriental and African Studies University of London* 28 (1965): 319–335.

Lawrence, T. E. *Seven Pillars of Wisdom*, Chapter 33, pp. 188–196. Garden City, NY: Doubleday, Doran, 1935.

Lawrence, T. E. 'The Evolution of a Revolt'. In *Oriental Assembly*, A. W. Lawrence (ed.), pp. 103–134. New York: E. P. Dutton, 1946.

Lefever, Ernest. W., ed. *Ethics and American Power*. Washington, DC: Ethics and Public Policy, May 1985.

Leinveber, R. *Mit Clausewitz durch die Rätsel und Fragen Irrungen und Wirungen des Weltkrieges*. Berlin: B. Behrs, 1926.

Lepingwell, John W. R. 'The Laws of Combat? Lanchester Rexamined.' *International Security* 12 (Summer 1987): 89–134.

Liddell Hart, Basil H. *Greater Than Napoleon: Scipio Africanus*. London: William Blackwood, 1930.

Liddell Hart, Basil H. *The Ghost of Napoleon*. London: Faber & Faber, 1933.

Liddell Hart, Basil H. *Thoughts on War*. London: Faber & Faber, 1944.

Liddell Hart, Basil H. *Strategy*. New York: New American Library, 1974.

Linnebach, K. 'Die Wissenschaftliche Methode in Clausewitz' Werk "Vom Kriege".' *Wissen und Wehr* 14 (1993): 477–501.

Luttwak, Edward N. *Strategy*. Cambridge, MA: Harvard University Press, 1987.

Luvaas, Jay, ed. *Frederick the Great On the Art of War*. New York: The Free Press, 1966.

Luvaas, Jay. 'Napoleon on the Art of Command.' *Parameters* 15 (Summer 1985): 30–36.

Luvaas, Jay, ed. *Napolean On the Art of War*. New York: Free Press, 1999.

Lynn, John A. *The Bayonets of the Republic: Motivation and Tactics in the Army of Revolutionary France 1791–1794*. Urbana: University of Illinois Press, 1984.

Lynn, John A. 'War of Annihilation, War of Attrition, and War of Legitimacy: A Neo-Clausewitzian Approach to Twentieth Century Conflicts.' In *Marine Corps Gazette*, October (1996): 64–71.

Machiavelli, Niccolo. *Machiavelli: The Chief Works and Others*, 3 vols. Translated by A. Gilbert. Durham, NC: Duke University Press, 1965. *The Prince*, vol. 1, pp. 5–96; *The Discourses*, vol. 1, pp. 175–532; *The Art of War*, vol. 2, pp. 561–726.

Machiavelli, Niccolo. *The Art of War*. Translated by E. Farenworth. Introduction by N. Wood. Indianapolis: Bobbs-Merrill, 1965.

Machiavelli, Niccolo. *The Prince* (2nd revised edition). Translated by Harvey Mansfield. Chicago: Chicago University Press, 1998.

Machiavelli, Niccolo. *The Prince and the Discourses*. Introduction by Max Lerner, translated by Luigi Ricci, revised by E. R. P. Vincent. New York: The Modern Library, 1950.

Maguire, Miller T., ed. Translated by Miss Maguire. *General von Clauewitz on War*. London: William Clowes, 1909.

Mahan, Alfred Thayer. *The Influence of Sea Power Upon History 1660–1783*. Boston: Little, Brown, 1894 and New York: Dover, 1987.

Mahan, Alfred Thayer. *The Life of Nelson*. Boston: Little, Brown, 1897.

Mao Tse-tung, *Mao Tse-tung on Guerrilla Warfare*, trans. with an introduction Brig.-Gen. Samuel B. Griffith. New York: Praeger, 1961.

Mao Tse-tung. *Selected Military Writings of Mao Tse-tung*. Peking: Foreign Language Press, 1963.

Mao Tse-tung. *Selected Readings from the Works of Mao Tse-tung*. Peking: Foreign Languages Press, 1971.

Maoz, Zeev. *Paradoxes of War*. Boston: Unwin Hyman, 1990.

Marey, E. J. *La Méthode Graphique dans les Sciences Expérimentales et Principalement en Physiologie et en Médicine.*, 2d ed. Paris: G. Masson, 1885, pp. 71–73.

Marwedel, Ulrich. *Carl von Clausewitz: Persönlichkeit und Wirkungsgechichte seines Werkes bis 1918*. Boppard Am Rein: Harald Boldt, 1978.

Masterman, J. C. *The Double-Cross System*. New Haven, CT: Yale University Press, 1972.

Matthews, Lloyd. J. 'On Clausewitz.' *Army* 38 (February 1988): 20–24.

McNeilly, Mark. *Sun Tzu and the Art of Business: Six Strategical Principles For Managers*. New York: Oxford University Press, 1996.

McDonald, John. *Strategy in Poker, Business and War*. New York: W. W. Norton, 1950.

Metz, Steven. 'A Wake For Clausewitz: toward a Philosophy of 21st Century Warfare,' *Parameters*. Vol. 24, No. 4 (Winter 1994/1995): 126–132.

Metzsch, Horst von. *Clausewitz Katechismus*. Berlin: Bucholtz und Weisswange, 1937.

Militargechichtliches Forschungsamt, *Operational Thinking in Clausewitz, Moltke, Schlieffen and Manstein*. Bonn: E. S. Mittler, 1988.

Moltke, Helmuth von. *The Art of War: Selected Writing*. Edited by Daniel J. Hughes, translated by Daniel J. Hughes and Harry Bell. Novato: Presidio, 1993.

Montagu, Ewen. *The Man Who Never Was*. Philadelphia: J. B. Lippincott, 1954.

Montgomery, Field-Marshal. *The Path to Leadership*. London: Collins, 1964.

Moran, Lord D. *The Anatomy of Courage*. London: Constable, 1945.

Moran, Daniel. 'Clausewitz and the Revolution.' *Central European History* 22 (June 1989): 183–199.

Morgenthau, Hans. *Politics Among Nations*. 5th edn. New York: Alfred A. Knopf, 1973.

Münkler, Herfried. 'Instrumentelle und existentielle vom Krieg bei Carl von Clausewitz.' *Leviathan* 16 (June 1988): 235–251.

Mure, David. *Master of Deception*. London: William Kimber, 1980.

Murray, Stewart L. *The Reality of War: An Introduction to 'Clausewitz'*. With a note by Spenser Wilkinson. London: Hugh Rees, 1909.

Murray, Williamson. 'War, Theory, Clausewitz, and Thucydides: The Game May Change but the Rules Remain.' *Marine Corps Gazette* (January 1997): 62–69.

Neilson, Keith and McKercher, B. J. C., eds. *Go by the Land: Military Intelligence in History*. New York: Praeger, 1992.

Niou, Emerson M. S. and Ordeshook, Peter C. 'A Game-Theoretic Inter-pretation of Sun Tzu's *The Art of War.' Journal of Peace Research* 2 (1994): 161–174.

Nohn, Ernst August. 'Clausewitz contra Bülow.' *Wehrwissenschaftliche Rundschau* 5 (1955).

Nohn, Ernst August. 'Der unzeitgemässe Clausewitz. Notwendige Bemerk-ungen über zeitgemässe Denkfehler.' Beiheft 5 der *Wehrwissenschaftliche Rundschau*. Frankfurt: A. M., 1956.

Nohn, Ernst August. 'Moralische Grossen im Werke 'Vom Kriege' und in einem unterzeichneten Beitrag. zur 'Neun Bellona' des Jahrgang 1801. *Historische Zeitschrift* 186 (1958): 35–64.

Nohn, Ernst August. 'Jomini und Clausewitz.' *Politische Studien* 107 (March 1959): 175–181.

Nooy, Gert de, ed. *The Clausewitzian Dictum and the Future of Western Military Strategy.* The Hague: Kluwer van International, 1997.

O'Dowd, Edward and Waldron, Arthur. 'Sun Tzu for Strategists.' *Comparative Strategy* 10 (1991): 22–36.

Offer, Avner. *The First World War: An Agrarian Interpretation.* Oxford: Oxford University Press, 1988.

Palsson, G. 'War and State in The Prince of Machiavelli.' Ph.D. dissertation. Buffalo: University of Buffalo, 1986.

Parel, Anthony. *The Political Calculus: Essays on Machiavelli's Philosophy.* Toronto: University of Toronto Press, 1972.

Paret, Peter, ed. *Makers of Modern Strategy.* Princeton, NJ: Princeton University Press, 1986.

Paret, Peter. Clausewitz: 'A Bibliography Survey.' *World Politics* 17 (October 1964): 272–286.

Paret, Peter. 'Clausewitz and the Nineteenth Century.' In *The Theory and Practice of War*, edited by Michael Howard. London: Cassell, 1965.

Paret, Peter. *Yorck and the Era of Prussian Reform, 1807–1815.* Princeton, NJ: Princeton University Press, 1966.

Paret, Peter. 'Clausewitz.' *International Encyclopedia of the Social Sciences*, vol. 2, pp. 511–513. New York: Macmillan and the Free Press, 1968.

Paret, Peter. 'Education, Politics and War in the Life of Clausewitz.' *Journal of the History of Ideas* 3 (1975): 394–408.

Paret, Peter. 'Nationalism and the Sense of Military Obligation.' *Military Affairs*, 34 (1970): 2–6.

Paret, Peter. *Clausewitz and the State.* Oxford: Clarendon Press, 1976.

Paret, Peter. 'Clausewitz's Bicentennial Birthday.' *Air University Review* 31 (May–June 1980): 17–20.

Paret, Peter. 'Clausewitz.' In *Makers of Modern Strategy*, edited by Peter Paret. Princeton, NJ: Princeton University Press, 1986.

Paret, Peter. 'Continuity and Discontinuity in Some Interpretations by

Tocqueville and Clausewitz.' *Journal of the History of Ideas* 1 (1988): 161–169.

Paret, Peter. *Understanding War: Essays on Clausewitz and the History of Military Power.* Princeton. NJ: Princeton University Press, 1992.

Parkinson, Roger. *Clausewitz.* New York: Stein and Day, 1971.

Pelletiere, S. C., Johnson, D. Z., and Rosenberger, L. R. *Iraqi Power and US Security in the Middle East.* Carlisle Barracks, PA: Strategic Studies Institute, 1990.

Phillips, Gen. Thomas R., trans. *Frederick The Great: Instructions for His Generals.* Harrisburg, PA: Military Publishing Co., 1944.

du Picq, Col. Ardant. *Battle Studies: Ancient and Modern Battle.* Translated from the 8th edition by John N. Greely and Robert C. Cotton. New York: Macmillan, 1921.

Pieri, P. 'Niccolo Machiavelli.' In *Klassiker der Kriegskunst*, edited by Werner Hahlweg, pp. 103–118. Darmstadt: Wehr und Wissen, 1960.

Pilcher, Major-General T. D., ed. with commentary. *War According to Clausewitz.* London: Cassell, 1918.

Pillar, Paul R., *Negotiating Peace: War Termination as a Bargaining Process.* Princeton, NJ: Princeton University Press, 1983.

Plutarch. *Lives.* (Dreyden translation). New York: Modern Library, 1992.

Polybius, *On Roman Imperialism*, abridged, with introduction, Alvin H. Bernstein, trans. Evelyn S. Suckburgh. Lake Bluff, FL: Regnery Gateway, 1987.

Powell, General Colin L. 'Why Generals Get Nervous.' *New York Times*, 8 October 1992.

Ramsey, Douglas K. *The Corporate Warriors.* Boston: Houghton Mifflin, 1987.

Rees, David. *Korea: The Limited War.* London: Macmillan, 1964.

Reynolds, Charles. 'Carl von Clausewitz and Strategic Theory.' *British Journal of International Studies* 4 (1978): 178–190.

Reynolds, Charles. *The Politics of War: A Study of the Rationality of Violence in Inter-State Relations.* New York: St. Martin's, 1989.

Ritter, Gerhard. 'Die Lehre Carl von Clausewitz vom politischen Sinn des Krieges.' *Historische Zeitschrift* 167 (1943): 41–65.

Ritter, Gerhard. *The Sword and the Scepter*, vol. 1, *The Prussian Tradition 1740–1890.* Translated by Heinz Norden. Coral Gables, FL: University of Miami Press, 1969.

Roques, P. *Le General de Clausewitz: Sa Vie et Sa Theorie de la Guerre.* Paris: Berger-Levrault Editeurs, 1912.

Rose, J. Holland. 'The Prophetic Instinct in Nelson.' In *The Indecisiveness of Modern War*, edited by J. Holland Rose. London: G. Bell, 1927.

Rosello, Victor M. 'Clausewitz's Contempt for Intelligence.' *Parameters*, 21 (Spring 1991): 103–114.

Rosinski, Herbert. 'Die Entwicklung von Clausewitz' Werk "Vom Kriege" Im

Lichte Seiner "Vorreden und" "Nachrichten".' *Historische Zeitschrift* 151 (1935): 279–293.

Roskill, Captain S. W. *The Art of Leadership*. London: Collins, 1964.

Rothfels, Hans. *Carl von Clausewitz: Politik und Krieg: Eine ideengeschichtliche studie*. Berlin: Dummler, 1920. Reprinted 1980.

Rothfels, Hans. 'Clausewitz.' In *Makers of Modern Strategy*, edited by Edward Mead Earle, pp. 93–117. Princeton, NJ: Princeton University Press, 1943; also in *Clausewitz in Perspektive*, edited by Günther Dill, pp. 261–290. Frankfurt: Ullstein, 1980.

Rousseau, Jean-Jacques. *The Government of Poland*. Translated by W. Kendal. Indianapolis: Bobbs-Merrill, 1972.

Rudin, Harry. *Armistice 1918*. New Haven, CT: Yale University Press, 1944.

Rylander, R. Lynn. 'Mao as a Clausewitzian Strategist.' *Military Review* 61 (August 1981): 13–21.

Sawyer, Ralph D. *Sun Pin: Military Methods*. Boulder, CO: Westview Press, 1995.

Sawyer, Ralph D., trans. *The Seven Military Classics of Ancient China*. Boulder, CO: Westview Press, 1993.

Schelling, Thomas C. *Arms and Influence*. New Haven, CT: Yale University Press, 1966.

Schelling, Thomas C. *The Strategy of Conflict*. Cambridge, MA: Harvard University Press, [1960] 1976.

Schering, Walther Malmsten. *Die Kriegsphilosophie von Clausewitz: Eine Untersuchurg über ihern systematischen Aufbau*. Hamburg: Hanseatische Verlaganstalt, 1935.

Schmelzer, Paul. 'Clausewitz and Mao.' MA thesis. Colorado State University, Ft. Collins, Summer 1989.

Schmitt, Carl. 'Clausewitz als Politischer Denker: Bemerkungen und Hinweise.' *Der Staat* 6 (1967): 479–502.

Schmitt, Walther E. 'Lenin und Clausewitz.' *Wehrwissentschaftliche Rundschau* 11 (1961): 243–257.

Schneider, James J. and Izzo Lawrence L. 'Clausewitz's Elusive Center of Gravity.' *Parameters* 27 (September 1987): 46–57.

Schössler, Dietmar. 'Revolutionare Praxis und ihre Theorie.' In Max Kaase, ed. *Politische Wissenschaft und politische Ordnung*. Opladen: Westdeutscher Verlag, 1986.

Schössler, Dietmar. 'Das Wechselverhältnis von Theorie und Praxis bei Carl von Clausewitz.' *Archiv für Geschichte der Philosophie* 71 (1989): 39–62.

Schössler, Dietmar. *Carl von Clausewitz*. Hamburg: Rowohlt, 1991.

von Schramm, Wilhelm R. *Clausewitz: Leben und Werk*. Essen: Bechtle, 1977.

Schurman, Donald M. *The Education of a Navy*. London: Cassell, 1965.

Schurman, Donald M. *Julian S. Corbett 1854–1922*. London: Royal Historical Society, 1981.

Seabury, Paul. 'Taking Necessary Risks.' In *Ethics and American Power*, edited by Ernest W. Lefever. Washington, DC: Ethics and Public Policy Center, 1985.

Seeckt, Hans von. *Thoughts of a Soldier*. London: Ernest Bueur, 1930.

Seeckt, Hans von. 'Clausewitz.' In *Gedanken eines Soldaten*, pp. 23–29. Leipzig: K.F. Koehler, 1935.

von Senger, H. *The Book of Stratagems: Tactics for Triumph and Survival*. Translated and edited by M. B. Gubitz. New York: Viking, 1991.

Senghaas, Dieter. 'Ruckblick auf Clausewitz.' In Detlef Bald, ed., *Militarische Verantwortung in Staat und Gesellschaft*. Koblenz: Bernard und Greife, 1986, pp. 61–76.

Seychab, Carl A. 'The 36 Stratagems: Orthodoxy against Heterodoxy.' In C. A. Syeschab, A. Sievres, and S. Szywkiewicz (eds), *Society, Culture, and Patterns of Behavior*, pp. 97–155. Bad Honef: Hore Lemann, 1990.

Shepard, J. E. '*On War*: Is Clausewitz Still Relevant?', *Parameters* 20 (September 1990): 85–99.

Shultz, George P. 'The Ethics of Power.' In *Ethics and American Power*, edited by Ernest W. Lefever. Washington, DC: Ethics and Public Policy Center, 1985.

Shultz, George P. *Turmoil and Defeat: My Years as Secretary of State*. New York: Charles Scribner & Sons, 1993.

Shun-te, L. *Business Management and the Art of War*. Taipei, Taiwan: CTS Enterprises, 1993.

Shy, John. 'Jomini.' In *Makers of Modern Strategy: From Machiavelli to the Nuclear Age*, edited by Peter Paret. Princeton, NJ: Princeton University Press, 1986.

Smith, Hugh. 'The Womb of War: Clausewitz and International Politics.' *Review of International Studies*, 16 (1990): 39–58.

Snyder, Jack. *The Ideology of the Offensive: Military Decision Making and the Disasters of 1914*. Ithaca: Cornell University Press, 1984.

Stahel, Albert A. 'Clausewitz und Sun Tzu: Zwei Strategien.' *Schweizer Monatshefte* 61 (1981): 859–870.

Stamp, G. *Clausewitz im Atomzeitalter*. Wiesbaden: Rheinische Verlag-Anstalt, no date.

Stinemetz, Steven D. 'Clausewitz or Khan?: The Mongol Methods of Military Success.' *Parameters* 14 (Spring 1984): 71–80.

Strachan, Hugh. *European Armies and the Conduct of War*. George Allen & Unwin, 1983.

Stuart, Reginald C. 'Clausewitz and the Americans: Bernard Brodie and Others on War and Policy.' In *War and Society*, edited by B. Bond and I. Roy, pp. 166–172. New York: Holmes and Meier, 1977.

Stumpf, Reinhard, ed. *Kriegstheorie und Kriegsgeschichte Carl von Clausewitz Helmut von Moltke*. Frankfurt am Main: Deutscher Klassiker Verlag, 1995.

Sumida, Jon Tetsuro. *Inventing Grand Strategy and Teaching Command: The Classic Works of Alfred Thayer Mahan Reconsidered.* Baltimore, MD: Johns Hopkins University Press, 1997.

Summers, Harry J. 'Defense Without Purpose.' *Society.* November/December (1983): 4–17.

Summers, Harry G. *On Strategy: A Critical Analysis of the War in Vietnam.* Novato, CA: Presidio Press, 1982.

Sun Haichen, ed. and trans. *The Wiles of War: 36 Military Strategies from Ancient China.* Beijing: Beijing Foreign Language Press, 1991.

Sun Pin. *Military Methods of the Art of War.* Translated by Ralph D. Sawyer. New York: Barnes and Noble, 1995.

Sun Tzu. *The Book of War: The Military Classic of the Far East.* Translated by Captain E. F. Calthorpe. London: John Murray, 1908.

Sun Tzu. *The Art of War.* Translated by L. Giles. London: Luzac, 1910; also published during the Second World War as: *Sun Tzu Wu: The Art of War.* Introduction and notes by Brigadier General T. R. Phillips. Harrisburg, PA: The Military Service Press Publishing Co., 1944.

Sun Tzu. *The Art of War.* Translated by Chang Lin. Shanghai: The World Book Company, 1946.

Sun Tzu. *The Art of War.* Translated by M. Tai. Taipei, Taiwan: 1954.

Sun Tzu. *The Art of War: Military Manual.* Translated by Chang Lin. Hong Kong: Far East Book Press, 1969.

Sun Tzu. *The Art of War.* Translated by Samuel B. Griffith. New York: Oxford University Press, 1971.

Sun Tzu. *The Art of War.* Edited by James Clavell. Translated by L. Giles. New York: Delacorte, 1983; also London: Hodder and Stoughton, 1981.

Sun Tzu. *The Art of War.* Translated by A. Chen and G. Chen. Singapore: Graham Brash (PTE) Ltd, 1982.

Sun Tzu. *The Art of War.* Translated by T. Cleary. Boston: Shambhala, 1988.

Sun Tzu. *The Art of War.* Translated by L. Giles. Singapore: Graham Brash (PTE) Ltd, 1989.

Sun Tzu. *The Art of War: The Book of Lord Shang.* Translated by J. J. L. Duyvendak, with an Introduction by R. Wilkinson. Ware, Herts: Wordsworth, 1998.

Sun Tzu. *Sun-Tzu The Art of Warfare.* Translated by R. Ames. New York: Ballantine Books, 1993.

Sun Tzu. *Sun-Tzu: The New Translation.* Translated by J. H. Huang. New York: William Morrow, 1993.

Sun Tzu. *Sun Tzu: The Art of War.* Translated by R. D. Sawyer. New York: Barnes & Noble, 1994.

Sun Tzu. *Sun Zi Speaks: From the Works of Mao Tse-tung,* trans. Brian Bruya. New York: Doubleday, 1994.

Sun Tzu. *The Strategic Advantage – Sun Zi and Western Approach to War*. Bejing, China: New World Press, 1997.

Sun Tzu. *The Lost Art of War: Sun Tzu II*. Translated with commentary by Thomas Cleary. New York: Harper San Francisco, 1996.

Sun Tzu. *The Complete Art of War: Sun Tzu, Sun Pin*. Translated with an introduction and commentary by Ralph D. Sawyer. Boulder, CO: Westview Press, 1996.

Sun Tzu. *Sun Tzu's Art of War*. Edited by Khoo Kheng-Hor, translated by Hwang Chen-Mei. Pelanduk Publications, Selangor Darul Ehsan, 1996.

Sun Tzu. *Sun Tzu The Art of War and Strategy: A New Translation of Sun Tzu's Classic The Art of War*. Translated by R. L. Wing. New York: A Dolphin Book, Doubleday, 1988.

Sun Tzu. *The Art of War*. Adapted and introduced by Stefan Rudnicki. West Hollywood, CA: Dove Books, 1996.

von Szczepanski, Max. 'Hans Delbrück und Karl von Clausewitz.' *Deutsche Revue* 25 (1920): 14–21.

Tang Zi-Chang. *Principles of Conflict: Recompilation and New English Translation with Annotation of Sun Zi's Art of War*. San Rafael, CA: T. C. Press, 1969.

Taylor, F. L. *The Art of War in Italy 1494–1529*. Cambridge: Cambridge University Press, 1921.

Thucydides. *The History of the Peloponnesian War*. Translated by Richard Crawley. New York: E. P. Dutton & Co, 1950.

Thucydides. *The Landmark Thucydides: A Comprehensive Guide to the Peloponnesian War*. Edited by Robert B. Strassler. (A newly revised edition of the Richard Crawley translation.) New York: The Free Press, 1996.

Trotsky, Leon. *Military Writings*. New York: Merit, 1969.

Troht, Jack and Ries, Al. *Marketing Warfare*. New York: McGraw-Hill, 1986.

U.S. Army. *Operations FM 100–5*. Washington, DC: Headquarters, Department of the Army, 1986.

U.S. Marine Corps. *Warfighting FMFM1*. Washington, DC: Department of the Navy, Headquarters, United States Marine Corps, 1989.

Vad, Erich. *Carl von Clausewitz: Seine Bedentung heute*. Herford: E. S. Mittler, 1984.

Vollrath, Ernst. 'Das Verhältnis von Staat und Militär bei Clausewitz.' In *Staatsverfassung und Heeresverfassung in der europäischen Geschichte der frühen Neuzeit*, edited by Johannes Kunisch, pp. 447–461. Berlin: Duncker and Humblot, 1986.

Vollrath, Ernst. 'Neue Wege der Klugheit' Zum Methodischen Prinzip der Theorie des Handelns bei Clausewitz', *Zeitschrift Fur Politic*. Vol. 31, No. 1 (198): 53–76.

Vowinckel, G., ed. *Clausewitz-Kolloquium: Theorie des Krieges als Sozialwissenschaft*. Berlin: Duncker and Humblot, 1993.

Wagmann, Eberhard, ed. *Frieden ohne Rustung?* Herlord und Bonn: E.S. Mittler und Sohn, 1989.

Wagmann, E. and Niemeyer, Joachim. *Freiheit ohne Krieg?* Bonn: Dummler – Clausewitz Gesselschaft, 1980.

Walt, Stephen M. 'The Search for a Science of Strategy.' *International Security* 12 (Summer 1987): 140–165.

Watts, Barry D. *Clausewitzian Friction and Future War.* Washington, DC: National Defense University. McNair Paper No. 52, October 1996.

Wavell, Field Marshal A. P. *Generals and Generalship.* The Lee Knowles Lectures, Cambridge, 1939. Harmondsworth: Penguin, 1941.

Wavell, Field Marshal A. P. *Speaking Generally.* London: Macmillan, 1946.

Wehler, H. Ulrich. '"Absoluter" und "Totaler" Krieg: von Clausewitz zu Ludendorff.' In *Clausewitz in Perspektive*, edited by Günther Dill, pp. 474–510. Frankfurt: Ullstein, 1980; also in *Politische Vierteljahresschrift* 10 (September 1968): 220–248.

Weinberger, Caspar W. 'US Defense Strategy.' *Foreign Affairs* (Spring 1986): 675–97.

Weinberger, Caspar W. *Fighting for Peace: Seven Critical Years in the Pentagon.* New York: Warner Books, 1990.

Weniger, Erich. 'Philosophie und Bildung im Denken von Clausewitz.' In *Schicksalwege Deutscher Vergangenheit*, edited by Walther Hubatsch, pp. 123–143. Düsseldorf: Dorste, 1950.

Whaley, Barton. *Stratagem, Deception and Surprise in War.* Cambridge, MA: Center for International Studies, MIT, 1969.

Wheeler-Bennett, John W. *Hindenburg: The Wooden Titan.* New York: Macmillan, 1967.

Wilkinson, S. *War and Policy.* New York: Dodd, Mead, 1900.

Williams, T. Harry. 'The Military Leadership of North and South'. In David Donald, *Why the North Won the Civil War*, pp. 23–48. Baton Rouge, LA: Louisiana State University Press, 1969.

Williams, T. Harry. 'The Return of Jomini – Some Thoughts on Recent Civil War Writing.' *Military Affairs* 39 (December 1975): 204–206.

Wills, Garry. 'Critical Inquiry (*Kritik*) in Clausewitz.' *Critical Inquiry* 9 (December 1982): 281–302.

Windsor, Philip. 'The Clock, the Context and Clausewitz.' *Millennium: Journal of International Studies* 6 (1977): 190–196.

Wohlstetter, Roberta. *Pearl Harbor: Warning and Decision.* Stanford, CA: Stanford University Press, 1962.

Woodward, Bob. *The Commanders.* New York: Simon & Schuster, 1991.

Zhang, Yuan-Lin. 'Mao Zedong und Carl von Clausewitz.' Ph.D. dissertation. University of Mannhein, 1995.

Index

CONCEPTUAL INDEX TO THE CLASSICAL STRATEGISTS

GENERAL REFERENCE INDEX